THE LIFE AND TIMES OF
CONSTANTINE
THE GREAT

THE FIRST CHRISTIAN EMPEROR

THE LIFE AND TIMES OF
CONSTANTINE
THE GREAT

THE FIRST CHRISTIAN EMPEROR

D.G. KOUSOULAS

Rutledge Books, Inc.

Danbury, CT

Copyright© 1997 by D.G. Kousoulas

ALL RIGHTS RESERVED
Rutledge Books, Inc.
107 Mill Plain Road, Danbury, CT 06811

Manufactured in the United States of America

Cataloging in Publication Data
Kousoulas, Dimitrios George, 1923-
   The life and times of Constantine the Great - the first Christian Emperor.

   ISBN: 1-887750-61-4

   1. Constantine I, Emperor of Rome, d. 337. 2. Emperor—Rome—
Biography. 3. Christian saints—Rome—Biography. 4. Church history—
Primitive and early church, ca. 30-600. 5. Rome—History—Constantine I,
the Great, 306-337.

937'.08 '091   97-66794

CONTENTS

PART THREE: CONSTANTINE, SOLE EMPEROR

The Economy
The Role of the Church

ACKNOWLEDGMENTS

I am deeply indebted to those scholars who studied and illuminated the events and the personalities of that period and to the ancient chroniclers who left for us their invaluable testimony. A biography for the general public (however non-scholarly it may be) cannot be written without such original and scholarly input. My research owes a great deal to the help and cooperation given me through the years by the Dumbarton Oaks Library directors Peter Topping and Angeliki Laiou and by the library staff, help which was indeed indispensable since so much is to be found there. I would also like to thank Dumbarton Oaks, the Worcester Art Museum, the Museum of London, the British Museum, the Library of Congress and the Croatian embassy in Washington for providing the illustrations included in the text.

My appreciation also goes to Margaretta Fulton of Harvard UP Humanities Editor who read the text and encouraged the effort, Felicia Kinney who reviewed the text with the eye of the general reader, Teri Boccuzzi and John Laub who guided the publication process, and above all, my wife Mary, who has been a source of encouragement and sensible advice throughout. Finally I would like to thank my son George who prepared the maps with meticulous care and provided Constantine's photo for the dust jacket. For any errors or inadequacies, I have no one to blame but myself.

PREFACE

This is an enriched biography of Constantine the Great. Without compromising historical accuracy, it brings before the eyes of the reader as vividly as possible Constantine's fascinating life, filling in the gaps by exploring the ancient records and the findings of modern scholarship, reconstructing events or offering plausible explanations to ancient riddles. I share the view that "it would be refreshing if historians would seek not only to be revisionist in their history but also in their writing style. The traditional approach to writing history and biography is to tell about what happened, rather than to describe what actually did happen, as a novelist might—in effect to tell a story."[*] Moving away from the traditional approach in order "to tell a story" has been my guiding principle.

The most astonishing fact I found while working on this biography was how little the broad public in the West knows about Constantine. Yet, he is the man who proclaimed freedom of religion for the first time in the history of the Western world, and ushered in the Christian era giving a new direction to civilized society. One may wonder whether Christianity would have survived if he had not embraced it with his imperial authority. In his day, Christianity was

---

[*] "Book World," *Washington Post* June 11, 1995.

only one of several "mystery religions" although one of the most influential. Some of those cults had many followers and their ethical precepts were not very different from those of the Christian faith. One of them, the cult of Mithras, was quite popular especially among the men in the legions. Why Constantine chose Christianity is one of the questions this biography hopes to answer.

Constantine's impact on our world is not the only reason for writing a popular biography. His life is so rich in excitement, drama, personal tragedy, intrigue, violence and high adventure that the story can be as engrossing as a good work of fiction. In this biography, Constantine and the other men and women in his life are seen as human beings with all their virtues and foibles, while their ambitious dreams, their motives, fears, intrigues and betrayals are explored as fully as the ancient records will allow. By probing the original writings and the findings of modern scholars I have sought to read between the lines, uncovering what really happened and why.

Although the early years of Constantine's life are shrouded in mist, we have hints, innuendoes, and legends to help us reconstruct what may have actually happened. Constantine, of course, did not appear suddenly on the world stage fully grown like Athena from Zeus' brow. To understand him and his actions in later years we must begin at the beginning, to see him as a child growing into manhood, and to view at close range the events and the people who shaped his character and his thinking. For this reason, several pages are devoted to the actions of the men who deliberately or not—mostly not—paved the way for Constantine's rise to supreme power.

The accurate but also vivid presentation of Constantine's life and times was made possible with the extensive use of the original sources in Latin and fourth century Greek. Access to those sources, especially those in the rich collection of the Byzantine Library at Dumbarton Oaks, was an invaluable advantage.

Several books have been published in the last hundred years

about Constantine and the late Roman Empire but practically all of them were written for scholars and readers with a special interest in the period. This biography is written for the general public because Constantine deserves to be more widely known. Decisions he made, and actions he took during his long reign, profoundly affected our world to this day. For a peasant lad born out of wedlock, the son of an innkeeper's daughter, his rise to the summit of imperial authority was spectacular by any measure. A novelist might have felt uneasy to invent such a character and such a life; his readers might have protested that the author had taken fiction too far, especially when so many fortunate incidents paved the way. For Constantine's rise to greatness cannot be attributed exclusively to his genius; luck deserves some credit. He was lucky that Emperor Carus plucked his young father from the legions and appointed him governor of Dalmatia; lucky that emperor Diocletian sent his father to serve as Praetorian Prefect to his co-emperor Maximian in Gaul; lucky that Diocletian decided to appoint two Caesars and that he chose Constantine's father as one of the two; lucky...but the list of events which opened one after another destiny's gates is much too long. This book covers those events in graphic detail, drawing on the ancient chroniclers.

Constantine was indeed the "first Christian emperor" but those who expect to find in him a pious believer in Christ's ethical and humane message are bound to be disappointed. He saw the God of the Christians as a powerful deity that could strike down his enemies and support his ambitious goals. Christian theology—difficult for him to fathom in the first place—attracted his attention only when it became the subject of controversy within the Church. Then, fearful that disputes of this kind might displease the Supreme Deity and deprive him of divine favor, he would step in and try to restore unity and peace in the Church, sometimes quite forcefully. His letters to feuding bishops are quite revealing.

Even though to the Eastern Church he is "Saint Constantine," he was no saint, not if a saint is a kindhearted, self-denying, charitable man. The Church, of course, had a most valid reason for bestowing on him this supreme accolade. He had assured the supremacy of the Christian faith in the Roman world and thus in the kingdoms and states that emerged in Europe and in the New World in the following centuries. If the Western Church has kept his memory at a distance, it is mainly because he moved the seat of the empire to Constantinople, a city he built in the East, challenging in this way the supremacy of the bishop of Rome.

Whatever the Church prelates in East and West may have thought of him, his life was not and could not be that of a saint. He was an emperor and he had to carry the burden of power. For this reason, if this biography differs from previous books, it is most of all in its focus on the personal conflicts, the many crises, the great achievements as well as the harsh, even cruel, deeds that fill the rich canvas of Constantine's eventful life. The darkest of these acts of violence occurred during the celebration of his twentieth anniversary as emperor. He had his wife Fausta brutally murdered for allegedly seducing his son Crispus and then having the young man executed. Fausta's was not the only violent death Constantine had on his conscience when he died in 337 at the age of sixty-five.

Still, with all the unholy deeds of his life, Constantine left a lasting mark on our world and deserves to be called Great as few men and women in history. The story of his life and times as it unfolds on the pages of this biography will hopefully bear this out.

MAPS

PART I

THE EARLY YEARS

CHAPTER I

CHILDHOOD

A FANCIFUL TALE

No seer would have risked his fame foretelling that Naissus (Nis), an obscure town, a *municipium*, in the backwoods of Illyricum (today's Serbia and Croatia), was to become the birthplace of a great emperor. One of the towns and villages nestled on the craggy hills and narrow valleys deep into the land we know today as the Balkan peninsula, Naissus was too ordinary to expect history to take notice. In the winter, the rooftops and the fields were covered with snow and the bitter cold forced the people to spend most of their time inside their small houses huddled around the crude fireplaces to keep warm, but in the spring the hills came alive with red poppies and cyclamens, and the fields were dotted with the blooming almond and apple trees. The villagers spoke mostly Dardanian with a smattering of broken Latin and Greek needed to communicate with travelers of foot soldiers and horsemen passing through, for the town was on the Roman highway which came from the city of Thessaloniki in the south, unfolding toward the north as it crossed the length of Illyricum, all the way to Pannonia (the Roman province where most of Austria, Hungary and Slovenia are today).

Life in Naissus was hard, and for the poor rather primitive, but also happy in its simplicity save for the fear that hordes of Sarmatians or Goths from beyond the Danube might elude the soldiers guarding the forts and the mountain passes and sweep down from the north.

The barbarians seldom reached the area because the men in the legions pushed them back beyond the Danube, yet the fear persisted.

It was a warm day in the middle of June in the year 271,[*] when Flavius Constantius, very likely a Military Tribune, came with his men to Naissus on his way back from one of those bloody encounters with marauding Sarmatians. As the sun was about to slide behind the hills to the west, Constantius ordered his men to halt for the night and pitch their tents in the fields. Then he walked to the nearest inn to have a decent meal and spend the night on a straw mattress. At age twenty-three, he was "tall, slender, of fair complexion and grey-blue eyes, with an elegant nose," an impressive figure in his uniform with its plumed helmet, embossed cuirass and flowing cape.

Flavius Constantius was not a stranger to the area, born to a peasant family in a small village not far from Naissus to the north. Until the time he was about seventeen, he had known only the simple life of his village, tending the sheep or helping his father till the land. All this had changed when he was recruited into the legions. He had been in the army six years at the time he stopped with his unit at Naissus, and in that short span of time the ignorant peasant lad had changed drastically. His native intelligence had blossomed, and he had gained a self-confidence and maturity that young peasants of his age could never hope to attain. In those six years, he had been tested time and again in the crucible of battle and had shown that he had an astute mind and a brave heart. In the legions, where no barriers of race or origin kept a man from rising as high as his abilities could carry him, for young Flavius Constantius the future appeared bright indeed.

The straw mattress must have felt like the epitome of luxury after many nights of sleeping on the hard ground, but the young tribune was restless. Desires he had suppressed, as long as death lurked behind every tree, came to the surface and "he felt the need to have a woman, i.e. to fornicate," to quote the monk who wrote down the

---

[*]At the time our story unfolds, the numbering of the passing years from the birth of Christ was yet to come, but for the convenience of the reader we shall use the Christian chronology.

story in Greek much later. He went to the innkeeper and "told him of his desire for unbridled ecstasy." It was not an unusual demand and ordinarily a village widow would have been called to spend the night with the young tribune. But the innkeeper, "impressed by the man's stature, gladly brought his young daughter Helena." She was sixteen years old and "had never been with a man."

Constantius made love to the slender, blond girl until the passion drained from his body and he fell asleep, the young girl nestled in his arms. In the words of the imaginative monk who recounted the story, Constantius saw in his sleep "the sun rise against nature from the ocean in the West and come to bathe in brilliance the house where Constantius and Helena were asleep. Constantius was awed by the vision, being superstitious, i.e. a fervent believer in his religion, and thought that it was Apollo who was seeing his actions from above. Terrified and speechless, he drew away from the erotic embraces, fearful that he might have offended the gods."

In the morning, as his men were preparing to move on and the air was thick with the shouted orders of the centurions, the neighing of horses and the curses of soldiers, Constantius called the innkeeper and gave him a pouch of coins and his own tribunal cape, its silver-coated buckle engraved with his initials and rank. "Keep the young maiden pure," he told the innkeeper, "and if by chance she were to give birth to a child, protect the infant as the apple of your eye." Nine months later a boy was born to Helena and she named him Constantine, little Constantius. The boy became for her the essence of her existence, but for Constantius who knew nothing about the birth of his son, even the memory of that night in Naissus had faded.

The life of Flavius Constantius took an unexpected turn nine years later. We may assume that by that time he had become a senior officer in the legion commanded by Diocles, another Illyrian of obscure origin, so obscure that some people whispered behind his back that he was the son of a slave.

Constantius was with the legions in Pannonia near the banks of the

Danube, not far from the town of Aquincum (today's Budapest), when he was summoned to the tent of Emperor Carus, the general the legions had chosen to be emperor following the murder of Emperor Probus some eight months earlier. It was an unusual summons but even more unexpected was the reason behind it. Carus wanted Flavius Constantius to become governor of Dalmatia, the Illyrian province along the Adriatic, which controlled the routes between the western and the eastern sections of the empire. With this leap up the hierarchical ladder, Constantius was suddenly raised to the status of a *vir perfectissimus*, a "most perfect man." He was thirty-three years old.

It was Diocles—at the time the commander of the elite force of the emperor's personal guard—who had persuaded Carus to give the coveted governorship to the young officer. At the time neither Diocles nor Carus could have imagined that they had set in motion a train of events that three decades later would signal the onset of the Christian era and change the course of history.

Helena must have heard of the new governor of Dalmatia from passing travelers, but whatever joy she may have felt must have been shattered by the realization that the gap which separated them had now widened. She was an innkeeper's daughter, a simple peasant woman who had no hope of ever marrying Constantius. She had not seen him since that night, ten years ago, and for all those years she had not even known whether he was alive. All that time she had no way of telling him he had a son. Now that she knew where to find him it was too late. Even if she were to go to Salonae, the provincial capital, the guards would not let her pass through the gates of the governor's mansion. Even if by some miracle she were allowed to see him, could she expect the mighty governor to acknowledge his son after ten years of silence? Being a practical and proud woman, Helena made up her mind to say nothing.

This might have been the end of the story and we would have never heard of a peasant boy in Naissus named Constantine had fate not intervened. It appears—if we are to believe the monk who wrote the story—that some horsemen were passing through Naissus and stopped for the night.

The next morning, Constantine, by now a mischievous nine-year-old, went to the stable and began to tease the horses, "thereby provoking the ire of the men who had stayed overnight at the inn." As one of them started thrashing the boy, Helena rushed to stop the beating, frantically yelling that the boy was the son of Flavius Constantius. The men who heard her cries and the claim that the boy was the governor's son, began laughing and making fun of her. "Woman," they said mockingly, "are you taking us for fools?" Indeed, how could this peasant woman, shapeless in her coarse, rough hewn clothing, her hands and face dirty from the oily pots in the kitchen, have anything to do with the governor of Dalmatia? "I swear to the gods that I am telling you the truth," she shouted back, angered by their taunting. "When Constantius was a tribune he slept with me one night on his way back from the war against the Sarmatians and I became pregnant and gave birth to this boy. And if you want to know the truth I can give you as evidence the reward for my going to bed with him." Whereupon she brought the cape.

The monk goes on to tell us that the commander of the unit reported the incident to Flavius Constantius, telling him "the boy is your spit and image, Domine." Constantius interrogated the man about the boy and his mother, and then probably more out of curiosity he sent a messenger to Naissus with orders to escort Helena and the boy to Salonae.[*]

---

[*]We have no written record of Constantine's childhood years. The story I have used here as the basis comes from a manuscript written by a monk centuries later. It may be the product of the monk's fertile imagination or more likely the retelling of an earlier legend. I found it worth using for three reasons. First, the story is plausible and amplifies what contemporary chronicles merely mentioned in a few words. Second, in the light of the prudish ethics of the Church, it would have been most unlikely for a monk to have invented such a raunchy tale. Third, the *bios*, written in Greek, begins with these words: "The Life and the Record of the blessedly departed pious, most faithful, great and first king of us Christians, Constantine, and his mother Helena. Father, give us your blessing." Clearly the story was not written by a hostile chronicler.

AT THE GOVERNOR'S MANSION

L ittle Constantine must have been in a daze as he entered the governor's mansion. Since birth he had known only the narrow world of the small town, the daily routine of the inn, cleaning the dining tables, feeding the pigs with leftovers, and playing with the other village children out in the fields.

Our monk tells us that "Constantius was overjoyed, embracing them and taking them inside the palace." Even though our storyteller speaks of a happy reunion we may assume that things were not as simple or as agreeable as he claims. No doubt Constantius accepted the little boy as his son otherwise he would have sent them both back to Naissus. He must have also understood that if he kept the boy he would have to keep the mother, too, because he could see how close they were.

Helena was twenty-six years old and the hard life at the inn must have left its marks on her, but evidently Constantius found her attractive since we know that the thought of marriage entered his mind. Very likely, her beautiful face and slim figure resurfaced once she was given the expert ministrations of women slaves and the drudgery of the kitchen was washed away. The sixteen-year-old peasant girl had matured into an attractive young woman. Constantius, whatever his feelings about Helena, was facing a knotty legal problem. As a member now of the equestrian class he was forbidden by law to marry a humble peasant like Helena. He could have kept her, of course, without the benefit of a legal union, but that would have made the boy a *nothos*, an illegitimate child. Clearly, he did not want to let such a stain blacken his son's life forever.

All chroniclers of the time agree that Flavius Constantius did marry Helena, but in a *matrimonium concubinatum*, a form of marriage the law allowed in similar cases. Legal though it was, this type of marriage gave the son limited rights when it came to inheriting from the father, and it also made divorce easier. But what mattered most to Flavius Constantius was that his son would now be regarded as legitimate.

Constantius faced more problems with the two persons that had come so suddenly into his life. Both Helena and Constantine were illiterate, speaking only Dardanian mixed with a few Latin and Greek expressions picked up from passing travelers. Constantine had to be educated. At his young age, of course, he could learn easily, but with Helena it would not be as easy. A governor's wife had to act as the hostess in banquets and other social gatherings. True, Constantius did not often give elaborate banquets. He was a frugal man and on occasion he had to borrow plates and utensils from wealthy neighbors to serve his guests. Still, there were times when he had to entertain high-ranking officials visiting the provincial capital. Helena could not stay out of sight forever.

The first years must have been rather trying for both Helena and Flavius Constantius, but the tutors had strict orders to work hard with their two pupils and before long both mother and son began to show progress. The boy, intelligent, ambitious and eager to make his father proud, worked hard and so did Helena, who spent almost all her waking hours studying. With slaves and servants doing all the housework, she had plenty of time.

For Helena and little Constantine, life in the governor's mansion was a source of constant fascination. The day they arrived from Naissus, they saw for the first time in their lives the sea, a fascinating sight. Since then, they could see every day from the governor's mansion the bay and the islands in the distance resting on the water, and inside the harbor the cargo boats and the triremes, with their three banks of oars on each side. The bay and the harbor were well protected against the angry waves of the winter storms, offering a welcome haven to weather-beaten seamen.

Inside the *praetorium*, as the governor's mansion was formally called, a large staff of scribes, accountants and record-keepers (*cornicularii* and *commentarienses*) kept busy looking after the administration of the province. Several household servants and slaves did the daily chores. A military garrison was quartered in a large building next to the mansion, to keep order in the town and protect the governor. The soldiers had a thousand tales to tell from their battles with the barbarians and it is easy to imagine that every time the tutor gave him permission Constantine would rush over to the barracks to listen to those exciting stories.

The little peasant boy was changing rapidly, his quick, curious mind taking in every snippet of knowledge, every new experience, doing exceedingly well in his schooling and in the athletic exercises that were part of his daily routine. Constantius was proud of his son and could look to the future with confidence, but neither he nor Helena could have the slightest notion that someday the precocius boy would become the emperor who would destroy the ancient idols and usher in the era of a new faith. All that was far into the future, yet the Fates were already spinning their golden threads.

MURDER OPENS THE WAY

As Constantine entered his eleventh year, a chain of events, seemingly unconnected to each other or to Constantine's future, unfolded many hundreds of miles away, in far off Mesopotamia, the land between the two great rivers, Euphrates and Tigris. This fertile land between the Persian kingdom and the Roman Empire was trampled upon by these two giants, passing from one to the other and back again. In the year 283, the Romans found conditions turning to their favor.

Carus and his legions crossed the Bosporus in the spring, marching through Asia Minor and Syria and in a great battle north of Seleukia, they annihilated the Persian army. Thirsting for more glory in spite of his age—he was over sixty—Carus wanted to move on and invade the Persian heartland, with dreams of repeating the feat of Alexander. Before he had a chance to march along Alexander's path, a heart attack ended his life "as if he were struck by a thunderbolt".

Carus had earlier elevated his two sons, Carinus and Numerian, to the rank of Caesar—a sort of vice-emperor. In the Roman tradition, seldom had an emperor been succeeded by a natural son and even more rarely, an emperor raised a son to the rank of Caesar while the father was still alive. But Carus had dreams of founding a dynasty. To his older son, Carinus, a bold, ambitious young man, he had already given command of the western part of the empire which covered the

Italian peninsula, Gaul (today's France), Spain, the British Isles and northern Africa along the Mediterranean coastline west of Libya. Carinus, intoxicated by his sudden rise, began to confuse imperial power with license. Even before his father's death, rumors were reaching the legions with tales of violence and debauchery. When Carinus reached Rome, we are told, "he executed the city's Prefect and replaced him with Matronianus, a crony of his and a procurer who had always served him in his debaucheries...By frequent marriage and divorce he took nine wives altogether, and threw some of them away even while they were pregnant. He filled the palace with actors, pantomimists, harlots, singers and procurers." Obviously this unflattering portrait was not recorded by a friend, but from what we know it does not appear to have been overdrawn.

By contrast, Numerian was a timid, pleasure-loving youngster who made a pitiful soldier. He was with his father at the time he died and the legions immediately proclaimed him emperor. The elevation of the young man to the dignity of Augustus was engineered by his father-in-law, Lucius Aper (whose last name meant Wild Boar in German), and by Diocles who as the commander of the emperor's personal guards had a great deal of influence. Each of these two men had designs to wrest the purple[*] away from Numerian at the right moment. They had to shelve their plans for a while, until the legions had solidified control of Mesopotamia and had returned safely to their bases in the Balkans.

The moment came outside of the small town of Nicomedia (today's Izmit), a short distance south of the Straits of Bosporus. Numerian had been suffering from an eye infection and, to avoid the dust the horses and the foot soldiers kicked up, he was riding inside a litter carried by a team of Numidian slaves.

As the legions were approaching Nicomedia, the dead body of Numerian was discovered by a slave who immediately told Diocles.

---

* Latin purpura from the Greek porphyra, a mantle of deep red fabric, erroneously rendered in English as "purple." It was the symbol of imperial authority.

He moved swiftly. As the commander of the *Protectores Domestici*, he was responsible for the emperor's safety. Now that the emperor was dead, he had to find and apprehend the perpetrator of the crime. Since he had not ordered the killing, he had no doubt that Aper was behind the foul deed. Lucius Aper had been Carus' Praetorian Prefect,[*] and Numerian had kept him at the same powerful post. Aper was in a good position to move and claim the *purple* and become the next emperor. For Diocles the moment of truth had come. Without wasting one minute, he sent messengers to two of the legion commanders he trusted most, Valerius Maximianus and Gaius Galerius, and when they came he told them of Numerian's death and of his suspicion that Aper was the mastermind of the crime. The time had come for them to act.

With the decisiveness that was the hallmark of his life, Diocles went to Aper's tent in the middle of the night with a squad from the *Protectores Domestici*. They swiftly overpowered the few guards outside and entered the tent. Before Aper had a chance to resist, the soldiers clamped the irons on him. Only then did Diocles summon the other legion commanders and showed them Numerian's foulsmelling corpse that he had ordered to be taken from the litter and placed on the ground outside of Aper's tent.

Aper angrily denied any part in Numerian's death and Diocles wisely promised an open hearing to give the accused a chance to defend himself. The following morning, on the 20th day of November in the year 284, the legions gathered in a wide meadow some three miles outside of Nicomedia. Diocles' plan was to have himself proclaimed emperor with the aid of Maximianus and Galerius. He wanted his elevation to appear as an orderly decision of the legions, but events did not follow the script.

After Numerian's body was consumed by the flames of the funeral

---

[*] The post was initially associated with the Praetorian Guard in Rome but for the previous one hundred years the Praetorian Prefect had been the emperor's chief aid, a sort of prime minister in modern terminology.

pyre, Diocles walked to the top of a knoll facing the ranks. It was just high enough for the men to see him. He stood silent for a moment and surveyed the impressive host. The legion commanders, on horseback and in full regalia, were in front, the plumes on their helmets fluttering in the morning breeze, while behind them stretched a sea of some fifty thousand men, lines upon lines of foot soldiers "with walls of shields in red, green, yellow, white and black" stretched to the far ends of the valley, "the glittering scale armor and conical helmets of the heavy cavalry" shining under the autumn sun, next to "the Moorish javelin men with their small round shields, and the German units with their trousers and sleeveless tunics, and above them a forest of lances and javelins, punctuated by the legionary eagles and the long, silk dragon pennants fluttering in the wind."

After a short speech, Diocles turned to the prisoner who was brought up to the knoll in chains. "Lucius Aper," he shouted, "you have heard the charges. What is your answer?"

Aper gave Diocles a murderous look and spat the ground. "The guilty are accusing the innocent," he shouted to the men. "I did not need to kill Numerian. He was my son-in-law and I was his Praetorian Prefect."

Diocles let a few moments pass so that Aper's words could reach the end of the columns. Then, he addressed the legions.

"For the past four days, legion commanders Valerius Maximianus and Gaius Galerius have been asking Lucius Aper to arrange a meeting with the emperor. Their requests were denied by Lucius Aper. I, the commander of the *Protectores Domestici*, asked Lucius Aper about the emperor's health. I was told that he was suffering from an ailment of the eyes. I did not become suspicious until a faithful soldier reported to me that for days the emperor had not left the litter even to relieve himself." Diocles went on with a brief retelling of what had followed. He ended his harangue, pointing an accusing finger at Aper, with the words "He is the murderer."

Aper reacted with the fury of a wounded lion. "He is the murderer, not me," he cried out. "Are you going to believe the words of a plotter, the words of a filthy son of a slave..."

The last words hit Diocles like a savage lash on the face. For him to be called the son of a slave was the ultimate insult. With a swift motion he drew his sword and plunged it into Aper's rib cage. The stricken man doubled over and with the blood gushing from his wound he slumped to his knees and then to the ground. Even those battle-hardened men in the ranks froze at the sight of the killing.

At that moment, Valerius Maximianus rushed to the top of the knoll and, without giving the men time to recover from the shock, shouted in a booming voice: "Romans, this is a moment of destiny. The future of Rome is in the hands of her legions. Hail the Augustus, Hail Gaius, Aurelius, Valerius Diocletianus, Dominus, Pontifex Maximus, Restorer and Protector." With these words, he raised high Diocles' hand still holding unsheathed the bloodstained sword. From below, Galerius repeated the words "Hail Augustus Diocletianus..." The front ranks picked up the chant and in seconds the sound of cries and the striking of swords and spears on shields rolled like a thunderous wave all the way to the end of the columns. "Hail Augustus Diocletianus..."

The Roman Empire had a new emperor.

A Husband's Revenge

The new emperor was forty years old, a man of medium height, with a broad forehead, penetrating almond-shaped eyes, thinning brown hair, and a strong, athletic body developed through years of strenuous work on the land as a youngster and later in the legions. He was married to Prisca, possibly the daughter of a landowner from Sirmium (today's Mitrovica), and they had a daughter, Valeria, seven years old at the time.

The dramatic rise of the new emperor was to shape Constantine's future and the course of world history, but at the time the little boy in Salonae had no inkling of what the Fates had in store for him. Neither did his father who learned of the events outside of Nicomedia several weeks later when he received the first official dispatch from the new emperor. It appears that Diocles—soon to be known as Emperor Diocletian—had been his mentor for years. The future appeared very promising indeed. The boy had brought him good fortune.

Diocletian reached Sirmium just before the celebration of the Saturnalia[*] and we can visualize the elation of his wife and daughter. He had left them over a year ago as plain Diocles, a legion commander from the village of Doclea, and he had now returned as the

---

[*] Festivities dedicated to Saturn, celebrated in late December with merriment, the exchange of gifts, good food and drinking.

Augustus. We may assume they were proud but also apprehensive.

His elevation to the imperial rank had not sealed the future. In the western part of the empire, Carinus had also been raised to Augustus by his legions soon after his father's death. When he learned of the tragic events outside of Nicomedia, he denounced Diocletian as a murderer and usurper. A clash was inevitable and would certainly come in the spring. Diocletian had to use the winter months to prepare for it. As soon as the festivities for the Saturnalia were over, Diocletian went to Salonae. He wanted to talk to Constantius who as governor of Dalmatia controlled the area that stood between east and west.

Young Constantine was probably disappointed to see that the emperor looked so human. He had never seen an emperor before and in his imagination an emperor was a mythical, god-like presence. Judging from what happened later, the eleven-year-old boy came most likely to the conclusion that emperors were only human and that he, too, one day could become an emperor—if only he were loved by the gods. The conviction that he needed the gods' love and benevolence was to remain with him all his life and guide his steps later when, at the pinnacle of power, he was shaping the world of the future.

The clash came in the spring at Margus, near the river Savus (Sava), not far from present day Belgrade. Carinus' legions fought fiercely. By midday, the ranks of Diocletian's legions began to weaken and fall back. He faced the dismal prospect of having his reign of less than six months turn into a pathetic footnote in Roman history. He galloped frantically to Maximian's legion and shouted orders for a counterattack. Maximian moved quickly in front of his men and with his sword raised high he called on them to drive a wedge into the advancing enemy forces. Galerius also led his men to a fierce attack from the side, while the archers under Constantius unleashed their arrows against the rear of the enemy. After a momentary confusion Carinus' forces regained the initiative. Both sides were fighting with savage ferocity. The outcome of the fight now hung on the balance.

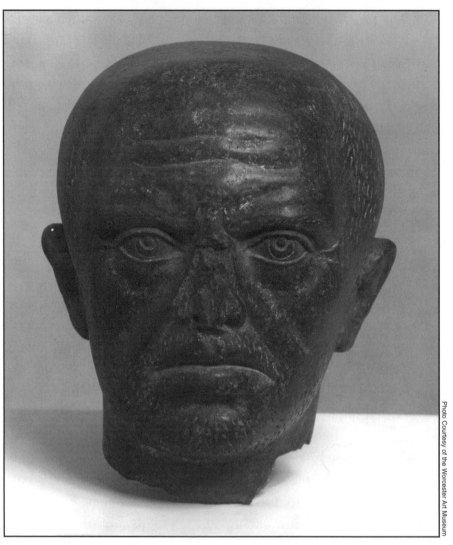

Photo Courtesy of the Worcester Art Museum

Head in black basalt believed to be that of Diocletian.

Then, at this critical moment, something strange happened. The bugles sounded retreat and Carinus' forces, turning around, ran to the hills leaving the battlefield. There, they stopped as if waiting for new orders.

Puzzled, Diocletian sent couriers to his legion commanders with orders to halt and wait. They did not have to wait long. Within minutes two horsemen peeled off from the Carinus ranks and galloped to where Diocletian waited on horseback flanked by a maniple of horsemen from his imperial guard.

One of the two enemy horsemen turned out to be a legion commander who as soon as he came within hearing distance reined his horse in and raised his arm in salute. "Augustus, Gaius, Aurelius, Valerius, Diocletianus, your legions salute you," he called out at the top of his voice, adding, "Carinus is dead."

The words swept through the ranks and the sound of the jubilant cheers and the striking of swords and spears on shields reverberated on the hilltops and the mountains beyond. Diocletian had won.

What had happened?

Later in the day, soldiers brought to Diocletian the body of his slain opponent. A sword had been plunged deep into his back. That was strange since he was too far from the hand-to-hand fighting to have been killed by an enemy soldier striking from the rear. Diocletian ordered an investigation and within two days the truth came out. A dishonored husband, a young Tribune, had killed Carinus. It appears that the lecherous emperor had "forced his lust" on the Tribune's young and beautiful wife, and the dishonored husband had waited for the right moment to avenge his shame.

"I do not want to know his name. Otherwise I will have to punish him and that will be the ultimate ingratitude," Diocletian told the man who had delivered the report.

It is almost comical to think that a quarrel over a woman had saved the day for Diocletian. If Carinus had won at Margus, Diocletian would have been finished and so would have Flavius Constantius—and so would have Constantine's prospects of leaving his mark on history.

One can easily imagine the joy that must have swept through the governor's mansion the day the victors came back, their faces darkened with dust and sweat but their eyes shining with a happy glow.

Diocletian was now the sole, undisputed emperor.

ONE STEP HIGHER

Diocletian was not given much time to savor his victory. Less than three months after the battle at Margus, alarming reports came from Gaul which had been left defenseless when the legions moved to Italy and Illyricum to fight for Carinus. The Germanic tribes from across the Rhine were again on the move, the invading bands leaving charred ruins in their path and forcing thousands of peasants to abandon the farms and seek safety behind the strong walls Emperor Probus had built around the towns a few years back. Before long, gangs of young marauders began to criss-cross the deserted countryside, pillaging whatever the Germanic invaders had not burned or taken away, and killing and raping those who had not yet abandoned the exposed hamlets. As time went on, the roving, unconnected hordes swelled in numbers and coalesced into two strong armies of savage outlaws who called themselves "Bagaudae," a Celtic word meaning "valiant." Then, they raised two of their leaders—Aelianus and Amandus—to the dignity of Augustus. The fertile valleys of eastern Lugdunensis and Viennensis (Loire and Rhone), one of the richest farming regions in the empire, were at the mercy of those wild bandits.

Diocletian could not possibly ignore the urgent pleas of the local people. In the end, his fertile mind came up with an ingenious new twist to a familiar arrangement. In the summer of 285, at an impressive ceremony in Mediolanun (today's Milan), he raised his close friend Maximian to the rank of Caesar, bestowing on him at the same time the special title *Filius Augusti* (Son of the Augustus). Maximian was now Caesar Marcus Aurelius Valerius Maximianus. Diocletian had rewarded the man who had rushed to his side and hailed him as the Augustus while Aper's lifeless body lay on the ground. At the same time he had wisely set the stage for a division of responsibility in governing the sprawling empire.

The new "Caesar" was assigned control over all the legions that Carinus had commanded only a few months before. The legion commanders had shifted their allegiance to the victors because being practical men they had no reason to remain loyal to a dead emperor. Maximian now commanded a formidable force of over fifty thousand men and hundreds of horsemen. His first task was to destroy the Bagaudae. Soon after the ceremony, Maximian left for Gaul and set up his headquarters at Moguntiacum (Meintz). From that strategically located stronghold, he directed the operations not only against the Bagaudae but also against the Germanic tribes.

Like Diocletian, Maximian was of Illyrian stock, born at a village near Sirmium, a strict disciplinarian and a good military commander. He had been a legion commander for over three years when at the age of thirty-six he was elevated to the dignity of a Caesar. He was a gruff, humorless man but a brave and fair-minded commander who knew how to win the loyalty of his men. Above all, he was fiercely loyal to Diocletian and that was the quality the emperor valued most.

Maximian had a job to do in Gaul and he was determined to prove that he was worthy of the great honor Diocletian had bestowed on him. In the following months, the Bagaudae were hunted like mad dogs by small detachments of mounted archers. By the spring of the following year, the roaming bands were decimated, Aelianus and Amandus were dead and those few who were still alive retreated into the forests or melted into the nameless crowds of the larger towns.

Maximian had barely broken the back of the Bagaudae, when

another threat rose. Frankish pirates form Germania Inferior (Belgium, Holland and the northwest corner of today's Germany), emboldened by the weakening of the Roman Fleet patrolling Fretum Galicum (the Channel), unleashed devastating raids on the merchant ships that plowed the waters between Gaul and the British Isles. Those sea raiders swept down with their fast boats on the lumbering cargo ships, playing havoc with the vital trade between the two shores. Maximian had no experience with the sea. A man who had spent all his life on firm ground, he inevitably found the ocean a mysterious and frightening element. His legion commanders were just as ignorant of the ways of the sea. He needed an experienced seaman to lead the fight against the pirates. He chose Carausius, a seaman and the son of a seaman, a Gaul from Germania Inferior, who had risen in the legions to high military command.

Carausius caused such devastating damage to the pirates, that in January 286 Maximian proclaimed victory in the north sea, giving generous praise to his successful commander. He should have waited. Three months later, Carausius moved with his fleet to the British Isles and there, near Eboracum (York), he was proclaimed by his legions Augustus and Dominus of a new, independent *Imperium Britanniarum* which covered the Roman lands in Britain and most of the northern section of Gaul, from the Atlantic to the mouth of the Rhine.

Diocletian was in Pannonia when the news reached him. In his eyes, Carausius had unsurped the *purple* with treachery and should not be allowed to survive. Otherwise, other ambitious men in every corner of the empire might elevate themselves to the dignity of Augustus, breaking up the empire.

Diocletian also knew what titles meant to people. Carausius was now calling himself an Augustus. As long as Maximian remained a Caesar he was at a disadvantage. A few weeks later, in April 286, Diocletian held a symbolic ceremony at Mediolanum and elevated Maximian to the dignity of Augustus.

To prepare for the destruction of Carausius, Diocletian and

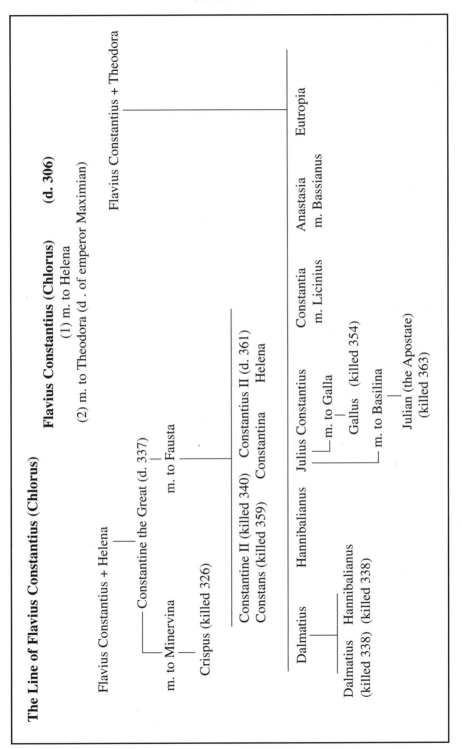

The Line of Flavius Constantius (Chlorus)

Flavius Constantius (Chlorus)   **(d. 306)**

(1) m. to Helena

(2) m. to Theodora (d . of emperor Maximian)

Flavius Constantius + Helena

Flavius Constantius + Theodora

Constantine the Great (d. 337)

m. to Minervina   m. to Fausta

Crispus (killed 326)

Constantine II (killed 340)   Constantius II (d. 361)

Constans (killed 359)   Constantina   Helena

Dalmatius   Hannibalianus   Julius Constantius   Constantia   Anastasia   Eutropia

m. Licinius   m. Bassianus

Dalmatius   Hannibalianus

(killed 338)   (killed 338)

m. to Galla

Gallus   (killed 354)

m. to Basilina

Julian (the Apostate)

(killed 363)

Maximian launched a great offensive against the Germanic lands, attacking with large forces, Maximian from Gaul and Diocletian from Pannonia and Raetia (today's Hungary, Czechoslovakia and Switzerland). The operation was so successful that a local orator had this to say in a *panegyric* during a victory celebration at Moguntiacum. Some degree of exaggeration was acceptable on such occasions but this time the panegyrist was close to the truth. "When did the Rhine shrink in its bed," he intoned, "after a long spell of dry weather without making us shiver with fear? When did it ever swell to a flood without giving us a feeling a being secure?" In other words, the danger of invasion from the Germanic tribes rose and fell with the water level of the Rhine. "But now," the panegyrist went on, "all our fears are gone. The river may dry up and shrink until the water has no strength to roll even a pebble, and none will be afraid. As far as I can see beyond the Rhine, all is Roman." At least at the time he was uttering those words he was not overstating the truth.

Maximian, now in control of the Rhine, used the next two years to build a formidable fleet. In the spring of 289, he gave the signal for the invasion of Britain. The operation failed dismally. His fighting ships were destroyed as soon as they sailed out of the mouth of the Rhine into the open sea, while the larger ships carrying the soldiers, the horses, and the provisions never came out of the river.

On top of this misfortune, Maximian lost his trusted and capable *Praetorian Prefect* Afranius Hannibalianus. With the thorn of Carausius still piercing his side, Maximian needed not only a capable administrator but also a man who understood strategy and tactics and who could lead men to battle. Diocletian recommended the governor of Dalmatia, Flavius Constantius. By another twist of fate, Constantine's father had moved up to become second only to Emperor Maximian.

Constantine had just turned eighteen when the family left Salonae in late February 290 on the way to Moguntiacum. He was now a tall, athletic young man, with an aquiline nose and large, penetrating eyes. One could hardly recognize in him the peasant boy that had come to Salonae eight years ago.

For Constantine and his mother this was a move to a different world far removed from what they knew at Salonae, where life—however more complex than the simple life in the town of Naissus—had by now become familiar and comfortable. What they did not know at the time was that the dramatic rise of Flavius Constantius would be even more fateful for his son's future.

SON OF A CAESAR

A few months after his arrival to Moguntiacum, Constantine entered the cadet school of the *Protectores Domestici*. It was the beginning of his military career.

The ancient chroniclers have very little to say about Constantine's training as a cadet. It is doubtful that he was treated differently from other cadets only because his father happened to be the Praetorian Prefect. Favoritism would have been out of character for Flavius Constantius and out of step with Roman tradition. In fact, being the son of Flavius Constantius was one more reason to try harder and excel. Constantine must have been a good student in the arts of war, but his successes in later years indicate that he was learning much more than how to fight. He evidently was following with a keen eye what was happening around him, and how the senior Augustus was strengthening the empire, step by step, using military force and clever diplomacy to blunt the barbarian threat and solidify his power.

A little over six years had passed since that fateful day outside of Nicomedia when Diocletian had plunged his sword into Aper's heart. They were difficult years but Diocletian could look back with satisfaction. He had many reasons to be pleased. True, Carausius still was left unpunished, and there were occasional disturbances in Syria and Egypt, but after the great offensive of 288 the Germanic tribes had been pushed far to the east and the land beyond the Rhine was secure, a treaty with Persia had stabilized the Orient, and a determined campaign against the Sarmatians and the Goths had brought peace along the banks of the Danube in the Balkans. Optimism had returned with this feeling of security and with it the supply of food became more abundant now that the peasants could safely till the land and bring in the harvest. Most important, Diocletian had survived. He had not been slain in a palace coup, nor had he faced treason from his brother Augustus as many had predicted. Both, their victories and their reverses had strengthened their bonds of loyalty.

Diocletian had wisely rewarded those loyal to him, making some of his generals governors of new provinces and opening the way to younger men to move up to higher command in the legions, creating a new aristocracy that held the reins of authority in a broad net with all its strands ending in the hands of the emperor. Maximian had willingly and wisely accepted Diocletian's supreme authority, not out of fear but out of genuine respect for the wisdom and ability of the senior Augustus. It will not be inaccurate to say that, since the days of Marcus Aurelius a century earlier, the Roman Empire had not seen at the helm a man of such extraordinary sagacity and imagination.

Knowing well the value of symbolism, Diocletian decided to have in February 291 a magnificent celebration in Mediolanum. Maximian would come from Moguntiacum and Diocletian himself would travel from Illyricum.

Both Augusti turned the journey into a triumphal procession. In every city they passed, the local notables organized elaborate receptions and festivities. An imperial visit was always an expensive affair for the local people but it also offered them the opportunity to present to the emperor in person their requests and seek favors of all kinds.

As the two emperors and their retinue moved from town to town converging on Mediolanum, jubilant crowds greeted them at every stop, and eloquent panegyrists extolled their glory in orations full of flattery and exaggeration but which nevertheless left for us valuable images of contemporary life and history. The local panegyrist in the town of Massalia (Marseilles), describing Maximian's passing through the countryside, sketched the procession with vivid phrases. "The closer you came, and the more people recognized you, the more the fields filled with crowds, not only of men rushing to see, but also with shepherds and their herds leaving the pastures and the woods. The peasants raced to report to the villages what they had seen. Fires were lit on the altars, incense thrown in, libations poured, victims slaughtered for the sacrifice. Everywhere there was jubilant dancing and cheering." Even though we may doubt the genuine joy of the celebrants, there is no question that in the drab life of the peasant the event was indeed a cause for celebration.

Diocletian reached Mediolanum with his retinue two days after the arrival of Maximian. Already waiting for the two Augusti, were the senior senators from Rome, attired in their traditional white togas.

The leading citizens (*curiales*) of Mediolanum had spared no expense, proud that their city now rivaled Rome in dignity.* A panegyrist, referring to Rome, said on the occasion: "She sent the illustrious men of her own Senate, gladly sharing with Mediolanum, a blessed city, the brilliance of her majesty. So, the capital of the Empire appeared to be where the two Augusti met." He was stating a plain fact. Rome remained the eternal city, encrusted in ancient glory and tradition, but the actual center of power was where the emperor happened to be at the time.

Three days after their arrival, the two Augusti took part in an

---

* The inhabitants of Mediolanum and those who came from the neighboring towns were treated to performances of ludi scaenici on stage, munera gladiatoria in the arena, and ludi circenses in the circus, expertly organized by the city decurions with contributions from wealthy citizens and city funds. As always, the gladiator fights drew capacity crowds. The spectators were mostly men, for the gory spectacle was certainly not for the squeamish. The fighting was fierce as desperation drove even the least strong or skillful to unbelievable feats of endurance and courage. As the gladiators fought for their lives, the roar of the crowd rose with every masterly blow, every gush of blood, the tumult of the shouting merging with the clanging of swords and shields. The professional gladiators were pitted against criminals condemned to death for murder, treason, or arson. In a way, the Romans had found a way to turn a public execution into a spectator sport. The criminals had chosen

impressive ceremony at the circus where they offered sacrifice to Jove—the supreme god the Greeks called Zeus and the Romans, Jupiter. After the sacrifice, the chief *haruspex* studied the entrails of the sacrificial bull and pronounced the omens favorable. Then the high priest of the temple of Jupiter Optimus Maximus who had come from Rome, proclaimed Diocletian son of Jove. It was a symbolic gesture implying that like Jove—the ruler of the universe who had slain the evil Titans—Diocletian would also rule supreme and destroy the enemies of the empire.

Next, the high priest proclaimed Maximian son of Hercules, the legendary hero who had defeated all his enemies, even the many-headed Hydra. Maximian the Herculean would destroy even those

---

to fight in the arena in the hope that they might survive, as some did, and escape death on the executioner's block.

Even more popular were the chariot races in the circus where betting was heavy and the spectacle exciting. The thrill of a race was not so much in its speed which did not exceed twenty to twenty-five miles an hour. The race was a contest of skill. Each race had seven laps going around and around the spina, the marble wall that ran down the middle of the long, elliptical arena, the entire race lasting some fifteen minutes. But what a thrill it was as the horses crashed into each other, wheels came loose, axles broke, and charioteers lost their precarious footing and fell off their chariot, dragged behind on the ground, desperately trying to cut with their knives the leather straps that still held them tied to the chariot, hoping that the deadly hoofs of horses racing past would not land on their head. With four horses hitched to each chariot and four teams racing side by side, the arena was a crowded place and accidents were not rare.

In the ludi scaenici, the stage performances were mostly given by mimes, acrobats, jugglers, and puppeteers. Most of the people in the audience were not literate enough to grasp and appreciate the subtlety of language in a play by Terentius or Plautus. They preferred simple skits with short plots of violence and sex, of adulterous liaisons and entanglements, recreations of simple myths, the show usually ending with scantily dressed young actresses dancing and stripping on stage to the boisterous delight of the audience.

Each time during the festivities that Diocletian and Maximian appeared at the imperial podium of the circus or the amphitheater, they were cheered wildly by the large crowds. Most of the spectators had not seen the two men before and the cheering was hardly a sign of personal affection. But people knew what was expected of them and saw no reason to offend with silence or jeers those who held supreme power. Besides, those two men had brought stability and a more secure supply of food and that was a very good reason for cheering.

Porphyry statue in St. Mark's Square, Venice, possibly taken from Constantinople in 1204 by the Crusaders who occupied the city. It immortalizes the *Tetrarchy* in the persons of four co-emperors, each Augustus embracing his Caesar.

barbarians who rose like the legendary Hydra with a new head rising when one was cut off.

Knowing that the gods are most helpful when their priests are happy and grateful, Diocletian reciprocated by giving strong support to the ancient religion which in those days was being challenged by the mystery religions, such as those of Mithras, Mani, or Christ. His generous gifts pleased the priests even more and turned them into avid champions of the benevolent emperors. The traditional pagan religion was not organized in a consolidated hierarchy but any sign of support from the imperial center traveled through the empire and priestly favor translated into one more instrument for public support.

The celebration was not the main reason for the meeting of the two fellow emperors. For the first time, Diocletian discussed with Maximian a novel idea he had been pondering in his mind. The empire was too large even for two men. Each of them needed a trusted assistant, a loyal Caesar, to be responsible for part of the empire. They needed a *Tetrarchy*. This was definitely not a division of the empire, only a division of responsibility among four men. The principle of *patrimonium indivisum* (the undivided patrimony) would remain in tact.

Unquestionably the identity of the two new Caesars was of paramount importance. They had to be not only capable men but most importantly loyal men—men the two emperors could trust. Diocletian selected as his Caesar the general who had led the cheers acclaiming Diocletian as the Augustus on that fateful November day outside of Nicomedia. Gaius Galerius was to become Caesar under Diocletian, responsible for the Orient. As Caesar under Maximian, the two emperors chose Flavius Constantius. Young Constantine was about to become the son of a Caesar. At the moment, of course, he had no inkling of what was being decided by the two emperors. Neither could he imagine at the time what would be the price for his father's meteoric rise.

Diocletian told his brother Augustus that he wanted to solidify the bonds of loyalty with the ties of matrimony. Gaius Galerius would be asked to divorce his wife and marry Diocletian's daughter, Valeria, who was twenty-three years younger than Galerius.

Flavius Constantius should also divorce his wife Helena and marry Maximian's step-daughter Theodora, who was from his wife's

Cities and Towns

1. Corduba
2. Caesar-Augusta
3. Pons Aelius
4. Eboracum
5. Londinium
6. Gesoriacum
7. Lutetia
8. Augusta Treverorum
9. Lugdunum
10. Moguntiacum
11. Arelate
12. Massalia
13. Augusta Taurinorum
14. Mediolanum
15. Ravenna
16. Aquileia
17. Carnuntum
18. Aquincum
19. Sirmium
20. Salonae
21. Naissus
22. Thessalonica
23. Novae
24. Durostorum
25. Serdica
26. Hadrianopolis
27. Byzantium
28. Nicomedia
29. Nicaea
30. Ancyra
31. Tarsus
32. Nisibis
33. Antioch
34. Berytus
35. Caesaria
36. Aelia Capitolina
37. Alexandria
38. Athens
39. Carthage

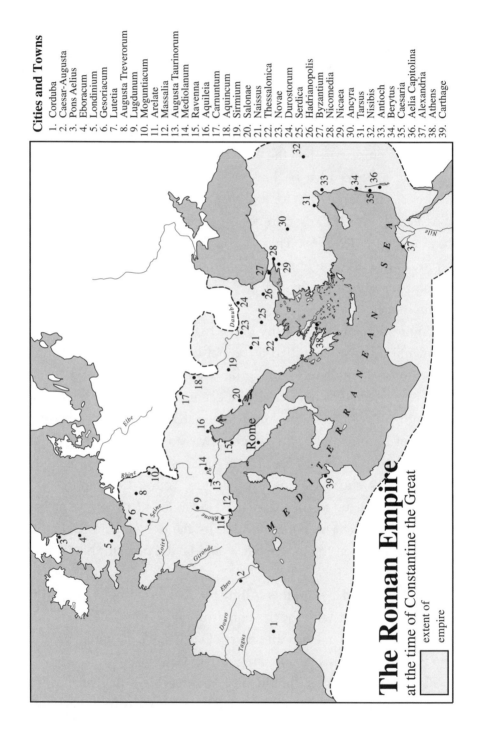

The Roman Empire
at the time of Constantine the Great

extent of empire

previous marriage, twenty-six years younger than Constantius. Maximian had a daughter of his own with his wife Eutropia. Her name was Fausta, but at that time she was only two years old. He also had a son, Maxentius, just over five. Both Fausta and Maxentius would play important and tragic roles in Constantine's life but at that time Constantine was hardly aware of their existence.

CHAPTER II

THE LONG WAIT

DIVORCE

Soon after his return to Moguntiacum from the festivities in Mediolanum, Maximian decided to move his imperial household to Arelate (Arles) in southern Gaul. With the Rhine now secure, he had no reason to stay in the drab and forbidding Moguntiacum. Flavius Constantius as the *Paetorian Prefect* moved with the imperial household.

Helena must have found Arelate a delightful place. The market was full with an amazing variety of goods brought from the Orient, from Africa, from Spain and Italy. Across the river over the pontoon bridge one could cross to the west bank and the suburb of Tinquetailla which was studded with private villas, pottery kilns, and vegetable stalls with fresh vegetables and fruits from the nearby farms. The city itself was impressive. The arena (well preserved to this day) was a smaller version of the famed Flavian Amphitheater (the Colosseum) in Rome, and the open theater showed the strong Greek influence left since the days when the Greeks had set up the nearby colony of Massalia. The theater was adorned with a fine collection of Greek and Roman sculptures, an imposing statue of Octavius, the first Augustus, and two beautifully crafted altars of Apollo. Those who had said that Arelate was the little Rome of Gaul were not bending the truth.

As a junior officer in the Imperial Guard, Constantine moved to

Photo Courtesy of the Library of Congress Collection

The Amphitheater in Arles (Arelate) as it is today.

Arelate and that made Helena's happiness complete. All she wanted was to be close to the two men who gave meaning to her life. But the happy days in Arelate did not last long. Helena's world crashed suddenly the day Flavius Constantius told her that he had to end their marriage because Diocletian wanted him to marry Maximian's stepdaughter, Theodora, before he raised him to the dignity of Caesar. We do not know exactly when Flavius Constantius divorced Helena. Most likely it happened before the end of the year, a few months after the great celebration in Mediolanum.

The realization that the forthcoming rise of Flavius Constantius would help the future of her son must have softened the blow. Helena, a practical and proud woman, most likely tried to keep her grief to herself, even though her heart was bleeding. The ancient sources do not tell us at what time in her life Helena embraced the Christian faith but we may not be very wrong to assume that it was during those painful days in Arelate that she turned to Christ seeking solace and hope.

From the record left to us it appears that Constantine was at first angered and bewildered by his father's decision. This was a natural reaction. The two people he loved most were to part. It was probably his mother who tried to calm him by saying that what mattered to her most was his future and that if she had to pay a price to help him rise to the mountain top no suffering was too great. This was for Constantine the most excruciating crisis in his young life and could have easily broken the bonds of love that tied him to his father. That those bonds remained strong tells us that he was told, and that he accepted, that the divorce was a necessary sacrifice his parents had to make for his sake. For Flavius Constantius to reject Diocletian's demand would have signaled the end of his career and the crashing of the high hopes he had for his son.

In the spring of 292, Helena, with a small escort for protection on the road, left Arelate for the village of Drepanon, a few miles south of Bosporus. It seemed as though Flavius Constantius was exiling Helena to the end of the world. But he had a good reason and his decision shows how thoughtful a man he was. One of the conditions for his elevation to Caesar was that Constantine would be transferred to Diocletian's imperial guard. The village of Drepanon was located a few miles from Nicomedia which for the past four years had become Diocletian's official capital. With young Constantine serving in Diocletian's imperial guard and spending much time in Nicomedia, Drepanon was not a far away place of exile but a place where Helena would be near her son.

Soon after Helena's departure, Flavius Constantius married Theodora. He was now a member of the imperial family of Maximian Herculeus. Exactly one year later, he was elevated to Caesar by Maximian at Mediolanum on the same day Diocletian elevated Galerius in Sirmium. The panegyrist who delivered the traditional oration spoke of the felicitous number four, reminding his audience that there are four seasons, four elements, four continents, and that now the empire was blessed with four rulers jointly defending its peace and prosperity.

As was the custom, new coins of excellent quality were minted commemorating the event and saluting the *Jovi et Herculi Conservatori Caesares*.

The day after the investiture, Constantine left for Sirmium to join Diocletian's imperial guard. He was only a centurion but he was also the son of a Caesar. The peasant lad from Naissus had traveled already a long way.

NICOMEDIA

From Sirmium after the festivities, Diocletian with his "sacred retinue"—this strange mixture of high ranking civilian office-holders and military officers of his personal guard—went on an inspection tour through the Balkans, accompanied by Galerius, now his Caesar. The route and the dates for Diocletian's journey have come down to us in the rescripts and edicts issued by the emperor and his Caesar while en route. The area they toured was to be part of Galerius' domain, and evidently Diocletian wanted to make all understand that from now on Galerius was the man with the highest authority for his region.

Born to a peasant family in the village of Romulianum in Moesia (today's Bulgaria), Galerius was a lowly herdsman before he was recruited into the army. He was a tall, huge man with a barrel chest, a thick dark beard, and a booming voice. That he was also flat-nosed and slightly myopic did not make his appearance less formidable.

It was almost autumn by the time Galerius went back to Sirmium and Diocletian with his traveling retinue reached Byzantium on his way to Nicomedia. Byzantium was a strategically located town perched on the slopes of the European side of the Straits of Bosporus, the home of fishermen and boatmen who made a modest living from the sea and from ferrying passengers from one side of the Straits to the other. Every time a large force came to cross the narrow seaway between Europe and Asia, the boatmen of Bosporus were as happy as farmers after a bumper crop.

This time more than a thousand men and many dozens of horses, mules and wagons had to be ferried to the Asiatic side. For young Constantine this was a novel experience. He saw for the first time such a large number of people and animals transported across the sea. The crossing was difficult. The current in the narrow seaway was strong and treacherous and only the seasoned seamen of the Bosporus could navigate safely the short span between the two shores. Accidents did happen and sometimes men and horses fell into the dark water and were swallowed by the unseen forces that lurked beneath the surface. When a boat, pushed by the current, yawed and heaved and the boatmen frantically struggled to steer it back on course, the frightened horses could capsize the boat with their sudden and jerky movements. Most of the time, the boatmen managed somehow to take their cargo and their passengers safely across. But the crossing was also exhilarating, as the salty breeze and the spray from the breaking whitecaps brushed against one's face.

For the first time in his life Constantine stepped on Asia as the boat on which he was riding reached the opposite shore. A new chapter in his life was about to begin.

The following day the imperial train reached Nicomedia. The town was nestled in the inner loop of a small bay which came out to the Sea of Marmara. New piers had been added to the harbor and many cargo ships, galleys, and barges were moored alongside, stevedores emptying or loading them, seamen moving about, merchants haggling over prices, mule wagons waiting to be filled with merchandise. To the east, the old town was now surrounded by many villas, their marble porticos glowing white inside luscious gardens, perched on the hills that sloped toward the bay. Those were the homes of the new aristocracy that had risen around Diocletian's imperial power.

Nicomedia had been Diocletian's capital for almost four years and the effect of the imperial presence on the small town was stunning. New, imposing public buildings were rising in every empty space. A large amphitheater and a circus were already under construction, and in the midst of it all was Diocletian's imperial palace with the adjacent large barracks for the *Protectores Domestici*. In the main square, right across from the sprawling bulk of the palace, the Christians had an imposing church.

The church had been there before Diocletian built his palace and he had decided to let it stand. He saw no harm in it. As Pontifex Maximus, he was legally the head of the Roman religion. But the Romans were usually tolerant on religious matters and often accepted in their pantheon new gods and goddesses from the regions they conquered. The Christian sect had been around for some three hundred years and it was benignly ignored most of the time even though their ways were vexing to many people. The Christians differed from the followers of the other mystery religions, such as that of Mithras or Osiris, in that they rejected totally the traditional gods, being devoted exclusively to a young Jew who had been crucified in Aelia Capitolina (Jerusalem) some thirty-five years before the city's destruction by (later) Emperor Titus.

Today, the Turkish town Izmit shows no traces of all the splendor that was Nicomedia in Diocletian's days. Most of the great buildings were destroyed in a series of earthquakes not long after Diocletian was gone, and the emperors who came after him let the ruins crumble even more. Constantine, who in 293 was a young centurion in the imperial guard, would one day, as emperor, build a new capital on the Straits of Bosporus, to be named Constantinople, the City of Constantine. But all that was far into the future, and on the day the young centurion came to Nicomedia for the first time, he could only spin secret dreams.

For the next eleven years Constantine was to remain a member of Diocletian's "sacred retinue," traveling with the emperor on his inspection tours and on his military campaigns. It was a time of learning the secrets of governing by watching a master who was inventing some of the rules himself as he went along. It was also a time to be patient and self-effacing and Constantine prudently kept himself out of the lime-light.

For a keen mind there was much to observe and learn. Diocletian was remodeling the administration, the economy, the army and the defense of the empire. He had introduced a rigid protocol in the palace—the few who were admitted to the emperor's presence were required to bow and kiss the hem of his robe, the gesture he called by the Greek word *proskynesis*—and he limited the provincial governors to civilian duties, giving the military tasks exclusively to military officers. The orators of panegyrics at the time often spoke of *duces* and *judices*, the first term applying to military commanders, the second to civil governors. To make the administration more manageable and more effective, he cut up the provinces into smaller geographic areas, increasing the number from forty-eight to one hundred and ten and placing them under twelve dioceses covering large areas, such as the entire Gaul or the entire Italian peninsula, each supervised by a vicar. At the same time he opened the way for the appointment of many more capable and loyal men to high positions.

Constantine enjoyed the luxury of observing and learning without being responsible for solving the major problems the emperor was facing every day. It was an unplanned but valuable apprentice-ship that one day would pay off.

THE SIEGE OF GESORIACUM

T he unspoken truce that had followed Maximian's failure to invade the British Isles four years earlier was soon to come to an end. Coins minted in Gaul showed the two Augusti, Diocletian and Maximian on one side, and on the other Jove with his thunderbolt destroying a Titan and Hercules lifting and crushing Antaeus. The implication was clear. The two fellow emperors were saying that the time to deal with Carausius was fast approaching.

Caesar Flavius Constantius was chosen to lead the assault. Always a methodical man, he chose a two-stage strategic plan. First, he would take control of northern Gaul with its ports, dockyards, and forts, and most important its people who were familiar with the ways of the sea. Maximian was to have under his direct command only the legions needed to keep watch on the Rhine.

In early August, Flavius Constantius launched his campaign into northern Gaul. In a proclamation, he pledged not to punish those who would surrender and come over to his side, no matter how high their rank. Flavius Constantius needed as many men as he could bring under his command, so his leniency had a purpose. Every time he was about to unleash an attack, he had his heralds read to the opposing troops the contents of the proclamation. It worked. A few officers who tried to prevent their men from going over to the other side were slain. Constantius' much stronger force was, of course, another, very convincing argument, and so one unit after another shifted allegiance to the new Caesar. In the time-honored tradition of the legions, allegiance went to the leader who held the power.

Three weeks after Flavius Constantius had launched his drive to the north, his forces stood under the walls and the bastions of Gesoriacum (today's Boulogne)—the most important seaport on the northern coast of Gaul on the Fretum Gallicum (the Channel). He knew that if Gesoriacum fell, the other ports along the coast would fold without a fight.

When the garrison commander refused to surrender, Flavius Constantius laid a masterful siege. He surrounded the city from land but he also constructed with rocks a barrier blocking the entrance to the harbor. With no supplies coming from across the Channel, famine reduced the inhabitants and the garrison to eating dogs and rodents. In the end a deputation of the local decurions went to the commander and implored him to accept Constantius' generous terms. He refused. That same night he was murdered by one of his guards. The next day the officer who now commanded the garrison sent a delegation to Flavius Constantius. The famed legion XXX Ulpia Victrix was prepared to surrender the city. The following day, Caesar Flavius Constantius entered the city as the starving people came out into the streets cheering wildly at the sight of the long column of wagons bringing food.

The news that Gesoriacum had surrendered spread rapidly throughout the towns and forts along the coast. One after the other, they sent delegations pledging their allegiance to Augustus Maximian and Caesar Flavius Constantius. The first stage in the strategic plan had been completed before the celebration of the Saturnalia in December.

Two months after the fall of Gesoriacum, Flavius Constantius received a heartening report. Carausius was dead, murdered while asleep. The man behind the murder was his best friend, Allectus, his "economic minister," the man who, seven years before, had planted in his mind the idea of betraying Maximian.

Before long, Allectus, now claiming the dignity of an Augustus, began to issue coins stressing the benefits of peace and making subtle overtures for reconciliation. Diocletian was adamant and so was Maximian. Nothing but total surrender and the dismantling of the *Imperium Britanniarum* would be acceptable. Still, until Flavius Constantius was ready to cross the Channel and set foot on the British Isles, they would let Allectus play the Augustus.

With his customary efficiency, Flavius Constantius set up more shipyards to build ships for fighting at sea and for transporting troops and supplies, while at the same time training at feverish pace the men in the legions how to fight at sea, seize an enemy vessel, land later on the beaches, and above all how to shed their fear of the angry seas—not an easy task with soldiers who had lived all their lives on dry land.

IN THE SERVICE
OF DIOCLETIAN

W hile his father was preparing for the invasion of the British Isles, Constantine got a first taste of real fighting. In the spring of 294, Diocletian left Nicomedia at the head of a large force, moved through Thrace and Moesia, and crossed the Danube. At the same time, Galerius with another strong force left Sirmium and marched toward the great river. The two armies moved deep into the territory of the Sarmatians and the Goths, attacking them in a pincer movement from east and west. In the carnage, thousands perished, men, women and children. For the first time in his life, young Constantine saw what war was really like.

Combat was not the only experience—violent but also exhilarating—young Constantine had during this campaign. He was also given a firsthand look into Diocletian's mind as a holder of the imperial power. Shortly after the slaughter ended, and most of the barbarian warriors were either dead or maimed or fleeing to the forests for their life, Diocletian sent messengers to some of the surviving Sarmatian and Goth elders and invited them to a meeting. We do not have a verbatim record of the negotiations but we know in broad strokes what was proposed and what was accepted.

Diocletian reminded the elders—who hardly needed any

reminding—of the harsh consequences of warfare and offered them the benefits of peace. Their land which had now come under Roman control would be given back to them, their people allowed to return to their homes and live in peace under the protection of Rome. Roman garrisons would be posted in their major settlements, and their sons would be permitted to join the legions. If all went well and peace was kept, their people would someday become Roman citizens. Moreover, they could expect to be protected against hostile tribes pressing from the north.

They found the terms generous and they accepted them. With a deft combination of force and diplomacy, Diocletian had extended Roman rule beyond the Danube and, as he had done earlier along the Rhine, he had made the lands on both sides of the great river secure. His strategy was not entirely novel. Since the early days, the Roman empire was built on this wise mixture of force and diplomacy. The Romans conquered the lands, placed them under the control of Roman garrisons and then allowed the local people to live their lives and eventually become Roman citizens. Most important, a person's ethnic or tribal origin never stood in the way of his rising as high as his ability and good fortune could take him.

The Danube was now at peace but trouble was brewing else-where. Urgent dispatches from the Roman governor in Egypt spoke of heavy losses inflicted on the trade caravans by black horsemen sweeping from the south and the desert in the east, killing the traders and making off with the merchandise.

"These bandits who call themselves Blemmyes make the collection of taxes very difficult, and undermine the authority of Rome. What is the good to be under the protection of Rome if Rome cannot protect us, is what they all say, even to my own face," wrote the Roman governor with brutal honesty.

Egypt had been a valuable Roman possession for over two and a half centuries. The Greek aristocrats—the descendants of Alexander's warriors—were arrogant and self-centered, especially those in Alexandria, looking down on anyone else. But they knew how to cooperate with Rome and—with the exception of the Alexandrians, who since Caesar's days were exempt from taxation—paid their taxes and their *annona* (payments in produce), as long as they could have the native Egyptians till the farms and bring in the harvest. Egypt was too valuable a province. The raids of the black bandits could not be allowed to go on.

Diocletian chose Galerius for the task. Since those marauders were attacking on horseback, in small bands, coming suddenly out of nowhere, Galerius formed small detachments of archers on horseback who could hunt the bandits, moving swiftly and suddenly after them. The detachments even used fake caravans to draw out the bandits.

Galerius destroyed most of the bands by the end of the year and, satisfied that he had brought the situation under control, he started on the long trek back, reaching Nicomedia in late February. He stayed there for a few days to go over the campaign with Diocletian, before going on to Thessaloniki which had become his capital now that the Danube was secure. Constantine had not gone to Egypt with Galerius, since he was in the service of Diocletian, but we can be sure discussions of the campaign must have been a hot topic among the officers and men. The tactics Galerius had used were another valuable lesson for a keen and curious mind.

During the days Galerius stayed in Nicomedia, he told Diocletian about the Manicheans, another mystery religion that Mani, a Parthian nobleman born some eighty years ago, had started in Persia. He apparently had a vision that he was the last of the great teachers, after Zoroaster and the Jew that the Christians worshipped as a god. Like the cult of Mithras, the Manicheans, too, claimed that there is a world of light (good) and a world of darkness (evil) and that in the end the light will win out.

To Diocletian, another mystery religion would be of little concern. But Galerius told him that the Persian king, Narses, had taken this sect under his wing, had given money to their preachers and sent them to the lands west of the Euphrates, and especially to Egypt where they had set up many close-knit communities, with bishops and priests, and teachers and with sacred scriptures they claimed Mani had received from God.

Diocletian was not overly concerned with matters of theology but the information that the Persian king was using this sect could not leave him indifferent. There was more. The governor in Thebes had intercepted a letter by one called Paniskos. He was writing from the town of Coptos to his wife in Philadelphia in the north, telling her that their group of "select men" was gathering weapons and that more and more men were joining the worship of Mani every day. Paniskos was arrested and tortured but he died before he revealed the purpose for the weapons or other useful information. His wife killed herself as soon as she heard what had happened to her husband.

Without delay, Diocletian sent a dispatch to the governor in Egypt ordering him to keep an eye on the Manicheans and report on their activities. Time would soon prove that he had good reason to be concerned.

Constantine was now twenty-two years old. There is no reason to doubt that he did his share of drinking and whoring just like his fellow officers. But then he met Minervina and he fell in love.

She appears to have been the daughter of a lowly sandal-maker. We have no description of her but she must have been very attractive to win over a strapping young man who was also the son of the Caesar. This last, of course, presented a special problem. Because of Constantine's status, marriage between them was out of the question. Very likely Constantine did not think of starting a family at first. But then Minervina became pregnant and Constantine decided to marry her, resorting to the same type of marriage his father had used to marry his mother. History was repeating itself.

We can only imagine his mother's conflicting feelings. She could see herself in Minervina and feel compassion for the young girl but she could also see that the marriage would be a barrier blocking her son's way to the top, his status forcing him some day to divorce the unfortunate girl as she, too, had been cast aside. But Constantine was in love and young lovers seldom listen to reason. Besides, Helena was probably already a Christian and could not oppose the marriage now that the girl was pregnant. Her God would never forgive her if she even thought for a moment of solving the problem by having Minervina destroy the child she carried in her womb. So, in the spring of 295 Constantine married Minervina with the same form of marriage Constantius had with Helena.

A few weeks later, in April, Constantine left with the force of *Protectores Domestici* escorting Diocletian on an inspection tour of the forts along the banks of the Danube. By the time he returned with the imperial host in early June, Minervina's pregnancy was well advanced, and in late summer, she gave birth to a beautiful little boy, with dark curly hair. She apparently died at birth. In all the ancient sources, we find no further mention of her, not any reference to a later divorce. She just disappears in the shadows of history. Helena named the little infant Crispus, the boy with the curly hair, and that little boy became the joy of her life.

THE INVASION OF BRITAIN

Across Europe, in Gaul, Flavius Constantius was ready for the invasion of the British Isles. His plan was devious. His Praetorian Prefect, Asclepiodotus, was to lead the main landing, sailing toward the south coast of Britain, near the island of Vectis (Isle of Wight). Flavius Constantius himself would lead a smaller force from Gesoriacum to the southeastern coast. But Constantius wanted Allectus to think that the main invasion was to take place under his command further to the east, near today's Dover. He instructed Asclepiodotus to start the preparations for an invasion in a very ostentatious fashion, letting everyone know that his troops would land at the southern coast of Britain. Allectus was bound to hear all this from his spies and he would most likely think that the Asclepiodotus expedition was a ruse to deceive him while the main thrust would come to the southeast under the command of Constantius. After all, how could Constantius allow someone else to lead the invasion and snatch the glory? Allectus fell for it and deployed his forces along the southeastern coast, southeast of Londinium (London).

In the second week of March, Asclepiodotus sailed from Gesoriacum with great fanfare, his standards and insignia in full view. Allectus' spies were given every reason to believe that this was a show designed to fool the master of the *Imperium Britanniarum*.

Britain and Northern Gaul

at the time of Constantine the Great

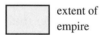 extent of
empire

Allectus decided to wait for Constantius' main invasion along the southeast coast.

The landing of the Asclepiodotus force turned into an epic undertaking. To keep the element of surprise, he had all his ships use remote beaches, instead of the British ports on the Channel. The boats were brought close to the shore so that the men could jump into the water up to their waist and walk the rest of the way. When the shore was sandy the boats had no problem. But in many of the landing sites, treacherous reefs and underwater rocks played havoc with the boats.

"Let the boats sink," Asclepiodotus ordered his commanders. "We won't need them to go back." He meant that retreat was not in his plans. In carrying out this command, many of the boats were crushed on the rocks but not before most of the men on them were safely ashore. The next day the legion started its march toward Londinium. It met no resistance. Allectus' forces were many miles away in the southeastern part of the island waiting for the main invasion!

When Allectus was told that a large force was marching from the west, he made a frantic effort to move his forces from the southeastern coast but only a few cohorts managed to regroup and move westward to meet the enemy. The opposing forces met in a wide plain a few miles southwest of Londinium. Allectus' force was annihilated. Himself, never much of a soldier, threw away the imperial cloak and all his insignia and tried to escape as a simple soldier. He was one of those who died. His body was not found until two days later during the gory job of burning the corpses.

Heavy seas prevented Constantius from landing before the death of Allectus. For three days, within sight of the white cliffs, his ships battled the heavy seas, the men fearful and miserable, vomiting constantly over the balustrades, the horses threatening to break the planks in the keel with their hoofs, the steersmen struggling to avoid the huge waves from hitting the boats sideways and capsizing them. On the third day, the weather subsided and the force landed safely.

To his surprise, Constantius' force met with no resistance. An officer from the legion II Augusta, one of Allectus' premier units, came to report that Allectus was dead and that the legion waited south of Londinium to join the forces of Caesar Constantius. He added the vexing piece of news that some of the Franks in the legion had rebelled and were heading for Londinium with plunder on their minds.

The Frankish deserters came up to the city walls but they had no way of scaling them, no way of forcing the heavy gates. They started milling around, searching in vain for some opening. They were still searching when Constantius' archers galloped up at top speed, unleashing their arrows. The Franks tried to fight back but they were doomed against a strong and disciplined force. We are told that some of the townspeople went up to the top of the walls and from there, as though they were watching the fight of gladiators in the arena, they enjoyed the gory spectacle, cheering with delight as one deserter after another fell to the ground. Few Franks survived and drifted north, seeking refuge in the woods.

The next day practically every person living inside the walls of Londinium came out to the streets to greet the victors. Constantius with Asclepiodotus at his side rode toward the center of the city, followed by the legion commanders, the tribunes and the centurions with their units, under the happy cheers of the multitude that had lined the narrow streets, relieved that their city had escaped the ordeal of a siege. The gold medallion that was struck to commemorate the victory showed on one side Constantius on horseback and a man on his knees with the walls of the city behind him expressing his gratitude. Struck around the periphery were the words *Redditor Lucis Aeternae*, the Restorer of Eternal Light. On the other side of the coin was a cameo of Constantius' head and upper chest, in military uniform, with the golden diadem of the Caesar and round the periphery the abbreviated words Flavius Constantius, Noble Caesar.

A panegyrist describing the events spoke of Allectus with derision, but also with a faint trace of regret for the errors that had led to his dismal end. "He failed to deploy his troops properly, or use all the forces at his disposal, instead he rushed straight into battle, with all the closest companions of his conspiracy, as well as bands of German mercenaries, abandoning the early defensive preparations he had made." But then the panegyrist shifted to the expected praise of the victor. "It was a further blessing on the Roman Empire, Caesar, that by your own fortune the victory was won with barely the death of a single Roman citizen. I have heard it said that the plains and hills were strewn with corpses, but only those of our worst enemies." For good measure, the panegyrist described in vivid detail the slaughter of the rebellious Franks and the delight of the citizens who witnessed the carnage from the tops of the walls.

The propertied citizens of Britain were happy to see the *Imperium Britanniarum* go. True, they did not have serious grievances against Carausius, or even Allectus, and at first they had been flattered by having an *Imperium* of their own. But being cut off from the other side of the Fretum Gallicum had eventually begun to hurt business even though some trading was allowed. Now the Channel was open and that meant more business and greater profits.

They were delighted to hear Flavius Constantius promise to restore the trade with Gaul, keep the currency strong, and carry out with fairness and common sense the new tax policies Diocletian was putting gradually into effect. He even assured those who had collaborated with Carausius and Allectus that they faced no punishment as long as they stayed away from any conspiracies and intrigues. Constantius kept his word and before long he was as popular as Carausius had been in his heyday.

This military success and the wise treatment of the people won the admiration of Diocletian and solidified the imperial status of Caesar Flavius Constantius. In the long run, this was to bring his son Constantine even closer to the summit of power.

TROUBLE IN THE ORIENT

The victory of Flavius Constantius in Britain was to have great impact on his son's future. Constantine was now the son of the victorious Caesar who had extinguished the *Imperium Britanniarum*. Prudently, Constantine kept to himself whatever ambitious thoughts filled his mind. In this, he must have followed his father's advice and his mother's constant reminders that he was safer if others did not know what goals he had set for himself.

The elation brought to the court of Nicomedia with the retaking of the British Isles was soon dampened by the reports that in August the Persian king, Narses, had invaded Armenia. Tiridates, Armenia's king, in an urgent message to Diocletian asked for help. The Persians, he wrote, were using elephants in battle, and the huge beasts were terrifying his soldiers. He had been forced to retreat to the mountains where he was now holed up with some two thousand men.

It was not only Armenia, an independent kingdom friendly to Rome, which faced Persian aggression. Even more disturbing to Diocletian was the loss of control over much of Mesopotamia, an important source of grain. He had no alternative but to wage war against the Persians and push them back to their own lands. He assigned the task to Galerius.

After an exhausting march at top speed through Cappadocia and into Armenia, Galerius met Tiridates and together they marched

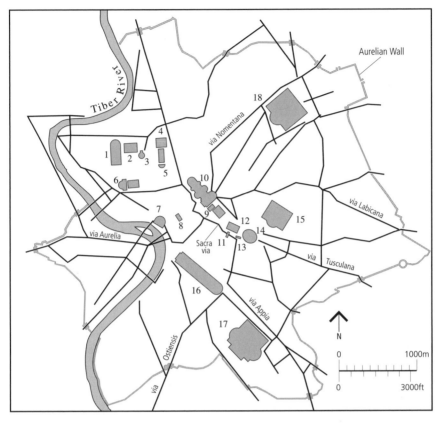

Rome
at the time of
Constantine the Great

1. Stadium of Domitian
2. Baths of Nero and Severus Alexander
3. Pantheon
4. Temple of the Divine Hadrian
5. Temple of Isis
6. Theater of Pompey
7. Theater of Marcellus
8. Temple of Jupiter
9. Roman Forum
10. Imperial Fora
11. Arch of Titus
12. Temple of Venus
13. Arch of Constantine
14. Flavian Amphitheater
15. Baths of Trajan
16. Circus Maximus
17. Baths of Caracalla
18. Baths of Diocletian

southwest. They came upon the Persian force at the plain of Callinicum, just south of Carrhae, at the same spot where three centuries before the Parthians had destroyed a Roman force under Crassus. The battle was fierce and at one point Tiridates himself was surrounded and would have been killed or captured had he not jumped with his horse into the river. He was lucky that the water was not very deep at that point otherwise he would have drowned under the weight of his panoply. He reached the other side of the Euphrates and, with those of his men who had survived, rode away to the protective mountains to wait for another day.

Galerius grasped quickly that he had no alternative but to retreat in good order before it all ended in a rout. To his surprise, Narses and his generals did not press their advantage. They just let Galerius and his forces walk away.

Some ancient sources give a graphic but most likely overdrawn description of Galerius' meeting with Diocletian in Syria upon his return from the campaign. They say that Diocletian had Galerius walk on foot like a slave while he rode his chariot, humiliating his Caesar in front of his men and the local people. The senior Augustus was no doubt angered and he probably used harsh words when he was alone with Galerius but he was too wise to treat his Caesar in public in such an insulting manner. Besides, what Diocletian did next does not reflect a rift between the two men.

In a war council, the senior Augustus asked Galerius to stay in Syria, strengthen his forces with new recruits, train his men and prepare for a more decisive confrontation with the Persians. Reports reaching Diocletian in Antioch said that Narses, emboldened by his victory at Callinicum, had begun to use his Manicheans in Egypt to foment unrest in that valuable province. Diocletian decided to deal with the problem in Egypt personally. As an officer in the imperial guard, Constantine marched along.

REVOLT IN EGYPT

The Greek aristocracy in Egypt had never fully accepted the Roman rule. The simmering discontent erupted into a violent revolt soon after the governor, Aristius Optatus, promulgated the new tax laws in March of 297. The laws were actually favorable to the Egyptian peasants but they listened to the Greek landowners who had to pay most of the taxes. With the Manicheans fighting by their side, the local Greeks and the Egyptian peasants attacked the Roman garrisons which were not strong enough. Within weeks the cities of Coptos, Ptolemais, Busiris, Caranis, and Theadelphia came under the control of the rebels led by a Lucius Domitius Domitianus who claimed the rank of Augustus. Before long, he even issued his own coins. One of them had the old pattern of the Ptolemies as a sign that the rebels wanted to restore the old Greek kingdom. But on the other side, in the familiar offer for reconciliation, the coin had the faces of Diocletian, Maximian, and Domitianus, as the three Augusti.

Other reports said that this Domitianus was only a figurehead and that the real power was in the hands of another man who called himself Achilleus. No matter who was the real leader, the rebellion had to be crushed.

With a strong force of five legions, Diocletian set for Egypt from Antioch in the late summer of 297. Constantine, a 25-year-old tribune in the imperial guard, marched with the rest of the army. As they passed through Palestine, one of Constantine's biographers, Eusebius, saw him for the first time. "We saw him as the army marched through Palestine, with the senior of the kings who had him (Constantine) at his right, a very impressive man for those who saw him, having a royal air about him." The description very likely is colored by Eusebius' later friendship with Constantine, but no doubt the young tribune cut an impressive figure.

The troops crossed the desert north of the Red Sea (through the Sinai desert) and entered Egypt. It was already the late part of October when they came near Alexandria, the largest city in the empire after Rome. Constantine saw the city, now under rebel control, from a distance because Diocletian decided to bypass it and move against the smaller towns. It was a sound strategy. He knew that a siege of Alexandria would take time, while the smaller towns were much more vulnerable. Besides, the grain did not grow in Alexandria.

With his strong force, Diocletian took one town after another. By the middle of December, he had brought under his control most of Egypt and was ready to lay siege to Alexandria.

At the other end of North Africa, beyond Libya, Maximian launched a successful campaign against the tribes that lived on the Atlas mountains and at the edge of the desert. They had become a menace to the towns and settlements on the northern coast of Africa, in Mauritania, Sitifensis, and Numidia (today's Morroco, Algeria and Tunisia). The rebellious tribesmen were decimated by Maximian's legions, and those who survived were pushed far into the desert. Maximian proudly wrote to Diocletian of his success as the senior Augustus was preparing for the siege of Alexandria.

The siege lasted almost four months. Early on, Diocletian had sent his heralds under the city walls to proclaim his pledge to spare the lives of everyone, even of the rebel leaders, if the city surrendered peacefully. Achilleus in his reply was as contemptuous as he could be. He used the Greek words "Molon Lave"—the famous words "come and take it if you can"—the Greeks had flaunted at the Persians seven centuries before at the battle of Thermopylae. Angered, Diocletian vowed publicly that when his troops entered Alexandria the slaughter would not stop until the blood reached his horse's knees.

Constantine saw now for the first time how the siege of a great city was carried out. He saw how the catapults and the *ballistas* breached the walls here and there weakening the city's defenses and how, in the end, the men had to scale the walls and fight their way through the gaps the siege machines had opened, while powerful rams crushed the gates after consistent pounding, allowing more men to pour into the city. It was for him a valuable experience.

When Diocletian's forces finally entered the city of Alexandria in the early spring of 298, the slaughter seemed to have no end. Achilleus and Domitianus tried to escape in the confusion but they were captured and executed. After two days of carnage, Diocletian decided to end the violence. But since he had vowed not to stop the killing until the blood reached his horse's knees, he made his horse stumble so that its knees were bloodied, and so he ordered an end to the slaughter while remaining true to his pledge. Later, we are told, the Alexandrians built a statue to Diocletian's horse. There is no record regarding Diocletian's reaction to this dubious gesture.

Constantine did not return to Nicomedia until late in the summer of the following year. He remained in Egypt with Diocletian. The senior Augustus was determined to bring the valuable province back into the fold of the empire, and so he did with an iron hand during the spring and summer after the fall of Alexandria. Those who were suspected of disloyalty, and that included many of the Manicheans, were shackled in irons and sent to the salt mines and the stone quarries. At the same time the new tax laws and the land census were put into effect by hard-fisted administrators working under Diocletian's watchful eye. Needless to say, the Alexandrians lost the privilege of not paying taxes, which they had enjoyed since Julius Caesar granted it to them for the sake of his lover, the Greek queen, Cleopatra.

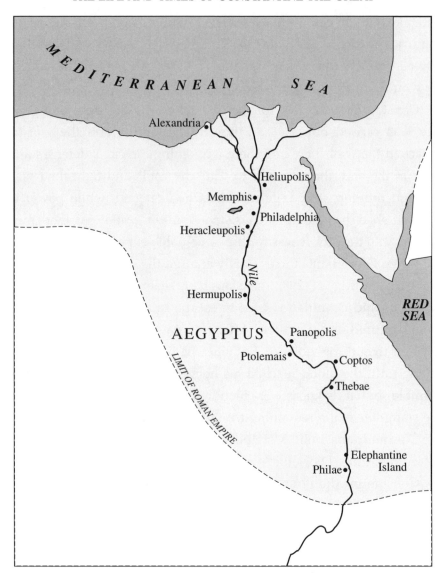

Egypt
at the time of Constantine the Great

As in the old days of the Pharaohs, Egypt was divided by Diocletian into two parts, Thebais in the south with Thebes as its capital and Aegyptus Jovia in the north with Alexandria the seat of its governor.

Constantine, now a senior tribune in Diocletian's personal guard, followed the emperor down the Nile all the way to the first cataract and the town of Philae next to the Elephantine Island in the river. Not far from this spot, Constantine must have seen the huge granite obelisk the ancient Egyptians had started to curve from the rock but for some reason had left unfinished. (Tourists can still see it today at the same place.)

Diocletian, pleased with what had been accomplished, ordered the construction of an arch in Philae to commemorate his victory and to mark the farthest end of the empire in the land of the Nile. Then, he moved back toward the north, and in the town of Thebes he visited the ancient temple where he made a sacrifice to the bull-god Apis, one of the gods of the ancient Egyptians. It was a well calculated gesture designed to please the native Egyptians and spite the arrogant Greeks. He even dressed like a Pharaoh and went through the ancient ritual with every prescribed gesture and sacred word. With his keen mind, Constantine would not have missed the meaning of the gesture. Bowing to old customs and rituals that men held dear could be used at times as a powerful tool to win over the minds of simple people. Constantine had in Thebes another glimpse into the intricacies of statecraft.

For the rest of the year, with three legions, II Triana, II Herculia, and III Diocletiana, maintaining order, the emperor's civilian administrators moved ahead with a land survey and the repair of the irrigation canals, bringing more lands under the plow, pushing away the relentless desert.

Constantine could not have failed to see that order had been restored but that the resentment ran deep against the Roman presence which was costly and oppressive. Still, however sullen and resentful, the locals had no choice but to cooperate with their masters—and they would do so as long as Roman spears wrote the rules.

Those Manicheans who had survived the persecution tried to disappear into the shadows of Egyptian life, hiding their hostility to the

Greek and Roman gods and holding to their faith, hoping to survive in obscurity, but Diocletian continued their persecution because he saw them as the agents of the Persian king, not merely as a secretive religious sect. In a directive to proconsul Julianus, he ordered that "their founders and leaders be subjected to the most severe punishment, burned in the flames together with their abominable writings. Their followers and especially those who are fanatical shall suffer capital punishment and their goods shall be seized for our fiscus. And if any officials or persons of rank or distinction have gone over to this infamous sect of the Persians, you shall confiscate their estates and deport them to the mines..."

The news of the Manicheans' persecution must have given a chill to the Christians in Egypt and elsewhere and must have caused Constantine concern for his mother's safety. Of course, the Manicheans differed from the Christians. They were accused of being the perfidious agents of the Persian king, while the Christians were loyal citizens and no one had accused them of treason. The last persecution of the Christians had been in the days of Emperor Valerian, almost half a century ago. But the fear persisted.

Diocletian was in Thebes in the early summer when he received a long dispatch from Galerius informing the senior Augustus that he had completed his preparations and was ready to cross the Euphrates.

This time Galerius was successful because he used imaginative military tactics. He came upon the Persian army as it was marching towards the mountains of Armenia and for several days he shadowed its movements, using scouts, keeping his main force out of sight. Then, after a swift march, the legions closed on the Persian forces while they were passing through a narrow valley at the eastern edge of Cappadocia. In a surprise attack which military men for years afterwards discussed with genuine admiration, Galerius' legions came over the mountain ridges and fell on the Persians, throwing their ranks into confusion. The elephants that were supposed to spread terror to the enemy turned against the Persian soldiers, trampling them underfoot, totally out of control. The raging assault of the elephants threw the horses into panic, and the crazed animals bolted toward the slopes crashing into each other and throwing off their riders. At the same time, Tiridates' horsemen, thirsting to avenge past humiliations, swept down into the valley and with their Roman allies put to sword the bewildered foot soldiers. Thousands perished that day. Narses himself was wounded and would have been captured were it not for one of his bodyguards who lifted him on his own horse and galloped through a ravine until he and his king were away from the field of battle. In his flight, Narses left behind his family, his concubines, his magnificent tents and large chests full of gold coins.

The might and splendor of great Persia had been crushed into the dust. Galerius with his victorious legions marched unopposed to Nisibis and then on to Ctesiphon. Mesopotamia was again under Roman control. Diocletian, who had come back to Antioch from Egypt, received the report of the great victory around the middle of November. Constantine had also come back to Antioch and the news of the Persian defeat must have filled his heart with joy for a personal reason. Diocletian would have now no reason to stay in Syria. Soon he would start with his legions on the trek back to Nicomedia and that meant that young Constantine would see again his mother and his little boy now almost four years old. But Diocletian had other plans. While in Antioch, he had received a message that the Persian king wanted to negotiate a peace treaty.

Diocletian agreed but he insisted that the Persian delegation should be of the highest level. Narses accepted this and selected his chief minister, Apharban, and the head of the army, Barbaborsus.

Diocletian traveled to Nisibis where he received the Persian delegation in person, having Galerius at his side. The victorious Caesar sat a few paces away from Barbaborsus, the defeated Persian general, a giant of a man. It must have been quite a sight.

The treaty that was signed did not reflect a desire for mindless punishment of the vanquished, nor excessive lust for land on the part of the victors. The territory that passed to the Roman side was clearly needed for the defense of Mesopotamia. Armenia received some Persian lands including the old royal city of Ecbatana but that land was also needed for the defense of Armenia. Diocletian set up a new vassal state in the Caucasus to cut off communications between the Persians and the Scythians and to block the passage of Gothic tribes into Pontica and Asiana (Asia Minor). But all in all, Narses had come off with no heavy territorial losses. If he still lusted for land, he would have to turn to the northwest or the east, to Bactria or India.

Diocletian did not know it at the time but the realistic and moderate treaty he had signed with the Persians was to last for over forty years, long after he had passed from the stage. One week after the signing of the treaty, he left for Nicomedia. After almost three years, Constantine was about to see again his mother and his little boy. Galerius also returned to Thessaloniki where he was given a glorious welcome. A month later he commissioned a team of architects, sculptors, stonecutters and builders and gave them instructions to build a marble arch in Thessaloniki over Via Egnatia to commemorate his victory against Persia. The arch still stands today in the northern Greek city.

Taming the Economy

This was the fist summer in many years, that from the British Isles to Egypt and from Numidia to Mesopotamia and along the Rhine and the Danube, the Roman Empire was at peace. In all the previous years, every summer the legions had been fighting in one frontier or another to hold back the menacing barbarians. Now, Diocletian could turn to the other problems that pressed for his attention.

Even though the farmers could now sow, and reap and thrash the wheat in safety and the harvests were good, prices continued to rise. Diocletian could find no other explanation than the greed of unscrupulous merchants who were driving the prices to the sky, reaping huge profits, and bringing misery to the common people in the towns. For a soldier, and the emperor remained a soldier at heart, amassing riches by gauging the people was a despicable crime. The problem was how to punish so many, especially when so many were high in the social ladder, paying taxes, taking part in local governing, holding the fabric of the empire together.

Diocletian studied the matter, sought expert opinion, consulted the members of the *Consistorium*, the imperial council he had established, and in January of the year 301, he issued the decree *De Pretiis* (On Prices), imposing a rigid system of price controls for virtually every commodity and service. It is a fascinating document which gives us a detailed list of the commodities and services that a Roman citizen of that time used in his daily life.

The decree—following the decree on the coinage six months earlier—reflected Diocletian's anger against the greedy speculators.

> "As we recall the wars we have successfully fought, we must be grateful for a tranquil world, reclining in the embrace of the most profound calm, and for the blessings of peace won with great effort...Therefore, we who by the gracious favor of the gods stemmed the ravaging tide of the barbarians by destroying them, must guard this peace...with the due defense of Justice."

After this self-congratulating preamble, the emperor lashed out against the villains.

> "Since the only desire of these unbridled madmen is to have no concern for the common welfare, because for them being immoderate and unscrupulous is almost a creed...and they will not curb their plundering until forcibly compelled to do so...We, the protectors of the human race are agreed that justice must intervene...There can be no complaint that our intervention is untimely or unnecessary or unimportant, because the unscrupulous have perceived our silence over so many years as a lesson in restraint, but have been unwilling to imitate it."

It is worth quoting the next paragraph because it reflects most vividly what he saw as the evidence of the speculators' greed.

> "Who...is unaware or has not perceived that immoderate prices are widespread in the commerce and in daily life of cities, and that unbridled lust for gain is not lessened by abundant supplies or fruitful years? Truly the evil men engaged in business actually try to predict the wind and weather by watching the movements of the stars; for they cannot stand the rains nourishing the fertile fields and promising rich future harvests...Who does not know that whenever the public safety requires our armies to march, the profiteers...extort prices for merchandise not four-fold, not eight-fold, but so great that human speech cannot describe."

It is interesting to note that Diocletian had to resort to this extensive diatribe to justify his decree. Modern leaders will find his reasons quite familiar. Once he had pointed the finger against the speculators, he turned to the main object of the decree.

> "We have decreed that maximum prices for sale must be established. We have not set down fixed prices because we do not think it just to do so since many provinces occasionally rejoice in the good fortune of low prices...Since it is agreed that in the time of our ancestors it was customary to pass laws prescribing a penalty because a situation beneficial to humanity is rarely accepted spontaneously, and since experience teaches that fear is the most effective guide and regulator for the performance of a duty, we decree that anyone who violates the provisions of this decree shall, for his daring, be subject to capital punishment. And let no one consider the penalty harsh, because one can easily protect himself by simply being moderate..."

Then followed the long list of goods, raw materials, clothing, as well as wages and charges for various services. The Edict set a price limit for every different kind of meat, every type of clothing, every construction job, every type of service. At the same time, it specified wage limits for workers, herdsmen, mule-drivers, carpenters, bakers, plasterers, stonecutters, teachers, scribes, seamen and others. It was a comprehensive effort to promote economic and social justice through government imposed controls, but whatever its intentions, the plan to legislate economic stability and ignore the dictates of the marketplace was doomed to fail. After the first shock, the marketplace asserted itself. The best food disappeared only to be sold under the counter to those who were willing and able to pay the higher price. The same with other commodities. Artisans charged more than the law allowed and were paid secretly behind closed doors. The black market appeared in all its glory and the emperor soon found out that he had not enough soldiers to check violations and executioners to punish the guilty. Yet, conditions improved because with peace came a more abundant supply of goods.

The constant rise in prices was caused only in part by the greed of hoarders and speculators. For decades, the state had resorted to a Roman style of printing money—it reduced the content of silver in the coins, replacing it with copper until by Diocletian's time a *denarius* was just a copper coin dipped in melted silver to give it a shine and the illusion of value.

The experience with the edict *De Pretiis* was a lesson in basic economics that Constantine evidently understood. In later years, when he himself was the emperor, he sought economic stability not in price controls but in creating a stable currency that people would accept with confidence.

The Tentacles of the State

If Diocletian could not tame the economy, he could at least fashion to his liking the administration of the empire. Constantine had a rare opportunity during those years to learn how valuable an elaborate machinery of administration and control could be to the

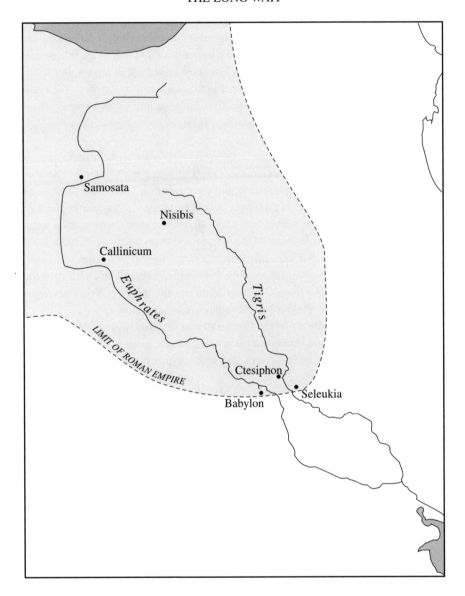

Mesopotamia
at the time of Constantine the Great

governing of a sprawling multi-ethnic domain. In later years, he would craft even more finely Diocletian's advanced design. The old emperor had profited from what he had learned in Egypt concerning the governing practices of the Pharaohs and in the end he fashioned a system in which every citizen had his life tied to the state machinery in one way or other.

In the countryside, the lease-holders (*coloni*) were responsible to the landowners who were then responsible to the state for paying their taxes and their deliveries in kind (*annona*). Besides, the state was the biggest landowner of all and that made things easier. In the towns, artisans, craftsmen and merchants were organized in *corpora* and *collegia*, occupational and professional associations tied to the machinery of the state. The system put curbs on the free-wheeling life of the old days but after more than a century of constant turmoil security and stability had become a supreme necessity and the people were willing to pay the price.

The tetrarchy was now more than a word describing the system of having two Augusti and two Caesars. Diocletian remained the senior Augustus, respected and honored by his associates in the purple, but within their domains, Maximian, Galerius and Constantius reigned at the apex of their own pyramids. In each of the four imperial sections, the chain of command stretched from each Augustus or each Caesar to their respective Praetorian Prefects, from there to the Vicars and then to the governors of the provinces, reaching finally the local magistrates and the towns' *decuriones* and *curiales*. From its earlier days, the administration of the Roman Empire relied on a well structured and disciplined bureaucracy. What Diocletian had done was to develop the system further, make it more elaborate and then tie the citizen more closely to the state.

To pay for this elaborate structure, Diocletian and his associates needed funds. But with money being such an uncertain and capricious element, he opted whenever possible to having taxes paid in kind or in services. To introduce greater fairness to the system he changed the basis for assessment. Land holdings of the same size were no longer taxed equally. The tax was related to the fertility and the use of the land. One *jugum* of vineyard was taxed much more than one *jugum* of land growing wheat on a poor soil.

Since the ancient times, the law was for the Romans the foundation of civilized society. Diocletian revered the law and with the help of two learned secretaries, Gregorius and Hermogenianus, he codified the basic laws to ascertain that throughout the empire men would know what was lawful and what was not. Even though he had embraced some of the ceremonial trappings and administrative practices of Egypt and the Orient, he rejected polygamy or marriage between brothers and sisters, a move that was in keeping with Roman traditions, but also a move that received the praise of many Christians.

CHAPTER III

THE PERSECUTION OF THE CHRISTIANS

Religion in the Empire

The gods had indeed been good to Diocletian and, being as superstitious as any man of his time, he wanted everyone to pay appropriate homage to them. To make sure that the gods would continue to crown him with their benevolence, he donated money from the public treasury to restore the temples to their ancient splendor and supported the priesthood with lavish gifts, knowing that only a foolish emperor would make enemies of the priests. Constantine later would show that he, too, appreciated the influence of religion but, unlike Diocletian, he understood that the ancient religion was fading and that a new religion was emerging.

The traditional gods the people worshipped in the Roman empire at the time Constantine was growing into manhood were many. Those of the highest rank, known by their Latin names, were long identified with the Greek gods who dwelled on Mount Olympus. Jupiter was the Latin name for Zeus and as in the Greek "pantheon" he was the highest among the gods. Even these gods were occasionally given special identities and were worshipped as the protectors of a city. During the centuries that the Romans were building their empire, they came to know and accept many other gods from the lands they conquered. Religion to the average Roman citizen was a strange mixture of beliefs and ceremonies ranging from the dignified worship of the major gods to the crudest superstitions and rituals.

They also had gods of a lesser stature, even household gods with special attributes suitable for offering aid and solace to a family on every occasion. In this tolerant and cosmopolitan climate of the Roman cities and towns, gods from different lands were welcome and their religious myths were woven together with those of the Greek mythology.

In the rural backwoods the people worshipped their own pagan gods following the local traditions. It was only when they were drafted into the legions that their young men were exposed to the gods of the Roman pantheon. Then they were expected to offer sacrifice to them, at least by joining in the prescribed rituals. They seldom found this difficult to do. The traditional gods were not overly demanding. The faithful needed only to offer the sacrifices required by tradition.

For centuries, the gods of the Roman pantheon were worshipped with a deep-rooted, sentimental attachment by the people in the major cities and towns on the Italian peninsula, above all by the inhabitants of Rome. As time went on, the members of the provincial upper classes in the cities and towns of the newly conquered lands from Spain to Mesopotamia, whatever their ethnic or tribal origin, embraced the gods of the Roman pantheon with the zeal of new believers, determined to prove their "romanization." Once firmly within the empire, they were steeped, generation after generation, in the Greek and Latin classics and were surrounded by the art and architecture which embodied the glory of Rome and Greece. Both literature and architecture were entwined with the traditional gods and this reinforced the emotional ties. But this was not a profoundly theological faith. It was more of a sentimental attachment to annual rituals and festivities which broke the routine of daily life. Still, as humans have been doing since time immemorial, the people in the Roman Empire would often turn in time of sickness or danger to the god or goddess of their choice and pray for health and safety.

The more sophisticated in the upper classes were likely to adopt the religious philosophy of the Neoplatonists and focus on a Supreme

Deity as the Creator and Ruler of all. They were further attracted by the teachings of the neoplatonists who advocated a higher morality as the most compelling evidence that an individual had indeed reached a superior level of existence. The neoplatonist call for a pure and honest life was a departure from the demands of traditional religion. The ancient gods did not set specific moral rules for the faithful. They did not raise the specter of sin and eternal damnation, nor did they promise eternal life after death to those who lived a pure life. This was left to the mystery religions which came mostly from the Orient, except for the ancient mysteries of Eleusis which were Greek. In the third century, many people were turning to the mystery religions such as that of Mithras, Mani, Osiris, or Christ. Their promise of eternal life after death offered a hope and gave human life a deeper meaning and a higher purpose.

The mystery religions found most of their followers in the cities and larger towns where newcomers, slaves, freedmen, traders, and seamen, cut off from their native religious cults were searching for new sources of solace and hope to brighten their hard, drab lives. The mystery religions also found converts in the army where men from diverse cultures came together. Most of the followers of the mystery religions came, then, from the low and lower middle classes in the urban centers of the empire. The mystery cults hardly ever penetrated the rural areas where the people were strongly attached to their local deities.

Once a mystery religion gained a secure foothold among the underprivileged and downtrodden, it branched out and gradually gained followers in the upper levels of society, among the more sophisticated, wealthy citizens who were no longer satisfied with the traditional religion or who could not find answers or solace in philosophy. Most of them were people who had profound questions about the purpose of life, man's relation to the Supreme Divinity (*Summa Divinitas*), or the awesome mystery of what happens after death to the human soul.

All mystery religions offered a "revealed theology" which could be told only to the faithful, and even then in successive stages of initiation. In virtually all mystery cults, the prospective follower was subjected to rituals and mystic instructions in a physical setting designed to impress and eventually overwhelm the initiate in a process which in reality amounted to a form of brainwashing. Because the claims and religious myths of those cults were so outlandish, the prospective follower had to shed all doubt and accept their claims and fables with unquestioning faith.

Going beyond the teachings of the philosophers, the spokesmen of the mystery religions claimed that their teachings were not just the product of philosophical reasoning but the divine word of the Supreme Deity. Their founders claimed that the ultimate truths were revealed to them by the Supreme God and for this reason their truths could not be disputed or questioned. One of their most powerful revelations was their assurance that those who believed and accepted the divine truths and who lived pure and honest lives would have an eternal and blissful life after death. At the same time, they all focused on the concept of sin and evil and warned the sinners that they would be denied a happy life in eternity. But even sinners were given hope if they repented, and practically all cults prescribed rituals of purification.

The mystery religions flourished in the first three centuries after the birth of Christ, apparently because many people were thirsting for something mysterious and outlandish that offered answers neither the traditional religion nor the more rational philosophy could give.

"Mystery Religions"

One of the earliest cults was that of the Great Mother of Pessinus and her consort Attis. During its spring festival, the followers commemorated the death and the resurrection of Attis, while those who had been accepted to the inner circles of initiation participated in a secret sacramental meal where the worshippers "ate from the drum and drank from the cymbal" and became the communicants of Attis. With much pain and suffering in their lives, many sought solace in the assurance of a future life beyond the grave. The followers of this cult were told that as Attis was slain and rose again, so those who believed in him and joined in mystic communion with him would live beyond the grave in blessed happiness. It was a powerful promise indeed.

Another mystery religion was that of Isis with her consort Serapis and their son Horus, a trinity represented in human form with the father a bearded man, Isis a beautiful woman, and Horus a small child, all in a style of sculpture reflecting the Greek art tradition. The priests and the rituals, however, showed Egyptian influence. Just as in the case of Attis, Serapis was slain by Typhos, the embodiment of evil, and his body was cut to pieces. Isis recovered the severed parts and Serapis was resurrected. This religious myth was enacted every year, and again the resurrection symbolized the defeat of death and the hope for eternal life.

Another ancient cult—which had spread into the Roman Empire some two centuries before the birth of Constantine—was that of Mithras. Of Persian origin, this cult had very ancient roots. Mithras was a luminous presence, the embodiment of justice and truth fighting against the dark powers of evil. By the end of the second century, the cult had begun to spread rapidly through the Roman Empire, primarily among merchants, slaves and seamen but most importantly among the men in the legions. The Roman emperors tolerated and even supported the cult of Mithras because it espoused the belief that the reign of emperors was sanctioned by the Supreme Deity. The initiates passed through seven stages (degrees) signifying the seven planetary spheres presumably traversed by a soul in its ascent to heaven. Most of the faithful reached only the third degree of *Miles* (soldier), pledged to wage a holy war against evil. Those who entered the higher degrees were admitted to a sacred meal of bread, wine and water given the initiate as proof of his communion with Mithras. The followers believed in heaven and hell, in the constant warfare between good and evil and in the final triumph of good, in eternal life for those who remained morally pure and upright, and in eternal punishment on the hands of *Ahriman*, the spirit of evil, for those who persisted in their wicked ways, and in the resurrection of the dead at the time of the fiery destruction of the Universe and the final judgment. In some aspects Mithraism resembled Christianity and for at least three centuries it remained its major and most persistent antagonist among the mystery religions.

Another widespread cult was that of Mani. Diocletian's harsh persecution of the followers of Mani in Egypt did not extinguish Manichaeism. Mani, a Persian by birth, did not claim to be a god or the son of God. He presented himself only as the last and most perfect messenger of God who had received the ultimate truths through divine revelation when he was around twenty-five years old. At the age of thirty he began to proclaim his new religion in Persia during the reign of Shapur I and then as he traveled to the east as well as to the west of Persia. His disciples also traveled and preached in many parts of the Roman Empire. Eventually, he was persecuted by the Zoroastrian priests, the Magians, and executed during the reign of Bahram I, in 276. Not unlike the cult of Mithras, the Manicheans spoke of an uncompromising division between good and evil, between light and darkness. In the kingdom of Light, God reigns radiant with the virtues of love, wisdom, charity, fairness, under-standing, knowledge and insight, surrounded by angels. Opposing this kingdom of Light is the kingdom of Darkness which has spawned Satan and his demons. Those who accepted Mani's mes-sage, went through rigorous stages of initiation and those who reached the level of *eklektoi* (the chosen ones; the perfect men), were assured of eternal bliss after death in the kingdom of Light. Those who did not become "chosen" during their lifetime, would have to go after death through a severe process of purification (similar to the "purgatorium" of Catholic Christians) and if they passed the tests they might be admitted to the blessedness of Light. When the Light had emerged triumphant throughout the world, the end of all things will come. The God of Light with the angels and those who have been accepted into the kingdom of Light will come together for the final glorious defeat of Darkness. The angels who, according to Mani, sup-port the Earth will be relieved of their burden, while a tremendous conflagration will consume the world. The victory of the Light will be final and complete.

The ethical tenets of Manichaeism were extremely demanding and few could live the ascetic, self-denying life the "chosen ones" were expected to live. For this reason, the cult provided for a catego-ry of faithful (known by the Greek word *katechumenoi* or *auditores* in Latin) who were not subject to the strict moral discipline of the "cho-sen ones." Still, they too had to avoid the worship of idols, avarice, falsehood, sexual immorality, cruelty, and above all the killing of another human being. Like the Ten Commandments in the Bible Mani too, gave his followers ten commandments not much different from those in the Bible. Not surprisingly, Manichaeism became one of Christianity's rivals not only during Constantine's time but for several more centuries reaching into the Middle Ages—its tenets modified to be sure by the influence of Christianity.

CHRISTIANITY IN THE ROMAN WORLD

The early followers of Jesus of Nazareth believed that he was the Messiah (*Christos* in Greek, meaning the anointed one) as the Hebrews understood the concept—God's messenger who would descend from heaven and lead the people of Israel to freedom and the re-establishment of the kingdom of David. But within years from the death of Jesus, the Christian sect as it became known from the Greek word for the anointed one expanded beyond its Hebrew origins and presented a system of beliefs which could have a universal appeal. In the early years, some people, mostly among the poor, were attracted to the new faith by the prospect of mutual help and the communal spirit which prevailed among the members of the group. But they were soon exposed to the basic theological tenets of Christianity. Central to the Christian teachings was the belief in the divinity of Jesus and in his resurrection. Christianity was the only one among the mystery religions that raised to a level of cardinal tenet the belief that the human founder of the sect was not merely a prophet but the son of God, and that he had risen from the dead after his crucifixion. It was an extravagant claim but one which gave Christianity a unique source of power. Christianity further made as its central goal the salvation of the human soul. Men and women could "accept

Christ" and find salvation through simple but mysterious acts, the Holy Sacraments. Baptism was the ritual—sanctioned by Jesus himself when he was baptized by John the Baptist—which cleansed past sins and made humans capable of achieving salvation. Holy Communion, commemorating the Last Supper, united the faithful with Jesus and gave hope of immortality. Indeed, the immortality of the soul and the prospect of eternal life in Paradise were the most precious rewards for a righteous and moral life. Acceptance of the moral code, enshrined in the Sermon of the Mount and the faithful adherence to its precepts, was the hallmark of a true Christian and the only road to salvation, eternal life and resurrection on Christ's Second Coming. From the earliest days, Christians were convinced that the ultimate truth had been revealed to them and that their religion surpassed all others. Sacrifice to the pagan idols was an abomination that could cost a Christian his salvation and eternal life.

Their uncompromising refusal to even tolerate the traditional religion was bound to get them into trouble, and it often did. The first persecution we are told occurred in the reign of Nero in the year 64. The persecution was prompted by the Great Fire of Rome when a large section of the city was burned down. Many people at the time whispered that Nero had set the fire deliberately to make room for the huge palace he was planning to build. Tacitus in his *Annales* has a very brief reference to the killing of Christians in the arena not because he was concerned with Christianity but only to highlight Nero's vanity and cruelty. Christian writers, however, painted later a fantastic picture of the first persecution with dramatic descriptions of Christians hurled into the arena to be devoured by the wild beasts or burned alive like human torches. It is doubtful that the Christian sect was so well known or important thirty years after the death of Jesus. Most likely, Nero turned his praetorians against the poor people of the city using them as a scapegoat for the fire. Among those poor people many were Christians and among the condemned the Christians were the most defiant and the least fearful of death since they believed that dying for Christ was the road to salvation and eternal life. Nero probably was not even aware of what Christianity was. To Tacitus and to another contemporary Roman writer, Suetonius, the Christians were "a class of men given to a new and mischievous (*maleficus*) superstition." To the few Romans who were aware of its existence, Christianity was a mischievous superstition which set its followers apart from the rest of the pious and god-fearing people.

Pagan Romans began to deal more seriously with Christianity in the second century after the birth of Christ. The first written reference we have is dated in the fall of 112 and comes from Plinius the Younger (Pliny) who was sent to Asia Minor by Emperor Trajan as governor of Bithynia. In one of the towns, some local citizens came to Pliny and complained about the Christians in their town. In his report to the emperor, Pliny did not specify the reasons for the complaint. Reading between the lines, it appears that merchants and local butchers who were engaged in the slaughter and sale of sacrificial meat complained that business was poor because people were not making sacrifices to the gods. Evidently Pliny did not take the charges seriously because he wrote to the emperor that he found "flesh of sacrificial victims on sale everywhere." He also wrote that contrary to rumors about sinister activities (the slaughter of babies and the eating of their flesh), the Christians "were eating food of an ordinary, harmless kind." Pliny apparently had been shown pamphlets circulated in the area accusing the Christians of secret rites involving sexual acts and other "crimes."

Pliny wrote to the emperor for instructions but before he had a reply, he sent to the executioner several Christians who defiantly admitted of their faith. In his eyes, their crime was not their "superstition" but their "stubbornness and unshakable obstinacy." Defiance and contempt for a Roman governor "ought not to go unpunished," he wrote. The emperor in his letter praised Pliny for following "the right course of procedure" but he told him that "these people must not be hunted out" and that anyone brought before him on charges of being a Christian should be pardoned if he stated that he was not.

Referring to the pamphlets, Trajan wrote that "the pamphlets circulating anonymously must play no part in any accusation. They create the worst sort of precedent and are quite out of keeping with the spirit of our age." However moderate Trajan's words may appear, the incident indicates that less than one hundred years since the appearance of the new religion, many pagan citizens in the empire were hostile to the Christians, whether for economic or other practical reasons or because they were simply annoyed by their refusal to participate in the traditional rituals and sacrifices which they rejected with contempt and derision.

Less than fifty years later, the first serious commentary on the Christian beliefs appeared in the writings of Gallen, a philosopher and physician by training, born in the city of Pergamos, in Asia Minor, a major city some fifteen miles from the Aegean Sea. His language and culture were Greek but he was also versed in Latin. A highly educated man, Gallen moved to Rome in 162 and became a private physician to the family of emperor Marcus Aurelius. At the time Gallen arrived in Rome, a Christian community had existed for over one hundred years. It was not, however, a large or influential community, compared to those of other mystery religions. Still, the Christian community in Rome was the most significant among all other Christian communities in the empire and many Christian thinkers of the time made it a point to come to Rome and live for a while with their Christian brethren there.

Gallen did not write a specific treatise on Christianity, but while dealing with other topics he wrote several passages on the Christians in an effort to understand the new cult and to see it in the context of the intellectual and social setting of his time. He often spoke of Moses and Christ in the same sentence as though there was no distinction between Judaism and Christianity. In one passage, he criticized physicians who accept "what is commonly spoken by prominent people" without resorting to "cogent demonstration as if one goes into the school of Moses and Christ and hears talk of unproven laws." Again, criticizing the opinions of certain physicians, he wrote: "Those who practice medicine without scientific knowledge are like Moses who framed laws for the tribe of Israel, since it is in his method to write without offering proof, saying 'God commanded, God spake.'"

Gallen wrote as a philosopher would, rejecting the blind reliance on faith. Although he was not writing a rounded critique of Christianity, he was obviously turned off by the Christian claim of Jesus' resurrection. As a physician he knew that death was final; and since he was not willing to accept on faith the divine nature of Jesus, he could not possibly accept Christ's resurrection. He was not alone in this. The divinity of Christ and the claim of his resurrection were two of the most serious obstacles in the expansion of Christianity during the first two centuries.

Around the year 170, Celsus, a Greek philosopher, was the first pagan intellectual to write a rounded and well-reasoned critique of the Christian faith. We have extensive fragments of his book, *The True Doctrine*, only because Origen, the famous Christian theologian from Alexandria, wrote a book of his own—*Contra Celsum*—dissecting Celsus' arguments. From the excerpts preserved in *Contra Celsum* one can see how an educated person in the Roman world viewed the Christian cult in the second century after the birth of Christ.

Celsus pointed out that many of the ethical precepts advocated by the Christians "had been better expressed among the Greeks who refrained from making exalted claims and from asserting that they had been revealed to them by a god or by a son of god." It was an argument many students of philosophy could understand. But Celsus did not limit himself to such a broad criticism. He took issue with specific theological questions as he was evidently familiar with Christian doctrine.

He questioned the Christian claim that God came to earth from heaven to live as a man among men. This assertion, he wrote, "is most shameful." God was not the kind of being to "change from good to bad, from beautiful to shameful, from happiness to misfortune and from what is best to what is most wicked. God is immortal and perfect." How can a God who is by definition eternal and immutable become a human being? It was a stinging argument since the Christians also believed that God was "un-created, eternal, invisible, incomprehensible, infinite, with indescribable beauty, spirit, and power." To Celsus the claim that Jesus was divine was an affront to his concept of God, undermining the belief in one God—a hard-won advance in a world long accustomed to a variety of gods. He had more to say on this. If the Christians insisted that Jesus was indeed the incarnation of God who appeared in human form at a specific time in history, then what happened to the countless generations who lived before Jesus? "Is it only now after such a long time that God has remembered to judge the human race?" To Celsus the Christians were presenting an arbitrary and capricious God and so he argued that any person informed in theological and philosophical matters could see the contradiction and the irrationality of their doctrine.

Celsus took issue with the Christian belief in the resurrection of the dead. "What sort of body, after being entirely corrupted, could return to its original nature and to the same condition which it had before it dissolved? As [the Christians] have nothing to say in reply, they escape to a most outrageous refuge by saying that 'anything is possible to God.'" But God who was "the reason for everything that exists...would neither desire or be able to do anything contrary to reason or to his own character."

Celsus took issue with many other Christian dogmas including Jesus' birth or his miracles but this is not the place for a full coverage. Whatever its merits, his treatise is significant not only because of the high intellectual content of his arguments. It is even more important because it shows that a man of Celsus' stature and education would find it worth his time to study and discuss the beliefs of the Christians. Clearly by the end of the second century, Christianity had become an intriguing religion to Roman intellectuals who found hard to accept on faith its outlandish dogmas. It had also become a religion which attracted many people from different walks of life. Apparently they were not repelled by profound theological issues. They were drawn to the new religion by its promise of salvation and eternal life. And their numbers were already on the rise.

THE LAST PERSECUTION

We may assume that for Constantine, a young soldier, religious issues were far removed from his daily life. He most likely knew that his mother was close to the Christian sect, but he, himself, worshipped the traditional gods more out of habit than religious conviction. Like other young men of his age, he was superstitious and was careful not to offend the gods but instead to please them and secure their protection by offering the proper sacrifices. That was the extent of his ties with religion—any religion. He did not know it then but the time was fast approaching for a violent upheaval which would leave a lasting mark on his thinking.

The issue was first raised by Galerius in the summer of 302. The Christians, he argued, were offending all good citizens by treating the traditional gods with contempt. What was even worse and more dangerous was that disrespect to the gods was the first step toward disrespect to the emperor, which in turn was the gateway to treason.

In reality the Christian sect was not revolutionary in the sense that it had the inclination—let alone the means—to wage rebellion against Rome, but their claim that the founder of their faith was the son of God set the Christians apart—a secretive community based on an extravagant claim, with its tentacles spreading throughout the empire. Like the Jews, the Christians rejected as profane what the other inhabitants of the empire held sacred. But in contrast to the Jews who were an ancient people with their own time-honored traditions, the Christians were a recent sect which—a major offense in the eyes of many, including the Jews—worshipped a man as the son of the Supreme Deity, offering their exclusive devotion to him as to a god and turning many men and women away from the worship of the traditional gods.

Even though the treatment of the Christians by imperial Rome varied from an occasional violent persecution to benign indifference their sect was always regarded as an affront to the traditional gods. The letter Emperor Trajan wrote in 113, responding to a report by Pliny who was visiting Bithynia in Asia Minor as an imperial inspector, offers an interesting glimpse into the official view of the Christians in the words of one of the more enlightened emperors:

> "You have followed the right course of procedure, my dear Plinius, in your examination of the cases of persons charged with being Christians, for it is impossible to lay down a general rule. These people must not be hunted out; if they are brought before you and the charge against them is proved, they must be punished, but in the case of anyone who denies that he is a Christian, and makes it clear that he is not by offering prayers to our gods, he is to be pardoned... The pamphlets circulated anonymously must play no part in any accusation. They create the worst sort of precedent and are quite out of keeping with the spirit of our age."

The pamphlets mentioned by Trajan were usually crude scripts full of outrageous charges that the Christians slaughtered infants to drink their blood and eat their flesh as supposedly the founder of their sect had told them to do, and that in their secret ceremonies they engaged in "love feasts" which were nothing but sex orgies. Many believed those rumors.

With the passing of time, as more men and women of education and social stature joined the Church, Christian theology began to attract the attention of pagan intellectuals and philosophers. Celcus claimed that by elevating the founder of their sect to divine status, the Christians had set up a rival entity to the Supreme Deity that watched over the prosperity of the empire and protected the emperor. "Under those conditions", Celcus wrote, "there is nothing to prevent the abandonment and the desertion of the emperor..." Arguments of this type could easily frighten superstitious men vested with imperial authority.

During the reign of Diocletian, another philosopher, Porphyrios, became a most prominent critic of the Christian faith. Born in the city of Tyre, north of Palestine, he had a Greek education in philosophy, logic and rhetoric and his writings against the Christian teachings were so effective that for generations after his death in A.D. 305, Christian writers felt the need to refute his arguments. To educated men like Porphyrios, the Christian teachings and the Christians' total rejection of the traditional gods threatened to weaken everything which held the pagan society together.

Until the persecution of the Manicheans in Egypt—and Diocletian had persecuted them not for their religious beliefs but for their treasonous connection to the Persian king—the senior Augustus had shown little interest in the mystery religions of his time.

What eventually turned Diocletian against the Christians was their insistence to stay spiritually apart from the rest of the people; this did not sit well with his idea of a well-run, centrally controlled state. For the first seventeen years of his reign, Diocletian had been much too busy fighting the barbarians. The Christians seldom occupied his thoughts. Those in the army obeyed the orders of their superiors like every other soldier and seldom gave any trouble. A man's religion was his business and it was part of the Roman tradition to tolerate, even to embrace different gods.

Still, the argument that the gods who had been so good to Diocletian might be offended by the Christians' stubborn refusal to sacrifice at the altars was something a superstitious man of that time could not have easily ignored. Galerius had effectively planted the first seed. Lactantius blamed Galerius' mother Romula, a pagan priestess in her native Moesia (today's Bulgaria), "an extremely superstitious woman who worshipped the mountain deities," and who was enraged "by the contempt the Christians showed to her sacrifices...She incited her son, more superstitious than even herself, to turn against those people." Whatever his personal motives or his mother's influence, Galerius was the man who suggested to Diocletian that the Christians should no longer be allowed to offend the gods by refusing to sacrifice. A few extreme and rather unusual cases of defiance in the army fueled Galerius' arguments and gave them a sense of urgency.

Nonetheless, Diocletian was not eager to start another persecution. As was his custom, he tested the waters. In September 302, he visited several garrisons and frontier towns in the Balkans on an inspection tour. He took the opportunity to ask military commanders, civilian administrators, and local notables what they thought of the Christian sect. Most military commanders agreed that the Christians in their units were good soldiers, obeying orders and keeping their religious beliefs to themselves. The only complaint they had against the Christians was that they stayed away from public sacrifices to the gods, and that this practice certainly bothered most of the other soldiers.

Other officials told the emperor that the Christians were like a poisonous weed spreading across the empire. "Their numbers are growing," they said. "The army is full of them, and so is the civil list. Christian businessmen control commerce and are behind the constant rise of prices. Christian landowners contribute from their wealth to the coffers of this sect, and with the money they collect from the faithful their priests can be very dangerous because they have control of a tightly-knit cult of fanatical believers. "The Christians' first loyalty," they added, "is to a crucified Jew they address as *Dominus*, claiming that he is their Lord and Savior."

This last argument impressed Diocletian most. The first and foremost loyalty of every Roman citizen was to the emperor and to Rome. No other loyalty could be higher because, then, a rival authority could emerge, more insidious than the false authority of the usurpers he had to destroy in his path.

Still, Diocletian was undecided. In October, shortly after his return to Nicomedia following the inspection tour, he summoned a special meeting of high ranking civil officials and military commanders to hear their views on the Christians. One of them was Hierocles, the governor of nearby Bithynia and a prominent leader of the "Greeks"—the vigorous pagan intellectuals who supported the traditional worship. With Hierocles at the meeting, this was their best chance to convince the emperor of the need "to extirpate the Christians as enemies of the gods and of the established religious ceremonies." Hierocles, who was also a Neoplatonist philosopher and reportedly the author of two books attacking Christianity, led the argument in favor of persecution. "Do not think, Domine," he told Diocletian, "that this cult is like the cult of Mithras. The followers of Mithras never spoke against the gods. But the Christians consider our gods to be demons, unholy spirits, and claim that only the Hebrew rebel they worship is the one true god." Diocletian listened carefully but he was still reluctant to give the signal to open the floodgates of violence.

A Round
of Consultations

Lactantius was a harsh critic of those who led the persecution so we may believe him when he tells us that Diocletian was reluctant to start the persecution of the Christians. He writes that Diocletian, still searching for answers, "sent a haruspex to the oracle of Apollo at Didyme," near the ancient town of Miletus. Constantine, himself, was at the court when the reply came and years later he told the story to Eusebius.

"[The haruspex reported] that Apollo spoke from a deep and gloomy cavern through a medium, and the voice heard was not human. [The god] declared that the Pious on Earth were preventing him from speaking the truth, and that therefore the oracles that issued from his tripod were without value. This is why he hung down his hair in grief, mourning all the evils that will come to men from the loss of his prophetic spirit."

Constantine then told Eusebius; "I heard the senior Augustus asking his advisers: Who are the Pious on Earth? And one of the pagan priests replied: "The Christians, of course."

The Christians did indeed use the word *pious* or in Greek *evseveis* in referring to themselves. This brief passage is interesting for another reason. Assuming that Constantine was telling Eusebius the truth, it shows that the young tribune was not treated like an ordinary officer of his rank. We know the strict protocol Diocletian had instituted in the palace. For Constantine to be at a meeting where Diocletian was also present shows that he was treated as a member of the imperial family. If this assumption is correct, then the years Constantine spent in Nicomedia were immensely valuable for his learning the intricacies of statecraft, watching at close range Diocletian, a real master in the exercise of power.

It appears that the senior Augustus sought also the advice of Porphyrios. In a letter the prominent pagan philosopher wrote to his young wife, Marcella—he married her when he was seventy years old—he explained that he had to take a long journey "because of a need of the Greeks." At the time, Porphyrios lived in Rome and the reference to the "Greeks" is clearly related to those at the forefront of the fight to preserve the worship of the traditional gods.

These consultations took much time during the winter months. In the end, Diocletian gave in, "but he remained firm on the point that all should be done without shedding blood," pointing out that "these people have the habit of marching voluntarily to their deaths." The authorities should not help them become martyrs. He added that as far as he was concerned it would be sufficient to purge the palace and the army of those who refused to sacrifice to the gods. Whatever his real intentions, the edict he issued opened the way to violence and death.

THE EDICT OF PERSECUTION

D iocletian made up his mind around the end of January of
303. According to Lactantius, Diocletian consulted the
pagan priests "on the most favorable day to launch the projected action." They suggested the feast of the Terminalia, the 23 of
February. That day would be known later, Lactantius wrote, in the
words of Vergil (Aeneid IV, 169-170), "*Ille dies primus leti primusque
malorum causa fit*" (This day was the first cause of death, the first of
suffering).

We can reconstruct the scene using the vivid description left to us
by Lactantius. The city prefect, accompanied by military officers and
soldiers and officials of the Treasury (Fiscus), came at the crack of
dawn with axes and heavy iron bars to the church building which
stood on the other side of the square, across from the imperial palace.
While Diocletian and Galerius—who had come from Thessaloniki—
were watching the scene from inside the palace, the soldiers broke
down the main entrance and entered the building where they found
the holy scriptures and other religious objects. They carried them outside to the middle of the square and set them on fire. Already a large
crowd had gathered to watch the burning.

Galerius wanted to set the church on fire and burn it to the
ground but Diocletian prudently objected that the fire might spread
through the town and cause a catastrophe. Instead, a battering ram,

used by the army to break down the gates of a besieged city, was rolled ponderously to the front of the church building, poised like a monster ready to attack. Minutes later, the ram started pounding against the walls. It took some time before the building was reduced to rubble, but by the end of the day only a pile of broken beams, crashed benches, stones and tiles remained where the church had stood in the morning.

The next day, a parchment with the text of the edict was posted by a squad of soldiers on a pillar in the square, while copies were dispatched with couriers to all the governors in the eastern part of the empire. Maximian and Constantius had already been told about the projected action and were now asked in imperial letters to implement the policy within their domains.

The persecution that many Christians feared but few believed would ever happen again was now an ugly reality. Under the decree, church buildings were to be demolished, the holy scriptures surrendered and publicly burned, the sacred vessels (mostly in gold and silver) "seized for the Fiscus." The Christians were no longer allowed to gather and worship their God. Officials and dignitaries who refused to sacrifice at the altars of the traditional gods would be removed from their posts, deprived of all honors and distinctions. All Christians could face torture as punishment for their refusal to sacrifice. Besides, Christians no longer had the right to take someone to court and seek justice if they were the victims of assault or theft. No slave who professed to be a Christian could be freed even if his master wished to set him free. At least no blood was to be shed since the edict did not impose the death penalty for those who refused to sacrifice.

Diocletian apparently hoped that those measures would be enough to break up the tentacles of the "poisonous weed" and convince the Christians to come to their senses and abandon their silly superstitions. He counted without their strong convictions. Since a Christian believed that dying for Christ would bring him eternal life, many would seek death by insulting the emperor in court, and were condemned to die not so much for their religious beliefs as for their insolence. In the eyes of the judges who sent them to death such punishment had nothing to do with the religion of the condemned.

TORTURE AND DEATH

The very same day the imperial edict was posted in Nicomedia, a zealot Christian, a young man by the name of Euethius, tore down the parchment and trampled it on the ground shouting in front of onlookers: "Here are your Gothic and Sarmatian triumphs," referring tauntingly to Diocletian's titles "Gothicus" and "Sarmaticus" which had been bestowed on him after his victories over those barbarian tribes. The young man was immediately arrested by the home guards, the *scutarii*, and taken to a judicial magistrate. We have enough information to reconstruct the scene. The judge listened as one of the guards described the incident, then he turned to the prisoner.

"Is this all true?" he asked.

"Yes, it is," Euethius replied defiantly.

"You admit that you insulted the sacred person of the Augustus?"

"For me, only the person of Christ is sacred."

"If I condemn you, it will not be for your religion; it will be for your insolent act against the emperor."

"I insulted the emperor only because he insulted my Lord and Savior. If you kill me, you will not give me death but life eternal. I pity you."

"You are an idiot but the law does not exempt idiots from just punishment...Take him away. Torture and then burn him on the stake.

This is the sentence pronounced by this court."

The guards pushed Euethius out of the court and led him to the prison. For most of the night they flogged him while he was hanging naked from an iron hook, the ropes cutting through his flesh as his body twisted grotesquely with every lashing. By dawn his body was a bloody pulp. Half-conscious, he put up no resistance when he was taken to the square and tied to a pillar surrounded at its base with piles of fagots and dry branches. "He suffered death with admirable patience," to quote Lactantius. Euethius was the first victim.

Diocletian was furious when the story was reported to him. He did not want any blood, but those Christians courted death. "Yes, Domine," he was told by the priest of the local temple of Jupiter, "they believe that if they die for their Christ, they will have eternal life in what they call Paradise."

All Diocletian wanted—somewhat naively—was to make life difficult for the Christians so that they would come to their senses and sacrifice to the gods. But to the Christians a sacrifice to the pagan gods was an abomination. Such an act, they believed, would cost a Christian his salvation and his hope for eternal life. The more fanatical among them were ready to provoke their death by insulting the emperor, and find in death eternal life in Paradise.

Still, in the first weeks after the publication of the edict, few were forced to sacrifice and after Euethius no other Christian was put to death. Some churches were demolished here and there and some priests were taken to prison for refusing to sacrifice or surrender their holy books and sacred vessels. Many were flogged as part of their punishment. The worst part was the incarceration in filthy, rat-infested dungeons.

Maximian in his part of the world ordered the governors to pressure the Christian priests to sacrifice, but there too his governors tried to go easy on them. "Just make the gesture, drop a pinch of incense, it's only to comply with the law," the judges would say according to stories recorded in the *Passions of the Saints*. Some Christians agreed and dropped incense on the altars brought into the court for this purpose but others refused stubbornly and were sent to prison. In northern Africa where the Christians were most fanatical, many were sent to the salt mines and some perished under torture.

The persecution was milder in Gaul and Britain where Falvius Constantius went through the motions but never took a truly harsh line. His governors limited themselves to the demolition of the least imposing church buildings. Even in the area governed by Galerius few paid for their defiance with their lives during the first month after the publication of the edict. In most parts of the empire, the authorities simply closed down church buildings and forced the priests to surrender the holy books and especially the valuable sacred vessels. But then the fire in Nicomedia changed it all.

THE PALACE ON FIRE

A few weeks after the publication of the edict, Diocletian was awakened in the middle of the night to frantic shouts that the palace was on fire. One wing of the huge building was burning like an inferno, the flames leaping into the sky, heavy black smoke billowing from the roof, glowing cinders exploding in the air.

Constantine, together with other officers and soldiers from the *scutarii* unit sleeping in the nearby barracks, rushed to the palace to help put out the fire. The place was a madhouse, slaves and servants running with buckets full of water, officials half-dressed seeking shelter, scribes trying frantically under the direction of the Praetorian Prefect to gather official documents and stuff them into wooden campaign crates, guards tearing down curtains and banners and dipping them into water buckets to smother the flames, others breaking down wooden doors and benches and throwing them out into the square before they, too, could catch fire. Diocletian and Galerius had sought refuge at the other side of the building in their nightclothes, all imperial dignity and decorum gone. It was daylight by the time the fire died out. The wing with the sacred bedchamber and the family quarters was a mess of blackened walls, charred furniture, collapsed ceilings.

Later in the day, Diocletian with Galerius at his side inspected the destroyed part of the palace. The fire appeared to have started on the ground floor at the back, near the sleeping cubicles of several slaves.

Some of them had died in the fire before they had time to escape because the flames spread much too quickly.

Lactantius accuses Galerius for deliberately setting the palace on fire in order to blame the Christians and force Diocletian to take a harsher stand. True, Galerius insisted that the Christians must have set the fire but it is rather unlikely that he would have risked burning himself to death just to blame the Christians. Not only was he staying at the palace but so was his wife Valeria and his son Candidianus—Valeria had no children and they had adopted this boy Galerius had fathered with a concubine—as well as Diocletian and his wife Prisca.

Without waiting for the findings of an investigation, Galerius formally charged the Christians and called for revenge. Diocletian, too, was enraged but he wanted to find out who were the perpetrators of the foul deed before he would unleash the executioners. Four palace slaves were arrested and taken to prison where for the next two days they suffered on the rack. In the end, their bones broken, they were left to die without telling their torturers anything of substance. Very likely, they knew nothing.

The investigation continued but nothing came to light. Anthimos, the bishop of Nicomedia, was also interrogated under torture but being old and frail he died before he told his tormentors anything at all. Frustrated and angry, Galerius came up with a clever suggestion. Everyone knew that the Christians refused to sacrifice for fear of losing their chance to have eternal life. Here was a simple test to see who was loyal and who was not among those in the palace. "Why not hold a public ceremony to thank the gods for our salvation, and have everyone offer sacrifice to the gods. This will unmask the traitors."

Diocletian agreed. This loyalty test would be simple and bloodless. He summoned the priests from the temple of Jupiter and ordered them to prepare a public sacrifice with incense. Everyone in the palace, high officials, eunuchs, scribes, servants, slaves, all gathered in the inner courtyard. Even Prisca and Valeria offered sacrifice, leading the way after Diocletian and Galerius. After all, this was a sacrifice to Jupiter for saving their lives.

One after another, all who lived and worked in the palace went up to the altar and dropped a pinch of incense on the flames. Only Dorotheus and Gorgogianus, two of Diocletian's most faithful secretaries who had been with him for years, refused to drop the incense on the altar. It was a poignant scene. Diocletian made an effort to persuade them, saying "just one pinch will do." Dorotheus, speaking for his friend as well, gave a reply which was typical of a devout Christian in those days. "Domine," he said, "I have served you faithfully for many years. I would give my earthly life for you, but you are asking me to forfeit my eternal life. This I cannot do." Whatever their religious reasoning, those two men had publicly defied the emperor in front of everyone and could not be forgiven.

They were put in irons and taken away. During the night they were flogged while they were asked about the fire. They had nothing to say. They were beheaded in the morning. Still, the identity of the arsonists remained a mystery. Quite possibly the fire was an accident, not the work of arsonists, but in the charged atmosphere of those days Diocletian was not willing to accept a simpler explanation.

Then, fifteen days later, a second fire broke out in the palace. Constantine told Eusebius many years later that this second fire was set by lightning. Probably it was. The night had been stormy with heavy rain and much thunder and lightning. Even Alafius, the Praetorian Prefect, thought that the fire had been set by a thunderbolt which had struck one of the spires on the roof. The Christians, too, accepted the thunderbolt version which in their eyes meant that God had sent the fire from heaven to punish the persecutors of the *"euseveis"* (pious).

This time the rain kept the fire from causing too heavy damage, but Galerius, shouting that he had no intention of letting the Christians roast him alive, announced that he was immediately leaving for Thessaloniki with his wife and son.

Whatever the real cause, the fire was the last straw for Diocletian. He had tried to be lenient and in return those fanatics had attempted twice to burn him and his family alive. In the next few weeks, he sent angry messages to the governors ordering them to break up the Christian sect. Torturing and executions were to be used without hesitation. "Burn the godless at the stake because once the body is consumed by the flames nothing will be left for resurrection and eternal life," he wrote on the advice of Hierocles, the fanatical governor of Bithynia.

Violence now was the order of the day. Even though the ordinary pagans were not fired up with hatred (the record shows that very seldom did large crowds jam the courts and even less frequently did the spectators shout insults against the accused or call for their deaths), the more fanatical among the pagans welcomed this war against the godless Christians. The fanatical Christians on their part saw the final Armageddon approaching, bringing unspeakable suffering as the prophets had predicted, the times of turmoil ending with Christ's kingdom emerging triumphant on earth. Lactantius, who delights in describing the suffering of Christ's enemies, predicted in his *Divines Institutiones* (Divine Institutions) that nine-tenths of mankind would perish in the upheaval and that even one third of the "pious" would be lost.

Christian writers have recorded in much detail the trials, the torturing, and the violent deaths of many Christians who held up their faith to the end. It is impossible to give total figures but undoubtedly they were in the thousands. Some governors—as Datianus in Spain, Theotecnus in Galatia, Urbanus in Palestine, and Hierocles in Bithynia—carried out the orders of the emperor with exceptional ferocity. Others, and it appears they were in the majority, tried to scale down the violence. On their unwritten instructions many judges used every means in their power to persuade the accused to recant and return to the traditional religion. Some judges showed compassion out of a sense of humanity or even because they secretly favored the

Christian faith, while others did so because they hoped to bring many back to the old religion and gain praise from their superiors. We have stories of judges who would force a few grains of incense into the hands of the prisoner and at the same time sprinkle some of it on the altar declaring that the sacrifice had been performed and the prisoner was free to go. In other cases, the judge would ask the prisoner to sacrifice to the Supreme Deity (*Summus Deus*) without identifying the god he had in mind so that a Christian could sprinkle the incense on the altar while praying to his own God.

In some cases, judges tried to bribe prisoners into submission. "If you obey the governor," the judge told Saint Victor in Galatia, "you shall have the title 'friend of the Caesar' and a position in the palace." He chose death. Theodotus in Ancyra (today's Ankara, Turkey) was promised "the favor of the emperors, the highest municipal dignities, and the priesthood of Apollo." The prisoner declined by simply saying, "I am a Christian".

In other stories we find lenient judges driven to anger by the stubborn refusal of the prisoner to listen to reason. "Abandon your foolish boasting," Maximus, the Governor of Cilicia, said to a young man by the name of Andronicus, "and listen to me just as you would have listened to your father. You will gain nothing by following those before you who clung to their foolish beliefs. Pay honor to the emperors and our fathers and offer sacrifice to the gods."

The young man replied defiantly. "You do well to call them your fathers for all of you are the sons of Satan whose works you perform."

Governor Maximus made one more effort. He ordered the officers of the court to press on the prisoner's lips a morsel of sacrificial meat so that he could claim that the prisoner had complied and could be set free. Andronicus spat the meat with contempt crying out, "You despicable tyrant and those who gave you the power to defile my soul with your impious sacrifices, all of you will be punished for what you have done to the servants of God."

Angered, the governor retorted, "You, accursed scoundrel, how dare you curse the emperors who have given the world such long and profound peace?"

"I have cursed them and I will curse them again. May the immortal hand of God strike them so they can see what they have done to the Servants of God."

This was an intolerable insult to the Emperor and after a few more angry exchanges, the governor said, "I will make you die little by little in horrible pain."

"I am not afraid of your threats." Andronicus was young and fanatical and was convinced that by dying for Christ he was assured eternal life in paradise. Others were less insulting if not less adamant.

When Philippus, the bishop of Heracleia, was brought to the court, he said calmly, "I have obeyed the emperors all my life and when their commands are just I hasten to obey. For the Holy Scriptures order me to render to God what is due to God and to Caesar what is due to Caesar. I have kept this commandment without fail down to the present, but now I have to choose between the things of heaven over the attractions of this world. I am a Christian and I must refuse to sacrifice to your gods." *Christianus sum.* I am a Christian. Throughout the empire that was the reply and with this many died at the stake or on the executioner's block.

Still, the violent death of many did not bring the Christians to their senses as Diocletian had hoped. Most Christians were not known to the authorities and were never persecuted. They kept quiet but remained loyal to their faith. Those who paid the price were mostly members of the clergy or Christians who chose to declare openly their faith and seek punishment. But the persecution was waged at random, without system, and after several months of savage persecution the Christian sect remained as strong as ever. Diocletian began to realize that his harsh measures were not working. He had to find a way out without tarnishing his imperial prestige by admitting defeat. From his own personal experience, he knew the power of organization. He also knew that an organization is held together by its functionaries, those who direct the affairs of the organization and derive their influence, well-being and even livelihood from its existence. In the case of the Christian sect those functionaries were the bishops, the presbyters and the deacons.

"If we destroy those who manage the affairs of this sect, we will break its back. The mere followers will just give up," he must have told the meeting of senior officials he summoned to the palace to outline the new edict he was planning to issue.

FOCUSING ON THE CLERGY

The second edict came out in June, less than four months after the first. The target now was the Christian clergy. All bishops, presbyters and deacons were to be arrested and thrown into prison unless they surrendered their holy books, and sacred vessels and offered sacrifice to the gods. Some priests surrendered the holy books, or what they claimed to be holy scriptures, and a few even offered sacrifice. Later, they would be denounced as *traditores* for turning in the holy books and would be accused of betraying Christ, unfit to shepherd their Christian flock again. (Years later, Constantine as the emperor would have a great deal of trouble with this issue.) But most priests defied the authorities. The filthy dungeons that were built to hold murderers and thieves were now filled with Christian clergy.

Conditions in the crowded cells were abominable. Rats were biting at the feet of the prisoners, stealing the meager food the jailers were giving them. The stench from human excrement and urine was suffocating. There was hardly space for a man to sit, let alone lay down at night. And every day more were arrested.

Before long, several governors began to send urgent messages reporting to the emperor the problem they faced. "We have no room for criminals any more. Murderers walk free. Our townspeople complain that the streets are no longer safe and that they fear for their families," a governor wrote in his report. Even Hierocles, the governor of Bithynia who had advocated the persecution, wrote a report to Diocletian in which he decried the overcrowding of the prisons.

We have no reliable figures as to the number of Christians in Diocletian's time. The population of the Roman Empire in those days is estimated at some one hundred million. Of them, it would not be extravagant to say, five to six million must have been followers of the Christian faith. They lived mostly in the cities and towns, not in the villages where the traditional gods and especially the local deities held sway. Over two-thirds lived in the East, even though strong Christian communities flourished in northern Africa and Spain, and somewhat less numerous in Gaul and Britain. Italy also had many strong churches.

With the exception of Gaul and Britain, where Caesar Flavius Constantius kept the persecution to less violent levels, in all other parts of the empire many Christians suffered torture and death. But we have to understand that, as a rule, only bishops and priests were known to the authorities. Most of the ordinary people who worshipped the Christian God were not exposed to persecution because their connection with the Christian community was not necessarily widely known. Unless a vindictive informer—a disgruntled neighbor, for instance—told the authorities, they could go undetected, because the "security agencies" of the time did not have the means to keep complete lists of Christian worshipers. For the ordinary Christians the pain was not physical. It was the pain of seeing their church buildings being closed down or demolished, the holy scriptures and symbols burned, their bishops and priests dragged to prison and to the executioner's block. The first edict which did not single out the clergy did not cause as much violence as the second which was targeted at the bishops and priests who were known to the local officials. This explains why the prisons were packed with Christians after the second edict, to the point that the incarceration of so many became a public problem.

With his two edicts, Diocletian had opened a Pandora's box. For once his good judgment and imagination seemed to have deserted him. He was caught in a vise of his own making. A way had to be found to empty the prisons and end all this violence but without admitting that the persecution had been a failure.

In September, just before he left for Rome to celebrate his *Vicennalia* (twenty years on the throne), he issued another edict on the Christians, the third within less than a year. He presented it as a gesture of "clemency" and "benevolence," and the opening paragraphs seemed to order the release of the imprisoned Christians. But further down in the text, it posed a "simple" condition before one could be released. All a prisoner had to do to walk out of the prison as a free man was to offer sacrifice to the traditional gods. Those who offered sacrifice were to be released at once. Those who refused were to be tortured until they changed their minds. One way or the other, the crowding of the prisons would ease since those who complied would be set free and those who refused to sacrifice would not survive for long the ingenious tortures their jailers could invent. It was a "clever" scheme, probably suggested by a man like Hierocles.

Diocletian could not have chosen a worse way to end the violence. Since sacrifice to the traditional gods was an abomination for any devout Christian, the edict could not but bring more suffering and violence.

The stories we find in the ancient sources come mostly from Christian writers and may be overdramatized. Still, we know that even in our century, the savage treatment of human beings has taken appalling forms. Phileas, the bishop of Thmuis in lower Egypt, left a vivid description of the bloody ordeals he witnessed. "...Some had their hands tied behind their back and were flogged as they were hanging from gibbets...others had their limbs stretched by machines...Some died under torture, others were thrown back into the cells half-dead, and many died a few days later and found peace. Those who recovered were asked yet again to choose between touching the abominable sacrifice—whereupon they would receive the freedom that brought a curse with it—and when they again refused to sacrifice they were condemned to die, and without a moment's hesitation they went happily to their deaths."

Not everyone could stand the excruciating pain. Those who gave in and committed the cardinal sin of sacrificing to the "demons" and the "unholy spirits" would later find themselves reviled and despised by those who had remained faithful to Christ. The persecution was to leave behind not only the maimed bodies of tortured "confessors" but also a legacy of discord among the Christians.

At the same time, and this was most important for the future, the suffering steeled the conviction of the Christians that theirs was indeed the only true religion. Constantine, who witnessed the persecution from the vantage point of an officer in the imperial guard—and one who had the rare privilege of access to the palace and to the emperor himself—was impressed by the devotion of those Christians who faced torture and death without fear. Even more important for his political thinking was the realization that thousands of people were united in a strong, elaborate organization, with a common faith which brought them together whether they lived in Syria, Numidia, Spain, or Gaul, whether they spoke Greek or Latin or their native tongue. His mother, Helena, and Lactantius, the tutor of his son, Crispus, must have spoken to him during those trying days about their "Lord and Savior" who had the power to inspire such courage and dedication and to frustrate the emperor's savage efforts to destroy their community. Extensive evidence shows that Constantine was skeptical on the validity of Christian theology but he could not ignore the strength shown by the Christians in the face of horrible treatment. His later actions did not spring suddenly from nowhere. The seeds were planted during the years of persecution.

CHAPTER IV

THE ABDICATION
OF THE *AUGUSTI*

CELEBRATING THE VICENNALIA

However irritating the stubbornness of the Christians might have been to the aging emperor, their punishment was not the only issue occupying his mind. More than nineteen years had passed since that fateful day in November outside of Nicomedia when the legions had hailed him as the Augustus. He had reigned already longer than any other Roman emperor since Marcus Aurelius over one hundred years before. In those nineteen years he had brought peace and prosperity to the disintegrating empire and had restored its ancient glory. His ingenious decision to divide responsibility among two Augusti and two Caesars had made the governing and the defense of the sprawling empire more effective. He had every reason to look back and be proud of what he had accomplished.

As the time for the twentieth anniversary of his elevation to Augustus was approaching, several members of his Consistorium, his council of advisors, suggested that he should celebrate his great achievements with a magnificent triumph in Rome. The idea may have already crossed his mind because three years earlier he had ordered the construction in Rome of a colossal building of public baths which would bear his name and rival in splendor those named after Trajan or Caracalla.

As emperor, Diocletian had not been in Rome before and the celebration of the Vicennalia was a good reason for undertaking the long journey. He wanted to meet Maximian and discuss with him a thought he had been turning in his mind for some time. The Tetrarchy had worked well and it should be preserved as a system of governing for the good of the empire. But the system would break down in the end unless the two Caesars were raised soon to the dignity of Augustus and two new Caesars were appointed to their posts. This meant that Diocletian and Maximian should lay down the purple and return to private life.

It was an idea that virtually had no precedent in Roman history. Tiberius had gone to the island of Capri and his sexual orgies but he had not really given up the purple, trying to govern from afar, with little success to be sure. Nerva had retired after a few months, but Nerva was old and incompetent and he had done the empire a favor by passing to Trajan the imperial mantle. Diocletian was neither Tiberius nor Nerva. His plan to step down was a deliberate and calculated move to preserve the tetrarchy and assure that the system would continue. Being, as ever, a prudent man, he realized that such a drastic step should be taken while he was in full control, with his personal authority undiminished.

And so, shortly after issuing his third edict against the Christians in September of 303, he set off from Nicomedia on the long journey to Rome with his wife Prisca and his "sacred retinue" of palace officials, eunuchs, servants, and military men from his personal guard. Constantine, being one of the officers, accompanied the emperor. After almost ten years, he was to see his father again. At Sirmium, Diocletian was joined by Galerius and his wife, Valeria, and their retinue, and together they continued on to Mediolanum where they joined Maximian, Flavius Constantius and their wives. After a short rest at Mediolanum, they all started on the last leg of their journey to Rome to celebrate not only the *Vicennalia* of the two Augusti but also the *Decennalia* of the two Caesars who had already been ten years in their imperial posts.

Most likely it was at Mediolanum where Diocletian discussed with Maximian the idea of stepping down. Knowing Maximian's temperament we may safely assume that the idea did not sit well with the Augustus of the West.

Diocletian's assurances that they would retain their titles and their honors were not very convincing. Maximian knew full well that titles without the authority to punish or reward would be like blunted spears. But he could not possibly defy Diocletian. Since that day in Nicomedia when he had raised Diocletian's arm and proclaimed him Augustus in front of the legions, Maximian had accepted Diocletian's authority, bowing to his superior judgment and ability, and following his lead. He had been richly rewarded for his loyalty.

It was a balmy afternoon in late October when the imperial procession reached Rome. Thousands came out into the streets to see for the first time in person the men they had seen until then only on coins and on marble busts and statues.

The cheers of the jubilant public were not an empty show. For a long time Rome had been ignored, her ancient institutions reduced to empty relics. Rome was no longer the capital of the empire because the seat of power was wherever the emperor happened to be. Still, Rome was the eternal city, the spiritual center of the empire, the place where it all had begun over a thousand years ago. With his decision to celebrate the glorious anniversary there, Diocletian had solemnly recognized that Rome was indeed the "mother city." The Senate and the people of Rome were elated by this and were determined to make the most of this great event. With funds from the city treasury and with private donations, they organized the races at the Circus Maximus and the gladiatorial games in the Flavian Amphitheater so that they would be the most impressive the city had seen in a long time.

Already the construction of a triumphal arch was under way and four separate columns for each of the four emperors—the pedestals are still today in the Forum—were already completed. Diocletian visited the site of the arch and of the columns, and also of the baths less than a mile away, accompanied by several Roman senators in their traditional white togas, a sight which recalled the days of ancient glory. The senators reminded each other that Diocletian may have stayed away from Rome all these years but he had not entirely forgotten what Rome meant. The construction of the imposing baths was visible proof of that.

For the two Augusti and the two Caesars—all Illyrian soldiers at heart—Rome must have been a dazzling sight. No other city in the Mediterranean world could rival her magnificence. A visitor was overwhelmed by the numerous temples to the various deities, the basilicas where the Roman officials dispensed justice under Roman law, the gigantic baths, the colossal Flavian Amphitheater, the Pantheon, the Circus Maximus, the majestic temple of Jupiter Maximus on the Capitoline Hill, the Forum with the Senate building, the temple of the Vestal Virgins, the marble arch dedicated to Titus— an endless succession of marble porticos, statues, and colonnades lining the great avenues.

Rome was a city of over a million people who came from every corner of the empire, spoke a multitude of different tongues, and worshipped all the different gods that were made welcome in the eternal city. Under the gaze of the gleaming temples, the city was a busy, noisy place, with crowds milling about, shopping, arguing, talking in clusters, with mule-drawn wagons carrying produce to the markets, merchants peddling in loud voices their merchandise, open-air stalls selling freshly-baked bread and sweet-smelling corn cakes, praetorian soldiers patrolling the streets, small boys playing with fake wooden swords and holding leather or wicker shields for protection, beggars asking for alms in a sad, singing voice, and Roman aristocrats being carried through the narrow streets or the wide avenues to their destination in curtained litter chairs.

In the weeks which followed the arrival of the Augusti, the Caesars, and their wives, the scions of the old patrician families set aside their usual aloofness and gave lavish banquets and parties in honor of the imperial visitors. Some had to set aside more than ancestral pride. Several families had suffered under Maximian who on several occasions had accused prominent senators of wrongdoing and had some of them executed. The charges were not always well-founded and the cynics claimed in whispers that what Maximian wanted was not so much to punish the guilty as to seize the properties of the falsely accused. Some of the families that had been mistreated stayed away from the festivities, going to their country villas instead, to be away from Rome. But the rest of the Roman aristocracy fawned on their imperial guests with a servility that must have made Diocletian's stomach turn.

Constantine, who had come to Rome as an officer in Diocletian's personal guard, had the opportunity to see his father again. They had not seen each other since the day Constantine left for Diocletian's court almost ten years ago. We have no record of their meeting in Rome but subsequent events which are written down in considerable detail can guide our steps. The meeting must have been very cordial and Flavius Constantius must have been impressed by his son who was now a strapping thirty-one-year old senior Tribune in the emperor's personal guard. The last time they were together, Constantine was still bitter because of his parents' divorce. But now the old wounds had healed and Flavius Constantius must have felt a powerful surge of pride at the sight of this young man.

Thirty-three months later, a dying Flavius Constantius would ask his legion commanders at Eboracum to elevate his son to the purple. But in the fall of 303, Constantine could not foresee what was to happen in the not too distant future.

The residents of Rome had heard stories about the triumphal processions of the past, when the victorious generals and emperors had paraded down Via Sacra, followed by hundreds and hundreds of captured barbarians and their kings in chains and by long convoys of mule-drawn wagons loaded with the spoils of war. But most of them had not seen in their lifetime the celebration of a triumph.

On the day of the parade, the weather was unusually mild for late November, the sun's rays bathing in light the marble colonnades of the temples. The crowds were in a jubilant mood, heartened by the promise of generous handouts of grain and wine.

The triumph staged by Diocletian differed from those celebrated in ancient times. Nobody was paraded in chains and no spoils of war were on display. Instead, the Augusti and their two Caesars rode on their magnificent horses, followed by several maniples of *Scutarii* and Praetorian Guards on Horseback, the standard-bearers carrying on poles the bronze Roman eagles, the plumes on the helmets of the tribunes and the centurions fluttering in the breeze. Maniples of foot soldiers followed the horsemen, each maniple headed by its own centurion and its standard-bearers, and then several heavy machines of war, the catapults and rams that had breached the walls of Gesoriacun or Alexandria, and finally a long procession of mule-drawn wagons with painted and sculptured depictions of the emperors' great victories across the Rhine and the Danube, in Britain, in Egypt, in northern Africa, in Mesopotamia. For the victory against the Persians, the artists had reproduced images of Narses' captured family and concubines in colorful oriental dresses as the artists had imagined them.

From Via Sacra, the procession turned into the Clivus Capitolinus, the avenue leading uphill to the magnificent temple of Jupiter Optimus Maximus with its marble columns gleaming at the summit of the hill. With their task completed, the wagons with the gaudy displays peeled off and turned into the Vicus Jubarius on their way to the Campus Martius where they were to disband.

The horsemen and the foot soldiers lined up in formation at the foot of the hill along the Clivus Capitolinus, facing the temple. Already most of the senators, resplendent in their white togas, had taken their places near the temple, those of consular rank in front. Next to them stood the *hieration* headed by the senior priests and the Vestal Virgins. On all sides of the hill, hundreds of ordinary people elbowed each other trying to get a better view of the uncommon spectacle. On this occasion, Diocletian as Pontifex Maximus was to offer the sacrifice in the place of the high priest of Jupiter.

The two Augusti and their two Caesars dismounted and slowly ascended the steps leading to the temple. The hearty cheers of the spectators filled the air as the four men, impressive in their uniforms with the deep red capes flowing from their shoulders, went up the steps and reached the level ground in front of the temple.

A few minutes later with a signal from the senior haruspex, a bevy of slaves brought from the side of the temple a white bull and led the animal to the altar set in front of the temple. A strong dose of a numbing potion had been secretly given to the animal by the senior haruspex to help the slaves hold the powerful bull still. Diocletian drew his sword and with a swift motion sliced the back of the animal's neck, cutting the spinal cord. Bright red blood shot out and splattered the emperor's uniform, the bull's legs buckled and the animal keeled over, under the people's jubilant cheers.

After the sacrifice and the reading of the entrails by the haruspex, who found the omens most auspicious, Diocletian and Maximian walked into the temple. In the subdued light, the marble statue of Jupiter Maximus must have been an awesome sight. As agreed before, Diocletian asked Maximian to join him in taking an oath before Jupiter that when the time came both of them would return to private life so that the system of *tetrarchy* would be preserved.

That night a boisterous public celebration began. With countless flasks of cheap wine donated by the rich men of Rome, the merriment turned into an all-night orgy, with bawdy songs, sex in the streets, drunken quarrels, loud curses and obscenities. The wild celebration did not end with daylight. It went on for days and nights as though mass madness had gripped the city. And with the Saturnalia coming up in less than three weeks more could be expected. Diocletian, a rather prudish man, was appalled by the debauchery which deeply offended his sense of order and decorum. The inhabitants of Rome were turning into a farce a great event which ought to be celebrated with dignity.

THE EMPEROR IS
GRAVELY ILL

Diocletian was expected to stay on for a few more weeks, to be vested on the first of January consul for the ninth time, but he was so disgusted with what was going on in the streets of Rome that he decided to leave in the middle of winter. It took the imperial convoy ten days to reach Ravenna on the Adriatic after a miserable journey in rain, sleet, and bitter cold. The road that led to Ravenna through the mountain passes was covered with slimy mud brought down from the hillsides by the heavy rain, making the riding of a horse a hazardous undertaking. Diocletian had to use a litter. But even the litter could not keep the cold out and by the time they reached Ravenna he was down with fever. The physicians resorted to the usual remedies, potions and bleeding the veins, and the emperor improved enough to take part in the ceremony of his investiture with his ninth consulship. But the effort tired him out and in the evening the fever returned. He had to give up any thought of leaving Ravenna any time soon. He remained there until spring. Galerius also stayed on with Valeria, to the relief of Prisca who was understandably unhappy to be left alone with the ailing emperor in this strange town she was visiting for the first time in her life. Constantine, too, stayed in Ravenna with his unit of imperial guards.

As the weather began to improve with the coming of the spring, the emperor's health also showed signs of improvement and, shortly after the Ides of March, they decided to move on. From Ravenna they followed the coastal road to Aquileia where they stayed for a few days so that Diocletian could rest, and then they moved on to the flatlands of southern Pannonia, traveling toward the Danube. Diocletian's plan was to follow the river until they reached Moesia, then turn south toward Hadrianopolis and on to Byzantium where they would cross the Bosporus and a day later come to Nicomedia where he could be in the comfortable and familiar surroundings of the palace.

Things did not work out as he hoped. In Pannonia the fever returned and his condition grew rapidly worse. The "sacred retinue" had to stay in the small frontier town of Novae on the Danube and since there was not enough room many officials were sent back to Nicomedia.

It was at Novae that Galerius brought up again the problem of the Christians. He told the ailing emperor that he had received reports of revolts in the Orient and of Christians in the legions fomenting rebellion. With their stubborn refusal to become part of traditional society, he added, they were challenging the very authority of the emperor. This time, he said, they should declare the Christian cult an unlawful religion, just as Diocletian had done in the case of the Manicheans. Weakened by fever, and vexed by his failure to bring the Christians to their knees, Diocletian agreed and, in April of 304, he issued his fourth edict on the Christians. It went much further than the other three by reviving the policy of total persecution that Emperor Decius had imposed half a century earlier. The Christian faith was flatly declared *religio illicita*, an illegal religion. Just being a Christian was now a capital offense. It is hard to understand why Diocletian agreed to this. He ought to have known by then that death was not punishment in the eyes of those who believed that by dying for Christ they were gaining eternal life in Paradise. The new edict could only open up the floodgates of violence and death.

It did, especially in the East. Eusebius in his "Ecclesiastic history" in Greek gives a vivid picture of the new horrors.

> "Some of the victims suffered death by beheading, some by fire. So many were killed in a single day that the ax, blunted and worn out with slaughter, was broken into pieces and the executioners relieved one another from time to time to rest."

However exaggerated Eusebius' story may be, there is little doubt that many died a gruesome death during the summer months of that year. Again we must see the situation in perspective. Most ordinary Christians were not known to the authorities and as long as they stayed away from their places of worship they were safe. With most of the church buildings, especially in the East, closed down or demolished and most of the clergy in prison, in hiding, or dead, few Christians had the opportunity to go to church and be exposed to punishment. So, even though many thousands perished during the first two years of persecution, and many more would die in the following years, millions survived throughout the empire.

In the West, Maximian, who disliked the Christians as much as Galerius did, implemented the decree in his domain with some severity but Flavius Constantius virtually ignored it in Spain, Gaul and Britain. We have no evidence that Flavius Constantius was a Christian but he was certainly sympathetic to the Christian sect. We know that he had named one of his daughters Anastasia, and that was a Christian name honoring Christ's resurrection (*anastasis*).

The balmy summer weather and the enforced rest, if not the physicians' ministrations, helped the aging emperor regain some strength and in late July he decided to resume his journey. He wanted to return to Nicomedia and inaugurate the great circus that was now completed. The illness had made him realize that death was not a distant threat and this affected profoundly his thinking. It was not only the dedication of the circus that had to be carried out before it was too late. Much more important was his plan to step down together with Maximian to preserve the system he had created.

Constantine must have followed with grave misgivings what was happening. Being constantly near the emperor, he was astute enough to see that Galerius' influence on the old man was growing. That could only mean trouble in the future—especially if the emperor died—because Galerius was not Constantine's friend.

The journey through Moesia was uneventful. From the frontier town of Novae, they turned south to Augusta Traiana and then on to Serdica where Galerius and his wife together with their retinue left for Thessaloniki. It was already late August by the time Diocletian came back to Nicomedia. The ill-fated journey to Rome was over.

The inauguration of the new circus in Nicomedia was set for the third day after the Ides of October. As visitors had swarmed into the city from nearby towns, the inns in Nicomedia were full and the merchants in the market place were doing a brisk trade. The whole town was alive with excitement, with people arguing over the merits of the competing teams of charioteers and betting heavily on the races that would follow the inauguration ceremony. The chariot races always had that effect on people.

On inauguration day the weather was on the cool side, with a brisk breeze coming from the bay. Diocletian, with some effort, donned his imperial regalia and rode to the circus where the stands were filled to capacity. He watched the first race but then he felt a chill and left for the palace. Feverish, he went straight to bed. For the next two months his condition went from bad to worse with only brief improvements that gave his physicians false hopes that they had tamed the disease. Then, in December, Diocletian fell into a coma. Gloom filled the palace as all feared for the worst. Officials and servants walked silently with long faces, some with tearful eyes, speaking to each other in whispers. The gloom spilled outside as the word spread thorough the marketplace that the emperor was near death.

Greece and the Balkans
at the time of Constantine the Great

Some even claimed that the emperor was already dead and that the palace officials kept the truth from coming out, waiting for Galerius to arrive from Thessaloniki and take over. The rumor appeared to have some truth in it, as most of the festivities scheduled to celebrate the Saturnalia were canceled and the year ended in Nicomedia with little of the traditional merriment. The rest of the empire knew nothing as yet of the emperor's grave condition.

We have no written record but we may safely assume that Constantine must have gone to visit his mother in nearby Drepanon to discuss the dangers the death of the emperor might bring to both of them. Certainly they could not trust Galerius. At the same time it was hard to accept that he would harm then and provoke the wrath of Flavius Constantius. Still, Helena must have spent many sleepless nights worrying not so much about her own safety but as to what vindictive men might do to her son. No doubt, she must have prayed with tearful eyes to her Christian God for Constantine's safety.

With Diocletian still in a coma, Flaccinus, the Praetorian Prefect, was ready to dispatch a message to Galerius asking him to come to Nicomedia when, to everyone's amazement, on the first day of the new year 305, Diocletian regained consciousness and even asked for food. For months he had been unable to hold much food down and that was one reason for his loss of weight. The physicians saw the return of appetite as a hopeful sign. The good news spread quickly through the palace and into the streets.

For the next two months, Diocletian's condition improved and, five days before the Ides of March, he made his first public appearance at the temple of Jupiter where he offered a sacrifice of thanks for his recovery. He made every effort to give the impression that he was a healthy man but those who knew how he looked before the journey to Rome could see how heavy a toll the illness had taken.

Before the last day of March, Galerius came to Nicomedia at the invitation of Diocletian.

FAREWELL TO THE PURPLE

L actantius claims that it was a brusk and over-bearing Galerius who forced Diocletian to retire. Even if he wanted, Galerius could not—and, most importantly, did not need to—have pressed Diocletian to make such a momentous decision. Diocletian had long before made his plans. For almost five years, stonecutters and masons had been working steadily to build a huge palace at Spalatum on the Adriatic, in today's Split. The location was certainly not suitable for the seat of the imperial government but it was ideal for the residence of a retired emperor—and that is exactly why Diocletian was building his palace there. The decision to retire was neither sudden nor forced on Diocletian by Galerius.

What Diocletian certainly discussed with Galerius was the selection of the two new Caesars who would be invested with the purple once Galerius and Constantius moved up to the dignity of Augustus following the retirement of Diocletian and Maximian. Lactantius has given us a lively description of that discussion but he could not have been present and his narrative is the product of his own quite fertile imagination. Still, the events that followed are certainly in line with what Lactantius claims and for this reason we may use some excerpts from his imaginative story.

Maximian's son, Maxentius, was now twenty years old and he had recently become the son-in-law of Galerius, married to his

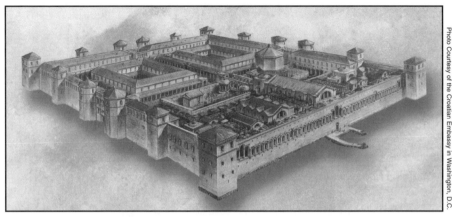

Photo Courtesy of the Croatian Embassy in Washington, D.C.

The palace as it was in Diocletian's time.

daughter from a previous marriage. One might have expected that Maxentius, being the son of Emperor Maximian and the son-in-law of the upcoming Augustus, would have a good chance to be chosen as the next Caesar of the West. But neither Diocletian nor Galerius—nor even his father, Maximian, if we are to believe Lactantius—had a good opinion of the young man.

"Maxentius is not worthy of being chosen. He insulted me when he was just a plain citizen; what is he going to do when he is elevated to the purple?" Galerius asked pointedly according to Lactantius. Diocletian apparently made no effort to support Maxentius' candidacy because he, too, had doubts about the young man's competence. With Maxentius pushed aside as a candidate, Constantine's chances to succeed his father faded rapidly. The son of Flavius Constantius was certainly a decent and intelligent young man and he had shown his unswerving loyalty to Diocletian all the years he had been in his service, but with Maxentius out of the picture he, too, had to be passed over, otherwise Maximian might have been offended— regardless of what he thought of his son. Besides, Constantine, too, lacked experience. He had never commanded a large force and his administrative ability had never been tested. Now that the two sons were out, Diocletian turned to the selection of the men who would become the next Caesars. According to Lactantius, it was Galerius who chose the men. Judging from the persons selected, we may accept what Lactantius tells us.

"So, who should be our choice?" Diocletian asked.

"Severus," Galerius replied.

Severus was a legion commander, a friend of Galerius and a man who would be acceptable to Flavius Constantius whose Caesar he was going to be. But Lactantius claims that Diocletian received the nomination with derision.

"What? This troublemaker, this drunkard who makes the night day and the day night?"

"He is worthy," Galerius replied coolly, "because he has shown his loyalty at the head of his soldiers. Anyway, I already sent word to Maximian that he may put the purple on him."

It is doubtful that Galerius would have spoken to Maximian about Severus before the man had been approved by Diocletian. To do so would have been a sign of unacceptable disrespect. Be that as it may, Lactantius tells us that the senior Augustus agreed readily.

"Very well. And who do you give me as the second Caesar," Diocletian said with a trace of irony.

Galerius suggested his nephew, the son of his sister, "a young man of semi-barbarian origin named Daia." (In the fashion of time, Daia had added the Roman name Maximinus.) Lactantius has only contempt and paints a dismal portrait of this man who was later to prove as hard on the Christians as his uncle. But Daia must have been a senior officer or even a legion a commander at the time and later he would show considerable ability as a Caesar.

"The men you have proposed to me are incapable and you are asking me to entrust to them the empire?" Diocletian said with dismay, to quote Lactantius.

"I am in a position to appreciate their merits," Galerius insisted.

To this, Diocletian supposedly replied, "It's your problem since you will take in your hands the reins of the empire. As for me I have worked long enough and I have taken good care to protect the integrity

The Mausoleum, ironically later converted into a church.

of the empire during my reign. If misfortune now comes, it will not be my fault."

Even if this dialogue was invented by Lactantius, it has a ring of truth because we know that Severus and Maximin Daia were the two men selected to succeed the two Caesars—Galerius and Constantius—

who were soon to be elevated to the dignity of Augustus. We also know that the two nominees were Galerius' personal choices and that alone shows that after his severe illness Diocletian had lost some of his vigor and judgment; otherwise it will be hard to understand why he accepted the two men without closer consultations with Maximian, and even more so with Flavius Constantius, especially with regard to Severus since this man was actually going to be the Caesar of the West under Constantius' supreme authority. Galerius might have gotten his way but the selection bore the seeds of trouble and developments would soon show how unwise the choices were.

On the first day of May in the year 305, twenty years after the battle of Margus in which Diocletian had emerged the sole emperor, Diocletian and Maximian returned to private life. Severus must have left Pannonia, where his legion was stationed, as soon as the decision had been made in early April because on the first of May he was in Mediolanum for the ceremony of his investiture by Maximian. Flavius Constantius did not come to Mediolanum for his investiture as the new Augustus of the West.

Lactantius, who was present at Diocletian's abdication, describes the event in vivid detail but again his flair for the dramatic may have played games with his accuracy.

> "Three miles outside of Nicomedia is the hill where [Diocletian] had received the purple. On the hill is a high pillar with the statue of Jupiter on top. The procession went up to this spot, while a great number of soldiers gathered round it. Tearfully, Diocletian addressed the soldiers telling them that he was now tired after so many years of ceaseless toil, and that he had earned the right to rest from his labors. He was therefore going to give up the purple and transfer the empire to younger and more vigorous hands and at the same time appoint two new Caesars. The vast

Photo Courtesy of the Croatian Embassy in Washington, D.C.

Today's Split with the remnants of the Diocletian's Palace occupying a large part of the town.

gathering waited in tense anticipation for the names to be announced. He then said that the two new Caesars were to be Severus and Maximinus."

At this point, Lactantius allows his reporting to be colored by his love for Constantine and his anger for having his idol bypassed. Constantine was certainly considered by many as a man worthy of being elevated to Caesar and, in fact, the mint in Alexandria had hastily issued a coin with the inscription of *Constantinus Caesar*, but on the day of the abdication the succession had been settled and there was no need for the dramatic incident described by Lactantius. Still, it will do no harm to reproduce it.

> "There was general amazement. Constantine stood prominently nearby, and men began wondering whether he had changed his name to Maximinus. But then, in the full view of everyone, Galerius reached back his hand, brushing Constantine aside, and drew Daia forward. He relieved him of the ordinary cloak he wore as a private man, and put him in the most prominent position. Everyone wondered who he could be and where he came from."

In his antipathy for Daia, Lactantius is obviously distorting the truth. First, Daia was not a private man, and second, as a high rank-ing officer he could not have been so utterly unknown to the soldiers. Besides, an incident such as that with Galerius pushing Constantine aside was rather unlikely because such important ceremonies were well planned in advance.

It was, in fact, Galerius who was vested first with the purple of Augustus by Diocletian with the words "Hail Gaius Valerius Maximianus Galerius, Sarmaticus, Persicus Maximus, Pontifex Maximus, Augustus."

Following the investiture Galerius thanked his mentor in words of the highest praise. "Hail Augustus, *Pater Patriae, Dator Lucis Aeternae*," father of the empire, the giver of eternal light.

It had been an impressive and dignified ceremony without precedent in Roman history. Two days later, Diocletian with his wife and a large retinue of assistants, servants and guards left for Spalatum and his newly—finished palace. The imposing building, which has survived to the present day, covered more than seven acres, a huge rectangle with strong outside walls and rising towers, situated right on the waterfront.

Even though the palace was built like a fortress, it was not an ugly, forbidding place. Marble colonnades, spacious gardens, sunlit walks and a profusion of fountains and statues made the palace a pleasant place to live. The private quarters of the family in the southern part of the building had a magnificent view of the Adriatic and their location was prudently chosen to shield the retired emperor from the intrusion of unwanted onlookers.

In Mediolanum, Maximian went through the ceremony with the solemnity required by the occasion but he showed no particular joy in laying down the imperial mantle. He only proclaimed Severus as the new Caesar of the West because Flavius Constantius did not come to Mediolanum, saying that he was having trouble at the moment with the Franks in Germania Inferior and preferred to stay in Augusta Treverorum (Treves) in order to keep an eye on the uneasy frontier. Probably he was unhappy with the way Diocletian had allowed Galerius to influence the succession, or he was already suffering from the illness that would end his life fourteen months later and for political reasons did not want his imperial colleagues to detect his condition.

A few days after the ceremony, Maximian left for his new home, a large villa in Lucania, situated in the midst of luscious gardens. It was a delightful place, but a life of leisure was too hard for this man who had lived much of his life fighting enemies, giving orders, and deciding on momentous issues affecting millions of people. He was only fifty-seven years old—not yet ready to content himself with growing cabbages like his senior colleague at Spalatum. He was restless and unhappy and this could spell trouble in the future.

PART II

THE RISE
TO THE SUMMIT

CHAPTER V

CONSTANTINUS AUGUSTUS

A HASTY DEPARTURE

Galerius never liked Constantine but he knew that Diocletian did, and as long as the old man was at the helm he avoided any show of open hostility to the son of Flavius Constantius. Now that Diocletian had turned over to him the reins of power, Galerius began to search for ways to keep Constantine shackled down in Nicomedia but without causing friction with his fellow Augustus in the West. He feared, not without reason, that if the young man went to join his father, he would sooner or later claim the dignity of a Caesar and disrupt the Tetrarchy. One plan that seemed to serve the purpose of keeping Constantine in the East was to give him a promotion and send him to far away Mesopotamia where he would be under the command of the new Caesar of the Orient, Galerius' nephew Maximin Daia.

As Galerius soon discovered, keeping Constantine out of the way was not such a simple matter. In late July, a special messenger brought to Galerius a letter from Flavius Constantius. The new Augustus of the West was asking his imperial colleague to send his son to Gaul as soon as possible. Considering the time needed for a horseman to travel to Nicomedia from Treves where Flavius Constantius was at the time, he must have decided to ask for Constantine as soon as he was elevated to the senior rank in May. Probably he had been thinking about this ever since he saw Constantine in Rome.

Galerius procrastinated for several weeks. His reply to Flavius Constantius was evasive, claiming that Constantine still had duties to perform as a senior tribune in the emperor's personal guard, and that he would certainly be released to leave for Gaul as soon as possible. But then a second, more pressing letter came from Flavius Constantius just before the Ides of September. Galerius could not possibly refuse now to let Constantine leave for Gaul without causing a dangerous rift with his imperial colleague. If he had learned anything at all from his long association with Diocletian, it was that it was unwise and even perilous to ruffle the feelings of powerful individuals who control the allegiance of mighty legions. Lactantius, who often writes more like a modern novelist than an ancient historian, describes Constantine's escape from Nicomedia in graphic detail.

"Galerius, who could no loner hold back, issued marching orders to Constantine in the evening but asked him not to leave until the following day, because he wanted to give him any last minute instructions that might come to his mind during the night. He either wanted to keep him under this pretext, or he wanted to send up ahead a letter to Severus, asking him to arrest [Constantine]. Suspicious of Galerius' intentions, Constantine took advantage of the moment the emperor retired after his supper, and hastened his departure. He set off at full speed, killing the horses in each post as he went ahead. The next day, the emperor who had deliberately prolonged his sleep until noon, called for Constantine but he was told that he had left immediately after supper. Indignation, fury. He ordered that they take the horses at the relay post and go after Constantine to force him to return. When he was told that the post no longer had any horses, he

could not hold the tears. In any event, after travelling
at incredible speed, Constantine reached his father."

Strangely, Lactantius, a Christian, finds the savage killing of the
horses not an act of cruelty but a clever stratagem for which his hero
could be proud.

Not so strangely, Zosimus repeats this tale in his *Historia Nova*.
Writing in Greek, almost two centuries later, this pagan historian glee-
fully tells us:

> "Fearful that he might be intercepted (because his love
> for imperium was already evident to many), he muti-
> lated the horses kept in the posts by the public trea-
> sury, and made them useless, cutting off in this man-
> ner the progress of those who chased him while he
> himself reached the nations where his father was.

Zosimus must have taken the story from   Lactantius' book "On
the Deaths of the Persecutors" (*De Mortis Persecutorum*). Being a
devout pagan, Zosimus was very happy to repeat a tale which testi-
fied to the cruelty of the man he despised for his support of the
Christians. But the tale is suspect for practical reasons. It would have
been impossible for Constantine to overpower by himself the guards
and kill or maim all the horses at the post. Besides, the killing would
have taken time, and Constantine had no time to waste.

If Galerius wanted to keep Constantine in Nicomedia overnight,
he did not need to play the charade described by Lactantius—giving
Constantine the papers with the imperial seal and then asking him to
wait until the next day. All he needed was to give orders that
Constantine was not to be allowed to go through the city gates during the night. Lactantius suggests that Galerius wanted to send ahead
a message to Severus in Mediolanum, telling him to arrest
Constantine, and that to gain time he wanted to keep Constantine a

few more hours in Nicomedia. If Galerius had indeed such a scheme in mind, he would have sent the messenger to Severus several days before giving Constantine his papers. But even the notion of having Severus arrest Constantine as he rode through his domain is rather improbable. Severus was the Caesar of the West under Augustus Flavius Constantius. Arresting the son of his Augustus under whatever pretext would have been a provocation that would certainly lead to a clash with Flavius Constantius' superior forces. Lactantius' account is picturesque but hardly believable. Galerius let Constantine go because he had no choice. The rest is most likely the product of Lactantius' flair for the melodramatic.

That Constantine traveled as rapidly as he could, especially in the early stages of his journey, is quite certain. What is not certain is whether he followed the main highways through Illyricum, northern Italy, and then on to Gaul through the Alpine passes. This would have been the normal route. But for safety reasons he may have followed *Via Egnatia* to Dyrrachium (Durres) on the Adriatic, from there crossing over to Brindisium by boat. Then traveling through the southern half of the Italian peninsula, he could have reached Neapolis (Naples) where he could easily find a cargo ship sailing for Massalia (Marseilles). With the exception of the usual dangers of a sea voyage, such a route would have been infinitely safer and even faster. If indeed Galerius had any designs to prevent Constantine from ever reaching his father, he could have arranged for an ambush by "unknown" bandits while Constantine rode through the mountains of Illyricum or through the Alpine passes where the bandits could have ended Constantine's life in a way that would have made it impossible for Flavius Constantius to blame Galerius or Severus for the death of his son. In any event, in late October, Constantine reached southern Gaul without mishap. His mother, Helena, and his little son, Crispus, apparently remained in Drepanon, unable to follow him in his perilous journey to Gaul.

CONSTANTINE SHOWS HIS METTLE

The first snow was already on the ground in northern Gaul as Constantine came to Gesoriacum, where his father was preparing to sail across the Fretum Gallicum (the Channel) to Britain. The barbarian tribe of the Picts in the northern part of the British isles—in today's Scotland—had launched raids into the south, across the Hadrian Wall, ravaging the fertile farms and the villages south of the Wall. The local garrisons had fought fiercely against the raiding bands but still many farmers were killed and many farmhouses and villages pillaged and burned. Flavius Constantius was determined to stump out this threat once and for all. Now he could count on his son to lift some of the burden from his shoulders.

We have no record of the scene. But it is not hard to imagine the moment Flavius Constantius embraced his son. Constantine must have been shaken by his father's appearance. The emperor was ill. He had aged rapidly since Rome; his once ruddy complexion was pale, his shoulders stooping. Yet, he wanted to lead the expedition against the Picts. We do not know if Constantine tried to dissuade his father, but if he did, he failed to change his mind.

At Gesoriacum, Constantine met Crocus, a Germanic chieftain who had been for some time a friend of Flavius Constantius and who

Photo by George W.D. Kousoulas

The head of Constantine the Great, part of the colossal statue which stood in his basilica in Rome. Currently in the courtyard of the Museo dei Conservatori in Rome.

had his men incorporated into the Roman legions. Constantine and Crocus hit it off well from the very first moment, and their friendship would one day soon help change the course of time.

The legions Flavius Constantius had assembled along the northern coast of Gaul were waiting for the weather to clear so they could sail across the Channel. But throughout the winter months of 306, the northern winds had been battering the sea with relentless fury, making the crossing a venture for insane men only. As the spring approached, the angry beast pulled back its watery claws, and so at the beginning of March the commander of the fleet told Flavius Constantius that they could now safely cross the Channel.

The orders went out to the legion commanders, and the boring inactivity of the winter months ended quickly. Preparations for the crossing began at a frantic pace. Many of the boats were already moored inside the harbor in Gesoriacum, but many more were in other ports along Gaul's northern coast and each legion had to move from its winter camp to the assigned port for embarkation. The sea marauders who a few years back had unleashed their assaults on the Roman ships from their hideouts in the delta of the Rhine no longer posed a threat. Still, moving thirty thousand armed men, hundreds of horses and mules, and tons of supplies across the Fretum Gallicum was a daunting undertaking. Few soldiers knew how to swim and even those who did feared the dark waters that could hide terrible monsters no man had ever seen. And then they had to cope with the heaving and rolling of the boats that made most of them puke up their entrails.

Organization had always been a hallmark of the Roman legions. It took less than two weeks to load men, animals, and supplies on some two hundred boats which moved the legions in stages, crossing the Channel three times back and forth. With the British harbors under the control of Flavius Constantius, the unloading of men, horses, and supplies was not a dangerous enterprise. Some ten days later, the legions reached Eboracum. After a brief rest there, they moved on to Pons Aelius, just south of Hadrian's Wall, where they set camp. On the way they had passed through a countryside scarred with the blackened ruins the Picts had left behind, and heard the wailing of women crying for their dead husbands and children. The Picts had to be punished in a way they would never forget.

At the war council Flavius Constantius held before the expedition, Constantine proposed a daring plan. The map they had was certainly crude but it did show a deep inlet north of the land of the Picts. Why not sail north with one legion along the coast until they reached the inlet. Then, have the troops land and attack the Picts from the north while the emperor with his forces attacked them from the south.

It was an ingenious but also a dangerous plan. Not one among those present at the council had ever been in that region. Besides, the map was old, drawn by Roman cartographers in the early days of the conquest of Britain. What if it was not accurate and there was no inlet at all? Constantine stood his ground and when Crocus offered to join Constantine with his force, the plan was approved.

It worked.

Caught between the two forces attacking them from north and south, the Picts were cut to pieces, their primitive villages burned to the ground. Those who survived were offered the familiar form of association with the Roman Empire. They would have to accept the protection of Rome and live in peace as long as they did not break the agreement. They accepted, too weak to refuse.

Constantine's imagination and bravery impressed Crocus and the other officers. Within a few weeks, he had won the respect of seasoned warriors and he had moved out of the shadow of his father.

CONSTANTINE IS PROCLAIMED AUGUSTUS

The campaign ended around the end of June, and an exhausted Flavius Constantius returned to Eboracum to rest. Constantine remained with Crocus in the land of the Picts, to put the agreement into effect and install the garrisons that would keep the peace. He was there when a horseman came from Eboracum bringing an urgent message from his father's Praetorian Prefect. He was asked to come to Eboracum without delay.

When, after a wild ride, Constantine arrived with his friend Crocus to Eboracum, he found his father in bed, gravely ill. In hushed voices the physicians told him that the end was near. The ancient sources tell us that the dying emperor asked his son to take under his protection his wife Theodora and his six children: the three boys, Dalmatius, Julius Constantius, and Hannibalianus, and the three girls, Constantia, Anastasia, and Eutropia. Dalmatius, the oldest boy was only twelve years old at the time.

Flavius Constantius was not destined to invest his son with the purple. He died on the 25th day of July in the year 306. He was fifty-five years old. Before he died he told Crocus and the senior commanders who had gathered around his deathbed that he wanted Constantine to be his successor. One of the panegyrists told his listeners that the emperor had died with his mind at rest "because he was assured of his heir and successor," and that "Jupiter himself had stretched his right hand to welcome him among the gods."

Zosimus in his *Historia Nova* notes that the "legitimate children" of the dead emperor "were not deemed worthy of the imperium"—actually they were much too young—and for this reason they were bypassed. The pointed reference to the "legitimate children" was a sly way of implying that Constantine was not "legitimate." On this, the pagan historian had allowed his personal feelings to take over. Under Roman law, the marriage of Flavius Constantius to Helena was legitimate and so was their son, even if he was illegitimate at the time of his birth. But the practice of distorting reality because of political enmity has a long tradition.

Zosimus adds one more detail to darken the picture. "The soldiers in the royal court seeing Constantine there, and hoping to receive magnificent gifts, placed on him the insignia of a Caesar." The pagan historian implies that bribery was behind Constantine's elevation to imperial rank. But it is quite doubtful that Constantine was in a position to dispense such lavish gifts. Not even his father could have done so because excess treasure was not normally carried along in a dangerous expedition.

Eusebius, one of Constantine's most ardent and consistent admirers, writes in his *Ecclesiastical History* that Flavius Constantius "who had not participated in the war [the persecution] against us," died "happy and thrice-blessed," leaving the imperium to his "legitimate son, the most wise and pious," who was "acclaimed Augustus by the military camps, and who followed his father's respect for our religion." It is worth noting that Eusebius uses the word "legitimate" (*gnisios* in Greek) with special emphasis as though he wants to counter Constantine's enemies who apparently continued to call him a "bastard."

We can draw on the ancient sources to reconstruct Constantine's elevation to Augustus. Eboracum was a frontier town, a *colonia*, very likely without a large palace or a decent circus. For this reason the funeral pyre was erected outside of the walls in an open field where the legions assembled with their officers in an impressive array of uniforms and colorful regalia. As usual, most of the townspeople came also to the valley to view the ceremony.

As the flames died out—Aurelius Victor tells us—Crocus with the consent of the other commanders called for the elevation of Constantine to Augustus in the place left vacant by the death of his father. Then, the cry of the senior legion commander, "Hail Flavius Valerius Aurelius Constantinus, Augustus," was taken up by the officers and the men in the legions and the thunderous cheer reverberated through the surrounding hills. The familiar tumult of thousands of swords and spears striking the shields filled the valley. The townspeople joined in, shouting at the top of their lungs, "Hail, Augustus."

Eusebius writes that "Constantine was invested with his father's purple," and that "all who saw him thought that his father had come back to life." We can accept that Crocus and the legion commanders placed his father's imperial cape on his shoulders because certainly no other imperial mantle was available. Apparently, someone had prudently removed the cape before the flames engulfed the body of Flavius Constantius.

One of the panegyrists claims that Constantine did not want to accept the purple and that indeed "he put spurs to his horse to shake off from his shoulders the imperial mantle." Much too melodramatic a scene to be believed. For the sake of propriety, Constantine may have feigned a reluctance he did not feel. He may also have said that he wanted first to write "to the senior princes" and ask for their wishes as to the choice of a successor, as the panegyrist claims. It is possible that he may have used such words before the funeral, in talking to Crocus and the senior commanders, to be able later to claim that the purple was forced on him. We know that he actually used this excuse when he wrote to Galerius a few days after the ceremony. But all this must have been only for show. Constantine was not about to refuse the purple or let others decide whether he was to have his dreams fulfilled.

In his letter to Galerius, Constantine spoke with deference and humility, and to show his good will, he sent along a bust of himself. Lactantius tells us that Galerius, livid with rage, almost hurled the bust against the wall and was about to order that the messenger be burned alive. But then he suppressed his anger and turned to his closest friends for advice. Certainly, Constantine's elevation to the purple by the soldiers was a return to the old days when the legions made the emperors, the days Diocletian wanted to end once and for all. On the other hand, Flavius Constantius as the Augustus of the West had every right to name his own Caesar. Now that he was dead, Severus should be elevated from Caesar to the rank of Augustus, and Constantine could be accepted as the Caesar of the West under Severus. With this arrangement, the Tetrarchy would be preserved and a dangerous conflict with Constantine avoided.

Galerius accepted this wise suggestion and, instead of sending Constantine's messenger to the flames, he sent him back with an imperial mantle as his gift to Constantine and a friendly letter in which he formally accepted him as the Caesar of the West, with a domain that covered Britain, Gaul, and Spain. Galerius had denied Constantine the rank of Augustus but that was not a sign of petty spite. The senior Augustus wanted to preserve the system of Tetrarchy the way Diocletian had initially organized it. The empire had again two Augusti, Galerius and Severus, and tow Caesars, Maximin Daia and Constantine. The Tetrarchy had been restored. It was not to remain unruffled for very long.

TROUBLE WITH
THE FRANKS

Constantine accepted the change in his title without any objection. He knew that those who have a future can wait. He, too, had learned a great deal all the years he had served Diocletian. It was not the title that mattered most but the reality of power. If it ever came to a clash with his imperial colleagues, the fight would be decided by the best army, not the title of the leader. Besides, Constantine already faced more important problems than the form of his title.

Constantine was still in Britain when he received the report that the Franks had violated a peace treaty his father had signed with them and were ravaging the lands in the northeastern part of Gaul. With the speed that would soon become the trademark of his military tactics, he marched with his legions to the ports in the southern coast of Britain, boarded the boats and crossed the Channel. Before the end of August the legions were marching toward the Belgica province and Germania Inferior, in pursuit of the Franks.

It appears that the major battle was fought to the northeast of the heavily wooded area we know today as the Ardennes. The Franks were annihilated. One of the panegyrists, praising the young Caesar, gave a harrowing description of the carnage.

"Those slain in battle were beyond numbers and those taken prisoner were even more. All their flocks were carried off or slaughtered and all their villages burned. Their young men who were too treacherous to be allowed to join the Roman army and too brutal to be used as slaves, were thrown to the wild beasts, and the savage creatures were tired out because they had so many to kill."

The leaders of the Franks, Ascaricus and Regaisus, were captured and brought to Treves in chains. They were among those who were thrown to the beasts. Constantine had shown to anyone who might still doubt his ability to rule that he had the iron will an emperor needed. Even though another panegyrist at another day would say that "his soul was so sensitive that he felt grief even when a wicked enemy perished," Constantine could be harsh, and even cruel, when the demands of imperium allowed no room for clemency.

When Constantine came to Treves from the battlefield, he was welcomed by a tearful Theodora with her little children around her. She was five years younger than Constantine and she was now his father's widow. He was told that when the invading Franks were approaching Treves she had refused to leave, confident that the walls were strong and that Constantine who was coming with his legions would drive the enemy away. Thirteen years before, when his father divorced his mother to marry Theodora, he had felt a deep resentment, even hatred for this woman, a young girl at that time getting married on orders from her step-father Augustus Maximian for the sake of imperial expediency. But that was a long time ago, and the wounds had healed. What mattered now was the promise to his dying father that he would protect his family. When Theodora graciously offered to leave the palace which by right was now his, Constantine replied that the palace was her home and that he was a soldier who never needed much space to live. He suddenly had a family with his half-brothers and half-sisters, small children that could have been his own. It was a novel experience for a man who had known for so many years only the life of the army.

Treves was a gloomy and unattractive town, and not a willing choice for a man who had spent so many years in the balmy climate of Nicomedia. But Treves was near the Rhine, in a strategic location. His father had made it his capital precisely for that reason. Now Constantine, for the same reason, decided to make it his own.

With peace restored in Gaul, Constantine turned to the affairs of daily administration. Governing was not as exciting as the heat of battle, but it was the stuff that held the empire together. All that he had learned watching Diocletian, both from the successes and from the errors of the old man, came back to him to guide his steps. He turned out to be a good administrator, imaginative and effective. But Treves was only a stopover for the new Caesar of the West, who had more daring dreams for the future. Still, for now he could wait. He was only thirty-four years old.

CHAPTER VI

A RIVAL IN ROME

THE RISE OF MAXENTIUS

I f Galerius believed that he had restored the Tetrarchy and that all was well now that Constantine had accepted the title of Caesar, he was in for a rude awakening.

Old Emperor Maximian had reluctantly moved to his villa in Lucania after the abdication, trying to adjust to the life of a retired emperor. All sources agree that he had not accepted happily his new status. His son, Maxentius, now twenty-one years old, a well-built, attractive young man, had made Rome his home and spent much of his time with courtesans and drinking friends. At the time, he had not shown openly any imperial ambitions and he had not complained publicly when Diocletian and Galerius rejected him as a possible Caesar of the West. After all, at that time they had also bypassed Constantine, "that bastard son of Flavius Constantius."

All this changed when Maxentius received the news that Constantine had been vested with the purple in Eboracum and that Galerius had formally named him Caesar under Severus, the new Augustus of the West. Probably his friends taunted him that "the bastard" had been made Caesar while he, the legitimate son of Emperor Maximian was left out. For Maxentius to feel resentment and envy would have been only human, but anger alone would have made not one dent in shaping the future—if it were not for what Galerius himself did unwittingly.

The residents of Rome had not paid taxes for centuries. It was a symbolic concession to the inhabitants of the "mother of cities," one of their few remaining privileges now that Rome no longer served as the real center of the empire and emperors no longer lived on the Palatine Hill. The tax exception was materially but also emotionally important to the patrician senators. The once powerful Senate was now an empty shell where the few surviving descendants of old, illustrious families and the more recent appointees spent their time debating idly over issues they had no power to decide.

The decline of the Senate is vividly shown in this story left by the ancient chroniclers. When Constantine was only three years old, in 275, Emperor Aurelius was murdered by a bodyguard acting on orders from a cabal of conspirators. But those who gave the order proved unable to produce a successor, and for the first time in almost two centuries, the Senate elevated its own choice, Tacitus, to the rank of Augustus. This was so unusual that Senator Florianus wrote to a colleague asking him "to tear himself away from the idle pleasures of Puteoli and come back to Rome. "The Senate," he wrote, "has returned to its ancient status. It is we who make Emperors; it is we who distribute offices. Come back to the city and the Senate. Rome is flourishing; the whole State is flourishing. We give Emperors; we make Princes; and we who have begun to create, can also restrain." This was the elation of a man who until then had felt to his bones the chill of humiliation. Soon the illusion of restored power and glory was shattered as Tacitus after one year was murdered by the military, and the legions once again became the king-makers. The letter of Senator Florianus reveals the pathetic yearning of those patricians in the Roman Senate for even the illusion of power. It was that frame of mind that would play into the hands of Maxentius at a critical moment.

It all started when Galerius issued an edict designed to implement more vigorously, and with greater sophistication, the tax legislation Diocletian had introduced a few years back. To collect the taxes, the authorities needed accurate and complete data on both people and property. This was the work of censors. "The census was imposed on all cities and provinces. The censors spread everywhere...measuring every vineyard, every tree, registering the animals of every kind, noting individually the names of the people in each city, gathering the population of each town and of the countryside...all families present with their children and their slaves." For those who dared to disobey or who tried to hide the truth, the penalties were heavy but that was not unusual. What was unusual was that for the first time the people of Rome were included in the census. Galerius sent explicit instructions to Severus who as the Augustus of the West had jurisdiction over the Italian peninsula. The people of Rome were to be taxed as everyone else. One might say that Galerius was only trying to be fair. He saw no valid reason for continuing a special privilege which existed only to give the residents of Rome a feeling of superiority. However fair his decision, it was politically unwise.

Young Maxentius saw in the census an opening. His patrician friends were enraged by this edict and by the arrival of the first censors sent by Emperor Severus. This time, as the edict touched directly on their treasure chests, their docility gave way to righteous indignation. Maxentius grasped the mood of the moment and approached them with a proposition. "Have the Senate elevate me to the purple and I will restore Rome's glory and power." The prospect was enticing but most of the senior senators felt that Maxentius was too young and too inept for such a serious step.

To convince them that his proposal was not as foolish as they seemed to think, he advanced two very significant arguments. The legions commanded now by Severus were the same legions that only two years before had been loyal to his father. If his father returned to his old imperial post, those legions would certainly rally around their old emperor. That Severus was not particularly liked by many of his legion commanders was not a secret.

The second argument was that the Praetorian Guards were enraged by rumors that Galerius had decided to break up their units and scatter them from Britain to Mesopotamia to serve in the legions. The Praetorian Guard, this ancient Roman institution, was not strong enough to fight against the legions of Severus but it was indispensable if action was to be taken by the Senate. They were the military muscle the Senate needed to protect its choice of Augustus during the early days after the proposed coup. Besides, with the legions under Severus shifting their allegiance to the returning Maximian, the Praetorian Guard would not be needed to defend Rome.

The senators were impressed by the words of Maxentius. The frivolous, fun-loving young man showed surprising maturity and intelligence. His proposal was not as idiotic as they had thought initially. They set, however, two conditions. First, they wanted convincing evidence that Maximian was willing to come out of retirement and resume his imperial post as Augustus. Second, they wanted proof that the Praetorian Guard would support Maxentius. Some other hurdles had to be cleared. Annius Annulinus, the prefect of the city, was apparently in sympathy with the elevation of Maxentius, but Abellius, the vicar for the Italian peninsula who resided in Rome and who had been appointed by Severus, was expected to move against Maxentius and the Senate with the troops he had at his disposal. To ward off such a threat, Maxentius told the conspirators, Abellius should be killed the night before the Senate action.

Within a few days, Maxentius had put together a promising coalition of political and military allies. He now faced the task of convincing his father.

Maximian listened to his son's proposal with skepticism. He, too, knew Maxentius as an indolent pleasure seeker. But the old man could not resist the enticing prospect of returning to his imperial post. In the end, he agreed to support his son's move if indeed the Senate vested Maxentius with the purple. We do not know if Maximian wrote a letter to the Senators. Probably he did, since Maxentius' word alone would not have been enough to convince them.

The conspirators were now ready to strike. On the night of 27 to the 28 of October in the year 306, a small detachment of Praetorian Guards went to the residence of Vicar Abellius, overpowered the guards and killed him in his bedchamber.

With the first crack of dawn, maniples of Praetorian Guards took positions around the Forum and the Palatine Hill as a show of support for the Senate. A few hours later, the Princeps Senatus opened the proceedings. After a debate which was less a debate than a litany of orators extolling the new-found virtues of Maxentius, the motion was introduced to elevate Maxentius to Augustus. With a show of modesty, which reveals the shrewd mind that was for so long hidden behind the frivolous veneer, Maxentius declined the lofty title and begged the Senate to name him merely a *princeps*. He added that he should earn in time with his deeds the highest dignity. His wily move had also left the place of Augustus vacant for his father. He knew that if Severus decided to move against Rome, as most likely he would, he needed the presence of his father at the helm.

Maxentius did not forget Constantine either. He knew that Constantine had no love for Galerius or Severus but politics make strange bedfellows. Constantine could either join forces with Severus and Galerius or he could stay out of the fighting leaving the field open to the others for an attack against Maxentius. Without wasting time, the new *princeps* ordered the casting of silver coins honoring the Augusti and the Caesars, recognizing Constantine's position as the Caesar governing Britain, Gaul, and Spain. Constantine accepted the overtures without showing any particular interest. He felt secure in his domain. This was a quarrel between Severus and Maxentius and he saw no reason to become involved at this stage.

Severus Marches on Rome

In the interest of building family ties with the house of Maximian, Galerius had given Maxentius in marriage his daughter from a previous marriage. The marriage had not put any curbs on Maxentius' drinking or sleeping with other women, and certainly it had not stood in the way of his ambitious coup. Now the marriage was not going to affect Galerius' decisions either. Lactantius says that Galerius "hated his son-in-law." If he did not hate him at the time of the wedding, he certainly had reasons to hate him now. At the very moment he had restored the system of Tetrarchy without a serious crisis, Maxentius had shattered the imperial order with his impudent coup. Galerius could not let it pass. Maxentius had to be eliminated.

Without wasting time, Galerius instructed Severus to march against Maxentius in Rome. Lactantius tells us that he told Severus "to reconquer the empire...and dislodge Maxentius". Without delay, Severus organized his legions for the campaign and on the second week of November he set off from Mediolanum marching south through the level valley of the Padus river with the Appenine mountains to the southwest.

Maxentius did not remain idle. The time to summon his father had come. Whatever misgivings or objections Maximian might have had against his son's unlawful act, he could not resist the prospect of returning to power. He had given up his imperium only out of loyalty to Diocletian. But all those many months in the isolated beauty of his villa, with his wife Eutropia and his daughter Fausta the only persons close to him to vent his anger, he had convinced himself that Diocletian's decision to step down was a folly.

When a messenger brought a magnificent mantle in imperial red, awarded to Maximian by decision of the Senate together with the restoration of the title of Augustus, the old man wasted no time. Escorted by a detachment of soldiers his son had sent along with the messenger, he left for Rome.

Before leaving his villa, he dictated a letter addressed to Diocletian. In it, he told the old man to lay aside the simple pleasures of his palace at Salonae and to resume, for the good of the empire, the power he had given up. Only the two of them, with their unique authority, had the ability to restore order and remove the seeds of contention that threatened to destroy all that they had built with so much toil. The old man was unmoved. In fact, Diocletian was disgusted with the pettiness and incompetence of the men who were now managing the affairs of the empire, and that above all meant Galerius, his own son-in-law. He did not respond to Maximian's letter.

On orders from Maxentius, a large detachment of the Praetorian Guards met Maximian outside of Rome and escorted him into the city where he was received by the people with the cheers befitting an emperor: "Hail Augustus!" He received the same salutation when he visited the Senate with his son standing by his side.

Severus was not facing young Maxentius alone. Now he had to deal with Maximian himself. Within days he found out what this really meant. The legions he was leading south toward Rome, were the same legions that only two years before were loyal to Maximian. The legion commanders had moved up the ranks through the many years of toil and blood under the leadership of Maximian, and here was now Severus, a man they respected little, asking them to fight against the man they idolized!

Zosimus writes that "troops from Mauritania" were the first to desert Severus. This may be true because as soon as the news of the coup reached Africa, the legions there declared their allegiance to Maxentius and his father Maximian—a move that in effect assured Rome of ample supplies of grain. As Severus moved further to the south through the Appenine passes, more and more men melted into the forests and the ravines. Then, his own Praetorian Prefect left for Rome to join Maximian. Severus, dispirited and fearful, ordered the troops that still remained with him to retreat to the city of Ravenna, "a well-fortified city, with a large population, and ample supplies of food." Ravenna was a coastal city on the Adriatic and Severus could easily keep in communication with Galerius by land or by sea, waiting for the spring when Galerius could come with a loyal army.

Maximian was not about to let this happen. Without wasting time, he reorganized the legions that had come to his side and, in the mid of December, he marched through the Appenine passes toward Ravenna. When Severus was told that the old emperor was outside of the walls of the city, he lost his nerve and agreed to surrender. In a dramatic gesture, he sent to Maximian the imperial purple Maximian had placed on his shoulders in Mediolanum the year before.

As soon as Severus came out of the city gate unarmed, Maximian gave the signal to his troops to start on the way back, to go through the Appenine passes before snow and mudslides made the crossing more difficult. Severus, a broken man, rode a few paces behind Maximian. When they reached Rome, he was taken to a villa on the Appian Way where, by decision of Maximian, he was to live in comfort but under guard. The brief reign of Severus was over.

After so many years, the people of Rome celebrated the Saturnalia with an emperor reigning in their city. In Treves, Constantine followed the events in Italy, keeping his distance. Even when Maxentius sent him coins he had struck with the image of Constantine included as an Augustus, he responded in a guarded and almost indifferent fashion.

GALERIUS SEEKS REVENGE

The surrender of Severus was a humiliating blow for Galerius. He had managed in the short span of two years to undermine with his inept policies the imperial order Diocletian had handed him as he left the stage. To restore his authority, Galerius had to fight both Maximian and Maxentius.

Knowing how he would have reacted under similar circumstances, Maximian understood that Galerius had no choice but to invade Italy. The outcome could be determined by the course Constantine was to follow. Should Constantine march into Italy with his legions in alliance with Maximian, Galerius would be faced with a formidable force on his rear. At the very least, the mere threat of a possible attack from Constantine's legions would force Galerius to hold back. On the other hand, if Constantine joined Galerius, Maximian and Maxentius would face a force much stronger than their own. With the Rhine secure after the brutal slaughter of the Franks under Ascaricus and Ragaisus, Constantine had moved many of his men to the south along the banks of the Rhodanus river (Rhone) in the vicinity of Lugdunum (Lyon), Arelate (Arles), and Massalia (Marseilles). If he sided with Galerius, the odds would be decidedly against Maximian and Maxentius. Constantine had certainly the power to decide the contest.

Maximian saw clearly that he had to prevent such an alliance between Constantine and Galerius, at all cost. With the first signs of the approaching spring, he sent for his daughter Fausta who had just turned eighteen, a beautiful girl with a lithe figure and an ambitious and calculating mind carefully concealed behind a facade of innocence and sweetness. As soon as she came to Rome from the villa in Lucania with her mother Eutropia, Maximian revealed his plan. He had written to Constantine suggesting that he take Fausta as his wife. Constantine had replied in the most positive manner, adding that he remembered their brief meeting in Rome during the celebration of the *Vicennalia*. A betrothal between Constantine and Fausta had been apparently discussed between Maximian and Flavius Constantius and both parents had agreed that this was a very desirable match. Now the marriage would also have a crucial political meaning. Constantine was now thirty-five years old, the right age for an eighteen-year-old bride. Although we have no written record of Fausta's reaction to her father's idea, we may reasonably assume that marriage to a man of Constantine's stature and impressive looks, not to mention the prospect of escaping the isolated life of the villa in Lucania and becoming the wife of a Caesar, would have thrilled almost every young girl at that time.

Maximian, with Eutropia and Fausta, set off for Gaul in early March, traveling by horse-drawn carriages over the Roman highways which led through the Appenine passes to the Padus valley and Augusta Taurinorum (Turin), the last major city before entering Gallia Narbonensis over the coastal highway going to Massalia and Arelate (Arles). It was a long and tiresome journey that lasted more than three weeks.

The wedding ceremony was held at the palace in Arelate, built near the river bank. Arelate was a delightful, cultured city—a little Rome without Rome's monstrous density of people. For Constantine, it was a place full of memories, not all of them happy. It was in this city that his father had divorced his mother, but the divorce had happened many years ago and the memory did not bring the pain it once did. Now the place was to be associated with other, pleasant images. He did not know that tragedy would strike again before long.

We have every indication that Constantine fell in love with his young bride. Fausta, on her part, was deliciously happy, being the wife of Constantine Augustus—because Maximian had brought to his son-in-law as a wedding gift the recognition that Constantine was no longer a mere Caesar but an Augustus and a legitimate member of the Herculean house, the dynasty of Maximian Herculius. This was a necessary gesture since during the winter the troops in Rome, elated with the victory over Severus, had raised Maxentius to the dignity of Augustus, next to his father. The Tetrarchy was turning into a pitiful joke with no less than four Augusti and one Caesar, the half-forgotten Maximin Daia in the Orient. We can imagine Diocletian's disgust.

Once the wedding festivities were over, Maximian turned to the pressing matters he wanted to discuss with his new son-in-law. (Maximian had been father-in-law to Flavius Constantius, Constantine's father, and so Maximian's grandchildren were also Constantine's stepbrothers and sisters. To entangle matters even more, Fausta's stepsister Theodora was now in a way her widowed mother-in-law!) Maximian asked Constantine to move against Galerius if the Augustus of the East decided to invade Italy. Although Constantine did not go along with this suggestion, he promised to remain in south Gaul as a potential threat to Galerius. Maximian had every reason to be pleased. The most critical aspect of his plan was to prevent an alliance between Constantine and Galerius. This, the old emperor had secured.

Galerius crossed into Italy around May. To his surprise he met with hardly any resistance as he moved from the area of Aquileia (east of Venice) through the Padus Valley to Ravenna and on to Fanum Fortunae (Fano) on the Adriatic coast. By then it was already June. From this point on, he had to march through the Appenine passes (following the same route used today by Italian highway No. E 78).

With Maximian still staying in Arelate—no doubt to make sure that his son-in-law did not strike a bargain with the advancing Galerius—Maxentius became his own strategist. He decided to draw Galerius as far away from his bases in Illyricum and in Asia Minor as possible, fortify Rome, secure food supplies within the city, and let Galerius try to take by force the "mother of cities." It was a risky strategy because it allowed Galerius to move almost unopposed all the way to Rome.

When Galerius moved his forces from Fanum Fortunae to Umbria and then to Interamna (Terni), Maxentius realized that Severus, being still alive and now within easy reach, could be rescued by Galerius and restored once again to the purple. So on the 25th day of July in the year 307, he sent a detachment of soldiers to the villa on the Appian Way. The commanding officer informed the prisoner that Maxentius was giving him a choice. He could take his own life in the way he chose or the soldiers would end his life in their own way. Severus ordered his personal slave to prepare a bath and a well-sharpened knife. When all was ready, he eased himself into the lukewarm water and with the sharp blade cut his wrists. "No one could have asked for a better death," Lactantius remarked. Legend has it that as the blood turned the water crimson, Severus said with dark humor, "now I am really giving back the purple." To conceal the crime, Maxentius gave Severus as impressive funeral. The official version was that Severus had committed suicide unable to bear the pain of humiliation.

Maximian became enraged when the true story reached him in Arelate. He had given his word to Severus that no harm would come to him. Now his own son had violated his father's solemn oath and had forced Severus to take his own life. He could find no excuse. If Maxentius was afraid that Galerius might rescue Severus, all he needed to do was move Severus to Rome. Before long, Maximian would have another reason to be angered with his son. In late August, Maximian was told that the legions in Spain, impressed by his return to the purple, had declared their allegiance to him.

This action was embarrassing to say the least. Spain was part of the area ruled by Constantine. Maximian was ready to denounce the shift of allegiance as an arbitrary and rebellious move, when he learned that his son had already welcomed the decision of the legions in Spain, stupidly offending Constantine at the very moment Maximian was seeking his cooperation. Seething with anger, the old man made no effort to find excuses for his son's action.

Maxentius was becoming overconfident, and arrogant—a fairly common affliction of successful leaders. During the summer months he had emerged victorious in his contest with Galerius, and was probably seeing himself already as the future ruler of the whole empire. He had won with hardly any fighting. Against all predictions, Galerius had not marched against Rome from the camp in Interamna. Reports he received told him that the city walls were fortified and that Maxentius had rich stores of foodstuffs for his army and for the city residents. A siege could take a long time and might fail altogether in the end. His legions, squeezed in the narrow valleys around the town of Interamna, were vulnerable to sudden attack launched by forces coming down from the surrounding hills. Already, archers on horseback were riding over the hills, unleashing their arrows against the soldiers below. Sensing the indecision of their emperor, many soldiers began to desert the ranks and drift into the countryside. Besides, being superstitious as most of them were, they saw an attack on Rome as a sacrilegious act the gods were not going to leave unpunished.

A dispirited Galerius sent a delegation to his son-in-law with an offer of compromise. Maxentius rejected the olive branch and demanded that Galerius and his legions leave Italy immediately. His argument was simple and to the point. Galerius was the Augustus of the East and had no jurisdiction over the western half of the empire. Since no one had crossed into his domain to challenge his authority, he should go back to his area and let those responsible for the West carry out their duties.

Apparently Galerius was already suffering from the early symptoms of the colon cancer that would eventually send him to his grave.

Even though he was only fifty-three years old, he was no longer the man who had humiliated the Persian empire. Enraged by Maxentius' refusal to let him save face through some show of conciliation, Galerius ordered his troops to start on their way back out of Italy, leaving behind a scorched earth, "taking away the flocks and the beasts of burden like booty taken from barbarians...to deprive of food any potential pursuers."

Strangely, Maxentius made no move to attack the retreating army and win an easy victory on the battlefield. Lactantius claims that "it would have been easy to capture Galerius if someone took the trouble to pursue him with a small force." For his own reasons, Maxentius allowed his father-in-law to leave Italy unopposed. Perhaps he wanted to keep his forces intact for the future. Or, perhaps he had promised to let Galerius go if he moved out of Italy and he saw no reason to fight since Galerius was doing just that.

Maximian, who received reports about the destruction wrought on the land by Galerius, found his son's inaction idiotic. Why not close in for the kill? Still in Arelate, he urged Constantine to cross with his legions into Italy, attack the retreating army of Galerius, destroy it, and then turn on Maxentius. The old man was convinced that the legions Maxentius commanded were in reality his legions, and that they would desert Maxentius the moment they realized their old emperor was back.

Constantine resisted the enticing prospect. Maybe he had already detected signs of insanity in his father-in-law. Someday he would have to fight against Maxentius but this was not the time. He kept his forces in Gaul while Galerius made his way through Italy. By September, Galerius reached Istria and crossed into Illyricum. A month later he was back in Nicomedia. Seeking escape from his gloom, he turned again on the Christians.

AN EMBITTERED OLD MAN

With Galerius no longer a threat, Maximian decided to set aside past grievances against his son and go back to Rome. He expected a glorious reception, but to his dismay he found Maxentius cold and arrogant. The young man, intoxicated by his easy victories over Severus and Galerius, told his father that he was welcome to stay in Rome as an honored guest but that he should give up any thoughts of governing. Maximian realized that his son had used him to overcome the threat posed by Severus and then Galerius and, now that the threat was gone, he was throwing him away like an old rag. This contemptuous rejection must have been unbearable for the old emperor. The contemporary writers have left us dismal portraits of both father and son. Eutropius describes the father as "an embittered, brutal man," while Lactantius writes that he was "childishly jealous and impatient when [his son] denied him the exercise of imperium." Aurelius Victor portrays Maxentius as a "man no one liked, not even his father," and repeats a story whispered by the gossips of the time that Maxentius was not even Maximian's son but the offspring of an amorous indiscretion between Maximian's wife Eutropia and a Syrian. Whatever one may think about these unflattering rumors, the fact remains that Maxentius treated his father shabbily as soon as he thought that he no longer needed his help. The daily humiliations must have affected the old man's sanity. His irrational actions later leave little doubt about it.

Fed up with his son's arrogance, Maximian decided to force the issue. In February 308, he summoned to Rome's Campus Martius a great assembly of the army and the people. He said he wanted to review with them the situation in the empire. We may assume that Maxentius agreed to have the gathering because without his consent the assembly would not have taken place.

Lactantius writes that the old emperor spoke at length on the problems facing the city and the empire. Very likely he brought up the destruction wrought on Italy by the retreating forces of Galerius. Everyone knew that Maxentius had allowed this to happen, so few were surprised when Maximian turned to his son, who was standing by his side, and pointed an accusing finger, denouncing him as the cause of whatever had been going wrong. Then, according to Lactantius, he snatched in a dramatic gesture the imperial mantle from his son's shoulders.

Most likely Maximian expected the soldiers to rally around their old emperor and desert Maxentius. He was dismally surprised. Maxentius had gradually and carefully replaced many of the officers up and down the ranks. Having control of the public treasury, and with substantial gifts from his wealthy patrician friends and merchants, he had used generous donatives of silver and other goods to win over both officers and men while his father was in Arelate. The army in front of Maximian was no longer *his* army. Maxentius had been arrogant and disrespectful because he knew that he could rely on the officers and men in the legions.

Maximian's theatrical gesture to strip his son of the purple—already a sign that his mind was not entirely sane—did not rally the soldiers and the people to his side. Instead of raising their voices against Maxentius, they turned against the old man with insults and curses. Maxentius was now their idol, and they saw in the old emperor a stubborn troublemaker, too stupid to understand that his time was over. When young Maxentius raised his arms in salutation, the multitude responded with a jubilant, wild acclamation. Trembling with rage, the old emperor left the rostrum and rode away.

Maxentius was shrewd enough to appear magnanimous in victory. He let his father leave Rome, humiliated but unharmed, even though he knew that the old man was going to Constantine and that with Constantine's help he could again cause trouble. Probably, he had already detected that his father was losing his mind and that he was going to be more trouble for Constantine than his brother-in-law anticipated.

For the second time, Maximian left Rome in the spring of 308, going back to his son-in-law in Arelate, and, once again, Constantine received him with all the deference and honor befitting an emperor. Constantine was in love with Fausta and for her sake he was willing to treat her father with respect and even affection, ignoring the unpleasant memories of the past. Maximian had now the opportunity to settle to a quiet, family life, living with his two daughters, Theodora and Fausta, and enjoying his grand-children—the children of Flavius Constantius and Theodora—and the grandchildren that soon were to come from the union of Constantine and Fausta who was already pregnant. But Maximian was not ready to settle for the joys of a simple life. He was still being tormented by dreams of imperium and glory.

MAXENTIUS AND
THE CHRISTIANS

C onstantine must have been disappointed when Fausta gave birth to a baby girl, since even humble peasants craved for a son. But they were both young and some day soon his beloved Fausta would give him a son. Besides, he had already Crispus, and his first born held a special place in his heart. Crispus was now almost fourteen and in another year or two he would be ready to enter the cadet school. He was still staying in Nicomedia with his grandmother and his tutor, Lactantius, the future author of *De Mortis Persecutorum*.

Helena apparently had refused to move to Gaul. For her, Arelate was full of sad memories. It was there that her life with Flavius Constantius had ended so dismally. Constantine might have insisted on her moving to Gaul to live in the royal household, but with Maximian an almost perennial guest—and with Theodora living at the palace with her children, the children of Flavius Constantius—life for Helena would have been a daily torture. He let her stay in Drepanon, near Nicomedia, convinced that she was safe. Fortunately, Galerius had never tried to use her as a pawn in the dynastic quarrels. She lived in obscurity and obscurity was her shield. That applied to Crispus, too.

Around this time Maxentius became the father of a baby boy. Bursting with pride and joy, he gave the infant the name Romulus in honor of one of the two mythical founders of Rome. He already had dreams of starting his own dynasty, with Rome as the center of his domain. With Constantine absorbed in the governing of his own territories, and with Galerius too weary to attempt another invasion of Italy, Maxentius felt secure. To imitate the great emperors who had left their mark on the "mother of cities" with magnificent buildings, he ordered the construction along Via Sacra of an enormous basilica with five entrances, to house the courts of justice. Even in ruins today, the basilica is deeply impressive and has often provided a unique setting for symphonic concerts.

To show his independence, Maxentius pointedly ignored the edicts against the Christians and he even adopted a benevolent policy toward them. One may doubt Eusebius' assertion that Maxentius feigned at first to be a Christian himself, but it is certainly true that, whatever his motives, he ordered his officials to cease any persecution of the Christians in his domain and especially in Rome.

At the time of his elevation to the purple, the Church in Rome was without a bishop. Marcellinus had died of natural causes in 304, and with the persecution going on, the Christians in Rome had postponed the selection of a successor. Now that Maxentius appeared to be kindly disposed toward them, they decided in the summer of 308 to elect a new bishop. They selected Marcellus, a kindly man who had survived the persecution without betraying his faith. He soon found out that his task was far from easy. With the end of the persecution, many of those accused of being *traditores* (the clerics who surrendered to the authorities the holy books during the persecution) pressed Marcellus to restore them to the offices they once held. Those who had withstood the persecution opposed this fiercely. Marcellus, in an effort to reconcile the rival factions, decreed that apostates should not be barred from the Church forever, and that they could be restored to communion after expiating their sin with penance. As to the *traditores*, however, he ruled that they would not be allowed to return to any official positions in the Church.

For those who wanted to return to their former posts, this compromise was not a solution at all. The feuding went on for almost a year and in the end Maxentius decided to step in. He banished Marcellus from Rome and told the Christians to find a successor. They selected one named Eusebius but the change at the top of the hierarchy did not put an end to the dispute. A dissident faction elevated one by the name of Heraclius as a rival bishop of Rome. Four months later Maxentius banished both Eusebius and Heraclius to Sicily, hoping as he said to restore unity in the Church. These quarrels among the Christians in Rome are worth noting because they show clearly that Maxentius had indeed stopped the persecution in his domain, otherwise the Christians would have no incentive to fight over positions and titles which during the persecution were a source of mortal danger for the incumbents.

Before the end of the year, Maxentius, with a bizarre sense of humor, asked the Senate to bestow the consulship for the next year on Diocletian and Galerius. He had heard the rumors that his father and the other two senior Augusti were planning to meet somewhere in Pannonia. It is not clear whether he offered the consulship to placate Diocletian and Galerius before the meeting or to remind them that he was the master of Rome. As it turned out, they were not particularly impressed.

REVOLT IN AFRICA

Constantine was receiving a constant stream of reports from his agents in Rome concerning the activities of his brother-in-law, but he had decided for the time being to keep his distance. The time for a decisive clash with Maxentius was yet to come. Old Maximian, however, was impatient. He wanted revenge for the humiliations he had received at the hands of his son. After long discussions, he persuaded Constantine to organize secretly a revolt in northern Africa, to deprive Maxentius of grain and other foodstuffs. The old emperor had many followers in the legions stationed in Mauretania and Africa Proconsularis and his agents found a fertile ground. The men in the legions agreed with the agents that Maxentius had treated his father in a way that was reprehensible. To show their indignation and their devotion to the old emperor, they refused to obey orders until their commanders had declared their allegiance to Maximian. The agitation reached the point that even those officers who were beholden to Maxentius eventually agreed. For reasons that are not entirely clear, they did not proclaim Maximian as their Augustus but turned to the Vicar of the African provinces, a Phrygian by the name of Lucius Domitius Alexander, and elevated him to the dignity of Augustus. Domitius Alexander was a man advanced in years, a competent civil servant but not a man with the qualities of an emperor. He was virtually forced to accept the imperial position and he did so against his will probably because he knew that if goddess Fortuna smiled to Maxentius again, he would be the first to lose his head.

An inscription found in Africa Proconsularis leaves the impression that Constantine was indeed behind the conspiracy. Taking the African provinces away from Maxentius was a sound move. There can be little doubt that Constantine was already planning for the day when he would have to deal with Maxentius. Cutting off his supplies from Africa was one way to weaken him. True, the loss was not irreparable since Maxentius could still count on Spain, but Constantine knew that Spain would fall in his lap once he decided to move in with his legions. The clash with Maxentius was still three years away, yet Constantine, being a cautious strategist, was already preparing the ground for the decisive moment.

We have no direct record of old Maximian's reaction to the decision of the legions in Africa to elevate Domitius Alexander instead of declaring their allegiance to him. In his deranged mind he probably blamed Constantine, and what he did in the following months seems to support this.

In Rome, Maxentius received with dismay the reports on the events in Africa. Zosimus claims that he turned, as he often did, to the soothsayers seeking their advice. After reading the omens they told him that the time was not propitious for him to go to Africa and put down the revolt. Partly because of this reading of the sacrificial entrails, and partly because of his fear that Constantine might invade Italy if he sent his legions to Africa, Maxentius prudently decided to stay home. Domitius Alexander would have a few more months to play the Augustus and worry about his future.

THE CONFERENCE
AT CARNUNTUM

T he empire was now fragmented into five domains, under Constantine, Maxentius, Galerius, Maximin Daia, and now Alexander. Diocletian's system was in ruins. Once again, Galerius asked his father-in-law to leave his gardening for a while and help him restore the imperial order.

In the past, Diocletian had turned down all such suggestions. This time he agreed, probably persuaded by what Galerius told him in confidence about his malady. The bleeding was getting worse and the physicians could find no cure.

Some years ago, when Diocletian was gravely ill, Galerius had cheered him up by saying that he was to bury them all. Galerius was turning out to be a prophet. Diocletian had outlived Flavius Constantius and Severus. Now Galerius had not much time left. Diocletian agreed to meet with Galerius and Maximian to see what could be done to stop the fragmentation of the empire. He could no longer remain indifferent, content with the small pleasures of pastoral life, while his life's work was crumbling.

Maximian had received the message about the meeting while he was in Arelate. The meeting was set for early November in a frontier town called Carnuntum—some twenty-seven miles from today's

Vienna. The message radically changed the old emperor's sullen mood. At long last he would have a chance to persuade Diocletian to come out of retirement so that the two of them could resume their imperial duties and stop the disintegration of the empire.

Constantine, on his part, did not find the meeting threatening. Even if the two senior Augusti decided to resume their posts, he could expect to be recognized as one of the two Caesars. His personal relationship with Diocletian was good and would remain so until the end. Three years after Carnuntum, a panegyrist praised Diocletian highly in the presence of Constantine—and we know that he would have never uttered such words unless he knew that Constantine approved. "That divine statesman," the panegyrist said, referring to Diocletian, "who was the first to share his Empire with others and first to lay it down, does not regret the step he took...since even in retirement, such mighty Princes as you offer him the protection of your deep respect. He is upheld by a multiplicity of Empires' he rejoices in the cover of your shade."

Traveling in late fall to where Austria is today was not easy for the two old emperors. Diocletian was sixty-six and Maximian sixty. Galerius was younger, only fifty-four, but the malady was already taking its toll.

Maximian was surprised to see Galerius accompanied by a legion commander by the name of Licinius. At first he thought that he was there to provide security even though such a task did not call for the presence of a legion commander. The mystery was soon solved. Galerius spoke to his two senior colleagues about his grave illness and stressed the need for a young, healthy man, capable of taking over the burden when he was gone. Then, he proposed that Licinius be raised to the dignity of Augustus. This was an unusual proposal, not in keeping with the system Diocletian had invented. No one was to be legally elevated to Augustus without being Caesar first.

In terms of seniority, Maximin Daia, the Caesar of the Orient, was certainly in line for reaching the highest level, but evidently Galerius did not think that his nephew was worthy of the honor. Neither Diocletian nor Maximian had much affection for Maximin Daia and raised no objection to letting him remain with the rank of Caesar. But Galerius' proposal to elevate Licinius to the rank of Augustus without having first served as Caesar was a departure from the Tetrarchy system, and that gave Maximian the opening he wanted. Why elevate Lincinius or anyone else for that matter? In his view, it was he who should resume his duties as the Augustus of the West with Constantine as his Caesar. In the East, Galerius should continue as the Augustus of the East having as his Caesar fot the Orient his nephew. That was the proper way to restore the Tetrarchy and put an end to the fragmentation of the empire.

If it were not for his old age and the weakening of his mind, Maximian's argument would have been most convincing. But Diocletian knew his old friend better than anyone else. In his familiar manner, that was soothing and hard as steel at the same time, Diocletian reminded his old friend that both of them had taken a solemn oath before Jupiter to give up the purple. They had done so in dignity. Now they should entrust the fate of the empire to younger men. Licinius was a capable commander and a good administrator. Maximian, seething with rage, saw again his attempt to resume his imperial authority blocked—this time by his closest friend. It was a heavy blow to his weakening mind. He argued for hours but Diocletian did not give in. In the end, Maximian folded, and unhappily he accepted Licinius. A few days later, in a brief ceremony at Carnuntum, Licinius was invested with the purple as Augustus. The following day, Maximian, still boiling inside, left for Gaul. Licinius left for his new capital at Sirmium, Diocletian back to his palace at Spalatum, and Galerius continued for Nicomedia.

The empire had now Galerius and Lincinius with the rank of Augustus, and Constantine and Maximin Daia as the two Caesars. Maxentius was denounced as a usurper and so was Domitius Alexander.

Constantine received a full report from his father-in-law who was still enraged by the decision of his old friend to keep him out of power. Constantine, who apparently had in those days a playful sense of humor and the ability to separate in his mind the essential from the trivial, accepted with equanimity his demotion to Caesar again. In his own mind, he was the Augustus regardless of what games others were playing. Apparently he was not disturbed by the elevation of Licinius to Augustus. He had known Licinius since the days they were in Nicomedia and they liked each other. Licinius was a capable man. Constantine did not join his father-in-law in his angry tirades against the new Augustus.

Constantine may have accepted the decisions at Carnuntum without any overt show of resentment, but Maximin Daia exploded as soon as he received the news. The letter he wrote to his uncle and senior Augustus reflected his rage which was evident even through the restrained language of the court. Maximin Daia told Galerius that he had every right to be named Augustus. He had been a Caesar for almost five years, he wrote, and he had performed his duties well. Is it that the Augustus does not want to lose a faithful servant and so he has decided to keep him where he was?

Galerius, too weary because of his illness to fight back, replied that Maximin Daia and Constantine would be named *filii Augusti*, sons of the Augusti, as an additional title of dignity. Maximin Daia rejected the idea as meaningless and then moved to have his legions acclaim him Augustus. On a pleasant spring day in the fields outside of Antioch, with the breeze blowing gently as usually from the coast, Maximin Daia was proclaimed Augustus. Symbolically he placed the red mantle on his shoulders himself, while the men in the legions and the assembled civilians gave him a rousing acclamation. Within six months from the conference at Carnuntum the arrangements approved there were laying on the dust like broken shields.

Galerius accepted what he could not change. Then, to remove any cause for further dispute, he elevated Constantine, too, to the dignity of Augustus. The lofty titles were losing their meaning. Six men claimed now the tile of Augustus: Galerius, Licinius, Constantine, Maximin Daia, Maxentius, and Domitius Alexander. Two more, Diocletian and Maximian, were retired Augusti entitled to the dignities if not the powers of the rank.

Constantine received the letter from Galerius vesting him with the dignity of Augustus and, judging from his reply, he found the entire matter rather ludicrous. He sent back a polite message telling Galerius, with a trace of mockery in his words, that he was content with the title of Caesar. He was truly indifferent to the changes brought to his title by Galerius or anyone else. In his eyes he had received the purple from his father, the legitimate Augustus of the West, and his elevation had been sanctioned by the will of the legions. All the rest was irrelevant.

In March, Constantine ordered most of his legions to move to southern Gaul, and set up their camps in the provinces of Narbonensis Prima, Viennensis, Narbonensis Secunda and Alpes Maritimae. Was Constantine preparing to invade Italy? Maybe he was, but events that followed held him back.

TRAGEDY IN ARELATE

It was around this time that Constantine sent for his son, Crispus. Maximian had told him that Galerius was seriously ill with the "evil malady" and Constantine did not want to leave the boy at the mercy of Maximin Daia if anything happened to Galerius. We have no report regarding Helena. Very likely she stayed on at the small village of Drepanon which had been her home for more than sixteen years. But Crispus, evidently accompanied by his tutor Lactantius, came to Arelate in the spring of 309. He was approaching fifteen now, a handsome, dark-haired youth, with an athletic body and features that reminded Constantine of Minervina. The last time Constantine and Crispus were together, Crispus was ten and his father was a senior tribune. Now his father was the Augustus. The ancient sources do not tell us how Fausta and Theodora treated the young boy. Probably they resented his presence, but knowing how Constantine felt about his son, they needed no warning to behave decently. In any event, a few months later, Crispus entered the cadet school at Autun and moved out of the palace.

In the summer of 309, Constantine received reports that some Frankish tribes, emboldened by the transfer of his legions to the southern provinces of Gaul and with the crossing of the Rhine made easier as the river became shallow at certain points in the summer months, had invaded some of the eastern regions, plundering frontier towns and villages. Without much delay Constantine put together a relatively small but very mobile force and left Arelate for Moguntiacum, determined to teach the marauders a lesson. Evidently, the killing of their kings by the beasts in the arena of Treves had not been enough.

The campaign was progressing well when Constantine received a strange report. Old Maximian had spread the rumor that Constantine had been killed in battle and that to hold the empire together he was resuming his old post as the Augustus of the West. Only an insane man would have concocted such a lie. With Constantine very much alive the false rumor could not survive long. At first, Constantine could not believe that his father-in-law was repaying his hospitality and friendship with treachery. But the report was verified. Was this the deed of an insane man or had Maximian staged the coup hand in hand with his son Maxentius? If such a conspiracy was behind Maximian's action, Constantine was facing a most serious threat. Unless he moved quickly, the legions in Gaul could join up with the legions it Italy. Before long Maxentius would be the sole ruler of the West because Constantine had no doubt that Maxentius would again throw the old man to the dogs as soon as his usefulness was over.

Constantine did not waste much time in idle speculation. Swiftly, he called together a small force of horsemen and rode at full speed toward the river Rodhanus (Rohn). Within three days they had reached the river. At Lugdunum, he seized every floating vessel, every fishing boat, every barge. When he could not find any more boats he ordered his men to tie together logs and make rafts strong enough to hold men and horses. The river Rohn is a smooth waterway with a steady, swift current but without dangerous rapids. The makeshift armada Constantine had put together was far from impressive but it was exactly what he needed to carry out his plan. He wanted to reach the area of Arelate as soon as possible and the river offered the fastest way. We find a rather amusing passage in the seventh panegyric in which the orator claims that the men showed their eagerness to move fast by refusing to accept the *viatica*, the extra travel money they were normally given before an expedition. The reason? "They did not want the extra weight to slow down their swift march." This is an obvious exaggeration used by the orator to illustrate the soldiers' loyalty to their young leader. But whether they accepted the traveling money or not is immaterial. The way they were traveling on the river they had little chance to spend the money anyway. What matters most is that they reached Arelate within days instead of weeks.

Like fire in a dry forest the word spread that Constantine was back. The legions which had sworn allegiance to the old emperor when they were told that Constantine was dead, changed swiftly and acclaimed Constantine again as their Augustus. Maximian, who had already received reports that his son-in-law was approaching rapidly, panicked and left Arelate for Massalia with a small number of followers, but not before loading on a wagon Constantine's treasure chests.

What did Maximian hope to gain? Massalia was well fortified but he had no forces to defend the city. Constantine knew that his father-in-law was doomed and he had no intention of laying a siege. The old man would have to give up without a fight. Lactantius claims that when Constantine and his troops appeared under the walls of Massalia, Maximian hurled insults from the top of the walls (*ingerebat maledicta de muris*) while Constantine from below reproached him for his ingratitude. The description is certainly colorful, and many will find it overly melodramatic, but one cannot reject it as impossible or even unlikely. It would have been only human for Constantine to vent his anger and respond in kind to Maximian's curses. The exchange had no trace of the imperial dignity and decorum Diocletian had introduced long ago to his court. The entire affair bordered on the ludicrous, anyway. In the end, Constantine sent into the city emissaries who assured the old man that his life would be spared. Maybe it was a promise Constantine had made to Fausta. Maximian did not give in easily, but after a few days of wrangling, he agreed to come out of the city and surrender. They rode back to Arelate where

Maximian was accepted as the patriarch of the family as though the treachery had never taken place. Fausta used the approaching Saturnalia to bring some gaiety to the palace and dispel the gloom. The whole affair was charged to a misunderstanding. Maximian, the people were told, had accepted in good faith as true the report that Constantine was dead and he had acted to preserve the allegiance of the legions and the safety of the empire. It was a far-fetched explanation but Constantine gave the impression that he was accepting it. At least this way he would be able to keep Fausta happy and avoid more friction within the family.

Constantine was not a fool and one may find it difficult to understand why in the face of Maximian's evident treason he was so lenient. Most likely it was Fausta who persuaded him to go easy on the old man. But Constantine may have been lenient for another reason. Maximian had the opportunity to leave by boat from Massalia's harbor at any time before Constantine rode under the walls or even while his troops were surrounding the city on the land side. If Maximian were in league with his son in Rome he would have certainly taken a boat to go to Maxentius as soon as he saw that the coup had failed. That he did not, must have convinced Constantine that what had happened was not the sinister deed of a conspirator but the folly of a deranged mind, tormented by wild visions of power.

Maximian had now one more chance to accept the realities of old age and find contentment in the company of his grandchildren and his two daughters. He certainly had at the palace in Arelate all the conveniences and comforts befitting the father-in-law of the Augustus. Today, only a very small section of the palace survives, but in that small portion one can see the elaborate baths where the water was heated up in large urns to supply large bathing basins through ingenious pipes and ducts. Maximian had indeed the opportunity to live his remaining years in peace and comfort, honored by Constantine and loved by his family. During the Saturnalia he appeared calm and even happy. But the events that followed a few weeks later show that his contentment was a facade and that such tranquil existence had no appeal for the old emperor.

Lactantius gives us a very dramatic account of what happened in January 310. One may question the entire story or only some of the details but it will do no harm to repeat it here. According to this imaginative chronicler, Maximian, still bent on recovering his lost imperium, tried to enlist the help of his daughter Fausta in a plot to kill Constantine. All she had to do, he told her, was to remove the guards from outside Constantine's bedchamber so that the killer could enter unopposed. Maximian must have lost all reason to have made to Fausta such a proposition. His offer to find for her another worthy husband was certainly idiotic. Not surprisingly, Fausta told Constantine about the plot. Determined to capture the killer red-handed, he ordered one of the eunuchs in the palace to lay down that night in his bed. He warned him not to fall asleep but to keep his eyes open so that no harm would come to him.

Maximian—to continue with Lactantius' story—rising in the dead of night, told the sentries that he had a strange dream and that he wanted to tell his son-in-law about it right away. If the story told by Lactantius were accurate, the reason given by Maximian to gain access to Constantine's sleeping quarters was certainly childish, but the guards were evidently instructed to let him pass. The old man entered Constantine's room and in the darkness he cut off the head of the hapless eunuch who had made the fatal mistake of falling asleep. As he rushed out shouting that Constantine was dead he was confronted by Constantine himself. Maximian, his sword still dripping blood, froze and stood there "speechless as Marpesian flint." Lactantius goes on to say that Constantine upbraided the old man for his vile treachery and gave him the choice of dying by his own hand or under the sword of the executioner. Maximian withdrew to his private quarters and hanged himself, "drawing, as Virgil had said, the noose of a shameful death from the lofty beam."

One may find it hard to believe that Maximian would have tried to kill Constantine with his own hand, but very likely he had no choice. He could not entrust the murder to anyone in Constantine's imperial household and he could not easily bring a killer in from the outside. By now, hardly any man was prepared to risk his life for the fallen emperor. Whatever colorful details in Lactantius' story may be questioned, the plain fact is that Maximian engineered the attempt against Constantine's life and that when the treachery was uncovered he committed suicide.

This was the dismal end of the man who had helped Diocletian restore the Roman Empire to its ancient glory and power. Other ancient historians support Lactantius' main story if not all the dramatic details. Eusebius, in his *Ecclesiastical History*, reiterates that Maximian hanged himself. Aurelius Victor simply notes that he "justly perished." The author of the Seventh Panegyric said some time later—in front of Constantine—that the young emperor had offered Maximian his life but that "he deemed himself unworthy of living" (*nec se dignum vita judicavit*) and committed suicide. Many Christians, of course, remembering their suffering when Maximian was at the height of his glory, felt that at long last he had paid for his crimes.

One can easily imagine the dark mood that must have engulfed the palace in Arelate after the tragic events. Constantine, evidently in an effort to console Fausta, gave her father an elaborate funeral worthy of an emperor. Departing from the old custom he did not burn the body in a funeral pyre but had it embalmed and placed, richly decked in the imperial regalia, inside a lead coffin inserted in a marble sarcophagus. This was a Christian custom ("you are of the earth and to the earth you must return") and Maximian's daughter, Theodora, who was very likely a crypto-Christian (the Spaniard bishop Hosius lived in the palace as her confessor, while her daughter Anastasia was named by this Christian name honoring Christ's resurrection) may have persuaded Constantine to bury the body instead of committing it to the flames. According to one story the sarcophagus was discovered in the eleventh century and thrown into the sea by decision of then archbishop Raimbald of Arles.

In Rome, Maxentius claiming that Constantine had murdered his father ordered all Constantine's statues in any part of his domain destroyed. One may doubt the sincerity of Maxentius' anger for his father's dismal end, but the event offered him a good excuse for tarnishing Constantine's name and preparing public opinion for the clash that Maxentius, too, regarded as inevitable.

CONSTANTINE
RECOVERS SPAIN

As soon as the weather improved in the spring, Constantine summoned a military council and discussed with his top military commanders the two problems they faced: the Franks to the northeast and the loss of Spain to the southwest. The traitors in Spain, he told them, have been allowed to enjoy the fruits of their treason for much too long. He had to regain Spain. But if they moved the legions to recover Spain, the Franks would cross the Rhine and play havoc again with the eastern provinces of Gaul.

They all agreed that before they marched against Spain they had to neutralize the Franks. This time Constantine was determined to end the threat once and for all. The campaign was set for April and until then every day was to be spent in training and preparation.

Around the middle of April, the legions left their camps in the southeast of Gaul and set off for Moguntiacum and the Rhine. The spring flowers were already dotting the countryside as they always did that time of the year and a soft breeze cooled the air. Far in the distance one could see the snow-covered Alps rising majestically against the eastern horizon.

Constantine had ordered the legions to carry ample supplies of food and other necessities so that the men would not have to turn to the villages along the way for food, except for fresh meat and vegetables. He did not want to go back to the old days when the passing of the legions through an area was worse than the passing of locust.

On his way to the Rhine, Constantine stopped at the shrine of Apollo to pray for victory and, in the words of a panegyrist speaking in the presence of Constantine a year later, he had a vision: "...you saw Apollo, I believe, oh Constantine, accompanied by Victory holding crowns of laurels out to you, each crown foretelling thirty years [of reign]." This was the vision of a pagan god and Constantine himself must have been the one who told others about it. Whether Constantine saw Apollo or not is immaterial. Very likely he believed that he did, while the prophecy of thirty years of reign is certainly uncanny since he did reign for thirty years. The story of the vision spread through the ranks by word of mouth and this gave the men renewed confidence in their upcoming victory.

Within days, the legions reached the western bank of the Rhine and, using the boats constructed the previous years, started the crossing. They met no resistance. Within two days the entire force of some forty thousand men and several hundreds of horses and countless supply wagons had moved across, with not one man or horse lost in the swift current. The training in rapid embarkation and landing that Constantine had now made part of the preparation of every campaign was paying off.

After a brief rest, the cohorts fanned out, marching through an empty land with deserted villages and no sign of Frankish warriors. The picture was deceptive. The Frank chieftains had learned through their spies and scouts that Constantine was approaching with a large army and they had decided to withdraw into the forests where the legions were more vulnerable.

Constantine did not fall into the trap; he had encountered the same tactic before. To deceive the Franks, he had one legion continue in the direction of the forests while the rest of the army marched at a rapid pace toward the east, deep into Frank territory, bypassing the

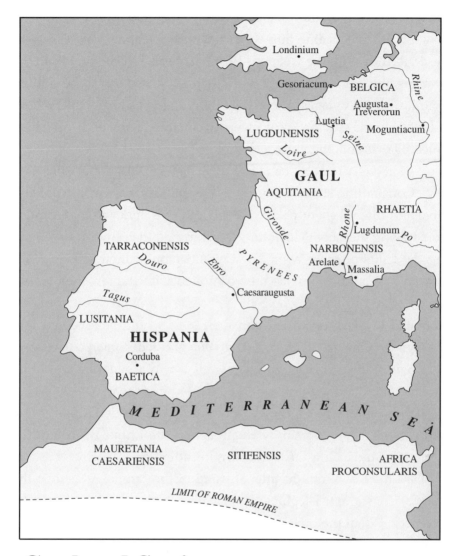

Gaul and Spain
at the time of Constantine the Great

forests. Then they turned sharply to the north. Two days later, the legions attacked the defenseless Frankish settlements from the rear. The slaughter was beyond belief. Constantine's forces put the villages to the torch, killing young and old without mercy. The Frankish warriors were forced to leave the forests and rush to the defense of their people but by the time they came thousands had already perished. When the Franks came into contact with the legions, the clash was fierce. Armed with the weapons they had copied in the past from the Romans, the Franks fought bravely, their fury fired up by the sight of their destroyed villages. The savage fighting took a heavy toll on both sides but in the end the Franks were decimated, many of their leaders killed or maimed, their strength broken.

As Diocletian had done many times before with remarkable success, Constantine summoned the few Frank notables who were still alive and offered them peace. They could live under Roman protection, having their own chieftains, worshipping their own gods, enjoying the fruits of their labor. They would rebuild their villages with Roman help and as long as they complied with the law they would have nothing to fear. To keep the peace, Roman garrisons would be stationed in their territories, and their sons would be accepted into the legions. One day, they might even be granted Roman citizenship. Otherwise, those Franks who were still worth a denarius would be sold as slaves and the rest would be treated like savages.

It was not much of a choice. When the parley ended, Constantine had extended his domain by treaty across the Rhine, deep into the Germanic lands. Now, he could turn his attention to Spain.

Less than two months after the end of the campaign against the Franks, Constantine's legions set off across Gaul in the direction of the Pyrenees. When the men entered the province of Narbonensis Prima and saw in the distance the formidable mountain range, they were awed. Constantine had decided to follow an unorthodox route to enter Spain. An easier way would have been to invade Spain from the sea. But he was never at home with the ocean. Besides, he had known from experience that the mountains appear formidable from a distance but as one comes closer one can see that they are made of low hills, imposing peaks, jagged ridges, but also mountain passes and river beds that unfold from one ravine to the next, making the passage of an army possible.

As the legions started going up the mountain range, the scouts found convenient passes and hidden valleys between the peaks. The men never really had to climb to the mountaintops or scale the forbidding slopes. They had to use mules and donkeys to transport their supplies because it was almost impossible for the supply wagons to roll through the rugged terrain, but it was not the first time that the legions had to use pack animals instead of wagons. A few days after the legions had started the crossing they reached the other side of the mountain range and started going toward the lowlands of Spain. After that, their march was easy.

The renegade governors and legion commanders in Spain expected an invasion from the sea, convinced that the legions would never try to come over the mountains. So when frantic messengers brought the news that Constantine and his legions were already on the soil of Spain, they just folded without a fight. Those who had their seats inland took their families and closest friends and traveled as fast as they could to the coastal towns, where they joined the other notables who were frantically arranging for passage to Italy. With ample funds stolen from the official treasuries they paid handsomely for boats that could take them away from Spain.

With the governors and most of the legion commanders gone, the Spanish towns opened their gates to Constantine. During a lavish banquet given by the local notables in the town of Caesaraugusta, a panegyrist lauded in extravagant words Constantine's exploit of crossing the Pyrenees, and spoke of the joy felt by the people when they saw the glorious Augustus in their midst. "It was as though Sol Invictus, (the Unconquered Sun) had come down to earth to bring peace and prosperity to all. Your father, oh great Augustus, will rejoice in the Elysian Fields seeing his son crowned with unbounded glory."

THE END OF THE
REBELLION IN AFRICA

Constantine's success in Spain spelled serious trouble for Maxentius in Rome. Now he had no choice but to try to recover the African provinces, because without Africa and now without Spain, Italy was facing famine. To stretch out the food supplies he ordered rationing in October. Even this restrictive measure did not help much. As winter moved in, the supplies in the warehouses dwindled and the people of Rome began to lose their patience.

The trouble started in the old Subura, the crowded section of Rome where most of the poor lived. At first it was only talk, angered grumbling, muffled voices of protest behind closed doors. Most of the people liked Maxentius because he had saved them from Galerius' tax collectors, but people usually forget old benefits when they face fresh troubles. Rome was a slowly boiling cauldron.

The celebration of the Saturnalia that year was the worst in memory. One evening, drunk with the last wine they could find, some people came out into the streets of the Subura shouting insults against Maxentius. As it happens when popular anger and frustration have been building up, many others soon joined the crowd. Armed with clubs and stones and kitchen knives, they spilled out into the broad avenues of Rome, moving like an angry torrent toward the Quirinal Hill and Maxentius' palace.

The rippling roar of the angry mob alerted the Praetorian Guards who rushed out of their barracks in force. They fell on the huge mass of people, slicing ears and shoulders with their swords, cracking sculls, cutting throats. A massacre was averted when Maxentius came out of the palace and stepped boldly in front of the multitude, ordering the guards to stop their attacks on the people while calling on everyone to join forces to put out the fire which had broken out in the Temple of Fortune and threatened the city. In answering the voices from the crowd, he pledged that as soon as the weather permitted, the legions would sail to Africa to put down the rebellion and recover the grain-rich provinces. The mob was pacified and the fire was put out, but the riot was a terrifying experience.

The next day Maxentius called Rufius Volusianus, his Praetorian Prefect, and gave him orders to start preparing for an expedition to northern Africa. Less than two months later, in early March, thousands of Roman residents walked or drove in wagons from Rome to Ostia to see the legions sail for Africa. The last winter storm was over and March had come in with a smile. The emerald sea shimmered in the sunlight, and this time the omens were good. Maxentius himself rode on a magnificent horse, with Volusianus at his side, escorted by a maniple of Praetorian Guards, their helmets polished, their plumes dusted off, their breastplates shining in the sun.

Volusianus wore the military regalia of a legion commander but his cape was lined with a wide red stripe, a sign that he was in command of all three legions departing for Africa. One by one, the boats cast off, filled with men, horses, supplies, catapults for the siege and other weapons, the oars slicing the water rhythmically, the sails unfurled. It was a majestic sight. A little over a week later, the first legion landed in Africa Proconsularis, between Utica and Hippo Diarrhytus, near Carthage, and immediately marched toward the town of Hippo with its good harbor. The town was defended by only its garrison and the small force was no match for the well armed legion. The local notables did not need to press the garrison commander too hard to have him open the gates.

With the Hippo Diarrhytus secured, the rest of the fleet came into the harbor and unloaded in good order. Then the troops passed through the town and set up camp in the countryside. The landing had been accomplished with masterful precision.

Domitius Alexander had been recruited into the legions from his native Phrygia and had moved up the ranks. A few years before these events he had been appointed by Maximian to the post of vicar for the north African provinces. He was now in his late sixties and seldom had a man borne the title of Augustus less happily. The news that Volusianus had landed with a strong force near Carthage told him that the end was near. The siege lasted only three days. Domitius Alexander was arrested and strangled in his private quarters, spared the humiliation of a public execution. Volusianus punished severely the towns of Carthage and Cirta, extracting heavy sums and treasure from the wealthy inhabitants who, in his view, had profited by selling at a premium their grain to Constantine in Massalia and to Licinius in Thessaloniki. Volusianus did not need to fight his way through the other African provinces. As it had happened so many times in the past, the legions simply declared their allegiance to the victor and that was the end of the African rebellion.

Constantine was still in Spain, overseeing the administrative reorganizing of the area, when the report reached him that Volusianus had recaptured the African provinces. His brother-in-law would now have enough grain to keep his legions and the people of Rome happy, at least for a while.

Maxentius was elated when he received the report from Rufius Volusianus telling him that once again Africa was under their control. But his joy was marred by personal tragedy. His beloved son Romulus died in June. The little boy had fallen ill shortly after the Saturnalia with high fever and shortness of breath. The court physicians gave him all kinds of potions and by the middle of March he seemed to have recovered completely. Then, early in June, he fell ill again and this time his condition worsened rapidly. A few days later he died. Angered by the failure of the traditional gods to save his boy in spite of all the sacrifices on their altars, Maxentius decided to punish them by giving back to the Christians their old cemetery and a few more churches. Then he ordered the construction on Via Sacra of a magnificent *heroon* in the memory of Romulus, one of the last great monuments of Roman architecture.

Volusianus came back to Rome in late August. He had dealt harshly with all those who had actively supported the rebellion, sending them to the salt mines or the executioner's block and seizing their properties. The men he put in charge had their orders to make sure that the grain would start flowing into Rome's granaries again. With one of his legions left in Africa Proconsularis for security, Volusianus had several empty boats and he filled them with grain and other supplies. The report that Volusianus was sailing back with boats filled with foodstuffs reached Rome ahead of time and thousands came down to Ostia to cheer the returning legions and see with their own eyes the boats bringing the grain. It was a happy and excited crowd, full of praise for Maxentius.

Mindful of the role the people of Rome played, he decided to have a triumph in the fashion Roman generals and emperors had celebrated their victories in the old days. The people of Rome deserved their glorious spectacle for their patience and loyalty. The brief eruption in the streets of Rome during the Saturnalia was forgiven and forgotten.

Eight years had passed since the Vicennalia, when Diocletian had come to Rome to stage his triumphal procession, together with his brother Augustus, Maximian, and his two Caesars, Flavius Constantius and Galerius. It was only a short time but so much had happened in those eight years. By his own choice, the senior Augustus was growing cabbages in his garden at Spalatum; his brother Augustus had hanged himself in disgrace; Flavius

Constantius had died in far away Britain; and Galerius was racked by a horrible disease. The men who now claimed the rank of Augustus were not united by the ties of common loyalty that had once formed the foundations of the Tetrarchy.

Maxentius was regarded by the others as a usurper but he could not care less. After the recovery of Africa, he could look to the future with confidence and pride. He was only twenty-five years old, and in the four years since he had vested himself with the purple he had beaten Severus, Galerius, and now Domitius Alexander. Even Diocletian had been unable to undermine his authority by calling him a usurper. Success filled his head with visions of grandeur and he saw himself as a future ruler of the world. Pleasure was the only purpose of life, he declared to anyone who would listen. After the death of his son, it seemed as though he were trying to forget his sorrow in an excess of drunkenness and debauchery. Eusebius tells the story of Sophronia, the beautiful, young wife of the city prefect, who chose to plunge a dagger into her heart instead of following the soldiers who had come to take her to the Quirinal and Maxentius' bed. Sophronia was not the only one. Maxentius and his friends spent many nights in banquets and orgies. But a life of extravagance was expensive and he found, we are told, an ingenious way to fill his private purse. His imperial favor was not to be given freely. Those who wanted to be his friends had to earn his friendship with lavish bribes he called "munerum specie" (in the form of gifts). The practice did not earn him many genuine friends.

In the ninth panegyric the author, speaking in front of Constantine, calls Maxentius "stupid and worthless animal" (*stultum et nequam animal*) and asserts that whenever he spoke to his soldiers he ended with the words "*Fruimini, Dissipate, Prodigite*" (Enjoy, Stay loose, Live it up). At the time the orator of the panegyric was heaping invective on Maxentius, the Augustus of Rome was dead, and it is a triusm to say that defeated princes seldom escape abuse from the victors. To those who sought Constantine's favor, Maxentius was a monster.

As the year 310 came to a close, the streets of Rome were alive with the boisterous celebrants of the Saturnalia. With Africa secure, the supplies of grain were arriving regularly and the people of Rome no longer faced the specter of famine. Maxentius was again popular. But, except for the times when he was in a drunken stupor, he could not completely ignore the fact that Constantine and his legions were lurking in Gaul, and Licinius with his in Illyricum and Pannonia. No less ominous were the reports that Galerius, his father-in-law, was gravely ill and could not last much longer. What was to happen in the eastern part of the empire when Galerius was gone? Maxentius was not the only one having such dark thoughts.

CHAPTER VII

TO THE MILVIAN BRIDGE

THE DEATH OF GALERIUS

B oth Lactantius and Eusebius found morbid pleasure in describing Galerius' terrible affliction. Eusebius speaks of "an abscess in the secret parts of his body, and a deep suppurating ulcer, incurable, going deep into his entrails, with innumerable swarms of maggots coming out and a deathly stench rising..." Lactantius is no less graphic. "Galerius was in the eighteenth year of his reign when God struck him with an incurable disease. He got a malignant ulcer in the area of his genitals...and the tumor grew and grew. The more [the physicians] cut the tumor, the more it spread...The inside of his entrails was decaying and his genitals rotting...The stench was not confined to the palace, it spread throughout the city. Devoured by the maggots, his body was dissolving in rot, his suffering being intolerable."

However exaggerated these descriptions may be, written as they are by Christians who found pleasure in seeing one of their persecutors dying in unspeakable pain, the truth is that Galerius was dying of cancer, very likely of the colon, which had spread to the rest of his abdomen.

His wife Valeria had the court officials bring the most famous physicians, but to no avail. Then, Galerius turned to Apollo and Aesculapius asking for their help. Apollo, to quote Lactantius, prescribed one remedy but "the affliction simply spread more and grew worse." This chronicler recalls with powerful effect the lines from Virgil describing the anguish of Laocoon as the serpents coiled around his body, "his horror-stricken cries rising to Heaven like those of a bull as it flies bellowing from the altar."

When all other gods had failed him, Galerius turned to the God of the Christians. A deeply superstitious man, he was now convinced that his suffering was punishment for what he had done to the followers of Christ. He must have heard of the Christians' belief in punishment after death and, fearful of eternal damnation, he was probably anxious to seek forgiveness. Lactantius believes so. Galerius' surprising edict issued in the spring of 311 does not seem to reflect a genuine repentance but he did ask the Christians to pray for his salvation.

Before issuing the edict, Galerius had copies of the document dispatched to Licinius, Constantine, and Maximin Daia, in order to have the edict promulgated in their name as well as his, so that it would remain in force even after he was gone. Licinius and Constantine agreed to sponsor it but apparently Maximin Daia declined. We do not find his name included in the edict's opening lines.

Late in April, Galerius, sensing that the end was near, asked to be taken to the town of Romulianum in Moesia (today's northern Bulgaria), the land where he was born. The imperial train left Nicomedia and traveled as far as Serdica (Sofia). There they stopped because Galerius was too sick to travel any further. It was at Serdica on the last day of April that he signed the edict. Five days later he was dead.

Eusebius in his "History of the Church" (*Ecclesiastiki Istoria*) gives the full text in Greek. It begins with the names and titles of the three Augusti sponsoring the edict. "Emperor Caesar Galerius Valerius Maximinus, invincible, Augustus, Pontifex Maximus...and Emperor Caesar Flavius Valerius Constantinus, pious, happy, invincible, Augustus, Pontifex Maximus...and Emperor Caesar Valerius Licinianus Licinius, pious, happy, invincible, Augustus, Pontifex Maximus." If Eusebius has quoted the edict accurately, one may note that the words "pious" (*evsevis*) and "happy" (*eutykhis*) are missing in the appellations attached to the name of Galerius. Probably he crossed out the words himself because he could not have claimed in good conscience to have been "pious" since he had been so deeply involved in the persecution of the Christians, and certainly could not have been "happy" suffering as he was at the time.

The edict is a remarkable document that offers insight into the thinking of the time.

"Among the measures which we have always taken for the well-being and advantage of the commonwealth, we had endeavored to regulate everything according to the ancient laws and the Romans' public discipline, and especially to help the Christians, who had abandoned the beliefs of their parents, return to the right state of mind.

But for whatever reason, they were taken over by such arrogance and folly that they not only refused to abide by the ancient traditions which very likely their own ancestors had instituted, but they made laws for themselves, according to their own fancy and willfulness, and brought together in different places all kinds of people.

And when our Edicts followed, to help them return to the ancient institutions and rituals, many submitted out of fear, but many more resisted and suffered all kinds of death. But because many insist on their foolishness and we see that they neither give the proper worship to the celestial gods nor to that of the Christians, we have turned to our clemency and to our constant habit of rendering forgiveness to all men, and

we have thought it best to extend willingly our forgiveness so that immediately all Christians will be able
to congregate in their houses of worship so that they
will do nothing against the law.

In another, letter we shall state to the judicial magistrates what they should do.

Therefore, because of our benevolence, [the Christians]
should pray to their God for our salvation, for that of
the commonwealth, and for their own, so that the State
will be safe and prosperous, and they themselves may
dwell in safety in their homes."

This was as direct a confession of failure as an emperor could
make. Galerius was clearly recognizing that, after years of persecution, the great majority of the Christians remained true to their faith.
Their tenacity had also impressed Constantine who saw the political
role this religious cult could play with its cells spread throughout the
empire. But the most interesting passage is at the end of the edict,
where Galerius is asking the Christians to pray to their God for his
salvation (*sotiria*). It is the cry of a desperate man as death is
approaching.

The edict did not imply, of course, acceptance of the Christian
faith. It was only a gesture of reluctant toleration, but after the harsh
years of persecution, even this was for the Christians a cause for
rejoicing. Eusebius writes vividly about their happy reaction, the
feelings of triumph as the prisoners were let out of the dungeons, the
emotional reunion of families and friends with those returning from
the mines to their towns and villages. Even pagans welcomed them,
happy to see an end to the violence. Those Christians who had
bowed to the pressure under the threat of torture or death, now
approached their more faithful brethren with humility and asked for

their forgiveness. In spite of all the hardship, the Christians had stood up to the persecution and had emerged out of the dark tunnel with their conviction even stronger that theirs was the only true God.

Galerius, with good reason, has not been treated kindly by the Christian chroniclers of his time. Yet, with his deathbed decision he had left to the Christians, however reluctantly, a precious gift: the freedom to worship their God. Lactantius and Eusebius have portrayed Galerius as an arrogant, cruel, vile ruler who was the sinister hand that had led Diocletian to launch the persecution eight years before. That he was a prime mover in the persecution there can be little doubt. But his anti-Christian actions represent only one side of his remarkable life. The shepherd boy, the *Armentarius*, had risen to the pinnacle of imperial power because of his abilities. Eutropius, another chronicler, may have been closer to the truth when he wrote that Galerius was "a man of moral stature and a consummate general" (*vir et probe moratus et egregius re militari*).

He was buried at his birthplace of Romulianum. The imposing mausoleum he had built for himself at Thessaloniki was never used as his burial ground. The domed rotunda was later turned into a church by Theodosius. During the Ottoman rule it became a mosque and its minaret still stands at its side even though today it is again a church dedicated to St. George.

LAND GRAB

Maximin Daia was in Antoich when, three weeks after the funeral, he learned that Galerius was dead. The end of his uncle had been expected for months, and he was not surprised by the news. Already he had worked out his plans for that critical moment. His most trusted commanders knew exactly what was expected of them. A few days after receiving the news, Maximin Daia marched with his legions through Cilicia and Cappadocia and within two weeks he had reached Nicomedia. Along the way, one after another the legions that had served under Galerius came over and pledged their loyalty to Maximin Daia. He had acted with speed and determination, and without bloodshed he had added to his domain all the lands Galerius once ruled.

Licinius heard the news and we can easily imagine his angry reaction. Since the conference at Carnuntum he had regarded himself as the legitimate successor to Galerius and therefore as the senior Augustus even though he was a relative newcomer to the purple. This notion spelled trouble because Maximin Daia, who had been wearing the imperial purple for the previous six years, claimed seniority and was not willing to accept Licinius' claim. Besides, he considered the decisions of Carnuntum a dead letter and in this he was right. Even though with the death of Galerius the Tetrarchy had been restored in a way, it was not in the form originally devised by

Diocletian. In practical terms, the empire was divided again as in the days of Diocletian into four parts, with Licinius and Maximin Daia ruling over the lands east of the Istrian peninsula and Constantine and Maxentius ruling in the West. They were all Augusti with no Caesars as in Diocletian's design, but that was not the only or the most significant difference. In the past, it was Diocletian who had held the empire together because he commanded the respect and the loyalty of his colleagues. Now, no one could play that unifying role.

Constantine could see that either the empire would break up into four separate and independent domains or one man sooner or later would unify the empire under his rule, restoring the *patrimonium indivisum* Diocletian had always tried to uphold. He had cast himself in this role but he knew that this would take time, careful planning, and a great deal of luck. Of more immediate concern to him in the summer of 311 was Maximin Daia's swift move to take over Galerius' lands.

We have no written record but we may assume that Constantine encouraged Licinius to act against Daia's coup. The ties that already existed between the two men, soon to be strengthened by Licinius' marriage to Constantine's half-sister, Constantia, support this view. In any event, Licinius could not remain idle. Inaction on his part would embolden Maximin Daia who then might attempt to seize Licinius' lands in the Balkans and in Pannonia.

In late July, Licinius marched with his legions all the way to the northern side of Bosporus but he did not cross over to the Asiatic shore to confront Maximin Daia on the battlefield. Instead he sent a high ranking delegation with a proposal that the two of them meet. The delegation told Maximin Daia that Licinius wanted to discuss peace. A few days later, the two men met on a boat in the harbor of the small town of Chalcydon (Kadikoy), on the Asiatic side of the Bosporus. The two Augusti agreed that the Straits of Bosporus and the Hellespont would mark the dividing line between their domains. This left to Maximin Daia all the lands he had seized after the death of Galerius. In exchange, Maximin Daia pledged to supply Licinius with grain.

Maximin Daia had secured the best part of the bargain but it was not because Licinius was magnanimous or kindhearted. By adding the legions once commanded by Galerius to his own, Maximin Daia had assembled a formidable force much stronger than the army Licinius could bring to the battlefield. It is an old truism that seldom can one win at the bargaining table what he cannot gain by force. Licinius could not possibly induce Maximin Daia to withdraw to the territory he controlled before the death of Galerius. All he could hope to achieve was some agreement to safeguard his lands until he could build a strong army to confront Maximin Daia on the field of battle. This he was able to accomplish at the meeting in Chalcydon.

Maximin Daia on his part had every reason to be pleased. He had almost doubled his domain without bloodshed, and he lived now in the palace Diocletian had built in Nicomedia. This in itself had in his eyes a powerful symbolism strengthening his claim that he was indeed the senior Augustus. To gain popular support he suspended the census and, setting aside his earlier objections, he instructed Sabinus, his Praetorian Prefect, to send a circular letter to the governors of Cilicia, Syria and Egypt ordering them to stop the persecution of the Christians. In the letter, Sabinus repeated the excuse for the persecution Galerius had presented in his edict. The emperors, Sabinus wrote, only wanted to lead all men back to a pious and correct life as dictated by the ancient traditions. Then he continued:

> "But since the mad obstinacy of certain people has reached the point that they are not going to be shaken from their resolve either by the justice of the imperial command or by the fear of punishment, and since a very large number of them have brought themselves to deadly peril because of their actions, it has pleased [the emperor] in his great compassion to send this letter to your Excellency.

If any Christian has been apprehended while observing the rituals of his cult, you must free him from all molestation or annoyance and not to inflict any penalty upon him, for a very long experience has convinced the Emperors that there is no way of turning those people away from their folly. Your Excellency shall write therefore to the judicial magistrates, to the commander of the forces, and to the prefect of each city that they are not to interfere with the Christians anymore."

This rescript, however favorable to the Christians, did not signify that Maximin Daia had abandoned his hatred of them. He remained a fanatical pagan and he continued to welcome to his court only the priests of the traditional gods, and to surround himself with all sorts of magicians and soothsayers. He even built in Antioch a temple to *Zeus Filios* (Jupiter the Friendly), an old deity with a new identity enriched with a special priesthood, and an oracle which he dedicated with imposing ceremonies that seemed to be parodies of Christian rituals. Some of the rites were gross and ludicrous. One of the highlights was a mechanical device which made the mouth of the god's statue open and close while a voice came through with oracles for the faithful. Paganism had moved a long way from the days when intellectuals of the stature of Origen or Plotinus argued over profound issues.

To show that he despised the Christians in spite of his official toleration, Maximin Daia encouraged pamphleteers to write parodies ridiculing the Christian doctrines. One of those pamphlets written by Theotecnus—whose name meant the "Child of God"—was titled *Acts of Pilate*. In this, Maximin Daia's most prominent propagandist pretended to have reproduced a text written by Pilate himself on his experiences with Christ. It was full of fictitious stories of scandalous incidents from Christ's life, ridiculing his teachings and holding up to contempt the Christian cult. Daia ordered many copies made and had the work read frequently in public. The most virulent passages were cut on brass or stone and posted in places where people could see them. Maximin Daia had reluctantly decided to tolerate those "obstinate" people who could not be shaken from their "folly" but that was all.

Still, realizing that one source of the strength and durability shown by the Christians against all odds came from their closely-knit organization, he decided to introduce a similar structure to the pagan religion. He set up a hierarchical structure throughout his domain, and even asked the pagan priests to wear their white robes at all times and to follow the instructions of their superiors.

He did not spend, of course, all his time dealing with affairs of state. At the time he came to Nicomedia he found still living in the palace Diocletian's wife, Prisca, and Galerius' widow, Valeria. Prisca had come to Nicomedia during Galerius' final weeks to help her daughter cope with the ordeal, and she had stayed on. At first, Maximin Daia treated the two women with respect, and when reports came that Licinius was advancing with his army toward the Bosporus, he asked them to stay in Nicomedia because it would have been dangerous for them to travel through Moesia and Illyricum to Salonae to be with Diocletian. They happily accepted his invitation. After all, Galerius on his deathbed had entrusted Valeria to the care and protection of his nephew.

Daia's kindness had ulterior motives. Soon after he came back to Nicomedia from his meeting with Licinius at Chalcydon, he took Valeria aside and told her that although it was now safe to travel to Salonae there was no need for her to leave. He confessed that he had been secretly in love with her for years and that he wanted her to become his wife. It is not hard to understand why Daia spoke to Valeria about marriage. Valeria was only thirty-four and quite attractive. Maximin Daia was fifty at that time and married to Eudoxia who was past her prime. But there was more to this declaration of love than the attraction of an older man to a younger woman. Maximin Daia wanted to strengthen his legitimacy as the senior Augustus by marrying Diocletian's daughter and Galerius' widow. The marriage would bring him into Diocletian's Jovian family and, the way people were thinking in those days, this was a matter of great importance.

Valeria indignantly rejected the proposal. Lactantius, the irrepressible gossip, claims to have knowledge of what she said. How could she think of marriage, she presumably replied, while she was still wearing mourning clothes for her husband whose ashes were not yet cold. It was monstrous for Maximin Daia to divorce a faithful wife and certainly it was not proper for the daughter of Diocletian and the wife of Galerius to stoop to a second marriage.

Whether the words are those actually spoken by Valeria we cannot be sure but we do know that Maximin Daia did propose marriage to Galerius' widow, and when she refused, he reduced her to poverty, persecuted with vengeance her friends who tried to help her, and eventually sent her and her mother to exile in Syria where, according to Lactantius, the two women wandered through the land like beggars.

After some time, Valeria found a way to inform her father of their plight. Diocletian sent with a messenger a stern letter to Maximin Daia asking him to send immediately his wife and daughter to Salonae. Maximin Daia took delight in ignoring the request. Now that Valeria had rejected with such contempt his proposal, he wanted to humiliate Diocletian and the house of Jove. Angered, the old emperor sent one message after another, but Maximin Daia did not even reply to the man who only six years earlier had placed on his shoulders the imperial purple and had bestowed on him the dignity of a Caesar. This contemptuous treatment must have been devastating for the old man. In the end he had to turn to a distant relative who was one of Daia's generals and ask him to speak to the emperor personally. Again Maximin Daia turned down the request. Diocletian was treated without even a pretense of respect or courtesy. He never saw his wife and daughter again.

CONSTANTINE
INVADES ITALY

Constantine had proven to be a thoughtful and effective administrator, drawing on what he had learned by observing Diocletian during the years he had served the old emperor in Nicomedia, but also on what his father had told him in his letters through the years. With a firm hand, but without unnecessary severity or cruelty, Constantine had brought peace and prosperity to Britain, Gaul, and Spain. Another man might have been content with what he had accomplished. He was not. He saw Maxentius as a thorn piercing his side and he was determined to destroy him and take over his lands in Italy and Africa. Eusebius, as always anxious to show every action of his hero in the best possible light, writes that "Constantine took pity of the tortured people of Rome...and moved with all his army." True, Maxentius' behavior was erratic and he often gave into avarice and to his lust for women, but on the whole the ordinary people were not badly treated and Maxentius was not unpopular. Many of his enemies came from the patrician families and the wealthy merchants who had to pay for his extravagance. Constantine did not act out of pity for them. He wanted to eliminate Maxentius and take over his domain, to emerge as the sole master of the entire western half of the Roman Empire.

To carry out his plans, Constantine needed to have Licinius on his side. At the very least, Licinius should agree to stay out of the fighting. Reaching such an understanding was not a problem. Their personal relations were quite good but more important their interests coincided at the moment. After the meeting at Chalcydon and the loss of Asia Minor, Licinius, too, needed Constantine's friendship to ward off any aggressive designs on the part of Maximin Daia.

In the fall of 311, Constantine sent an emissary to Licinius with a very personal message. In it, he suggested that Licinius marry Constantia, Constantine's half-sister. Not surprisingly, Licinius agreed most happily. He was forty-six years old at the time and Constantia was only sixteen. The idea of having such a young wife was reason enough. But more than that, by marrying the daughter of Flavius Constantius, he would strengthen his imperial standing with the bonds of matrimony. Family ties had a symbolic significance. One may also suspect that Constantine's suggestion, coming so soon after Valeria's angry rejection of Maximin Daia's amorous advances, must have given Licinius a feeling of sweet revenge.

Licinius' betrothal to Constantia was not kept secret. Soon, Maximin Daia and Maxentius learned about it and they saw in the proposed marriage a major step toward an alliance between Constantine and Licinius—an alliance directed against them. Maximin Daia was the first to act. In a letter he wrote in "a familiar, friendly style," he offered Maxentius his friendship and cooperation.

Maxentius, we are told, accepted the offer as if it were god-sent, but one should not overrate the practical usefulness of their agreement. Maximin Daia was too far away, and to be of military help to Maxentius he had to sail across the eastern Mediterranean with a large armada which Daia did not have. All he could do for Maxentius was to keep Licinius and his legions tied up in the Balkans'. That in itself was, of course, quite a lot, for Maxentius dreaded a combined attack by Constantine and Licinius. Maxentius had been able to defeat Severus because his father was there to call on the loyalty of his officers of old.

Then, Galerius had been forced to give up his march on Rome not only because of the city's formidable walls but also because of his painful malady. Maxentius had not won because of his bravery or his strategic genius. This time Maxentius could not expect such good fortune. If Constantine and Licinius joined forces and marched into Italy, his very survival could be threatened. Keeping Licinius out of the fighting was for him critical and Daia's proposal promised to do just that.

With his spies telling him that Constantine was preparing for war, Maxentius took steps to stir up the people in Rome and throughout Italy against his brother-in-law. Rather belatedly, he brought back the story of his father's death and with a pretense of righteous indignation he accused Constantine of murder. He wanted to convince the people that as a faithful son he was duty bound to avenge the death of his father. To dramatize the charges, he ordered his men to smash through-out his domain any statues of "his father's murderer," statues erected in happier days. Everyone could see now that the clash between the two rivals was approaching. For the ordinary people war was a fearful and dismal prospect because they usually paid the heaviest price.

During the winter months, Fausta and Theodora were busy with the preparations for Constantia's wedding. No date had been set but everyone expected it to be within a year or so. Fausta was pregnant with her second child and hoped that this time she would have a boy to make Constantine happy. The court in Arelate during the Saturnalia of that year was a happy place, even though the two women could see that Constantine was preoccupied, often lost in thought, holding frequent meetings with his military commanders.

Constantine was planning for war. He took advantage of the winter months, and of the military inaction the cold and the snow had forced on him, and speeded up the recruitment of soldiers and the gathering and storing of supplies. Many men of Germanic origin came into his legions from the territories beyond the Rhine he had conquered since he had come to the purple. More soldiers and many horses came from Spain and Gaul, and some even from the British

Isles. It was a substantial army but, if we are to accept the testimony of contemporary chroniclers, not as strong as that of Maxentius.

Constantine's plan was to lure Maxentius' forces to the northernmost mountain passes in Raetia (Switzerland) while his main army would enter the Italian peninsula through other passes further to the south.

In early April 312, he sent one legion in the direction of the Alpine mountain passes while spreading the word that his move was only defensive, to fight off an invasion by Maxentius who was marching through Raetia, planning to enter Gaul and move swiftly toward Lugdunum to cut Gaul in half. It was not true, but disinformation is not a modern invention. Maxentius saw in the reports a clever effort on Constantine's part to cover his tracks while he himself was planning to enter Italy through Raetia. The assessment seemed to be valid because other reports told Maxentius that Constantine had stored large quantities of supplies in the vicinity of the Raetian mountain passes.

The deception worked. A large force Maxentius had at first sent to the vicinity of Segusio (Susa) was moved north into Raetia to block Constantine's expected advance. With the rapid movement that had become one of Constantine's trademarks, his legions marched through the mountain passes further to the south (today's Mont Genevre) and came rapidly under the walls of Segusio (Susa).

Zosimus has given us a detailed account of the forces deployed by the two rivals. Maxentius, he claims, had 170,000 foot soldiers and 18,000 horsemen under his command. This was indeed a large force of some thirty legions. Constantine, even after extensive recruiting, could bring into the campaign no more than 90,000 foot soldiers and 8,000 horsemen, because he had to keep along the Rhine another three or five legions.

The author of the ninth panegyric, in recounting the campaign, revealed that many of Constantine's legion commanders voiced reservations not only in whispers (*non solem tacite*) but openly,

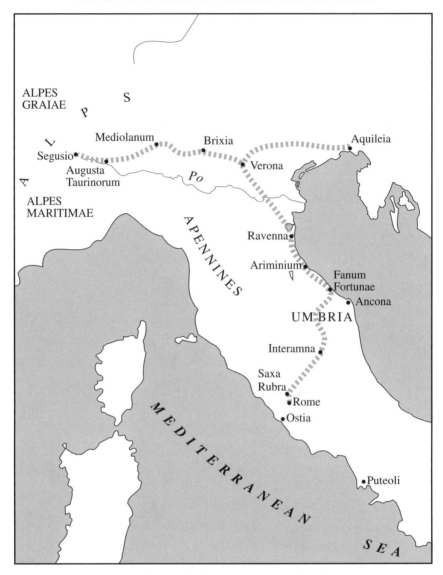

Constantine's March on Rome
312 A.D.

because they felt that their forces were not strong enough to defeat those of Maxentius. Such discussions before the launching of a campaign or a battle were common in the tradition of the Roman armies and ordinarily would not have been mentioned. But the orator spoke

226

of them on the occasion only because he wanted to emphasize that Constantine's force was smaller than that of Maxentius and that the victory was even more admirable because of that.

Segusio was a garrison town with strong walls, situated directly on the route leading from Gaul to the Padus (Po) Valley. (A highway and a railroad follow today exactly the same route.) The garrison was no match for Constantine's forces, but its commander rejected a call to surrender. After a few days of heavy pounding by the catapults and rams the walls began to crumble. Still, the garrison refused to give up. Exasperated, Constantine's men brought branches and logs from the countryside and piled them up during the night against the city gates. Then, they set them on fire, and when the wooden gates collapsed, consumed by the fire, they poured into the town through the gaping holes. The men in the garrison defended fiercely every inch of ground but in the end those who were still alive threw their weapons to the ground and surrendered.

As the fire from the burning gates spread to the nearby houses and threatened to engulf the entire town in flames, Constantine ordered his men to help the townspeople save as many houses as they could. Already he had issued strict orders to his troops to stay away from looting or raping. No harm, the soldiers were told, should come to the townspeople or to the soldiers who surrendered. This was not merely a humanitarian gesture. Constantine knew that what happened at Segusio, the first town in Italy to be taken over by force, would be reported throughout Italy in one way or another. The stories would reassure the people in other towns and weaken the resolve of the local garrisons to resist. He wanted to appear as the liberator because he evidently understood that popular perceptions would create a reality favorable to his cause. It is not a mere coincidence that, after the end of the campaign, the contemporary chroniclers called Maxentius "tyrant" exactly as the victor had branded him.

In Rome, Maxentius was unaware that Segusio had fallen. By the time the first report reached him, Constantine's forces were already marching toward Augusta Taurinorum (Turin), the gateway to the Padus Valley. Augusta Taurinorum was a large city with a strong force known by the Greek word *katafraktoi*, a special cavalry Maxentius had formed. As the Greek word indicated, the horsemen were fully covered with armored tunics and the horses with protective sheathing made of artfully jointed metal clips. This armor—which reminded Constantine of that used by the Persians—was cumbersome and cut into the mobility of the horsemen. Still, with their bodies protected against swords and spears, the *katafraktoi* could plunge into the enemy lines, trampling the foot soldiers under the hoofs of their horses and piercing the bodies of the men on the ground with their lances or slicing their necks with their swords. Against the opposing cavalry, the *katafraktoi* used long spears to push the horsemen off their mounts and then pierce their chests as they lay on the ground. They were a formidable force, almost invulernable—unless the horsemen were pulled from their mounts and thrown to the ground, if anyone, of course, could come close enough, without being pierced first by their deadly lances.

As Constantine's soldiers were approaching Augusta Taurinorum, they saw a large force of *katafraktoi* in front of the city walls, blocking the way. Constantine's spies had long ago reported to him about those frightening horsemen and he had come up with a special tactic to fight them off. He had his men trained for this and, when the order came that day, they responded with precision.

They let the armored horsemen approach and then, as they came close, they swiftly opened up their ranks and let the horsemen gallop through the middle. Before the horsemen had a chance to turn their mounts around, Constantine's soldiers closed ranks quickly, surrounding the *katafraktoi* who had no room to maneuver. Crowded in the narrow space, the horses began to crash against each other, while Constantine's foot soldiers, protecting themselves by their shields, pushed against the horses and began to cut their knees and hocks, the only parts of their anatomy not covered by the armor. Once a horse's tendons were slashed, the animal collapsed taking its rider down to the ground. Then, the armor that was to save a man's life became his coffin. Unable to move, the fallen horseman was as helpless as a turtle upturned on its back.

The clash did not last long. In the end, those *katafraktoi* who managed to escape in one piece from the deadly encirclement tried to reach the gates of Augusta Taurinorum only to find them shut. With Constantine's forces closing in, their commanders had no choice but to order full retreat. As fast as they could they rode away to join the forces deployed around Verona.

As Constantine and his army marched the next day up to the walls of Augusta Taurinorum, they found to their surprise the gates open and a deputation of city notables waiting outside with words of welcome. Most of the men guarding the city, they said, had left during the night and those who had stayed on were ready to join Constantine's forces. The people had heard of the way he had treated the inhabitants of Segusio and hoped that he would be as benevolent in dealing with their city. His decision to treat Segusio as "a city liberated from the tyrant" was paying off. He left one cohort to guard Augusta Taurinorum and without wasting time he marched toward Mediolanum (Milan), by far the most important city in Gallia Transpadana.

Constantine was prepared for a long siege because Mediolanum was protected by strong walls. Instead he found the notables of the city, flanked by a large crowd, waiting for him outside of the gates in a festive mood. After the fall of Augusta Taurinorum, he was told, the garrison of Mediolanum had been ordered to leave the city and move to Verona.

Constantine rode through the streets of Mediolanum as thousands of men, women and children cheered, happy to have escaped the hardship of a siege and the ordeal of plunder and rape. Nineteen years had passed since the day his father had come to this city to be vested in the *purple* by Maximian as the Caesar of the West.

Constantine was a youngster then, still embittered by his parents' divorce, but all that had happened a long time ago, and now he was in Mediolanum as the Augustus, reaching for an even higher mountain top.

The voluntary surrender of Mediolanum reminded Constantine of what had happened during the Severus and then the Galerius march into Italy, when they had been allowed to move toward Rome unopposed. The author of the ninth panegyric claims that not only Mediolanum but other cities, even Rome itself, had sent to Constantine deputations asking him to come and liberate them. However exaggerated the panegyrist's claim, it appears that Constantine's pledge that he was coming as liberator was gaining ground. Nevertheless, as a strategist Constantine could not ignore that this time Maxentius still had in the north a formidable force, under the command of Ruricius Pompeianus, one of his ablest legion commanders. Those legions were spread from Verona to the provinces of Venetia and Istria to guard against an invasion by Licinius. Constantine could have moved rapidly to the south, accepting the surrender of one town after another, but then he would have exposed his force to an attack by Pompeianus' force moving from the north against his rear. At a military council he told his commanders that before they moved south they should destroy this force in the north.

Pompeianus had his headquarters at Verona, a well fortified city on the banks of the river Adige, a swift flowing stream which surrounded the town on three sides leaving only one approach by land. It was a well-chosen stronghold.

Constantine stayed in Mediolanum only ten days to let his troops rest and to adjust his plans to the fresh reports he had received from the scouts and spies in the field. It was June by the time he gave the signal for the march on Verona where he did not expect Pompeianus to surrender without a fight.

As soon as Pompeianus learned that Constantine was marching on Verona, he dispatched a strong force of *katafraktoi* and regular cavalry to Brixia (Brescia) to block the way. Again Constantine's men used the same tactic, closing in on the armored horsemen, slicing the tendons of the horses' legs and killing the immobilized horsemen as they lay on the ground. With the force of the *katafraktoi* decimated, the regular forces, cavalry and foot soldiers from both sides fought against each other with savage tenacity. Many perished in the battle of Brixia, but at the end of the day, Constantine's army forced those enemy soldiers who were still on their feet to retreat all the way to Verona.

With the way now open, Constantine ordered his commanders to march with their troops swiftly against the city. His scouts had come back with a good description of the river and Verona's fortifications. The town was protected by the river and by the walls on the side facing the land. The walls on the side of the river were not very strong but the current was swift and treacherous and the catapults would have to be stationed at a distance across the river.

Constantine realized that it would be difficult to enter the city from the river but he wanted Pompeianus to split his forces. He ordered his scouts to find a broad and shallow spot in the river. They did find a good crossing upstream and Constantine sent several cohorts and two or three catapults across the river to the east bank and then south opposite the city walls. With those forces now across the city walls on the river side, the city of Verona was completely surrounded.

The siege lasted for many days. The rams and catapults did some damage to the walls but nothing decisive. Once or twice, Constantine's men tried to scale the walls facing the land but they were thrown back. Constantine intensified the pounding of the walls. Pompeianus was enough of a soldier to know that the walls could not withstand this forever. Besides, surrounded as he was, he had no way of contacting his forces in Venetia and Istria. He had to get out of Verona, reach those forces, and lead them back to attack Constantine's legions from the rear.

One night, disguised as a peasant, Pompeianus came down to the river where someone had a small boat waiting for him and, with the help of a well-paid river boatman, he slipped downstream until he was far away from any of Constantine's guards. The next day, he bought a horse from a peasant at the first hamlet he found and galloped north until he reached the first outpost of his legions.

A week later, Pompeianus, to the surprise of Constantine and his commanders, appeared at the head of a strong force. Constantine grasped immediately the simple fact that a defeat here would end his hopes to crush Maxentius. Invoking *Sol Invictus*, the Unconquered Sun, he exhorted his men to fight and win because then the way to Rome would be open.

The two armies clashed in sight of the walls of Verona. It was a savage battle and Constantine himself plunged into the fighting like a common soldier. A few years later, a panegyrist recounting the battle said that Constantine fought "like an angry torrent tearing away the trees on its banks by their roots and rolling down rocks and stones in its fury." When the battle was over and Constantine came back to his tent panting and sweating, with blood over his uniform and hands, his officers told him "with tears in their eyes" that he should not imperil the hopes of the world by exposing himself to mortal danger, and that "it is unseemly for an Emperor to strike down the enemy with his own hands and to sweat with the toil of battle."

They were right, of course, but Constantine could not stay at the sidelines as a spectator when so much was at stake. This was the bloodiest battle since his legions had entered Italy, and a defeat at this point could put an end to his drive. He won. By the end of the day Pompeianus was dead and his army broken and scattered. Those officers and soldiers who asked to join Constantine's legions were readily accepted. The rest who could still walk drifted away.

Just as he had done before, Constantine did not subject the people of Verona to the savagery of plunder and rape. Aquileia and the other towns in the Venetia and Istria regions opened their gates to the detachments he sent to accept their surrender and their people were treated the same way. The men in the town garrisons either deserted and went back to their villages or asked to join Constantine's legions. The army that could have destroyed his forces by attacking them from the northeast was no more. The way to Rome was now open.

THE MARCH ON ROME

The marketplace in Rome was buzzing with the news that
Verona had fallen and that Pompeianus was dead. The
prospect that Rome might now have to endure the hardships
of a siege cast a dark shadow over the city. True, the Aurelian walls
were strong, and Maxentius had added a parapet on top with open-
ings toward the countryside sheltering the defending soldiers.
Besides, covered arcades inside offered protected access as reinforce-
ments made their way from the city to the ramparts. Rome was well
fortified but they all knew by now that Constantine was a stubborn
and resourceful man.

We may accept the testimony of contemporary chroniclers who
tell us that many inside Rome wished that Constantine would take
the city and destroy Maxentius. Behind the cheers, many in Rome
hated him. His habit of granting favors to husbands in exchange for
having their young and attractive wives spend the night in his bed
had turned many men into enemies. His other habit of demanding
expensive "gifts" from the wealthy had not won him any friends.
Those disgruntled citizens of Rome had kept their feelings to themselves, knowing how harshly Maxentius treated those he feared or
disliked, but the resentment was smoldering beneath the surface.

Still, we should not exaggerate Maxentius' unpopularity. Most of
the poor people in Rome liked Maxentius because he supplied them

with free grain, while his heavy taxes and extortions did not fall on their shoulders.

Maxentius, on his part, seemed to be unconcerned. Even the fall of Verona and the breakup of his forces in Venetia and Istria had failed to shatter his confidence. He assured everyone that Constantine would have the fate of Severus and Galerius, and that the impregnable walls would bring the end of the "bastard." But if Maxentius truly trusted the walls of the city, he had other reasons to be apprehensive. He seldom came out of his palace on the Quirinal Hill, claiming that an oracle had told him to stay in. In reality he feared an assassin's dagger.

At the same time, as if peace reigned throughout Italy and Constantine and his legions were not moving toward Rome, he spent much of his time making plans for the triumphant celebration of the fifth anniversary since the day he had been vested with the purple. The anniversary fell on the twenty-eighth day of October and he was planning to hold the festivities on the twenty-sixth. To the warnings of his Praetorian Prefect Volusianus that they should send troops to guard the Umbrian passes in the Appenine mountains, Maxentius replied that he wanted all his forces intact to defend Rome. He was supremely confident that his brother-in-law would either do what Severus and Galerius did before—and go back to where he came from without even coming close to Rome—or his sister would soon be a widow.

In Arelate, Fausta was torn between her love for her husband and her concern for her brother. She knew that in this fight one or the other would meet his doom. It was only to be expected that she wanted her husband to win. Constantine's death would signal a dismal life for her and her children—she had just given birth to a second daughter—because she could never be sure of her brother's sentiments. He was too erratic and self-centered. And if it suited him he would certainly bring up the old story that she had betrayed her father to Constantine, and charge her with complicity in her father's "murder."

After the fall of Verona, Constantine and his legions moved slowly through the Padus Valley going south toward Bononia (Bologna) where they reached Via Emilia. With the Appenine mountain range to their right, the legions moved in the direction of Ariminium (Rimini). Both Bononia and Ariminium opened their gates, their small demoralized garrisons too weak to stand up to the victorious legions. From Ariminium, the legions moved to the Umbrian pass and on to Fanum Fortunae. Three years before, Galerius had made this town the staging point for his march against Rome, only to change his mind in the end and order a shameful retreat. Constantine had no plans for a retreat. He expected the town to be fortified and a large force blocking the way because Via Flaminia passed through Fanum Fortunae, and this Roman highway, snaking through the mountain passes, led directly to Rome. He met no resistance. Remembering that Maxentius had followed the same tactic when he was facing Severus and then Galerius, Constantine decided to proceed carefully. It was the end of September when he reached Saxa Rubra, nine miles from Rome. There, the legions camped, waiting for the final orders.

On the twenty-sixth day of October in the year 312, the streets of Rome were teeming with people milling around, waiting for the parade to begin. The celebration had a calming and reassuring effect on the populace because everyone agreed that with Constantine's legions just a few miles from Rome, Maxentius would not have gone ahead with the festivities unless he was indeed confident that the walls were impregnable.

The parade down Via Sacra was led by units of the Praetorian Guard in splendid uniforms, followed by several cohorts from the legions manning the city walls, and several units of *katafraktoi*, awesome in their armor, their long spears pointing to the sky. It was a magnificent spectacle Maxentius watched from a lofty throne set midway of Via Sacra, his high officials standing in a semi-circle on back and on the sides of the throne.

The people enjoyed the military parade but they were even more interested in the chariot races where they could lay bets and enjoy the thrills of the race; so, soon after the end of the parade, an impatient humanity jammed the Circus Maximus. The acrobatic feats of the *desultores* were spectacular but the people wanted to see the chariot races and soon started to shout rhythmically for the emperor to come to the Circus so that the races could begin. This rhythmic chanting was part of the ritual, good-natured, animated.

After awhile, Maxentius appeared on the marble podium with his Praetorian Prefect Volusianus at his side. He was greeted with thunderous applause. He basked for a few moments in the glow of public adulation and then he gave the signal for the first race to begin. The crowds appeared joyful, shouting excitedly as the chariots went around the spina, crowding each other, the charioteers using every trick to push a rival away and gain advantage.

The first race ended with cheers for the victors, especially from those who had winning bets. Suddenly a shout rose from the crowd, directed at Maxentius. "Are you afraid to fight Constantine in the open?" Another voice came from another section: "Are you a coward hiding behind the city walls?" Then, more and more voices: "Are you a coward?" rose from all over. It is very doubtful that this was a spontaneous demonstration. More than likely, wealthy individuals favoring Constantine had bribed many spectators who started shouting taunts against Maxentius. Although we have no written proof, we many speculate that Constantine had himself initiated the plan with his agents inside the city. He certainly wanted to avoid a siege on Rome. The isolated voices were soon joined by many more and before long the entire crowd, each man protected by the anonymity of the multitude, picked up the theme and filled the air with boisterous cries. "Are you a coward?"

Maxentius was startled at first. Minutes before the same people had been cheering him. He stood up expecting the shouting to die down but the multitude kept on shouting. A prolonged siege meant severe hardship for the ordinary people. What they were really asking was to have the issue resolved quickly on the battlefield. Even those who favored Maxentius could agree with this since in an open clash outside of the walls they expected Maxentius to emerge victorious with his force so superior in numbers.

Enraged, Maxentius turned his back to the multitude and, followed by Volusianus and his military escort, left the podium, stung by the taunting. He could not let the people think of him as a coward, cowering before his hated brother-in-law. As soon as he was back at the private home he was using as his residence for several days—we are told that for some superstitious reason, he had moved out of the palace—he called the senators entrusted with the custody of the Sibylline Books and in a dark mood he ordered them to have the books consulted for a prophesy.

The reply came the next morning. "Tomorrow, the enemy of Rome will perish."

To Maxentius, this was a magnificent omen. He ordered his men to spread the word throughout the city and also to let Constantine's soldiers hear about it. The sacred books had spoken. The enemy of Rome was to perish the following day. The meaning was crystal clear. The enemy of Rome could be no other than Constantine. He was the one who threatened the city. But Maxentius faced a problem. How could Constantine perish the next day unless there was a battle. He could not perish sitting safely in his tent at Saxa Rubra. Maxentius decided to follow the prophesy and force a clash with Constantine outside of the walls.

THE MONOGRAM

Constantine too learned of the prophesy, and so did his soldiers and his officers. Most of them worshipped the traditional gods and for them a prophesy from the Sibylline Books was a fearsome sign. Throughout the day, the twenty-seventh of October, Constantine searched for a way to dispel the gloom that had engulfed his army. His enemy had now a prophesy to galvanize and uplift his soldiers. To counter the prophesy and drive away the fear that had gripped his men, he too had to find some mystical sign.

In his *bios* of Constantine, Eusebius offers an insightful description of Constantine's state of mind on that fateful day. "Realizing that he needed something more than mere military strength, he searched for a helping god, placing second the power of weapons and the multitude of soldiers. He was pondering which God to select as his ally, and as he was searching, a thought came to his mind. The other emperors had placed their hopes on many gods, worshipping them with sacrifices and offerings, but their lives did not have a happy end. But the God of his father [note: here Eusebius implies that Constantine's father was something of a crypto-Christian] had given many signs of his power to his father, but also to those who had marched previously against the tyrant [meaning Maxentius] allied to many gods, only to have a dismal end; one of them [Eusebius refers to Galerius] was forced to retreat in shame empty-handed, the other

239

[Severus] finding death, his army slaughtered. Turning all this in his mind, [Constantine] came to the conclusion that it would be an act of folly if after so much evidence he allowed himself to be deceived and to waste his time honoring the non-existent gods; so, he decided that the only proper thing to do was to honor the God of his father [τον πατρωον Θεον]."

In this remarkable passage Eusebius is clearly telling us that what happened on that day resulted from a rational decision, not from dreams or supernatural signs.

It will be reasonable to assume that Constantine consulted Osius, the Christian bishop of Cordova, Spain, who had been with him during the campaign. For many months before Constantine's invasion of Italy, Osius had lived at the palace in Arelate and in Augusta Treverorum as the guest and confessor of Theodora, the widow of Flavius Constantius. We do not know what Osius suggested to Constantine, but before the end of the day Constantine ordered his men to draw on their shields the mystical sign with Christ's initials. According to Lactantius, who was also there, "Constantine was directed in a dream to cause the heavenly sign to be delineated on the shields of his soldiers and so to proceed to battle. They did as he had commanded and they marked on their shields the letter X with a perpendicular line drawn through it and turned in a loop at the top, being the cipher of Christ. Having this sign, his troops stood to arms." This is the earliest, direct account of the event, and judging by Lactantius' detailed description, the monogram must have not been very familiar even to him.

A persistent legend asserts that Constantine saw in the sky the sign of the cross formed by the rays of the sun and the words "*in hoc vinces*" or in Greek "*En Touto Nika*" (With this, emerge victorious). The legend started many years later by Eusebius (in his *Bios Constantini*) who claims that he was told of this by Constantine himself. "Constantine while he was preparing the campaign against Maxentius was worried as to how he could counteract the magical arts in which his rival was so adept, and he was seeking God's help...Wishing thus and ardently praying, a very strange god's sign (*theosimia*) came to the emperor. If someone else than the victorious king had told me this, I would not have easily accepted it, but he told me about it many years under oath when I had the privilege of speaking with him."

Here is what Constantine told Eusebius, in the words of this chronicler. "Around noon, as the day was already moving toward its end, he saw with his own eyes, he said, in the sky over the sun the sign of the cross composed of light, with an attached writing saying, "*touto nika*" [with this, emerge victorious]. The sight overwhelmed him and the entire army..." [Eusebius uses the Greek words *touto nika*, and we cannot tell whether Constantine claimed to have seen the words in the sky written in Latin or in Greek.]

Eusebius' story, published after the emperor's death, is not very convincing. First of all, the sign Constantine ordered his men to paint on their shields was not the sign of the cross, but a monogram, an abbreviation of the word "Christ" in Greek. The words "In Hoc Vinces" were not used on the shields. They were embroidered, many days after the battle at the Milvian bridge and Constantine's victory, in the *labarum*, the banner Constantine had ordered made. And, Lactantius, a fanatical Christian and an author who has described in a most colorful and vivid fashion many events even less spectacular than the one allegedly told to Eusebius by Constantine, would have certainly included this God-given sign in the sky in his detailed narrative of the events of the day, especially a sign "the entire army" had witnessed. Lactantius was there but he said nothing about a sign in the sky. Finally, Eusebius himself clearly implies that the events described by Constantine so many years later had not been told to anyone else before by him or any one else. It is hard to accept that such a miraculous event witnessed by the "entire army" would have not been reported by anyone of the thousands who, according to Constantine, saw it. We may also note that Eusebius in his

Ecclesiastical History written not long after the battle at the Milvian bridge and published twenty years before the biography, has nothing to say about a vision. He simply writes, "Constantine feeling sorry for those being harshly tortured in Rome, and seeking as his ally the Celestial God [ton epouranion theon] and his Word the Savior of all Jesus Christ, with his entire army marched on..." It is also strange that the panegyrist who was commissioned to praise Constantine's victory at the Milvian bridge has nothing to say of such a spectacular celestial sign. He was a pagan, to be sure, and he spoke of the "highest producer of things" (*Summus rerum Sator*) and of "God the Creator and Lord of this World" (*Deus ille mundi Creator et Dominus*) with no reference to Christ, but he could not have totally avoided any mention of the celestial sign.

Earlier when Constantine was marching with his army toward Italy, a spectacular celestial display of *Aurora Borealis* was indeed seen by the entire army. Nazarius, another pagan panegyrist delivering an oration four years after the event on the occasion of Constantine's tenth anniversary as emperor, did not leave out the spectacular sight in the sky. He said that "all Gaul was talking with awe and wonder of the marvelous sights in the sky".

The "northern lights" were not often seen so far south and it is not surprising that the soldiers saw them as a supernatural sign. As Nazarius told his audience, Constantine's soldiers had seen in the sky, "celestial armies marching in battle, their shields flashing". He also told them that they had heard the voices of those soldiers in the sky; "the soldiers of your father Constantius," crying out, "We seek Constantine; we have come to help Constantine." (*Constantinus petimus, Constantino imus auxillo.*) The other panegyrist who described in such detail Constantine's victory at the Milvian bridge and his triumphant entry into Rome would not have likely ignored the miraculous sign in the sky.

Many years later, (A/D/ 346) Kyrillos, the bishop of Jerusalem, wrote that Constantine's son Constantius saw a vision of the cross in the sky. In his letter to emperor Constantius, the bishop describes "a wonderful cross of light extending from Calvary to the Mount of Olives, which appeared in the air on the Nones of May, after the Pentecost." The bishop strangely adds that Constantius was more blessed than his father because Constantine "had only found the true cross in the earth, while his son had seen it in the sky." Apparently Kyrillos either did not know or did not accept Eusebius' story. Rufinus, a chronicler who lived over a century later, speaks only of a dream.

People in the fourth century, and in the centuries before and after for that matter, were eager to believe in supernatural signs and divine intervention, especially in moments of crises. Every Roman believed that Castor and Pollux had helped the Romans in their critical fight against Hannibal. Julius Caesar claimed that Venus Genetrix, the patroness deity of the Julian family, had rushed to his aid at the battle of Pharsalus to assure his victory. Octavius believed that Apollo himself had fought at his side at Philippi and at Actium. Divine help did not detract from the glory of the victor. On the contrary, it made the victorious general appear more formidable to his enemies since he was favored by the gods. Constantine was not breaking new ground when he attributed his victory against Maxentius to the mystical monogram.

The legend begins to take hold slowly, a long time after the battle of the Milvian bridge. But it is only a legend. The truth is actually presented by Eusebuis himself in the passage we quoted at the beginning of this section.

Modern scholarship points out that "the monogram was not exclusively Christian, but had already been used as a symbol of the Sun-god. Some forms which are nearly identical with this monogram have been found on coins in western Asia from an earlier period; in fact, one form was used in pre-Christian times on coins of Herod the First. The form which appears to be nearest to that adopted by Constantine is found on Phrygian and Lydian coins belonging to the time of the early Roman emperors, and seems to have become most common about the time of Septimius Severus."

It is quite possible that the early Christians in the eastern part of the empire were inspired by those earlier signs in fashioning a monogram which used the first two Greek letters of the word Christ (X and P, Khi and Rho) as a sort of secret or mystical identification of Christ. That the monogram has been found in the catacombs in Rome points to its use as a secret, mystical symbol, understood only by the initiated.

The legend of the vision aside, it is quite clear that when Constantine ordered his soldiers to draw the monogram on their shield, he saw it as a Christian symbol; after all, he attributed his victory to the God of the Christians—although not openly at first.

From the information that has come down to us, we may reconstruct the events of the two momentous days, twenty-seven and twenty-eight of October.

Claiming that he had been given (in a dream according to Lactantius) an even more powerful symbol of victory than any prophesy, he ordered all his soldiers to burn sticks and draw with the charcoal on their shields the magical monogram. He himself and his officers painted the monogram on their helmets. It is doubtful that he told even his officers what the monogram meant. Most of his soldiers were not Christians and telling them what the monogram represented would have destroyed its mystical effect. To them, it was a powerful talisman and that was all that mattered. In that superstitious age, the mystery covering the magic sign made all the difference. It may be difficult for us today to understand such beliefs in magical symbols, although even in our time millions of people believe fanatically in the mystical symbols of their religions and draw courage or solace from them. Be that as it may, Constantine had now a powerful magical symbol of his own to counter the strange prophesy of the Sibylline Books.

THE BATTLE

At the crack of dawn, Maxentius' forces came out of the city and marched in good order along Via Flaminia going north, a distance of some two miles, with the Tiber river to their left. To their right was a series of trenches and protective barriers dug up as an added obstacle to an enemy advancing against the city. Those earthworks could now be used to fight off Constantine's forces if they succeeded in crossing the river.

Rufius Volusianus had shown his mettle by planning the operation in the course of only a few hours. Under his plan, a strong force with the Praetorian Guards at the forefront would cross the river using the Milvian bridge, a narrow stone bridge, and another bridge made of pontoons, and attack Constantine's forces camped north of the river between and around Via Cassia and Via Flaminia. Another large force would cross the river, using other bridges further south, and march north to join the fray at the critical moment for the kill.

Volusianus counted on the element of surprise. Evidently he surmised with good reason that Constantine would never expect Maxentius' troops to come out of the city walls. Besides, at this early hour the enemy troops would be half asleep. Maxentius' forces would fall on the unsuspecting foe in an all-out, swift assault. Once this first phase of the battle was successfully completed, Volusianus would give the signal for his force to move back across the river. Part of his

245

stratagem was to use the pontoon bridge and trap as many of Constantine's soldiers on it as possible. The pontoon bridge had been constructed as part of Rome's defense perimeter and could be cut off midway by engineers protected while doing this hazardous job by experienced archers stationed inside a tower erected on the south bank of the river. According to Volusianus' plan, as soon as most of his troops were safely back across the pontoon bridge with the rear ranks about midway, the bridge would be cut in half, and Constantine's soldiers would be stranded on the northern half of the pontoon bridge, exposed to the archers in the tower and to those perched on the southern bank of the river. If the sibyline prophesy was accurate, Constantine would be dead by then and the threat to Rome removed. It was not a bad plan.

The dark sky was beginning to turn faintly grey and then purple and orange in the east behind the Apennines, when Maxentius' forces fell suddenly on Constantine's troops camped closest to the river. Many soldiers perished, some of them even before they had a chance to fight back, but the noise alerted the rest of Constantine's army and within minutes the men put on their uniforms, took up their weapons and formed their battle lines under their commanders.

Emboldened by his initial success, Volusianus ordered his troops to plunge deeper into the enemy lines, but by then the element of surprise was gone. Constantine saw clearly that Volusianus and his army were at a serious disadvantage. They had the river to their back, with not much room to maneuver. Constantine sent messengers to his commanders ordering them to spread their units along the low hills to the east and the south of Via Cassia, to crowd the enemy forces between the hills and the river. Volusianus saw what was happening and tried to break out of the trap. He ordered his men to attack Constantine's troops which were spreading their net along the hills, but Constantine reacted quickly, ordering his archers to unleash a thick shower of arrows against the enemy troops, breaking their advance. Then his horsemen galloped downhill with swords

unsheathed, shouting wildly as was their custom, while the foot soldiers, moving in a battle formation, attacked from the side.

With the Praetorian Guards fighting fiercely in the front lines and
prodding the other soldiers to hold their ground, Maxentius' horsemen and foot soldiers clashed with the oncoming cavalry and fought
with savage bravery, hundreds being killed and maimed on both
sides. The sun was already over the mountain ridges to the east when
Maxentius rode out of Rome to join his troops, certain that by then
they would have put Constantine's forces to flight. Instead, he saw
that the battle was raging and that his men were being pushed back
toward the river. The air was thick with the clanging of swords, the
cries of wounded men, the curses of warriors fighting for their lives,
the neighing of frightened horses, the smell of blood mixing with the
smell of sweat. Maxentius' appearance must have lifted momentarily
the fighting spirit of his soldiers but Constantine's men kept pushing
the enemy relentlessly toward the river, stepping over the bodies of
men already dead or dying, forcing many to jump into the river
where many drowned as they were pulled down by the weight of
their uniforms.

In a desperate move, Maxentius ordered his troops to pull back
and return to Rome to continue the fight behind the city walls. It was
a fatal mistake. To reach the city, his men had to cross the river again
in the opposite direction. They had crossed the river at dawn but then
they had marched in good order. Now they had to cross the river with
Constantine's soldiers on their heels.

The moment Constantine saw the enemy troops pulling back
toward the river, trying to reach the other side, he ordered an all-out
attack, himself leading the way on his horse with his sword raised
high. Hardpressed, Maxentius men retreated toward the river while
arrows rained on them. As hundreds descended on the bridges like a
herd of wild animals, the last semblance of order disappeared. Officers
who tried to hold back the stampede were swept away and trampled
over by their own men. Maxentius himself galloped to the Milvian

bridge, already crowded with retreating soldiers, and tried frantically to ride across. He never reached the other side. As men pushed each other in angry desperation, Maxentius was thrown off his horse and tumbled into the river. He tried to swim across but the current was too strong and within minutes the weight of his mailed tunic pulled him down, the water closing over his head. His body was found the next morning covered with mud, entangled in a clump of reeds.

The slaughter ended by mid afternoon. Many had died on both sides but Maxentius' army had suffered the heaviest losses. Thousands were wounded. Hundreds had drowned in the river. Those who were still on their feet had thrown their weapons to the ground and had given up the fight. Only a few hundred managed to cross the river and return to Rome to spread the word that Maxentius was dead. Constantine had won. He was forty years old.

Fear and uncertainty fell over the city like a heavy blanket. With all his foibles and excesses, Maxentius was a ruler the people of Rome knew. What did they know of this new man, Constantine? They had heard of his benign treatment of the cities he had conquered in northern Italy and that piece of news was reassuring. But the air of uneasiness stayed on during the first night.

Early the next morning detachments of soldiers began the gruesome task of burning the corpses of men and the carcasses of the slain horses. The stench from the burning was heavy in the air, carried all the way to the city by the breeze coming from the coast. The rest of Constantine's army was getting ready for the triumphant entry into the city of Rome. The soldiers cleaned their bloodied uniforms and polished with pig's fat their helmets and spears. The magical symbol they had drawn before the battle on their shields had faded by now but many used charred sticks to draw it again. It had given them victory. The emperor was right. The monogram was a powerful talisman.

On the twenty-ninth of October, Constantine, riding his horse, the deep red mantle flowing from his shoulders, entered Rome at the head of his battle-scarred legions as thousands of people lined the streets to cheer the victorious army. The cheers did not necessarily reflect genuine affection. The people cheered because, if for no other reason, it was in their interest to give the victor a warm welcome.

The parade entered the city through Porta Aurelia and the wide bridge of Aemilius (at the point where the bridge of Vittorio Emanuele leads today from the Vatican to the city of Rome). The pagan panegyrist Nazarius left for us a vivid description of the triumphal procession. "It was not graced," he said, "with captive chiefs or barbarians in chains, but by Senators who now tasted the joy of freedom again. Only the head of Maxentius whose features still wore the savage, threatening look which even death itself had not been able to remove, was carried on the point of a spear behind Constantine, amid the jeers and insults of the crowd." It was a gruesome trophy but a convincing proof that the reign of Maxentius was over. A few weeks later, Constantine sent the head to Africa to show everyone there that Maxentius was indeed dead and that any thought of rebellion should be cast aside.

The parade moved toward the Capitoline Hill but Constantine did not go up the steps to the temple of Jupiter as most people expected. It was a telling gesture. Constantine did not owe his victory to the help of Jupiter and he saw no reason to go to his temple and offer a sacrifice of thanks.

The next day Constantine visited the Senate. It turned out to be a glorious day for the ancient institution. All senators, even those who were old and feeble, came in their white togas to greet the young emperor who now controlled the entire western half of the Roman Empire. After an eloquent address by the Princeps Senatus, with words of praise and welcome, Constantine strode to the center of the well. In well-chosen, flattering words, he spoke of the eternal glory of Rome and of the Senate, the most venerable institution, and of his decision to restore the Senate's dignity. He made no move, of course, to revive the real powers the Senate once had but those powers were long gone and no one expected Constantine to bring them back. All

The Arch of Constantine in Rome as it is today.

that the senators wanted was to be treated with respect and to be spared of onerous tax burdens, and this he promised. Then, in a rather transparent effort to clip the wings of the ancient patrician families, he proposed to raise the status of the Senate by making it more representative (symbolically, of course). He told the senators that prominent individuals from other parts of the empire would become members of the Senate in Rome. It was a mixed blessing but they applauded his words knowing that there was nothing they could do to prevent this broadening of their ranks.

More genuinely welcome was Constantine's promise that no one would be punished for having been in the past a friend of Maxentius. That was good news for some of them who had been too close to Maxentius in his glory days. Another piece of welcome news was that those who had lost properties when Maxentius or his father were in power would have those properties restored to them.

The Praetorian Guard was to be abolished and the men sent to the legions stationed along the Rhine and in Africa. Most Senators disliked those arrogant and uncouth soldiers who had become Maxentius' willing henchmen, and they were not sorry to see that this ancient military force would be no more.

At the end of the ceremony, the Senate proclaimed Constantine "Augustus Maximus," Supreme Emperor, ranking above Licinius and Maximin Daia. Then, shortly before Constantine left Rome, the Senate bestowed on him and Licinius the office of consul for the coming year. Most likely Constantine himself had proposed to have Licinius honored to soothe the other man's feelings after his proclamation as Augustus Maximus. Constantine already had plans to form an alliance with Licinius.

Finally, in a special ceremonial session the Senate voted to erect a statue and a triumphal arch in Constantine's honor. The imposing arch stands today near the Coliseum in Rome. On it one can read chiseled on the marble this dedication:

> "To the Emperor, Caesar, Flavius Constantinus Maximus, Felix Pious, Augustus, the Senate and the People of Rome, because through the inspiration of the Divinity and the magnificence of his mind and with

Photo Courtesy of the Library of Congress Collection

The inscription on the Arch of Constantine.

his army he destroyed the tyrant and his faction with one stroke, vindicating the Republic, this distinguished triumphal arch we dedicate."

"Imp. Caes. Fl. Constantino Maximo
F P Augusto SPQR
Quod instinctu divinitatis mentis
magnitudine cum exercitu suo
tam e tyranno quam de omni ejus
factione uno tempore justis
Republicam ultus est armis
Arcus triumphis insignem dicavit."

The reference to "the inspiration of the Divinity" is very intriguing, too neutral an expression to tell us which "divinity" the Senate had in mind. Most likely, Constantine favored at the moment such vagueness.

Constantine stayed in Rome for a little over two months, reorganizing the administration of the lands he had just conquered and enjoying the festivities. To honor the new ruler, the Senate organized gladiatorial games and chariot races, in addition to lavish banquets and celebrations. A happy and proud Constantine sent for Fausta who came from Arelate and stayed at the Lateran palace which according to some sources she had received as part of her dowry when she married Constantine (if true, her father must have taken it away from its hapless owner under some pretext or other during his days as the Augustus of the West).

Fausta did not seem to have been overly distraught over her brother's violent death. Even when they were young children she had not liked him much because of his overbearing and unpredictable behavior. Now any trace of sorrow was swept away by her joy at being the senior Augusta, the empress of the western half of the Roman Empire. Besides, if Maxentius had won and Constantine were killed in the struggle, she would be now a pitiful widow in grave danger because Maxentius would very likely accuse her as an accomplice in the death of their father and send her to the block. She had every reason to be happy with her husband's victory.

Constantine did not entirely keep his promise to spare all those who were close to Maxentius. A few days after his entry to Rome, a squad of soldiers went to the palace on the Quirinal Hill where Maxentius' widow—Galerius' daughter—still lived with her little boy, Maxentius' second and only surviving son after the death of young Romulus. The little boy was around three years old. The soldiers took mother and son to one of the cellars of the palace and killed them, probably by strangulation. The male line of Maximian Herculius was now extinct.

A few more high officials in Maxentius' court were also killed. With these executions, "Rome", to quote Nazarius, "was reconstituted on a lasting basis by the complete destruction of those who might have caused trouble." Strangely, Rufus Volusianus was not among those punished. Instead, the following year he was appointed urban prefect for Rome and was elected consul the year after. Six years later he was

Praetorian Prefect to Constantine. One has every reason to suspect that Volusianus was working for Constantine while serving as Maxentius' top general. Was he the one who encouraged Maxentius to leave the protection of the city walls and confront Constantine in the open field? We do not know, but his elevation to high office by the victorious emperor must have been a reward for extraordinary service.

Before he left Rome, Constantine called the Christian bishop of the city, Miltiades, and offered him the Lateran palace as his official residence. Convinced that the god of the Christians had given him victory, Constantine had begun to repay his debt. Then, a few weeks later he had the powerful "monogram" embroidered on a deep red fabric with the words "*In Hoc Vinces*" fashioning in this way the banner which came down to history known as the "Labarum".

THE EDICT OF MILAN

M aximin Daia was in Antioch when he received the report that Maxentius was dead. This was another blow in a dismal year. His campaign against the Christian king of Armenia had failed while an outburst of the plague in the Orient had killed thousands, hampering sowing and harvesting and bringing famine to many parts of his domain. When he sold grain to Maxentius for gold he had used up much of the stored supplies and so, when the plague hit, there was not enough food to go around.

Then a second report came with the news that the Senate in Rome had proclaimed Constantine Augustus Maximus. This was an intolerable affront to Maximin Daia who considered himself to be the senior Augustus having been in the purple longer than both Licinius and Constantine.

But his irritation with the action of the Senate was overshadowed by his anxiety over the reported cooperation between Constantine and Licinius. He had hoped that Constantine and Licinius would fight over the possession of Italy and open the way for him to take over Licinius' lands in the Balkans. After all, under the arrangement decided at Carnuntum, Licinius was assigned control of Italy which at the time was ruled by Maxentius, and now that Maxentius was gone he was legally entitled to the area. But when Constantine took over Italy, Licinius did not claim the land. Being a prudent man, he realized that if he clashed with Constantine he would be facing two hostile armies, those of Constantine from the West and those of Maximin Daia from the East. He had no way of fighting off such formidable odds. Besides, he had already bowed to reality even before Constantine had launched the invasion of Italy, when he agreed to marry Constantine's stepsister Constantia as a token of their understanding. Maximin Daia saw now with dismay that Constantine and Licinius remained friends and that with Maxentius out of the way they were likely to turn against him.

Blaming the Christians for all his troubles, Maximin Daia revived the persecution with new vigor. He even encouraged petitions from several towns asking for the suppression of the Christians who, the petitioners claimed, had brought many evils to the people with their contempt for the gods. In a response to such a petition from the town of Tyre (Sur), recorded by Eusebius, Maximin Daia said that "if there have been calamities and cataclysms to what else can they be blamed on than on the vain and pestilential errors of the villainous Christians?" To please the traditional gods, he sent to the executioner's block Peter, the bishop of Alexandria, Methodius, bishop of Olympus in Lycia, and Silvanus, bishop of Emessa in Syria, and those were only the best known. But those acts of violence against defenseless men failed to improve his fortunes.

Before he left Rome, Constantine sent a message to Licinius suggesting that they meet in Mediolanum (Milan) in February for the wedding. Maximin Daia's worst fears had come true. His rivals were closing ranks and he was their target.

The wedding party, escorted by over three hundred courtiers and many squads of *scutarii*, left Arelate on the Kalends of February. It is not hard to imagine that Theodora, the bride's mother, and Fausta, her aunt, were not very happy to travel in the middle of winter, but Constantine was anxious to meet Licinius and gain his support on a radical policy he was planning to launch. As always, he traveled on horseback, protected by a heavy cape against the cold and the rain, but the women preferred to use litters carried by strong-armed slaves, although the litters were not very comfortable in the winter because no matter how much the artisans tried to insulate them, the cold wind penetrated through the curtains, chilling the occupants to the bone. Not even the heavy furs could keep them warm, but they chose the litters because the carriages could get bogged down in the mud or slide down a slippery, ice-covered hillside and overturn.

Whatever misgivings young Constantia might have had at first about marrying Licinius must have been pushed away by the exciting thought that she was going to be an Augusta like her aunt Fausta. Licinianus Licinius was much older to be sure, but so was her father when he married her mother who had told her so many times how happy she had been with Flavius Constantius.

The imperial train reached Mediolanum four days after the Ides of February, and one may assume that few people were ever happier to see the walls of the city and find a fireplace crackling with fire than the ladies in the wedding party. They had been on the road for almost three miserable weeks and the old, familiar palace, appropriately cleaned and refurbished by the servants, was a heavenly sight.

Licinius had already arrived from Sirmium to give them a cordial welcome. The wedding celebration, attended by most of the city notables and even a few senators from Rome, was a very elaborate affair similar to Constantine's wedding to Fausta. The ceremony was followed by a lavish banquet in honor of the newlyweds.

Constantine had invited Diocletian to the wedding but the retired emperor replied that he was too old to travel in the middle of winter. He was over sixty-eight years old and of failing health. The last years of Diocletian's eventful life have a tragic quality. After all that he had done for the empire, he was now alone, helpless, unable even to protect his own family from Maximin Daia's wrath. He still lived in his magnificent palace at Spalatum but the palace seemed now to mock his insignificance. In the less than eight years since his voluntary abdication he had been reduced to a useless relic of the past.

Understandably he did not want the people at the wedding to see him as an old, frail man, a shadow of his imperial image.

Constantine appears to have been offended by Diocletian's refusal to come to the wedding but if the report is accurate, it was a minor and passing ripple. After all, the old man was nearing his end. "With his spirit in anguish," to quote the ever descriptive Lactantius, "Diocletian moved from one corner of the palace to the other, unable to eat or sleep, sighing, groaning, crying without respite. So, this emperor, the favorite of fortune of twenty years, suffocating by the outrages which had turned his life into horror, let himself die of hunger and sorrow." Diocletian died alone a few months later, weary, bitter, having nothing left to live for. The *Epitomator de Caesaribus* says that he chose to poison himself to avoid a less glorious death. Probably Lactantius is closer to the truth. The old emperor died of a broken heart.

Licinius to his credit had the decency to make arrangements for Diocletian's burial in the mausoleum the old emperor had built for himself on the palace grounds. It was an impressive octagon building surrounded by a colonnade, its entrance flanked by two lions made of black marble. It remains in remarkably good condition to this day. Diocletian was interred in a sarcophagus of red marble with a symbolic relief on its side—Meleager confronting a wild boar. The hunter was Diocletian himself and the boar was Aper whose Germanic name meant wild boar. For several years the sarcophagus remained covered with the imperial purple. At least in death, Diocletian was again treated for the last time with imperial dignity.

Licinius' wedding with Constantia was only one of the reasons for Constantine's journey to Mediolanum. In the following days he spent many hours discussing with Licinius the problems of the empire. The economy had stabilized and the barbarians across the two great European rivers, the Rhine and the Danube, were quiet most of the time. Now that Maxentius was out of the way, the two of them controlled the largest part of the empire. If and when Licinius eliminated

Maximin Daia, he would bring under his control all the lands east of the Istrian peninsula, and then, the two of them would rule together just as Diocletian and Maximian had done with so much success before the madness set in.

In Constantine's eyes part of that madness was the savage persecution of the Christians. Licinius was a pagan, or more likely an agnostic, who had never been committed to a rabid anti-Christian stand. In the three years since Carnuntum, and even before the edict Galerius had issued from his deathbed, Licinius had not applied actively the anti-Christian edicts of Diocletian, which were legally still in effect. Licinius did not care much nor did he understand the Christians' outlandish claims about a rebel Jew who had risen from the dead and who, they said, was the Son of God, and he did not like their stubborn refusal to offer sacrifice to the traditional gods, but he saw no reason to send them to the executioner's block or to the salt mines just for that. So, he raised no serious objections when Constantine proposed that they jointly issue rescripts to the provincial governors in their domains telling them that from this point on every man was free to follow the religion of his choice.

In the next few days, they worked out the outlines of their religious policy and then they ordered the scribes to write down the text they had approved. Even though Eusebius speaks of an "aforementioned law" (τω νομω ον προειρικαμεν), we have no record of a formal Edict and if they issued one the text has been lost. What we have is the text of official letters (rescripts) addressed to specific governors and preserved by Lactantius and Eusebius. It is reasonable to assume that if Constantine and Licinius had issued a formal edict, both Lactantius and Eusebius would have used its text instead of quoting letters (*litteras*) in which the second person singular (*tuam, tuae*) is frequently used. In any event, this document which is usually called the Edict of Milan is a landmark not only in the history of the Christian religion, since it recognizes the Church as a legitimate corporate body under Roman law, but also in the religious history of mankind because for the first time it proclaims the principle that freedom of religion is a fundamental right.

Here is the text of this historic document from Eusebius' Greek original:

> "Already long ago, when we were considering (σκο-πουντες) that liberty of religion should not be denied, but that to each one's thought and volition authority should be given to practice divine things according to each one's individual preference, we had ordered (note: apparently this refers to the last Edict of Galerius, which they, too, had signed) that Christians should also have the freedom to maintain the faith of their own sect and religion; but since many different conditions appear to have been added to that rescript which granted such authority to those same persons, it is possible that after a while some of them were not observed.
>
> When I, Constantine Augustus, and I, Licinius Augustus came for a happy event to Mediolanum and discussed all matters relating to public advantage and safety, we came to the conclusion that among the things which would benefit all men nothing demands more immediate attention than those matters which relate to the reverence and respect due to the Divinity, that is, that we should give the Christians and every-one else freedom to follow the religion each may want (ελευθεραν αιρεσιν), so that whatever Divinity may exist in the heavens will be willing to show benevo-lence to us and to all those who live under our author-ity. Accordingly, we have resolved with sound and most correct reasoning that no one should be denied in

any manner the right to follow and choose either the Christian observance (παραφυλαξιν) or religion and to give everyone the right to dedicate his mind to the religion he considers most fitting for himself, so that the Divinity whose worship we follow with free minds will provide us with all things with its usual care and benevolence."

This is indeed a most eloquent and straightforward proclamation of freedom of religion: "...give everyone the right to dedicate his mind to the religion he considers most fitting for himself..." The edict of Milan did not declare the God of the Christians as the only God. Instead, it spoke of "whatever Divinity may exist in the heavens..."

No doubt this was a concession to Licinius who did not share Constantine's growing attachment to the Christian religion. Still, Constantine was able to persuade his imperial colleague to approve certain stipulations which were specifically focused on the Christians. The edict went on:

"It is proper therefore that all these things which please us be transcribed so that by removing totally all conditions contained in our previous letters (γραμ-μασιν) to your Excellency (*dicationem tuam*, την συν καθοσιωσιν) concerning the Christians, which stipulations we consider to be too severe and alien to our benevolence, these (stipulations) are now being removed and that henceforth freely and simply every person who has chosen to observe the religion of the Christians will be free to do so without any hindrance or molestation.

We have decided to make known to your Excellency this in the fullest manner so that you will know that

we have granted free and unhindered right to these
Christians to practice their religion."

This clear provision that the Christians were from this point on free to
worship their God should not be interpreted as a first step in giving
the Christian religion a privileged status under the laws of the
empire. In the next sentence, all other religions are granted the same
protection and freedom.

> "And while, your Excellency, you see that we have
> granted this right to those persons (the Christians),
> you shall understand that a similar right for free and
> unrestricted observance is granted to all others to prac-
> tice their own rituals and religion (την παρατηρησιν
> και θρησκειαν αυτων μετερχεσθαι) as they wish, in
> keeping with the tranquillity of our times, so that each
> has the right to worship any divinity (Θειον) they
> would like (οποιον δ'αν βουληται). And this we have
> done so that neither from any ritual nor from any reli-
> gion whatever may we appear that we have detracted
> anything at all."

Still, Constantine was concerned with the well-being of the
Christians. After all, the effects of the long persecution were still evident. The edict goes on:

> "In addition we resolve the following with regard to
> the Christians. If any persons have purchased from
> the public treasury or from others the places where in
> the past (the Christians) had the custom of congregat-
> ing and on which a previous instruction was sent in
> letters to your Excellency, such places must be
> returned to the Christians without money (ανευ

αργυριου) and without any demand for payment, removing any subterfuge or doubt (υπερτεθεισης πασης αμελειας και αμφιβολιας.) And also that those who have purchased those places or have acquired them as a gift, if they have any claim on our benevolence, to appear before the local magistrate so that we may provide for them in our clemency. All these (properties) must be delivered without delay to the corporation of the Christians (corpori Christianorum)."

The official letter went on with details on the return of the confiscated properties to the "corporation of the Christians." This recognition of the Christian religion as a legitimate "corporation" was an extremely important change in the status of the Church because it strengthened drastically the Church's legitimacy under Roman law. The edict ended with the statement that the two emperors had taken those important steps because they wanted "the divine favor toward us, which in so many matters we have already experienced, to remain surely with us for all time (παντος του χρονου βεβαιος διαμειναι)."

The Edict of Milan did not establish Christianity as the official religion of the Roman Empire. It did not even say that the God of the Christians was the only true God. The two emperors spoke of "whatever divinity may exist in the heavens." What they said very clearly, however, was that every person should have the right to worship "any divinity" and to observe the rituals and the precepts of any religion. For the first time, freedom of religion was formally proclaimed by the state. The principle would last for a brief period, to resurface after many centuries in North America.

Apparently there was a practical reason for not having a formal edict issued at Mediolanum, if indeed no edict was issued. Licinius had to leave Mediolanum in haste. A report came to him with the ominous news that Maximin Daia had left Antioch with a large army and was preparing to cross the Bosporus and invade the Balkans. Maximin Daia, convinced that Constantine and Licinius would soon launch an attack against him, had decided to strike first, while his rivals were preoccupied with weddings and festivities in Mediolanum. It was to be a fateful move.

Chapter VIII

Master of the West

THE END OF
MAXIMIN DAIA

Maximin Daia had a good reason to conclude that the moment was right for him to act. Indeed, if he moved swiftly and invaded Licinius' territories, he could grab most of his rival's domain and eliminate him as a potential threat. Then, Maximin Daia would have to deal only with Constantine who, with Licinius out of the way, would find it prudent to accept reality, agree to keep what he had already conquered in the West and let Maximin Daia rule over all the lands east of the Istrian peninsula—not an unrealistic plan.

Soon after he received the news about Licinius' wedding, Maximin Daia, who was at Antioch with most of his legions at the time, ordered a forced march through Cilicia and Cappadocia in the middle of winter. Lactantius has left for us a rich account of what followed. "The unusually heavy snowfall, the mud, the cold, the exhaustion killed most of the beasts of burden, and the pitiful sight of their corpses at the side of the road foretold the soldiers that the war was already lost and that the same fate awaited them." After three weeks of marching through the mountain passes and the arid plains of Cappadocia and Cilicia, the exhausted army reached Bithynia at the

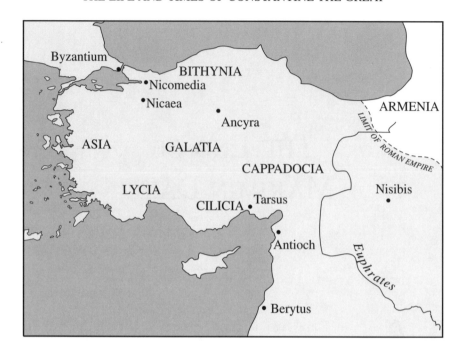

Asia Minor

at the time of Constantine the Great

beginning of March. By then the weather had improved considerably.

After spending a night in Nicomedia, Maximin Daia ordered his legion commanders to begin the crossing of the Bosporus. Moving almost seventy thousand men, many hundreds of horses, and volumes of supplies was a major undertaking, but within four days all his army had crossed to the north side of the straits.

At that point, Maximin Daia made a tactical error. Instead of marching on, he paused to lay siege to the town of Byzantium. Licinius had posted a garrison there to guard the narrow waterway but the force was not strong enough to pose any real threat to Maximin's army. He could have left the garrison behind, isolated, surrounded perhaps by a few hundred men. Instead, "he tried at first with promises of rewards to entice the soldiers in the garrison to surrender. When they refused to listen, he tried to intimidate them by ordering his troops to prepare for a siege." He was wasting precious time, because as soon as his forces had appeared on the Asiatic side, the garrison commander had dispatched a messenger to Licinius in Mediolanum telling him that Maximin Daia was crossing the straits— violating the boundary he and Licinius had agreed on at Chalcydon the year before.

For eleven days the garrison of Byzantium fought off the enemy. It was the middle of March when the garrison finally surrendered "not because of the absence of loyalty but because of exhaustion." Maximin still had ample time to advance rapidly through Thrace and Macedonia toward Dalmatia, but instead he paused again outside of Heraclea, some seventy miles east of Byzantium, and wasted more days trying to capture the town.

Licinius on his part moved rapidly as soon as he received the urgent message from the garrison commander in Byzantium. Most likely Constantine urged him not to waste a single day. Leaving his young bride with her mother Theodora and her aunt Fausta, Licinius rode at a fast pace to Sirmium. He had to assemble quickly a large enough force to fight off Maximin Daia. The messenger from Byzantium had told him that his rival had a large force of some thirteen legions. That was a serious threat indeed.

With his forces camped in Pannonia and Dacia along the banks of the Danube, Licinius had to send immediately messengers to his legion commanders with orders to bring south as many troops as they could. It took more than three weeks to assemble a force of some thirty thousand men, the equivalent of six legions. It was too small a force to match that of Maximin but Licinius had no time to recruit and train more soldiers. He had to move without delay with the troops he had available. And so he did.

By the third week of April, Licinius' troops reached Hadrianopolis in Thrace. In the meantime, Maximin had taken Heraclea and then Perinthos. But when he tried to move further to the northeast, he found the next station on the road, eighteen miles east of Perinthos, already occupied by Licinius' forces. The two armies were now poised against each other. A clash was imminent. Once again, Licinius thought that with reason and diplomacy a bloody fight might be averted, and he sent a delegation to Maximin Daia proposing a meeting between them. By then he knew for certain that his opponent had a force more than twice as strong. If he could persuade Maximin to go back to his domain, and to respect the agreement they had reached at Chalcydon the previous year, he could avoid a clash with such a superior force. But Maximin Daia was not going to let such an opportunity slip through his fingers. It made no sense to him to reach a compromise when he had the upper hand. Generals seldom show moderation when they feel strong. The meeting ended in failure.

At this point, the supernatural enters the picture. Quite possibly the story was invented by Licinius himself. After all, dreams are very personal experiences, not visible to third parties. The story comes from Lactantius and we may let him tell it in his own words. "At that point Maximin vowed to Jupiter that if he emerged victorious, he would sweep away the name of the Christians from the face of the earth, uprooting them completely. The following night, an angel of God came to Licinius' bedside while he was asleep and told him to get up immediately to pray to the Supreme God together with his army. If he did so, he would be crowned with victory. He dreamed then that he rose from his bed with the angel at his side instructing him in what manner and with which words he should pray. He woke up and immediately summoned his secretary and dictated the words of the prayer he had just heard:

> Supreme God—we beseech Thee
> Holy God—we pray to Thee
> We commit to Thine hands all just cause
> To Thee we entrust our salvation
> and to Thee we commit our *imperium*

Through Thee we live and through Thee
we gain victory and happiness
Supreme God, Holy God, hear our prayer
It is to Thee we raise our arms
Hear us Holy God, Supreme God!

It is difficult to resist the thought that Licinius was taking his cue from Constantine.

Lactantius goes on with his vivid narrative: "The emperor had the prayer transcribed into many copies and sent it to the commanders and tribunes to have each of them teach the prayer to their men. With this, the courage of the men redoubled, persuaded as they were that heaven had announced their victory."

Three days later was the first of May (*die Kalendarum Maiarum*), Maximin's eight anniversary as emperor. Licinius decided to have the battle on that day "in order to have him destroyed on the very same day of his feast, exactly like Maxentius had been destroyed in Rome [on his anniversary]."

Maximin Daia, on his part, decided to have the battle one day ahead of his anniversary, to celebrate it as the victor. So, very early at dawn on the last day of April, Maximin's army started marching in the direction of the enemy. Licinius' men alerted by the noise took up their arms, formed their battle lines and moved on to meet the opponent. With the sun now rising slowly over the distant hills to the east, the men in the opposing legions could see each other quite clearly across the barren field known as *Campus Ergenus*.

Suddenly, on orders from their officers, Licinius' men stopped, laid their shields on the ground, and took off their helmets. Then, led by their officers, they raised their arms to the sky and started reciting the prayer in unison more than once. Considering the length of the prayer, it is hard to imagine that the soldiers were able to voice more than the words "Supreme God, Holy God." If they said more, "they must have had angelic help, or breathlessness would surely have defeated them," to quote John Holland Smith's humorous remark in his *Constantine the Great*.

Licinius was not the kind of man likely to receive divine revelation, but he had seen how Constantine had fired the courage of his men with the mysterious monogram. Evidently he hoped that the prayer would have a similar effect on his men. And so, to quote Lactantius, "an army which was about to perish heard the murmur of those who were praying. After reciting the prayer three times, they felt full of courage and they picked up their shields from the ground and they put on their helmets." They were now ready to fight against Maximin's men—who were no doubt baffled by the strange behavior of their foes.

We may let Lactantius carry on with his story. "At the sound of the trumpets, the troops moved forward and penetrated Maximin's lines where the terrified soldiers could not even unsheathe their swords or shoot their arrows. Maximin ran from one end of the battlefield to the other trying to weaken the fervor of Licinius' soldiers, now with warnings, now with the promise of rewards. Not a single man listened to him. When an attack was launched against him, he sought refuge among his men. His army allowed itself to be cut to pieces without fighting back. Such a great number of legions, such a mass of soldiers was mowed down by a handful of men. No one among Maximin's soldiers remembered his fame, his valor, the many rewards he had given them in times past. Marching to their death like sacrificial victims and not like warriors who march to battle, that was the way the Supreme God chose to deliver them to their enemies who had nothing more to do than slaughter them."

Lactantius may have exaggerated the passivity of Maximin's soldiers, but the fact remains that his much larger army was indeed decimated. Seeing that the battle was taking a very different course from the one he had anticipated, Maximin "threw off his imperial mantle, put on the garments of a slave, hoping to avoid detection, and rode away as fast as he could" toward the Straits of Bosporus. "Half of his men were dead and the rest had either surrendered or were fleeing away from the battlefield, because upon seeing their emperor deserting them, they lost all shame and did the same."

Maximin rode away with other fleeing officers and soldiers all night, and in the morning, the day of his anniversary, he reached the Straits of Bosporus. Hastily he crossed to the Asiatic side and rode on for the rest of the day, arriving in Nicomedia late in the afternoon "having covered one hundred and sixty miles from the location of the battle."

One can imagine the scene at the palace in Nicomedia as Maximin came through the gate, clad in the garments of a slave, as Lactantius says. In a state of high agitation, he told his wife and children to get ready to leave. They left early in the morning, accompanied by some of the high officials in the palace and a few servants, a pitiful group of fugitives.

Apparently, Maximin Daia sent messengers to the commanders of the forces which were still stationed in Syria and beyond, because when he reached Cappadocia he found waiting several cohorts under the command of loyal officers. Several more units from the defeated army had managed to cross the straits ahead of Licinius' forces and had marched all the way to Cappadocia to be with their emperor. The sight of those forces restored Maximin's morale, "and he put on the purple again," to quote Lactantius' sarcastic remark.

With the forces he now had under his command, Maximin fortified the narrow passes in the Taurus mountains, hoping to block the way to Licinius' army and force a compromise. He was prepared to surrender Asiana and Pontica (Asia Minor) to Licinius and keep for himself Syria, Mesopotamia, Palestine, and Egypt—not a bad deal under the circumstances, if Licinius was willing to compromise.

Licinius was no longer interested in a compromise. Within days after the battle at Perinthos, he crossed the straits with his army and marched through Bithynia and Cappadocia, reaching the Taurus mountains in Cilicia in the third week of May. Already Maximin's forces had constructed barriers and towers on the slopes of the mountain passes.

Faced with this, Licinius chose from among his soldiers all those who had been shepherds and goatherders before they were recruited into his legions and sent them up the mountain paths, armed only with battle-axes and swords. They climbed to the top of the mountain ridges and appeared suddenly on the rear of Maximin's soldiers. Licinius' men fell on them like demons, splitting their skulls and cutting their throats, taking full advantage of the surprise. When Maximin Daia saw that his last effort to block Licinius had crumbled, he ordered his troops to retreat further south. He, himself, rode away in the direction of Tarsus.

Lactantius claims that once again Maximin had deserted his men. If indeed he had shown again such cowardice, he would have been finished. No officer or soldier would ever again rally around his standard. Maximin was not a fool. He knew well the rules of the game. For this reason it is quite possible that he withdrew to the coastal town of Tarsus to sail off from its harbor and go to Tyre (Sur) in Syria or even to Alexandria in Egypt. At the same time, his forces would move in good order south through Syria and join other units for a decisive battle at the barren peninsula (Sinai), blocking the way to Egypt.

If indeed Maximin Daia had such a plan we will never know because Licinius did not give him the time to carry it out. With his legions, he moved rapidly through the mountain passes and marched toward the coast where the town of Seleucia opened its gates and welcomed him. When Maximin was told of the fall of Seleucia, and that the other two towns of Elaeusa and Pompeionopolis on the road to Tarsus were ready to welcome Licinius, he prepared to sail off. But then he fell gravely ill, stricken most likely by cholera. The plague which had killed thousands the year before was still lingering on.

Lactantius, as always enjoying the graphic description of a foe's painful death, has written some ghastly details. "Unable to find relief from his pain and terror, he sought in death the deliverance from the evils God had heaped on his head. But first he gorged himself with wine and food like a man who wanted to enjoy himself one last time. He was in that condition when he took the poison and the food in his stomach counteracted and so he continued to suffer from the terrible pain of his malady. Eventually the poison began to take effect setting his entrails on fire. The unbearable pain brought his spirit to such a rage that for four days, prey to his madness, he was picking dirt from the floor and eating it, trying to put out the flames in his stomach. Then, after a thousand torments, he began to hit his head on the wall until his eyes burst out of their sockets. Now that he had lost his sight, he had a vision. God appeared to him, surrounded by his faithful servants clad in white, to pass judgment on him. Crying out like a man being tortured, he said. 'It was not me. The others did it all.' Then, as if he were still under torture, he confessed to Christ, praying continually and asking for His pity. This is how, moaning like a man being burned alive, he died, suffering a horrible death." In this much too graphic passage, Lactantius has given, no doubt, free reign to his overactive imagination and to his hatred against those who had persecuted his fellow Christians. Still, the fact remains that Maximin fell gravely ill and that to end the suffering he probably took poison. And if his repentance did not result from the supernatural intervention claimed by Lactantius, we do know that Maximin Daia tried in his final days, like his uncle Galerius, to mend his fences with the God of the Christians. From his deathbed, he too issued an edict. The document is given to us by Eusebius in his *Ecclesiastical History* and it deserves to be presented here because it testifies to the awe the God of the Christians had begun to instill in those pagan emperors, at least shortly before their death.

"Emperor Caesar Gaius Valerius Maximinus, Germanicus Sarmaticus, Pious, Felix, Invincible, Augustus. We have always endeavored by all means in our power to secure the advantage of those who dwell in our provinces, and to contribute by our benefits both to the prosperity of the State and to the well-being of every citizen. No one can be ignorant of this, and we are confident that each one who puts his memory to the test is persuaded to the truth. We found, however, some time ago that by virtue of the Edict published by our divine parents, Diocletian and Maximian, ordering the destruction of the places where the Christian were in the habit of assembling, many excesses and acts of violence were committed by our public servants and that the evil was felt more and more by our subjects every day, inasmuch as their properties were, under this pretext, unjustly seized.

Consequently, we declared last year by letters addressed to the governors of the Provinces that if anyone wished to join this sect and practice this religion, he should be allowed to do so, without interference, and that the Christians should enjoy complete liberty and be sheltered from all fear and all suspicion.

However, we have not been able to close our eyes completely to the fact that certain magistrates misunderstood our instructions, with the result that our subjects distrusted our words and were nervous about worshipping the religion of their choice. That is why, in order to do away in the future with all uneasiness and doubt, we have decided to publish this Edict by which all are to understand that those who wish to follow this sect have full liberty to do so, and that by the benevolence of our Majesty each man may practice the religion he prefers or that to which he is accustomed."

The edict went on to give the Christians the right to rebuild their houses of worship, and to order the return to them of all the properties "which were confiscated by the order of our divine parents or occupied by any municipality, or sold or given away." The reference to "the orders of our divine parents, Diocletian and Maximian" seems to echo Lactantius' colorful description of the dying Maximin telling God, "it was not me. The others did it all."

No less interesting is the similarity of this edict to the instructions issued by Constantine and Licinius at Mediolanum. Apparently a copy of what the two emperors had said about freedom of religion had reached Maximin Daia, and the palace official who drafted the edict on orders from the dying Maximin used the Mediolanum document for his guidance. That some high official composed the text is a fair assumption because if Maximin was as gravely ill as most likely he was, he would not have been able to draft such a well-reasoned document—well-reasoned but also blatantly hypocritical when he blamed on lower magistrates and on a misunderstanding his earlier policies of persecution.

Regardless of its content or its intent, Maximin's last edict was irrelevant. With his death, his opponent was now the sole master of the eastern half of the empire, from Pannonia to Mesopotamia to Egypt. On the 13th day of June, Licinius came to Nicomedia from Cilicia and staged a triumphal entry into the city with his victorious army. On the same day, he issued to all the governors in his realm instructions on the freedom of all citizens to follow the religion of their choice, exactly as he and Constantine had decided in Mediolanum. Freedom of religion was now the law throughout the Roman Empire.

TREASON SHATTERS THE BONDS

E mbracing freedom of religion and a benign stand toward the Christians did not mean that Licinius had accepted the ethical and humane teachings of Christianity. His instructions on religious freedom had hardly reached the provincial governors in his domain, when he ordered the execution of many high officials in Maximin Daia's regime, including the finance minister Peucetius, the imperial prefect of Egypt, Cuicianus, and the notorious pagan activist Theotecnus, the architect of Maximin's effort to organize the pagan priests into a cohesive structure resembling that of the Christians.

Licinius' mostly unnecessary cruelty did not stop with the death of palace officials. In the summer of 313, he turned against the surviving relatives of the dead emperors—Maximin Daia, Galerius, and even Diocletian. One of the first victims was young Candidianus, a son Galerius had with a concubine. His wife Valeria, Diocletian's only child, being sterile, had adopted the boy as her own son. When Valeria heard the news that Maximin Daia had been defeated by Licinius and had died in Tarsus, she took her mother and the boy and went to Nicomedia to seek Licinius' protection and support. Lactantius gives us a strange story at this point. Because she did not trust Licinius, he claims, "she joined his entourage in disguise to see what the destiny of Candidianus would be." It is hard to accept that she could send the boy to Licinius while keeping herself out of sight. Be that as it may, Licinius treated the boy with kindness at first, but then "at a moment [Candidianus] least expected it," he was killed. That ended the imperial line of Galerius. Valeria, terrified by the boy's murder, took her old and frail mother Prisca, Diocletian's widow, and left Nicomedia, both dressed as peasant women. They crossed the Bosporus in this disguise and started a difficult journey westward on Via Egnatia, trying to reach Thessaloniki on foot. After a few weeks, they came to that city hoping to find safety in obscurity.

Soon after the death of Candidianus, Licinius gave orders for the arrest of Severianus, the son of Severus, who was serving as an officer in Maximin's army and had followed him to the Taurus mountains after the battle of Perinthos. Accusing the young officer of "having dreams to assume the purple himself," Licinius ordered his execution. It was now clear that Licinius had decided to exterminate any member of the imperial families who could possibly be used as a rallying point to challenge his rule. He did not even spare Maximin's two little children, a son of eight and a daughter of seven. Incidentally, the little girl was to be Candidianus' bride when they both grew up. Maximin's widow had already been hurled to her death into the river Orontes. With their death, Maximin's line too came to an end.

Licinius could have stopped there but he did not. He gave orders for the arrest of Valeria and Prisca. Lactantius claims that Licinius wanted to take possession of Galerius' properties, by right of inheritance, and that Valeria refused to sign away her rights. Most likely, Valeria had no way of preventing Licinius from taking over anything he wanted. But if Licinius wished to give a legal veneer to his action, he needed a document signed by Valeria.

For several months, Valeria and her mother were able to hide in Thessaloniki under false names, passing for ordinary people. But as it often happens, someone who knew their real identities turned them in, most likely for gold, and they were arrested. It is quite possible that Licinius ordered the prefect of Thessaloniki to force Valeria to sign. But Diocletian's daughter was a strong-willed woman. Lactantius tells us that "in the same way she had refused Maximin's demand [to become his wife], in the same way she refused to turn over the possessions of Galerius." As soon as Licinius received the report of Valeria's refusal to sign, he ordered the execution of both Valeria and her mother. The two imperial ladies "were taken to their death in front of a large crowd. With the people in tears for their misfortune, they were beheaded and their corpses were thrown into the sea. So, their virtue and their rank became the cause for their doom." Lactantius, however, cannot resist a snide remark for the dismal end of all those who had not been Christians. "Thus," he wrote, "all the impious, by a just edict of God, suffered the evils they had inflicted on others." This could have hardly applied to seven- and eight-year old children.

We have no record of Constantine's reaction to this blood bath. But since he too had killed Maxentius' wife and infant son, he probably accepted Licinius' cruelty as the inescapable burden of imperial power. In any event, Constantine was much too busy with the administration of his domain, the suppression of minor incursions into Gaul from across the Rhine, pirate raids along the Spanish coast, and—something entirely new for a Roman emperor—becoming directly involved in the affairs of the Church, trying to settle disputes among Christian bishops in North Africa.

To cope with the heavy workload he decided to appoint his own Caesar. With his son Crispus being only eighteen, Constantine choose a more mature man. His name was Bassianus, apparently a relative of Licinius and a legatus in Constantine's army, a handsome man in his middle thirties, cutting an impressive figure in his uniform. It appears that Bassianus had been one of the guests at Licinius' wedding with Constantia in Mediolanum. Constantine's young stepsister Anastasia was also there and we should not be surprised that the idea of a match between Anastasia and Bassianus entered Constantine's mind. A few months later Anastasia and Bassianus were married. The young officer was now a member of Constantine's imperial family. He could not remain a mere legatus for long. Not surprisingly, in the summer of 313, Constantine elevated Bassianus to the rank of Caesar.

At this point, the record becomes unclear and one can reconstruct what may have happened only by probing like an investigator into the ancient sources and by reading between the lines.

Constantine was in Gaul, inspecting the military camps and shoring up the defenses along the Rhine, with Bassianus and his young bride in Mediolanum, keeping an eye on Italy. Being married to the daughter of legendary Constantius, and elevated to the rank of Caesar, should have been gain enough for a fairly young man like Bassianus—a gain he should have guarded like the apple of his eye. But it appears that the meteoric rise unhinged his mind because no sane person would have become entangled in the insane web of intrigue and treason he did.

The ancient sources do not tell who was the first to come up with the idea, but Bassianus' brother Senecius—whose Greek name meant a man of prudence—most imprudently became a central figure in the conspiracy. In the fall, Senecius went to Licinius with a wild proposition. Bassianus would engineer Constantine's death, taking advantage of his easy access to the emperor. With Constantine out of the way, Licinius would become the senior Augustus, in fact the sole Augustus. Then, he could either appoint Bassianus as his Caesar in charge of the West or even elevate him to the rank of Augustus just as Diocletian had elevated Maximian some thirty years before. Considering that Licinius was already fifty-one years old, Bassianus could one day become his successor and preserve their dynasty.

It is quite possible that Constantine's increasing involvement with the Christians had frightened the pagan priests who could see that lurking behind the lofty principle of freedom of religion was the growing supremacy of the Christian cult under the aegis of the emperor himself. It would be quite unrealistic to think that the pagan priests would accept their doom without resistance.

Licinius was not at heart a friend of the Christians. He had agreed with Constantine at Mediolanum only because under the circumstances such cooperation was in his self-interest. In his decisive clash with Maximin Daia outside of Perinthos, he had invoked the aid of the Supreme God but the supreme deity he spoke of was not necessarily the God of the Christians. He was a pagan—or more accurately, an agnostic—worshipping the traditional gods out of habit rather than fervent conviction. Still, he was a man the pagans could trust. If Constantine were eliminated, the pagan religion would be safe. Senecius' plan made sense. We have no evidence that Licinius objected to the plan out of loyalty to Constantine or that he tried to dissuade Bassianus. All the events that followed indicate that Licinius gave his blessing.

Zosimus, a pagan chronicler who disliked Constantine, claimed years later that "Licinius was not responsible while in his usual manner Constantine proved unfaithful." Since Constantine was the target of the conspiracy one cannot easily accept Zosimus' assertion. Constantine had taken Bassianus into his family and had raised him to the highest rank below the emperor himself. This alone shows that he considered Licinius a friend. Then, if Licinius had indeed done nothing wrong, as Zosimus claims, it would be hard to understand Constantine's actions in the early months of the following year when he uncovered the plot.

A conspiracy threatening the life of the emperor could not remain undetected for very long. When Constantine was shown clear proof of the plot, he reacted swiftly and without mercy. From Gaul where he was still staying, he sent to Mediolanum a few men he trusted, with orders to arrest Bassianus without giving him time to resist or rally his own personal guards. An unsuspecting Bassianus received Constantine's emissaries and apparently he was killed on the spot, or arrested and immediately sent to the executioner's block, because we have no evidence whatever that he resisted or that he was given time to escape or appeal to Licinius. Neither do we have any written record that Anastasia made any effort to save her husband by going to her stepbrother. Even if she did, her tears would have no effect. Constantine could never forgive treason, especially by a man who owed him so much.

Constantine's investigation uncovered the sinister role played by Senecius and in a letter to Licinius he demanded that the archconspirator be turned over to him for just punishment. In the letter, Constantine did not implicate Licinius. Apparently for political reasons he had chosen to ignore Licinius' perfidy and had shifted the blame to Senecius. It was a wise move. If he had accused Licinius he would have had no alternative but to break relations and wage war.

Eutropius claims that Constantine had already set his mind to conquer the rest of the empire and that he welcomed Licinius' treachery. He writes: "Constantine, a mighty man and one who always made sure that he achieved what he planned to do, once he had decided to rule the entire world, he provoked war with Licinius although bound to him by a treaty of friendship and by kinship, his sister being Licinius' wife." Eutropius wrote his chronicle seventy years after the death of Constantine. He was not an ardent admirer but as a secretary to emperor Arcadius in Constantinople he had access to surviving documents and his testimony is not without value. Nevertheless, it may be closer to the truth to say that Constantine, as was his habit, did not provoke the conflict but he took advantage of what Licinius did and carried out plans he had been drawing up in his mind for some time.

If that is what actually happened, Licinius played right into Constantine's hands. He refused to surrender his relative Senecius. Instead of sending the conspirator to Constantine in chains—a clear sign of his good will—he moved some of his legions into western Pannonia, much closer to Italy. Evidently, he feared Constantine's retaliation and wanted to be ready for it. It was a prudent military action but Constantine saw it as another provocation. Then, to add insult to injury, Licinius ordered the smashing of Constantine's statues at the frontier town of Emona, (today's Ljubljana). To quote Zosimus' apt phrase "as their enmity became evident, they began to prepare for war."

Zosimus has left us in Greek—and considering his dislike of Constantine—a fairly impartial description of the fight and we may let him tell the story. "Licinius assembled his army near the town of Civalis (Cibalae; Vincovci) in Pannonia, situated upon a hill. On the wider side of the town was a deep lake and on the other side the mountain of which the hill with the town was a part. Beyond that was a vast plain where Licinius set camp, deploying the main force below the hill and taking care to keep the two outside wings of his army strong. Constantine deployed his force on the mountainside, relying mostly on his cavalry which he considered to be his most effective force."

The battle started very early at dawn. "When both armies used up their arrows, they clashed with their swords and their spears until early in the evening, when the right wing which was led by Constantine himself won the day. When the enemy soldiers saw Licinius ready to mount his horse and leave, they, too, turned to flight. They did not waste one minute, not even to take time to have their evening meal; they ran, leaving their food, their animals and their gear behind, taking with them only the food they needed for that night. As fast as they could, they fled with Licinius to the town of Sirmium [Mitrovica], a town in Pannonia at the point where the river Savus runs into the river Istrus [Danube]. After cutting off the bridge on the river, Licinius left this town, too, and moved on, hoping to raise a new force from the villages in Thrace."

Zosimus leaves no doubt that Licinius' army was roundly defeated at Civalis (Cibalae). Out of 35,000 of infantry and cavalry, Licinius had lost almost twenty thousand men. Before he left Sirmium, Licinius took with him his wife Constantia, Constantine's stepsister, and his son Licinianus, an infant at the time. Only fifteen months had passed since the happy days of their wedding at Mediolanum.

Zosimus goes on with his vivid account. "Constantine, on his part, after he seized Civalis and Sirmium and everything Licinius in his flight had left behind, he dispatched five thousand men to pursue Licinius. But, not knowing the route Licinius had taken, they were unable to find him. In the meantime, Constantine reassembled the bridge on the Savus—the one Licinius had dismantled—and with his army he marched against Licinius. After he marched through Thrace, Constantine reached the plain where Licinius had set up camp. Since they had arrived at night, Constantine ordered his soldiers to rest and be ready to fight at dawn."

During the hasty flight from Civalis, Licinius had raised to the rank of Caesar his *dux limitis*, the general officer commanding his frontier troops. His name was Valens. On Licinius' orders coins were struck quickly inscribed with the portrait of Valens and the words Gaius Aurelius Valerius Valens, Caesar and Augustus on one side and the image of Jupiter the Preserver of Emperors on the other. This was a move with little practical value; still, Constantine saw the elevation of Valens to Caesar Augustus as a personal insult.

It appears that Constantine had not marched to Thrace at his customary quick pace. He had a good reason to be cautious. Already he had traveled a great distance from his home base in Gaul, and being a prudent general he wanted to reinforce his army before he clashed once again with Licinius. Still, the delay gave his rival time to bring in fresh troops from his legions in the Orient.

Constantine's army reached Philippopolis (Plovdiv) some five weeks after the battle at Civalis. At Philippopolis, he found a delegation from Licinius waiting to talk to him. Suspecting that Licinius wanted to use the talks to gain time to bring more troops from Asiana and Pontica (Asia Minor), Constantine dismissed the delegation and continued his march toward the southeast. A few days later, his forces arrived at nightfall—as Zosimus told us—to the wide valley of the river Evros (the river which today forms the border between Greece and Turkey) where Licinius had deployed his forces.

The battle started at dawn but during the day-long battle neither side won the upper hand. Later, in the night darkness, Licinius moved his forces to the north in the direction of Boroea, probably hoping to attack Constantine's forces from the rear. Constantine, on his part, finding the way open, pushed eastward to Hadrianopolis and then on to Bosporus, thinking that he was in pursuit of the retreating Licinius. He easily captured Byzantium but then he was told by his scouts that Licinius with most of his army was marching from the north, preparing to strike at any moment. This time, when Licinius sent another delegation led by Mestrianus, one of his highest officials, Constantine agreed to enter into negotiations.

The talks broke down almost as soon as they started because Mestrianus told Constantine that he was speaking for his two co-emperors, Licinius and Valens. Constantine cut him off angrily and told him that he recognized only Licinius as an emperor. He had not endured tedious marches, he said, and won a succession of victories only to share the purple with a contemptible slave. He added coldly that the first condition for peace was the removal of Valens and that Mestrianus would remain as a hostage until this demand was communicated to Licinius and word was back that Valens had been removed.

Without hesitation, Licinius ordered the arrest and execution of Valens. After this proof of Licinius' sincere desire for conciliation, the negotiations moved on smoothly. In the end, Licinius kept all the lands beyond the Straits of Bosporus—Asiana and Pontica, Syria, Mesopotamia, Palestine, Egypt and Libya—plus a foothold in the Balkans (the area of Eastern Thrace, now part of Turkey) on the north-eastern side of the straits. For his part, Constantine received Pannonia, Illyricum, Moesia and the Greek peninsula.

Included in the lands Constantine had added to his domain was the town of Naissus, the place of his birth. It is not hard to imagine his feelings as the agreement "was sealed with oaths by both as a guarantee that both of them would observe and be faithful to their treaties," to quote Zosimus. The circle was now completed. Forty-two years ago, he had been born in that small town, out of wedlock, the grandson of a humble innkeeper. He was now back as the senior Augustus, the *Augustus Maximus*, the master of an empire extending from the British Isles, to France, to Spain, to northern Africa, to Italy, to today's Switzerland, Hungary, the Balkans, all the way to the tip of the Greek peninsula. Since the Milvian bridge, his troops had marched under the *Labarum*, his powerful talisman. The God of the Christians had been a powerful ally indeed. He was now fully convinced that he had made the right choice.

Departing from Roman tradition as well as from Diocletian's idea of a tetrarchy, Constantine treated his empire as a family possession. He son Crispus was now twenty years old, a very impressive young man, intelligent, courageous, handsome, well-trained as a soldier. Constantine raised him to the rank of Caesar. Then, to calm down Fausta's inevitable displeasure, he raised to the rank of Caesar their own infant son, Constantine, who had been born in Arelate the year before. Following Constantine's example—and quite possibly by joint agreement—Licinius also raised to the rank of Caesar his own son, Licinianus, twenty months old at the time. The principle of succession by birth had now been introduced—a principle to be followed in dynastic succession for many centuries, until our own days, by the kingdoms which emerged later in Europe.

The reconciliation between the two brothers-in-law was sealed the following year in a symbolic fashion when the Senate in Rome—controlled by Constantine—appointed the two men as consuls for the year 315. The rift was healed, at least for a while.

CHAPTER IX

CONSTANTINE AND THE CHURCH

Embroiled in
Church Quarrels

T his was the first time that a Roman emperor paid attention to the internal affairs of the Christian Church. Constantine, under the guidance of Osius, his trusted advisor, felt that he had a responsibility to see that all was going well in "the legitimate and universal religion" (ενθεσμω και καθολικη θρησκεια). Convinced that his victory at the Milvian bridge was granted by the Supreme Deity of the Christians, he wanted to express his gratitude not merely with words but with deeds. Offering the Lateran palace to Miltiades, the bishop of Rome, for his official residence, was one first step.

In the spring of 313, a few months after the historic decision on freedom of religion at Mediolanum, Constantine sent a letter to Caecilianus, bishop of Carthage in North Africa. At the same time he dispatched another letter to Anulinus, the proconsul of Africa. It is worth quoting these two letters in full because they offer, in Constantine's own words, a revealing glimpse into his thinking.

"Constantine Augustus to Caecilianus, bishop of Carthage Inasmuch as it has pleased us to contribute towards the necessary expenses of certain servants of the legitimate and most holy all-embracing religion throughout all the provinces of Africa, Numidia and both Mauretanias, I have sent a letter to Ursus, the most illustrious official of finance (*rationalis*) and have instructed him to give to your Steadfastness three thousand purses (*follis*). When, therefore, you have received the aforesaid sum, take steps to distribute it among the above-mentioned persons in accordance with the instructions sent to you by Osius.

Should you find thereafter the amount insufficient to fulfill my purpose of showing my regard to all of you in Africa, you are to ask without delay Heraclides, our fiscal procurator, for whatever you may think necessary. For I personally instructed him when he was here to give without hesitation any sum of money your Steadfastness may request."

Constantine was certainly most generous in using public funds to support his favorite religion. But generosity was not the end of his involvement. Continuing his letter, he steps into a feud that had been simmering among the bishops in north Africa for quite some time.

"And since I have learned that certain persons of unbalanced mind (*quosdam non satis compositas mentis*) are desirous of misleading the people of the most holy and all-embracing Church with wicked and corrupting falsehoods (*improba et adulterina falsitate*) I want you to know that I have given verbal instructions to Anulinus, the pro-consul, and to Patricius, the Vicar of Prefects, to include among their other duties a close observance of this matter, and if it continues, not to overlook it. Consequently, if you find persons continuing in this madness (*in hac amentia perseverare*) do not hesitate to go to the above-mentioned magistrates and bring this matter before them so that they may punish the culprits in accordance with my personal instructions.

May the Divinity of the Supreme God (*Divinitas summi Dei*) preserve you for many years."

In the short span of only a few months, Constantine had traveled a long way in his religious policies. He was not merely being friendly and supportive to the Christians; he was prepared to use his imperial authority and even the state bureaucracy to deal with an internal Church feud.

His other letter to Anulinus is even more revealing of his view of the Christian religion and of its powerful God.

"Greetings to our most honored Anulinus. Considering that it is abundantly shown by many things that great dangers come to the State (τοις δημοσιοις πραγμασιν) when we neglect the religion in which the highest reverence of the most holy celestial power is safeguarded, while whenever it is upheld and revered properly it brings the greatest happiness to the Roman name and supreme felicity to all things belonging to men, in return for these divine benefits, we resolved that those men who live in the proper holiness and who offer their services to the holy religion according to this law shall receive the rewards for their toil, Anulinus most honored.

Therefore, it is our wish that those who live in the

province entrusted to you and who are members of the all-embracing Church (καθολικη εκκλησια) presided over by Caecilianus and who offer their own services to this holy religion and are called clerics as is their custom, to be relieved of all public functions once and for all, lest through some error or sacrilegious mischance (εξολισθησεως ιεροσυλου) they may be distracted from the service due to the Divinity (θειον), but rather without any interference carry out their duties. Thus, since they offer the highest adoration to the Divinity, it seems to me that they ought to receive the highest reward the State can offer."

This letter to a high government official is remarkable for its religious tenor. Constantine is forcefully telling Anulinus that the prosperity of all depends on offering homage and respect to the Divinity. He does not mention Christ but there is no doubt that he is speaking of the Christian God. Certainly for Osius, Caecilianus and the other Christian clerics, Christ was part of the Trinity and any reference by Constantine to the Supreme Divinity included in their eyes "Christ, the Son of God." It was the God of the Christians Constantine wanted to please. After all, in his letter, he orders Anulinus to exempt from public service the Christian clergy, "lest through some error or sacrilegious mischance" they neglect their duties of worship and by so doing anger the Supreme Divinity.

But more than the exemption from public service, it was Constantine's gold to Caecilianus that acted like the proverbial apple of discord. On the 15th of April, Anulinus sent a letter to Constantine in which he told his emperor that as soon as he had received his "celestial letter" he had carried out the instructions. "But," Anulinus went on, "a few days later certain persons came to me followed by a crowd and spoke against Caecilianus." They handed Anulinus a sealed package and an unsealed petition and asked him to "send them immediately to the sacred and venerable court of your heavenly grace."

The unsealed petition, signed by several bishops in northern Africa, read:

> "We appeal to you, Constantine, best of Emperors since you come from a just family, your father alone among his colleagues being the one who did not carry out the persecution and thus spared Gaul of that frightful calamity.
>
> A disagreement has arisen between us and other African bishops, and we pray that your piety will guide you to give us judges from Gaul."

The petition and the documents in the sealed package did not come entirely as a surprise to Constantine. In his own letter to Caecilianus he had spoken of "certain persons of unbalanced minds" trying to corrupt and deceive the common followers of the Christian Church with "wicked falsehoods." Osius had undoubtedly briefed him on the two clerical factions feuding in the northern African Church. The dispute was not over theology or religious dogma. Personal interests and ambitions accounted for the strife which had started nine or ten years earlier. Now Constantine's money had added envy and greed to the fire.

THE ORIGINS OF THE FEUD

W hat was it all about? The ancient records are unusually detailed but it will be sufficient to trace here the highlights and to bring to life the main personalities. A few years back, when Caecilianus was an archdeacon in the church of Carthage, "a very rich and very head-strong lady" (*pecunionissima et factionissima*) by the name Lucilla had the habit of kissing a bone before receiving Communion. She claimed that the bone came from one of the martyred saints and that it was a sacred relic. In those years it was not unusual to revere the bones of saints but Lucilla had no proof that her relic was genuine. Caecilianus reprimanded her repeatedly in public for her irreverence to the Holy Communion. For Lucilla, Caecilianus' action was an intolerable humiliation she would never forget nor forgive.

The feud reached a boiling point when Caecilianus was elected bishop of Carthage. At the time (A.D. 311) Maxentius was still reigning in Rome. It all started when one of the deacons in Carthage issued an insulting diatribe against Maxentius and then to avoid arrest sought sanctuary inside the church in Carthage. Mensurius, who was then the bishop of Carthage, refused to turn over to the authorities the deacon and he was summoned to Rome to explain to Maxentius the reasons for his refusal to surrender the culprit. Apparently Mensurius was able to placate Maxentius because he was allowed to leave Rome and go back to his post. But being an old man, Mensurius died on the way home. When the news of the old bishop's death reached Carthage, two deacons, Botrys and Celestius, pushed for the immediate election of a successor, hoping to be elected to the vacant post. Because Caecilianus was also a candidate, Lucilla became very involved, supporting the two deacons, one of them, we are told, living in her own house. Optatus, who left for us a very detailed account starting with the early stages of the feud in 305, tells us that both deacons were rejected by the faithful, and that Caecilianus was elected "by the suffrage of all the people." He was consecrated by Felix, bishop of Aptunga and two other bishops according to Church law.

Lucilla was furious and, with her encouragement, the two deacons attacked the election of Caecilianus. To quote Optatus, "the schism started with the hatred of a woman, fed by intrigue and strengthened by greed." Lucilla gained the support of a group of Church elders who refused to give to Caecilianus the religious objects Mensurius had entrusted to them before he left for Rome (with a precise list of all the items given to an old woman for safekeeping).

The group of elders led by Lucilla and the two deacons turned to the Numidian bishops and asked for their judgment. The Numidian bishops met and declared Caecilianus' election invalid on the grounds that one of the three bishops who had consecrated his elevation to bishop was a *traditor*. The bishop they accused of surrendering to the Roman authorities the Holy Scriptures during the persecution was Felix of Aptunga. It appears that no proof existed that Felix had indeed been a *traditor*, but the Numidian bishops accepted the accusations as valid and elected another cleric, a man by the name of Majorinus, to become bishop of Carthage. The city now had two rival bishops. The rift was complete. The faction opposing Caecilianus became known as the party of the Donatists, from the name of Donatus, the bishop who eventually succeeded Majorinus.

When Constantine on the advice of Osius recognized Caecilianus as the legitimate bishop, he walked right into this hornet's nest. With the petition Anulinus forwarded to Constantine, the bishops of the Donatist party were asking the emperor to convene a synod of bishops from Gaul—where there were not many *traditors*, thanks to the lenient policies of Constantine's father during the years of persecution.

"I Ordered"

In Constantine's eyes, feuds of this kind within the Church were bound to displease the Supreme Deity and this was unacceptable. He could not remain indifferent to the calamities this could bring, and he accepted the petition of the rival bishops as if he were the supreme authority of the Church. He instructed Miltiades, the bishop of Rome, to convene a synod. In his letter, Constantine told Miltiades that Caecilianus was accused of many wrongs by some of his fellow bishops in Africa. "I consider it very serious," Constantine went on, "that in those provinces which the Divine Providence (θεια προνοια) has given to my Devotion, and where large numbers of people live, an unruly crowd insists on false claims while bishops feud among themselves. Because of this, I have resolved that Caecilianus accompanied by ten bishops who believe that he is to blame and ten others whom he wants to bring on his side sail for Rome where in your presence but also in the presence of Reticius, Maternus, and Marius, your colleagues whom I have ordered (προσεταξα) to hasten to Rome for this purpose, he may be heard so that you may find out whether he has conformed to the most august law." He then told Miltiades that he was passing on to him the documents he had received from Anulinus, and that he expected him "to investigate and close this matter according to justice." He finished the letter with these words. "It should not escape your notice how much respect I render to the legitimate and all-embracing (ενθεσμω και καθολικη) church and that I do not intend to tolerate schisms or dissension anywhere. The Divinity of the Great God may protect you for many years, Most Honorable."

The Synod
at the Lateran

C onstantine was treating the Christian bishops as if they were
state functionaries. The word *prosetaxa* (I ordered) is quite
clear. In a way, he considered himself the man the Supreme
Deity had chosen to protect and strengthen the "legitimate, all-
embracing religion."

Miltiades did not follow, however, his instructions to the letter. To
broaden the panel of judges he added to the bishops from Cologne,
Autun and Arles, fifteen other bishops from the Italian peninsula.

They met in October 313 in Rome at the palace on the Lateran Hill.
Under Constantine's orders, Caecilianus had come to Rome with ten
other bishops from Africa who supported his claim. On the other side,
Majorinus had arrived with ten bishops opposing Caecilianus.

Constantine, who had just discovered the conspiracy against his
life, was anxious to see that these quarrels which could anger the
Supreme God would come to an end. And initially it appeared that
the matter would be closed.

At the first sitting, the judges examined the credentials of the witnesses and found that some of the bishops that had come with
Majorinus were individuals with questionable morals or improper
ordination. Majorinus and his closest ally, Donatus, bishop of Casae

Nigra, decided that the meeting was stacked against them and that it would not make any difference whatever they said. So, the next day, their witnesses simply said that they had nothing to say against Caecilianus. The judges refused to consider unsubstantiated gossip and the case against Caecilianus collapsed. On the third day, Donatus did not even appear. Still, in a last effort, they presented to the court a new list of charges against Caecilianus but they offered no witnesses. The proceedings were turning into a fiasco.

Miltiades, angered by this turn of events tried to bring back to the proceedings a semblance of gravity. Since the ordination of Caecilianus had been brought under question on the grounds that Bishop Felix of Aptunga was a *traditor*, the judges turned their attention to the meeting of the seventy bishops of Numidia who had declared Caecilianus' ordination invalid. They studied the record of those discussions and when they finished they decided that the decision of the seventy bishops was based on false and unsubstantiated accusations.

The case against Caecilianus had clearly broken down and the verdict was entirely in his favor. Miltiades wrote:

> "Since it is shown that Caecilianus is not accused by those who came with Donatus, as they had promised to do, and Donatus has in no way established his charges against Caecilianus, I find that Caecilianus should be maintained in the communion of his church with all his privileges in tact."

Then, in a spirit of reconciliation, Miltiades offered to send letters to all the clergy consecrated by Majorinus, proposing that where two rival bishops claimed the same see, the senior in time of consecration should remain while another see should be found for the other.

Clearly, the quarrel did not reflect disagreements on theology. It was the product of personal feuds over official posts in the Church, fueled by the prospect of lavish support from the emperor. With his well-meaning generosity, Constantine had opened a can of worms.

When he received Miltiades' report on the verdict of the synod, he thought with relief that the matter was closed. He was at the time embroiled in the dispute with Licinius over the conspiracy and he could not be bothered with the feud of small-minded clerics. But the Donatists were not prepared to accept the verdict and give up. In a petition to the emperor, they asked that he, himself, study the record and decide.

Constantine Steps
in Personally

With understandable anger, Constantine denounced the "rabid and implacable hatreds of the obstinate bishops" and at first refused to consider their petition. But the fear that the Supreme Deity might be displeased by his refusal to take action made him change his mind. In his letter asking Caecilianus to come back to Italy, he wrote that he wanted the matter settled "lest in the future, under the great glory of our God, things may be done by them, which may excite the greatest anger of the heavenly Provicence (*ne ulterius sub tanta claritate Dei nostri ea ab ipsis fiant, quae maximam iracundiam coelestis providentiae possiut incitare.*)

At the same time, he wrote to the Donatists. His letter vividly reflects his annoyance.

> "Since I know that some of your group are quarrel-some and pay little regard to a correct verdict and to the simple truth, and that it may perhaps come about that if the case is tried in your location the affair will not be terminated as it should and as the truth demands and through your excessive obstinacy something may occur which could both displease the

heavenly divinity and reflect badly on my reputation which I always wish to preserve unsullied, I have decided that Caecilianus should come here and I believe that in deference to my letter he will arrive shortly. I promise you that if in his presence you can prove anything on one single charge I shall regard this as if every accusation which you bring against him has been proven. May the Almighty God grant peace everlasting. (*Deus omnipotens perpetuam tribuat securitatem*).

The Donatists—pleased by Constantine's willingness to reopen the case and even to decide against Caecilianus even if only one charge were proven—came to Italy, ready to present their case to the emperor. But for reasons unknown, Caecilianus did not come. The Donatists, claiming that the case had gone against him by default, prepared to leave and go back to their sees in Africa. Constantine, who was in Mediolanum at the time and had not issued a decision on the dispute, was angered by this and ordered them arrested and brought to Mediolanum. When finally Caecilianus arrived, Constantine decided against trying the case. Instead he had Caecilianus, too, arrested and incarcerated at Brescia. Then, he sent two Italian bishops, Eunomius and Olympius, to Carthage with orders to consecrate a new, third, bishop for the city, to supersede the two rivals.

This merely added fuel to the fire. The Donatist followers staged violent riots and refused to accept the third bishop. When Eunomius and Olympius tried to point out to their leaders that a synod of nineteen bishops in Rome had decided the issue and that their decision was sacred, the Donatist partisans retorted that if the decision of nineteen bishops was sacred then the decision of the seventy Numidian bishops was more sacred. When Constantine received the report on the riots he ordered Domitius Celsus, the deputy prefect, to investigate the riots and punish the culprits. This action provoked more disturbances, and the victims of the repressive measures were acclaimed by the Donatists as "martyrs." The situation was getting out of hand largely because Constantine's hesitant policy had encouraged the Donatists.

ARBITER OF THE FAITH

O nce again reversing course, Constantine wrote a letter to Domitius Celsus ordering him to stop any action against the Donatists and at the same time to tell both parties that "with the favor of the divine piety (*pietate divina*), I shall come to Africa to most fully show what kind of veneration is to be rendered to the Highest Divinity and what sort of worship appears to please God...And since no one can gain the blessings of a martyr from this kind of people who seem to be alienated and divorced from the truth of religion, I shall without hesitation cause those I shall judge hostile to the divine law and the religion itself, and shall find guilty of violence against the proper worship (*competentis venerationis*), to pay the penalty which their mad and reckless obstinacy deserves. I am going to make plain to them what kind of worship is to be offered to the Divinity." Then, he boldly concluded:

> "There is no higher responsibility for me by virtue of my imperial office than to dispel errors and repress all rash thoughts so as to cause all to offer to the Almighty God true religion, honest concord, and proper worship."

In this remarkable passage, Constantine proclaims forcefully that as the emperor he is the supreme and final arbiter of what the "proper worship" should be.

Constantine, of course, did not go to Africa to resolve the dispute. He had more serious problems to face with Licinius. The two bishops, their mission a complete failure, left Carthage, declaring that Caecilianus was the only legitimate bishop.

Constantine was utterly disgusted by the whole affair. He had to deal with those petty feuds at a time when he had more pressing matters on his mind. His quarrel with Licinius was getting worse. Preparing for war, Constantine traveled to Augusta Treverorum (Treves) to mobilize troops for the upcoming fight. For some reason, he took with him the Donatist bishops, except for Donatus who was left in Mediolanum.

With the emperor in distant Gaul, Caecilianus and Donatus, who evidently were not heavily guarded, escaped and went back to Carthage where they resumed their feud with their familiar intensity.

THINKING OF
ANOTHER SYNOD

With all his other troubles, Constantine found the time, probably at the prodding of Osius, to decide on calling another synod, in the hope that a new, larger gathering of prelates from all his domain might put an end to the schism and "avert the heavenly wrath."

On February 26, 314, he released the Donatist clerics he had dragged with him to Treves and authorized the use of public transportation for their return to Africa. They were told that before long another synod would take up their claims. Somehow, Constantine was unwilling to brush the Donatists aside.

Before he left for his war with Licinius, Constantine took the time to set the stage for a second synod. With a forbearance unusual for a Roman emperor facing unyielding and unreasoning opposition, he called for a large gathering of bishops. But his frustration with the feuding bishops can be clearly seen in his letter to Aelianus, the proconsul of Africa. Constantine began by saying that he had fully expected to have the dispute ended with the verdict issued by Miltiades and his synod of bishops. He expected their decision to receive universal respect. But the enemies of Caecilianus remained as obstinate and dogged as ever, declaring that Miltiades and the other bishops had closeted themselves in a room and judged the case according to their personal wishes. They had clamored for another synod. He would give it to them.

The new synod would meet at Arelate (Arles). Aelianus was asked to see that the public posting service throughout Africa and Mauretania was placed at the disposal of Caecilianus and his party and of Donatus and his party and that they travel to Arles as soon as possible through Spain. He spoke of Donatus as the leader of the party although the rival bishop of Carthage was Majorinus. Donatus had been the leading personality because Majorinus was old and frail. He was to die the following year, to be replaced by Donatus. Later he was succeeded by another Donatus, a man of charismatic personality who eventually was given the appellation "magnus."

Constantine further instructed the proconsul to provide the bishops with imperial letters entitling them to public assistance during the journey (*tractorias litteras*) so that they might arrive at Arles by the first of August (314 A.D.). Revealing of his attitude toward the Christian clerics is his instruction to Aelianus to tell the bishops that "before they leave their diocese, they make the necessary arrangements whereby, during their absence, reasonable discipline may be preserved and no rebellion against authority or individual quarrels take place, because such actions bring the Church into great disgrace." He then expressed the hope that "when all those who are known to hold opposing views meet together in person, the quarrel may come to its natural and timely conclusion."

The closing paragraphs give us an intimate glimpse into Constantine's thinking.

> "For as I am well assured that you are a worshipper of
> the Supreme God, I confess to your Excellency that I
> consider it by no means lawful for me to ignore dis-
> putes and quarrels of such a nature as may incite the
> Supreme Divinity to wrath, not only against the

human race but against myself personally into whose charge the divinity by its Divine Will has committed the governance of all that is on earth. In its just indignation, it might decree some ill against me."

This is not the first time Constantine speaks of his fear that the "Supreme Divinity" may turn against him. But the passage is interesting for another reason. It introduces the notion of royal authority "by the grace of God," a notion which came down to our own days.

The next paragraph is no less significant. It shows Constantine's ambition to bring the entire human race into the "all embracing (Catholic) Church."

"I can only feel really and absolutely secure, and hope for an unfailing supply of all the richest blessings that flow from the instant goodness of Almighty God, when I shall see all mankind worshipping the most Holy God in brotherly unity of worship in the rites of the Catholic religion (*cum universos sensero debito cultu Catholiqae religionis sanctissimum Deum concordi observantiae fraternitate venerari.*)

Constantine found the time to address personal letters to all the bishops he wanted to come to Arles. Eusebius has preserved one of them addressed to Christos, bishop of Syracuse. In the letter, the Emperor instructs the bishop to reach Arles by the first of August and to ask Latronianus, the governor of Sicily, to provide him with a public vehicle. He even prescribes that Christos should bring with him two presbyters of the second rank and three personal servants. Constantine's attention to detail is all the more remarkable since at the time he was writing those letters he was actively engaged in the military campaign against Licinius.

THE SYNOD AT ARLES

The bishops came to Arles by the appointed day. Arles was one of the imperial cities, impressive with its large amphitheater and the imperial palace on the banks of the river Rhodanus (Rohn). We have no record of all those who attended. Later estimates bring the total to three or five hundred. The canons which were approved by the synod bear the names of thirty-three bishops, thirteen presbyters, twenty-three deacons, two readers, seven exorcists, and four representatives of the bishop of Rome, Sylvester, who had succeeded Miltiades upon his death. This was a synod of western prelates. Not a single bishop from the eastern part of the empire attended.

The synod examined with great care all the points raised by the Donatists but it is clear from the report sent to Sylvester that the Donatists presented no more convincing evidence against Caecilianus than what they had brought to Rome the year before. The synod heard the charge that during the years of the persecution, Caecilianus, a deacon at the time, had prevented the members of the Church in Carthage from giving help to their fellow Christians who were languishing in prison. The Donatists could offer no proof beyond unsubstantiated gossip. The old charge that Felix of Aptunga was a *traditor* and that he could not have consecrated Caecilianus was again reviewed and rejected as inaccurate. In a word, the synod at Arles endorsed the verdict of the synod of Rome. In the letter sent to Sylvester, the bishops assured him that "had he found it possible to join them, a more severe sentence would have been passed" on those "desperate men who have wrought grave injury to our law and our traditions."

They had been called by Constantine to resolve the Donatist controversy and with their damning decision they had done so. But such a wide gathering, "coming from diverse provinces," was a rare and valuable opportunity for taking up other Church matters. And so they did. In their letter to Sylvester, they presented twenty-two "canons" they had approved and which they transmitted to the bishop of Rome saying that because his diocese was wider than that of any other bishop, he was the most suitable to press their acceptance by the Church. It was a subtle recognition that the bishop of Rome occupied a special place in the firmament of the Church hierarchy.

One of the canons addressed a practical problem. In those days, Easter was celebrated at different times in the various parts of the empire. The synod recommended that Easter be celebrated on the same day throughout the whole word. Other canons dealt with problems facing them. One provided that the clergy should reside in the places to which they were ordained, another that soldiers deserting in times of peace be threatened with excommunication. Worthy of note is also the canon which decreed as unacceptable to the Church individuals connected with the arena or the stage such as charioteers, actors, or mimes.

Another canon decreed excommunication of clergy practicing usury. No canon on celibacy was included; only an exhortation that clerics who divorced their wives for being unfaithful should not marry again as they were entitled to do as long as the guilty partner was alive.

A New Petition

If the synod of Arles was quite productive in passing new rules designed to improve ecclesiastical discipline, it failed in its primary mission, that of putting an end to the Donatist schism. The Donatists refused to give up the fight and had the effrontery to ask Constantine for yet another investigation. The bishops of the West, they said, were prejudiced against them and their verdict was not impartial and fair. They wanted the emperor himself, "in his benevolence," to take over the case himself.

In the letter Constantine wrote to the bishops at Arles thanking them for their work, his anger for the new petition of the Donatists is quite evident. The letter is worthy of note for another reason. For the first time Constantine refers to Christ by name.

> "Certainly I cannot describe or enumerate the blessings which God in His heavenly bounty has bestowed upon me, His servant. I rejoice exceedingly, therefore, that after this most just inquiry, you have recalled to better hope and future those whom the malignity of the Devil seemed to have seduced away by his miserable persuasion from the clearest light of the Catholic law. Oh, truly conquering providence of Christ, our Savior, solicitous even for those who have deserted

and turned their weapons against the truth...I hoped, most holy brethren, to find a [benign] disposition to the stubbornest breasts...Now they clamor for a judgment from me who myself await the judgment of Christ (*meum judicium postulant qui judicium Christi expecto.*) For I say that, as far as the truth is concerned, a judgment delivered by priests ought to be considered as valid as though Christ Himself were present and delivering judgment. For priests can form no thought and judgment, except what they are told to say by the admonitory voice of Christ.

What then, can these malignant creatures be thinking of, creatures of the Devil, as I have truly said?"

These were harsh words. Yet, before long he changed his mind again and acceded to the Donatist demand for a rehearing. Did they have friends in high places, possibly among the members of the imperial family? We have no record. We can only marvel at their refusal to be intimidated by the emperor's wrath.

After hearing the case all over again, Constantine issued his decision on November 16, 316. He reaffirmed the innocence of Caecilianus and condemned his accusers. In a letter written to Eumalius, one of his vicars, Constantine wrote: "I saw in Caecilianus a man of spotless innocence, one who observed the proper duties of religion and served it as he ought..." The publication of the emperor's verdict was followed by an edict prescribing penalties against the schismatics. Three years after the Edict of Milan had proclaimed freedom of religion to all, Constantine was resorting to the force of state authority to suppress disunity within the Church. As in the days of the persecution, Church buildings were confiscated and schismatics were subjected to fines.

Yet, the Donatists did not give up. People who had faced the threat of torture and death less than two decades before were not intimidated by such a mild punishment as the confiscation of property. Four years later, in 320, we again find Constantine struggling with the problem. Since repression had failed to bring the schismatics back to the Catholic Church, Constantine decided to try gentle persuasion. In a letter to them after enumerating his repeated efforts to restore unity to the Church, he went on: "We must hope, therefore, that Almighty God may show pity and gentleness to his people, as this schism is the work of a few. For it is to God that we should look for remedy...Let there be no paying back injury with injury; for it is only the fool who takes into his usurping hands the vengeance which he ought to reserve for God...If you observe my will, you will speedily find that thanks to the Supreme Power, the designs of the presumptuous standard-bearers of this wretched faction will languish, and all men...by the grace of penitence, may correct their errors and be restored to eternal life."

Constantine's leniency and toleration proved just as futile as his more forceful measures. Donatus, the so called Magnus, who had been elected bishop of Carthage by the Donatist party, ruled the schismatics with an iron hand but he also won their unwavering devotion. A man of extraordinary personal gifts, eloquent, with an irreproachable private life, he dominated the scene for years. After 320, Constantine apparently paid no more attention to the Church in Africa. The Donatist schism remained strong for almost a century, long after the protagonists had passed from the scene.

CHAPTER X

YEARS OF PEACE

CELEBRATING THE
DECENNALIA

At the time the western bishops were holding their synod at Arles, Constantine was successfully concluding his campaign against Licinius. After the agreement which gave him Upper Moesia, Pannonia, Macedonia and the Greek peninsula, Constantine went to Sirmium (Mitrovica) to spend the winter months in the palace there. This was for him a familiar territory with many memories from his childhood. Naissus, the place where he was born, was not far to the south, and Salonae where his father lived as governor of Dalmatia, not far to the west.

But Sirmium was convenient for another reason. It was located in the heart of the new territories Constantine had won. From that vantage location, he could visit easily every part and organize the administration of his new lands in his methodical fashion.

He stayed there until the following summer when in early July he left for Rome to celebrate his tenth anniversary in the purple. Only ten years before, in July 305, Constantine had been acclaimed Augustus in Eboracum, in the British Isles, upon the death of his father. It must have seemed that this was a long time ago because so much had happened in those years.

This was Constantine's first visit to Rome since his victory against Maxentius three and a half years earlier. In those years, Constantine had spent his time in Mediolanum, in Augusta Treverorum (Treves), in Arelate, and most recently in Sirmium. Those were traditionally imperial cities, in locations suitable for overseeing the governing of the frontier provinces. But Rome was always the eternal city, the symbol of the empire.

For a whole month, the Senate organized triumphal celebrations to flatter the victorious emperor. True, many senators harbored secret resentments against the new men, mostly Christians, Constantine had added to the senatorial ranks. For the scions of old, pagan, aristocratic families, the changes Constantine was bringing to their world could not be happily accepted. But they had learned through long experience that was not prudent to reveal such thoughts to a powerful emperor. Already the Senate at the beginning of the year, at Constantine's suggestion no doubt, had elected Constantine and Licinius consuls for the year 315. The office was honorary but it carried great symbolic value, and under the circumstances it was a telling gesture of reconciliation and friendship.

The arch that the Senate had decided to build and dedicate to Constantine three years before was now completed and inaugurated in a grand ceremony on July 21. (It still stands today in Rome.)

Constantine accepted all the honors bestowed on him, but refused to make the traditional sacrifices to the pagan gods. Instead, as Eusebius tells us, he "ordered general celebrations, and offered prayers of thanksgiving to God the King of All, as sacrifices without flame and smoke." Still, he did not give up his title of Pontifex Maximus and the control it gave him over appointments of pagan priests. And, of course, faithful to the Edict of Milan, he did not forbid pagan sacrifices.

One month later, on August 20, he appointed one of the most respected pagan aristocrats, the aged Vettius Rufinus, to be prefect of Rome. Rufinus was a high priest of the Sun cult and also a priest at the temple of Mars on the Palatine Hill, but evidently Constantine wanted to show to the patrician pagans that he did not allow religious dfferences to interfere with affairs of state and that he expected them to do the same. But times were changing rapidily. The ancient world was slowly giving was to a new. Constantine was creating a new aristocracy, men beholden directly to him, and he was supporting a religion that until then the majority of people had rejected.

"Blessed Tranquillity"

C onstantine did not stay long in Rome after the celebration of
his *decennalia*. In the fall, he left again for Gaul where he spent
nearly a year in his favorite preoccupation, strengthening the
frontier fortifications, reinforcing city walls, constructing highways,
governing his empire, and from time to time trying to bring unity to
the feuding Christian factions of Carthage.

To underline his hope that the empire had entered an era of "blessed
tranquillity," Constantine removed from his coins the emblems of war
and spoke of peace. And it was to be peace until the summer of 323.

The effect of Osius' Christian teaching on Constantine can be seen
in some of the laws he issued during those years of "blessed tranquillity." In 319 a law banned the killing of slaves by their masters for
whatever reason, and a year later another law prohibited prison war-
dens from mistreating the prisoners in their charge, or for branding
convicts on the face "which is formed in the image of celestial beauty." Another celebrated law was that of 7 March 321, which established Sunday as the official day of rest. Since the days of Saint Paul,
Christians had gradually replaced the Jewish Sabbath as their day of
rest with the day of the Lord, the day they believed Christ had risen.

Still, in all the humane legislation he issued in those years we
cannot find anywhere the name of Christ mentioned. The Christian
religion was favored by the emperor to be sure but it was yet to

become the official religion of the Roman state.

Relations between Constantine and Licinius continued to be friendly, at least on the surface, as shown by the consulships for the years 318 and 319. In 318 the Roman Senate elected Licinius consul for the fifth time and Crispus for the first. The following year Constantine was elected consul for the fifth time and the infant Licinianus for the first. Considering that Constantine controlled the Senate, the selection of consuls had his approval.

In the following two years, Licinius seems to have been pointedly ignored. In 320 Constantine was elected consul for the sixth time together with his little boy, Constantine the Second. The following year, little boy Constantine was elected consul for the second time and so was Crispus.

The selection of consuls was not the only sign that something was not right in Constantine's relations with Licinius. In late 317, Constantine moved the seat of his administration from Sirmium to Serdica (today's Sofia in Bulgaria). Sirmium certainly made sense, especially in the two years after the agreement with Licinius. But Serdica was much too far from Gaul, Italy, Spain or Africa to serve as a central seat for the governing of the empire. To show that the transfer was not just for a short time, Constantine ordered his architects to expand the old palace of Galerius as if Serdica was to be his permanent capital. It was inevitable that Licinius would see Constantine's move as a prelude to renewed conflict.

Eusebius, both in the *Life of Constantine* and in his *Ecclesiastical History*, claims that Constantine turned against Licinius because the emperor of the East was mistreating the Christians in his domain. Licinius was not particularly interested in the Christian religion but neither was he hostile to the Christians because of their religion. Eusebius, the bishop of Nicomedia, (not the writer who is Eusebius of Caesaria), was a frequent guest at the palace and a personal friend of Augusta Constantia, Licinius' wife and Constantine's half-sister. A schism in the church of Egypt, led by Arius (we are going to see much of him later) and another by Meletius were treated by Licinius more like a nuisance than as a danger to his throne. He even allowed a synod by the churches of Asia Minor, the Orient, and Egypt to meet in Nicomedia, and decide what to do with the Arian "heresy."

Some of his decisions affecting Christians were probably seen as anti-Christian even though his motives may have been purely political. One edict, which Eusebius saw as a product of Licinius' "nature which was debased by sensuality," provided that men and women should not attend the Christian houses of prayer together, and that women should be instructed on religious matters only by women. With another law he ordered the congregations of the faithful to be held outside of the gates in the open. Eusebius argues that Licinius passed those laws because he could not accept that men and women could be virtuous. But it is quite possible that he was beginning to see the Christians as a potential "Fifth Column" inside his domain, a political force which favored his brother-in-law and could be a source of trouble in case matters boiled to an armed conflict.

We do have some evidence that, as relations with Constantine worsened, Licinius ordered the arrest of some bishops and tore down some churches. It may also be true that he sent one or two bishops to their death. But these actions were not inspired by religious opposition to Christianity in the way Galerius' persecution of the Christians had been. Licinius was most likely punishing with imprisonment or fines individuals who happened to be Christians but whose real crime was that they had spoken much too loudly in favor of Constantine or, worse, were suspected of secretly conspiring against Licinius.

Constantine on his part may have used Licinius' actions as a propaganda tool, but his real reason for preparing for a final conflict with Licinius was that he wanted to bring both halves of the Roman empire under his command.

PART III

CONSTANTINE, SOLE EMPEROR

CHAPTER XI

THE FINAL CONFRONTATION

CRISPUS IS HONORED

In the summer of 320, Constantine invited his son Crispus to visit Serdica and celebrate his fifth anniversary as Caesar. In the five years Crispus had served in Gaul, he had distinguished himself as a soldier and administrator. In the winter of 320, he had won a splendid victory against the Franks under great odds.

At the festivities held in celebration of the anniversary, panegyrist Nazarius, with the traditional hyperbole to be sure, spoke of Crispus "filling his young years with triumphant glories. Already the most Noble Caesar," he went on, "enjoys the respect of his father and all of his brethren, and presents himself before us as deserving the admiration of all. In this last cruel winter, with its fierce frost, he marched with incredible speed over vast distances, deep in snow to win a great victory. Is not thy breast filled with joy, oh Great Constantine, melting to see thy son after so long a time—and to see him a conqueror?"

Crispus had evidently done well, like his father and grandfather before him. He had followed their footsteps in another area, as well. He, too, had fallen in love with a young maiden of humble origin. Her name was Helena like that of his beloved grandmother. In 322, she gave birth to a baby boy. Constantine was evidently so happy that he ordered the release of prisoners to mark the occasion. Only "murderers, poisoners, magicians, and adulterers were excepted in keeping with an ancient ruling of the Twelve Tablets." (After the tragic events of 326, both Helena and her boy disappear into the shadows of history.)

PREPARATIONS FOR WAR

Father and son must have discussed the forthcoming clash with Licinius because Crispus, after a short visit back to Gaul, returned in the summer of 322 to be with his father. For several months, Constantine had been widening and deepening the makeshift harbor in Thessaloniki while his local administrators in the West were scouring every harbor, looking for ships capable of transporting troops and supplies. At the same time, the shipyards under Constantine's command were building fighting ships. By chartering, seizing and building ships, Constantine had gradually assembled by the summer of 323 some two hundred thirty-oared warships and two thousand transport barges. It was an impressive fleet but not as strong as that of Licinius who had over 350 larger and more dangerous triremes under the command of Avantos, his *Dux* of the Fleet.

The final confrontation started in a rather indirect fashion. In the autumn of 322, Rausimond, the king of the Sarmatians, crossed with his men the Danube into Moesia and spread havoc, destroying villages and taking many prisoners for ransom or sale into slavery.

Constantine with Crispus at his side marched against the invaders and, after a series of bloody clashes, they drove them away beyond the Danube. Constantine's troops continued the pursuit, crossed the river and attacked the fleeing Sarmatians. In a pitched battle, Rausimond himself was killed and his men were forced to free their prisoners and to sue for peace. The Sarmatians that were taken prisoner were, according to Zosimus, "distributed to the various towns." Constantine and Crispus returned to Thessaloniki and before long coins were struck for both the Augustus and the young Caesar with the inscription "Sarmatia Conquered." Evidently pleased with his son's performance, Constantine appointed Crispus *Dux* of the Fleet although we have no record showing that he had been trained in seamanship.

Some of Constantine's ancient critics claimed that the invasion of the Sarmatians, was engineered by him to find an excuse to start a war with Licinius. It is true that, as he was pursuing the Sarmatians, Constantine and his troops entered briefly lands which belonged to Licinius. But most of the fighting took place in the territories that belonged to Constantine so it is hard to see how the invasion was deliberately provoked or whether it was useful at all in providing an excuse for a clash with Licinius.

It may be that Licinius, too, was contemplating a war, probably to recover the territories he had lost to Constantine eight years before. Be that as it may, we know that he complained strongly to Constantine that he had violated their agreement and had entered territories which did not belong to him. Constantine in his response claimed that the incursion into the Licinius' lands was accidental, but even if it were not in every instance, it was certainly necessary to rescue people captured by the barbarians. The explanations should have ended the matter there. But Licinius rejected Constantine's justification and insisted that the incursion was a probing attack, for a full-scale invasion. Already he had dispatched messengers to the territories under his rule with orders to provide fighting ships and foot soldiers and horsemen. "Without delay, Egypt sent eighty triremes, the Phoenicians an equal number, the Ionians and Dorians in Asia sixty, the Cypriots thirty, and the Kares twenty, the Bithynians thirty and the Libyans fifty, while the infantry was around one hundred and fifty thousand and the cavalry fifteen thousand, mostly from Cappadocia and Phrygia."

A few weeks after the end of the Sarmatian invasion, Licinius moved a large force to Hadrianopolis, evidently as a defensive measure. The army camped there waiting to see what Constantine would do next. Constantine did not take action. He was still recruiting and strengthening his army. During the winter months, he brought together a force of some 120,000 foot soldiers and 10,000 horsemen. Now, he was ready.

A Decisive Clash

Crispus sailed in the spring of 323, southward from Thessaloniki in command of the fleet to rendezvous with the supply ships sailing from the port of Piraeus. Then, in the last week of June, Constantine's army crossed the frontier on the way to Hadrianopolis. Licinius had deployed his army in a strong defensive position on a hillside, just outside of the city.

Constantine's army, with the *labarum* held high by a standard-bearer protected by a detachment of horsemen, came to the west of the city of Hadrianopolis and camped near the banks of the river Evros (Maritsa). For a few days, the two armies faced each other without launching at attack.

At this point, we may let Zosimus tell the story. "Constantine realizing that the river was narrow at one point, this is what he thought up (μηχαναται). He ordered his soldiers to bring logs down from the surrounding hills, and to weave ropes as though he planned to forge (ζευγνηται) the river and move his forces across. Having thus deceived the enemy, he moved five thousand foot soldiers and a number of horsemen to a hill, thickly wooded and capable of concealing them. Then he took horsemen with him and crossed the river at one point where the river was passable (διαβατος) and fell unexpectedly on the enemy soldiers, slaying some, causing others to flee hastily, while others were standing there dazed by the unexpected crossing (κεχηνωτες επι τω της διαβασεως αδοκητον). Having thus established this bridgehead, he had the rest of the horsemen and his entire army cross the river."

Zosimus asserts that more than 34,000 of Licinius' men perished in the fierce battle that followed. The date was July 3, 323.

The savage fighting lasted the whole day. In the end, Constantine's army beat the enemy down. It is said that the fighting was so violent that at one difficult moment Constantine himself joined the fighting, moving close enough to the enemy to be wounded in the thigh by a spear. He managed to stay on his horse and fight on, inspiring his soldiers with greater determination.

Licinius fought just as valiantly. Many thousands of his soldiers were dead, and many more had deserted, before he decided to order retreat. During the night, he marched through Thrace "with those soldiers still with him" to reach his navy which was stationed at the point where the Hellespont meets with the Propontis (the Sea of Marmara).

"The next day after daybreak, all those of Licinius' men who were fleeing toward the mountains or the ravines, as well as those left on the field after Licinius' flight, surrendered to Constantine." Zosimus leaves no doubt that Licinius had suffered a serious defeat. But the war was not over. Licinius still had a large force and a fleet to prevent Constantine and his army from crossing to the Asiatic shore.

As in the past, the town of Byzantium held the key. And to Byzantium, Licinius went.

Constantine took two major steps. He moved with his army to lay siege to Byzantium. And he ordered his fleet to sail to the mouth of the Hellespont. At this point, Licinius' commander of the fleet, Avantos, missed the opportunity to destroy Crispus' thirty-oared boats with his superior triremes, by not moving out of the Straits of the Hellespont into the Aegean where his fighting ships would have ample room to maneuver. Instead, he remained in the narrow waterway where his ships could hardly move.

In a daring decision, Crispus and his naval commanders "chose only eighty thirty-oared boats, the best in the fleet, with men who knew how to fight at sea, and moved up into the Straits toward the Propontis. Licinius' admiral Avantos, highly contemptuous of the small number of the enemy ships, sailed [into the Straits] with two hundred ships of his own, thinking that he could easily overpower them. They raised their flags and signals and started moving against each other. Constantine's admirals sailing in good order attacked the enemy, but Avantos' ships moving with no order at all against their opponents, entangled with each other, hitting each other being so many, allowing their enemies to sink them and to cause every kind of damage, with many sailors and soldiers falling into the sea. With the arrival of the evening darkness, the sea battle came to an end. Constantine's ships docked in the Thracian port of Eleounda, while those of Avantos entered the port of Aeantion."

The next day, Constantine's entire fleet began to move toward the Sea of Marmara. Avantos had come out of the port of Aeantion thinking of engaging the enemy anew but when he saw the large number of Crispus' ships he changed his mind. To his misfortune, "a strong south wind forced many of his remaining ships to run aground or to capsize with all men on board so that he lost five thousand men and one hundred and thirty ships." Avantos escaped to the Asiatic shore with only four boats.

With the way now open, Crispus sailed with his entire navy through the Sea of Marmara toward Byzantium to join from the sea his father's forces besieging the strategic town from the land.

Licinius' position was hopeless but he refused to give up the fight. Constantine ordered his soldiers to build earthworks as high as the walls of the town and then to construct at the top of each mound wooden towers even higher than the walls. From their vantage positions, his soldiers were now able to attack with their arrows the defending soldiers. Then he brought rams and other machines, determined to take the town.

At last Licinius realized with dismay that he was doomed if he stayed on. Leaving behind a small force, he managed to escape from Byzantium and to go with a few trusted associates to the town of Chrysopolis, on the Asiatic side, hoping to gather a new army and resume the fight. In a desperate gesture of defiance, he declared that Constantine was no longer emperor and that he had elevated to the rank of Caesar his Magister Officiorum (the chief of the civil service) Marcus Martinianus. Nine years before, Licinius had played the same trick when he elevated Valens to the purple only to have him executed. One may wonder how Martinianus was persuaded to accept the unlucky title. In any event, Licinius' grandiose proclamation was an empty gesture which could only anger Constantine and his men.

THE END OF LICINIUS

S till believing that the war was not lost, Licinius sent
Martinianus to Lampsakos, on the southern shore of the
Hellespont, to bloc the passage of any of Constantine's forces
from the European to the Asiatic coast. Licinius himself deployed
whatever forces he had left on the hills and the ravines around
Chrysopolis.

Constantine was now confident of victory to the point that he
found time to celebrate Victory Games in honor of young Crispus. He
had a large number of ships and barges, and could have moved
directly to land in the vicinity of Chrysopolis, but the shore was very
rugged (δυσπρόσοδον) for the transfer of horses and cargo from the
boats to the shore. So, he moved a few miles away, until he found a
more accessible coast, and landed with his troops, his supplies and
his military machines. For the first time since he had left hastily,
almost twenty years ago, from the court of Galerius, Constantine was
back on the Asiatic side of the straits.

With understandable dismay, Licinius saw Constantine's army
taking positions on the hills in the vicinity of Chrysopolis. But he was
still determined to fight. He summoned Martinianus with the forces
under his command, and with valiant words to raise the morale of his
troops, he organized them for battle. It was a gesture of desperation.

Eusebius in his *Life of Constantine* gives a rather graphic description of Constantine's preparation for the coming battle. We may discount the divine intervention, but it will not be inaccurate to say that Constantine believed in it. If he did not, then he was a superb showman because he certainly spoke to his men with the holy conviction of a man who had heard the voice of God. Here is Eusebius' story:

> "He pitched his tent with the sign of the cross at a distance from the camp, and there he passed his time in a pure and holy way, offering prayers to God...He always acted in this way when he was meditating on the battle with an enemy...And praying thus continually to God, he was always soon visited by some token of His presence. And then, as if thrust into it by a divine command, he would suddenly rush out of his tent and give orders to his army to move at once, with drawn swords. When this happened, they would immediately launch the attack, fighting so fiercely as to win victory with incredible speed."

This is what Constantine did outside of Chrysopolis, according to Eusebius. The battle was fierce. Evidently Licinius made things easier for Constantine by coming out of the town to fight in the open, because none of the ancient chroniclers speaks of a siege.

According to Zosimus, only thirty thousand survived. Byzantium and Chalcydon opened their gates to Constantine's forces while Licinius with a few thousand foot soldiers and horsemen retreated to Nicomedia, his capital.

It seems that he was still prepared to fight but his wife, the Augusta Constantia who was in Nicomedia, persuaded him "in the course of a single night" that the war was lost. The next day she went to her stepbrother and implored him to spare her husband's life. Constantia was Constantine's favorite stepsister and for her sake he agreed. That same day, Constantia, Licinius and Constantine dined together. Licinius' reign was over and all his lands now belonged to Constantine. The grandson of a humble innkeeper from Naissus was now the sole master of the Roman Empire, from the British Isles to Egypt, from the Balkans to Mauretania.

The hapless Martinianus was "delivered to the spear-holders to die." Licinius was sent under guard to Thessaloniki where he remained under house arrest. Constantia with little Licinianus remained in Nicomedia as members of Constantine's imperial household.

A year later, "breaking his oath, as it was usual for him," to quote Zosimus, Constantine ordered the hanging of Licinius.

CHAPTER XII

THE ARIAN CONTROVERSY

GOD'S CHOSEN
INSTRUMENT

As soon as Constantine settled in the palace of Nicomedia, which he knew so well since the years he had spent in the service of Diocletian, he ordered in a proclamation the release of all Christians who were in prison or exiled to barren islands in the Aegean (a form of punishment which survived to this Century), and the return of any church or private properties that had been confiscated under Licinius.

In the proclamation which he sent to all the provinces announcing the measures (in Greek and in Latin), Constantine made a rather extravagant claim. Here is what he said:

> "Constantine, Victor, Supreme Augustus to the people of the Province of [the name of the province]. It has long been obvious to everyone that blessings are reserved for the Christians, while persecution of them leads to nothing but misery. Many a time, armies have been slaughtered or put to flight...and the perpetrators of those impieties have either met disastrous deaths of extreme suffering, or dragged out a pitiful

existence...What relief has the Supreme God devised? I myself am the instrument he chose..."

Constantine was now considering himself to be God's chosen instrument to guide the future of mankind. After all he had accomplished with the help of the Christian God, as he evidently believed, it was not difficult for him to take the next step and claim that he was the man God had chosen to secure the good life for all his people.

Such beliefs may turn a man to dangerous arrogance.

ENTER ARIUS

Constantine had washed his hands of the Donatists a long time ago. Their feud had nothing to do with profound issues of theology and still he had been unable to bring unity to the African churches. Now, as the new ruler of all the Roman lands in Asia and Egypt, he discovered that he was faced with an even more troublesome dispute, a dispute which centered on the most profound questions over the nature of God and that of his Son.

Disputes over the divine nature of Christ could be traced to the bishop of Samosata, Paul, more than half a century earlier. A flamboyant bishop with a scandalous personal life, Paul preached that Christ was not God because there was "only one God, the creator of all that exist in heaven and earth." Paul was eventually expelled but his ideas did not die. The Christian beliefs could not be easily reconciled with the logic the Greeks wanted to use to explain what could only be accepted on faith.

The ideas of Paul of Samosata were revived by Lucian, a priest in Antioch, who had known Paul and his teachings. Lucian was the head of a school supported by the partisans of Paul. Among the students were promising young Christians hoping to enter the church hierarchy, among them Arius, Eusebius (who later became bishop of Nicomedia and a friend of Augusta Constantia), Maris and Theognis, who later became bishops.

Lucian did not go as far as Paul of Samosata had done in his teachings. He taught that Christ was a heavenly Being, created by God, the Father, before all visible and invisible creatures. But he had not existed from all eternity since he was the Son of the Father. Before he was created by the Father, Christ the Son of God did not exist. This doctrine was less offensive than that of Paul of Samosata, and for a period of time had attracted little notice. But when one of his students, Arius, took up the torch after Lucian's death as a Christian martyr in the persecution, these ideas caused a tremendous upheaval in the Church especially in the East.

By 313, Arius was a priest in one of the local churches in Alexandria, known as Baucalis. His eloquence, regal bearing and austere personal life had begun to attract a large following. He was a tall, slender man, with magnetic eyes, always dressed in a simple white sleeveless tunic. Alexandria, the great center of learning with its long tradition of Greek thought, was precisely the place to welcome a theology based on pure reason.

Arius was very popular among the faithful to the point that at the death of bishop Achillas in 313, he was one of the candidates to succeed him as bishop of Alexandria. He was passed over in favor of another candidate by the name of Alexander but this did not cause any personal friction between the two. The trouble started two or three years later. Arius was becoming increasingly bold in his sermons, openly denying the godly nature of Christ. Alexander could not close his eyes to this blasphemy. The teachings of Lucian had been only those of a school; Arius, however, was preaching from the pulpit in the name of the Church.

At two private meetings, Bishop Alexander tried to persuade Arius to stop preaching his heretical views from the pulpit. Arius responded with the argument that what he was preaching was supported by logic and was bringing many more people to the Church. Alexander pointed out that to deny the godly nature of Christ was a negation of a most sacred tenet of the Christian faith. Arius did not yield. Undaunted he went on with his preaching.

Alexander had to take more drastic action. He summoned a provincial synod of a hundred Egyptian and Libyan bishops to judge the doctrines and the person of Arius. With several of his most prominent supporters, Arius appeared before the synod and boldly stood his ground.

What was the heart of the argument? Arius pointed out that if we speak of a Father and a Son, then we must assume that the Father was not always Father and that the Son did not always exist. And that since the nature, the substance of God cannot be divided ($\alpha\delta\iota\alpha\iota\rho\epsilon\tau\circ\varsigma$ $\epsilon\iota$) the Son cannot be of the same substance as the Father. But if the Son was not of the same substance like that of the Father, the Son could not be a true God, and "neither was he the true Word and the true Wisdom, having been created by the Word and the Wisdom which are only God's." Arius conclusion was that Jesus Christ could not be truly a God.

The majority of the assembled bishops listened with horror to Arius expounding what to them were abominable blasphemies, tearing down the very essence of the Christian faith. What Arius was saying made sense as a logical argument, but the Christian doctrines could only be accepted by faith. Logic, in fact, was irrelevant.

When Arius finished, one of the bishops put to him these questions.

"If Christ is a creature, then he must be subject to change like all creatures."

Arius agreed.

"Then if the Word of God, the Son of God, is subject to change, will it be possible for the Word to change, as Satan had changed, from goodness to evil?"

"Yes," came the answer. Arius had gone too far. He had implied that Christ could be evil.

With holy indignation, the assembled bishops excommunicated Arius and his supporters, including two bishops, Secundus of

Ptolemais in the Pentapolis, and Theonas of Marmorica, (both from Libya, Arius' birthplace) and six priests and six deacons. The Arian controversy had begun. A disagreement between a priest and his bishop had become a controversy that before long would engulf the entire Church, especially in the East.

THE DISPUTE DEEPENS

A rius was not a man that could be easily silenced. And he was not alone in his beliefs. Many bishops and other clerics in the East favored his doctrines. One of his fellow students at Lucian's school was now the bishop of Nicomedia, the imperial capital. Eusebius (no relation to the historian Eusebius of Caesaria) was close to the imperial family, especially to Licinius' wife Constantia. Arius, stung by the excommunication, wrote to his old friend:

"To my beloved master, the faithful man of God, the orthodox Eusebius, Arius, who is persecuted unjustly by bishop Alexander, for the sake of the all-conquering faith which you too uphold, sends greetings in the Lord...In view of your inborn love and affection for your brothers in God and his Christ, I must inform you that the bishop is persecuting us, employing every device against us, and has expelled us from the city as atheists because we do not agree with him when he says publicly 'Always God, always the Son. At the same time the Father, at the same time the Son...Not by a single moment does God precede the Son. The Son is of God himself.' And when your brother, Eusebius of Caesaria, and Theodotus and Aulinus and Athanasius and Gregory and Aetius, in fact, all the bishops of the East, declare that God is without beginning pre-existent to the Son, they have become anathema..."

Then Arius turns the tables and calls Alexander a heretic. "We cannot bear to hear the impieties of the heretics even if they threaten us with a thousand deaths. What we say and believe we have taught and still teach: that the son came into being by God's will before all times and ages, and before he was begotten or created, He did not exist...We are persecuted because we say: the Son has a beginning; God is without beginning....Farewell in the Lord, remembering our tribulations, fellow student of Lucian, truly Eusebius [playing with the Greek word *eusevis*, pius.]"

It is difficult for us today to grasp the intensity of feeling caused by those metaphysical arguments. After all, neither side could prove their point, not even by logic. Only on faith could the Christian doctrines be accepted. Yet, these disputes over the profound mysteries of the Church were not limited to learned theologians or philosophers. They had become a daily topic of the ordinary people. Even sailors and dock workers, we are told, and the idle rabble in the streets were arguing over the nature of Christ and singing excerpts from a poem Arius had written to popularize his views. He had titled his poem *Thalia*, after one of the nine Muses, and in it he ridiculed the views of his opponents. "Even in the pagan theaters, the pious words of the godly teachings were exposed to the ultimate ridicule [των απιστων θεατροις, τα σεμνα της ενθεου διδασκαλιας την αισχιστην υπομενειν χλευην]" to quote Eusebius.

The bishop of Nicomedia replied to Arius with encouraging words. "Your views are right; pray that all may believe as you do. It is plain to anyone that what is made does not exist before it comes into being."

Alexander, enraged by the report that the bishop of Nicomedia had taken up the cause of his rebel subject, sent out a circular letter to all the bishops of the East asking them to pay no attention to any communications from Eusebius. "Since," Alexander wrote with anger, "Eusebius, the present bishop of Nicomedia, who thinks that the affairs of the Church are in his hands, supports these apostates and has tried to write everywhere on their behalf in order to drag ignorant persons into this latest anti-Christian heresy, I have found it necessary, knowing what is written in the Law, to break my silence and to inform you all, so that you may know who the apostates are..."

At the time, Licinius was still the emperor of the East. Certainly without any objection or interference from him, Eusebius summoned a council of bishops in Nicomedia and placed before the assembled prelates the issue raised because of the dispute between Alexander and Arius. The synod approved Arius' doctrines and sent a communication to all bishops to receive Arius into communion—ignoring his excommunication by Alexander—and to bring pressure on the bishop of Alexandria to take him back.

Encouraged by this decision, Arius wrote a letter of conciliation to Alexander, but he opened it with a rather provocative sentence. "This is our ancestral faith, which we learned from you also, blessed father." Alexander reacted with understandable rage to this attack on his orthodoxy and circulated a statement with his beliefs asking the other bishops to subscribe to it. He gathered some two hundred signatures. Now a war of pamphlets had begun between the two sides.

Unyielding, Arius traveled to Palestine and asked his other fellow student, Eusebius, the bishop of Caesaria for help. Eusebius called a synod of Palestinian bishops who also sided with Arius, and asked Alexander to reinstate Arius to his parish church in Alexandria. They also asked Arius to accept the authority of Alexander to end the dispute. The bishops' decision was trying to reconcile views which were irreconcilable.

Alexander again rejected Arius' overtures and accused him of using "young women to parade through the streets in a disorderly fashion" praising Arius and his doctrines. Arius seems to have had great appeal to women. It is recorded that he had a special group of seven hundred holy virgins among his adherents, but it must be said that he was never accused of any sexual indiscretions. He would have been, if his opponents had the slightest evidence.

CONSTANTINE INHERITS
THE PROBLEM

While Arius and Alexander were carrying on their verbal attacks on each other, a much more violent war was approaching its end. The armed conflict between Constantine and Licinius was being decided in the Sea of Marmara and on the fields around the town of Chrysopolis.

A few days after Constantine entered Nicomedia as the victor and sole emperor, he was told by Osius, his informal advisor on matters of the Church, that a serious dispute was tearing apart the churches in the East. The dispute was more serious than that of the Donatists because it centered on matters of Christian doctrine.

Constantine had a fixation on the unity of the Church. He was truly fearful that dissension within the Church might displease God and bring God's punishment on him. In the midst of all the other problems of bringing his new territories under the imperial control, he had to act on this Church conflict.

He did not fully understand the esoteric doctrinal disagreements between Arius and his opponents. The letter he sent with Osius to both Arius and Alexander clearly shows this lack of understanding.

Eusebius has preserved the entire text but here we need only record some of the key excerpts. In the letter Constantine invoked as his witness "the ally of my endeavors and the Savior of all." His purpose, he wrote, was first of all "to unite all the nations in a single purpose around what is holy," and second "to heal a world suffering as though of an evil malady (χαλεπω τινι νοσηματι)." He went on to say that after "the intolerable madness which had gripped all Africa, provoked by those who dared with senseless levity to rend the worship of the people into separate sects," he hoped to find "the leading teachers for the salvation of the world," in the East, "whence the power of the light and the law of the holy religion had enlightened the entire world with a holy torch." Instead he had found a controversy "which no law required" but was the product of "misused leisure." The dispute should have been kept inside one's mind and never be allowed "to carelessly reach the public ear."

Their disagreement, he told them, was over "extremely trifling" (μικρων και λιαν ελαχιστων) matters. That remark must have surprised both Arius and Alexander since their dispute was certainly not over "trifling" matters of faith.

Constantine must have been told of the exchange between Arius and one of the bishops at the synod which had excommunicated him for "blasphemy," because in his letter Constantine clearly focuses on that exchange. Here is what he wrote:

> "This I understand was the cause of the present dissension. You, Alexander, asked your priests what each of them thought about some passage in the Scriptures, or rather about some frivolous question, and you, Arius, imprudently made an answer which should never have been conceived at all, or if conceived should have been committed to silence. Hence discord came between you, and the pious were rent asunder and separated from the harmony of the general body."

In Constantine's view, the entire controversy was reduced to an unimportant exchange of imprudent words, which could easily be forgotten.

> "Therefore let each of you, sharing an equal spirit of conciliation, accept the just advice your fellow servant of God offers you...Let us willingly move away from the temptation of the devil. Our great God, the common redeemer of all (ο κοινος απαντων σωτηρ), common to all he extended the light. Since as I said one is your faith and the dictates of the divine law this issue which has caused dissension among you should come to an end...Return to your mutual friendship, because friendship is often sweeter following enmity, once conciliation had come."

Then, in a rather emotional outburst, Constantine ended his letter in these words:

> "Give me back peaceful days and untroubled nights, so that I too may find some pleasure in the pure light and the joy of a tranquil life from now on...To help you understand the depth of my sorrow, I will tell you that the other day when I set foot in the city of Nicomedia, I was hoping in my imagination to travel further to the East. But the reports of your dissension kept me back because I did not want to see with my eyes what I could not bear to hear with my ears. Open to me by your agreement the road to the East, which you have closed by your mutual discord, and quickly forgive each other."

It is hard to imagine that the two hardened clerics would have been moved by the emperor's rather naive words.

Osius also spoke to them in the same spirit but without success. Eusebius writes that "the quarrel of the opposing sides increased much more while the force of the evil spread in all the eastern provinces, the work of envy, hatred and of a cunning demon."

Osius soon discovered that another dispute divided the faithful in Egypt. It had its origins in the days of the last persecution when Peter, bishop of Alexandria at that time, and Meletius, bishop of Lycopolis in upper Egypt, were in prison together. A disagreement arose between them over the future treatment of those who had "given in" to the authorities during the persecution. Meletius favored a very harsh policy: Clerics who had given in should never be permitted to resume their sacred functions. Peter urged a more lenient treatment for fear that people might be discouraged and fall away altogether if they had no hope of returning to the Church. Their arguments became so fierce that in the end Peter hung a curtain across the middle of the prison cell, and ordered all those who disagreed with him to leave his half of the prison. Several of the imprisoned bishops and priests moved to the side of Meletius and the two parties ceased to speak to each other.

After the end of the persecution, the dispute continued and eventually Meletius formed his own Church which he called "the Church of the Martyrs."

When Osius reported to Constantine what he had found in Alexandria, the emperor decided that a large synod was needed to restore the unity of the Church in the East, and soon issued invitations to the bishops in his new lands asking them to travel at public expense to the town of Ancyra (today's Ankara) in Galatia in the spring of the following year 325.

His plans changed when on the 20th of December, 324, the bishop of Antioch, Philogonius, died and a large assembly of bishops from Cilicia, Palestine and Mesopotamia, the provinces subject to the see of Antioch, came to the city to elect a successor. The synod was "packed" with anti-

Arian clerics who elected to the vacant throne of Antioch, Eustathius, a rabid anti-Arian. The bishops then went ahead with a review of the doctrinal issues and drafted a statement of faith which roundly condemned Arius' views. They had moved ahead of Constantine's proposed synod in Ancyra, prejudging the issues the synod was supposed to discuss. To add insult to injury, they excommunicated three pro-Arian bishops and sent a report with their statement of faith not only to all the bishops of the East but also to the bishop of Rome.

One can imagine Constantine's reaction to all this. Clearly seething with anger, he decided to summon a universal, ecumenical synod, representing the whole Church and, to keep some control of the outcome, he decided to preside over the synod himself.

In late March 325, he sent to all the bishops throughout the empire a letter in which he told them:

> "It is clear to all, I think, that nothing is more precious in my eyes than our religion. Although it was previously settled that the synod of bishops should convene at Ancyra in Galatia, it has now been decided for many reasons that it should meet at Nicaea of Bithynia, both because the bishops from Italy and the other parts of Europe are coming, and because of its pleasant climate, but also because I wish to be near to observe and take part in the work of the synod. I, therefore, inform you, beloved brethren, that I expect you to come to Nicaea as soon as possible. Each of you accordingly, faithful to his duty as I have previously said, must without delay urgently expedite his journey, so that you may observe the proceedings of the synod in person. May God preserve you, beloved brethren."

The time for the synod was set for June.

GATHERING IN NICAEA

In June of 325 they started arriving to the charming city of Nicaea, on the shores of the Ascanian like, only a few miles from Nicomedia. The response to the emperor's call was not as universal as Constantine had hoped. Over two hundred and fifty came from the East, but only a few came from the West because most of the clergy there had no interest in the dispute which appeared to them too esoteric. Sylvester, the bishop of Rome, excused himself because of his advanced age and ill-health but he sent two presbyters, Vito and Vincentius, to represent him. Eustorgius came from Mediolanum, Marcus from Calabria, and Capito from Sicily. Bishop Domnus came from Pannonia, and Theophilus the Goth came on behalf of the northern barbarians. No bishop came from the British Isles or from Spain. Hosius of Cordova attended, but as the emperor's personal adviser, not as the bishop of Cordova. Our old friend Caecilianus of Carthage came to Nicaea, probably interested more in strengthening his own position against the Donatists than in the doctrinal discussions.

Constantine was pleased to see that a few bishops came from countries outside of the empire. Two came from Cherson (the Crimea), two from the kingdom of Armenia, and one from Persia. Clearly, the composition of the Council was overwhelmingly from the East, and Greek, not Latin, was the language primarily spoken by the participants.

Eusebius has left for us a journalist's description of the arrival of the bishops accompanied by their deacons and servants, on carriages or mules. The public interest was intense not only among the Christians of the city but also among those who still clung to the ancient religion. Even before the official opening of the synod, the bishops had begun to gather in the inns where they were billeted, or in the principal church of Nicaea, engaging in debate with zest while waiting for the emperor to arrive.

Full of intellectual curiosity, even pagan philosophers came to debate the issues with willing bishops. In one such encounter, a bishop with little education but with earthy wisdom, replied to a pagan orator when all arguments were exhausted: "Christ and the apostles gave us no dialectical art and no vain deception but plain, bare doctrine which is guarded by faith and good works (γυμνην γνωμην, πιστει και καλοις εργοις φυλαττομενην)." He had given in a few words the essence of the issue. The Christian doctrine was not subject to proof by logical deduction; it was a matter of faith.

THE COUNCIL BEGINS

O n the 3rd of July, the first anniversary of his victory over Licinius, Constantine came to Nicaea. Eusebius, who was there, has not given us a detailed account of the debates, but he has reported nevertheless the highlights of the synod in a vivid, descriptive language. His account of the opening ceremony is quite impressive.

All the invited prelates came to the palace, escorted to the great hall where rows of seats were set on each side, and took their places "in proper decorum" (συν κοσμω τω πρεποντι). As the moment of the emperor's entry approached expectant silence fell in the hall. "The first, the second, and then the third of the emperor's officials came in, as well as others, not the usual armed guards but only his friends [who believed in Christ]." When the signal was given, they all rose from their seats, and Constantine entered. "He walked through the middle of the hall, as if he were a celestial angel of God, attired in a garment which was shining as though radiant with light, reflecting the glow of the deep red cape, adorned with gold and precious stones radiating a transparent brilliance. But this is about the body. His soul, however, was infused with the fear of God and with reverence, his eyes downcast, his face slightly flushed, his walk measured. He was taller than everyone else. When he had advanced to the front of the assembly he remained standing at first. A gilded seat was waiting for him but he did not sit until the bishops motioned to him to do so. And so did everyone else after the king. Then the bishop who was standing at his right [Theodoretus identifies him as being Eustathius, the bishop of Antioch] rose and gave a short speech, addressing the king, giving thanks to the Almighty God."

After the short speech, silence again fell in the room as everyone waited for Constantine to speak. We can understand the awe of the assembled prelates, many of them having suffered under previous emperors, seeing now for the first time face to face the man who had changed the status and the fate of their religion.

The whole scene was beautifully orchestrated. Constantine wanted to impress them enough to bring them together and end their offending disputes, but also to dazzle them with his imperial presence.

He gave his speech in Latin to underline the solemnity of the gathering by using the official language of the empire. Later during the meetings he spoke mostly in Greek which he spoke quite well since he had lived in the very same area as a youngster for many years.

"Gazing at all of them with tranquil eyes, gathering his thoughts, he gave his speech with a quiet and friendly voice." His message was clear. He expected them to set aside their disagreements and unite. His words reflected his superstitious fear of provoking the wrath of God, and his belief that he was indeed the chosen instrument of God to guide the fortunes of mankind. Here are a few excerpts from that speech as reported by Eusebius:

> "Brethren, it has long been my highest desire to see you assembled and now my wish has been fulfilled. I publicly give thanks to the King of All (τον βασιλεα των παντων) who in addition to all his other blessings has granted me this supreme blessing of seeing you all gathered together in a single spirit of concord

(ομονοια) May no malevolent enemy disturb our present peace. At this moment when, thanks to our Savior God (σωτηρα παντων), the tyrants who had raised their arm against God have disappeared, may no perverse devil expose the divine law to blasphemy. For my part, I hold any dissension within the Church of God as equally abominable as any war or battle, and much more difficult to bring to an end, and I am opposed to such dissension more than to anything else."

He concluded with a heartfelt exhortation which however sounded almost like an imperial order:

"Begin now to cast aside the causes of the dissension which exist among you, and eliminate the confusion caused by controversy by embracing the dictates of peace. For by so doing you will be acting in the manner most pleasing to the Supreme God, and thereby confer on me, your fellow servant, an extraordinary favor."

It is interesting to note that he spoke only of the "Supreme God." He evidently did not want to prejudge the outcome of the synod by declaring in some way that Christ was also God, equal to the Father. And with notable realism he said it was more difficult to bring an end to their disputes than to win an armed conflict. In war he knew how to win by force. With churchmen who had withstood even the horrors of the persecution, he had to rely mostly on persuasion.

On the day Constantine had arrived in Nicaea, he had found waiting for him many petitions submitted by bishops accusing each other of heresy, or political intrigue, or too close association with Licinius. In a dramatic gesture, "he took out of the folds of his toga the scrolls, had a brazier with burning coals brought in, and declaring under oath that he had not read any of them, he threw them upon the fire." It was a telling gesture.

THE OMOOUSION

Once the actual debates began, the dazzling impression of the opening ceremony rapidly faded, as contention and acrimony took over. The first issue to be discussed was the divine nature of Christ. As happens in large contentious conferences, three major groups emerged: those who sided with Arius, forcefully rejecting the doctrine that Christ the Son was a God of the same "substance" as the Father; those who denounced the Arians as despicable heretics; and those led by Eusebius of Caesarea who wanted to strike a balance that could preserve the unity of the Church. Alexander had brought with him from Alexandria a young priest named Athanasius, a man of small stature, thin, unimpressive, but a man with a brilliant mind and magnetic eloquence. In the course of the debates, Athanasius emerged as the leading opponent of Arius. He would carry the anti-Arian torch for the rest of his life.

It seems that soon after the discussion started, Eusebius of Nicomedia, as the bishop in the imperial capital, presented to the assembly a statement of faith to serve as the basis for their discussions. It was clearly a pro-Arian document. Many among the bishops rose in anger and literally tore the paper to pieces. It was now evident that a strong anti-Arian sentiment dominated the synod. But just as determined were those who supported Arius. At times the debates broke out into a shouting match, even in the presence of Constantine.

Then, Eusebius of Caesaria, who was already famous for his book on the history of the Church and who evidently had won the respect of the emperor, quietly offered for discussion the statement of faith being used in his diocese at the baptism of new members of the Church. Constantine told the bishops that the statement was a good basis for a more constructive debate.

Some of the sentences in the statement presented by Eusebius can be found in the formal statement of faith (Creed) eventually approved by the synod. But even the Eusebius statement had a rough sailing. The major stumbling block was what it had always been: the nature of Christ as the Son of God. They all agreed that Christ was the Son of God. But was he of the same substance as the Father? Was he a creature of God, like all other creatures? Did he have a beginning or was he without beginning (αναρχος) like the Father? For them, those were critical questions. They were also questions that could not be answered. No logic could really provide the answer, and no proof could be offered by either side. The answer could only be accepted by faith. Still, they debated as though the object of their debate was subject to proof.

Eusebius leaves the impression that it was Constantine who offered the magic word ομοουσιος. The word meant in the Greek "of the same substance," "consubstantial." Ironically the word could be traced to Paul of Samosata more than half a century before. He had been condemned for using this word (in addition to his punishment for a scandalous life). More recently Eusebius of Nicomedia had used the word in arguing against the opponents of Arius that if they declared the Son to be the "true God" they would have to accept that the Son was of the same substance (ομοουσιος) as the Father. To his surprise, the opponents of Arius embraced the word when it was suggested by Constantine. Some of Arius' more moderate friends tried to change the word by inserting the letters "oi" so that the word would be "ομοιοουσιος," meaning of a similar substance (*omoios*, similar), but their efforts failed.

In the end, the statement of faith that was produced by the

Council of Nicaea included the word ομοουσιος. It read:

> "I believe in one God, Father Almighty, the maker of all things, visible and invisible, and in one Lord Jesus Christ, the Son of God, the only-begotten (τον μονο-γενη) Light of Light, a True God from a True God, begotten, not Made, Omoousion to the Father who has made all things...And [I believe] in the Holy Spirit coming out of the Father (το εκ Πατρος εκπορε-υομενον) and glorified together with Father and the Son, [the Holy Spirit] which has spoken through the prophets..."

This was the text of the original statement of faith, which has come down through the centuries as the Nicene Creed. Some additions and some changes were introduced later, but these have not touched the central doctrine; above all, the *omoousion* remains. It could not have been otherwise. The Church was founded on the belief that Christ was the Son of God, in fact that he was God, a member of the Holy Trinity. Detracting from that belief was bound to weaken the appeal of the Christian religion and undermine its vitality. The men who assembled in Nicaea, though simple and unschooled many of them were in the intricacies of theological and philosophical thinking, clearly understood what made their religion strong. In the Creed they signed, they preserved the essence of their faith.

To make their position absolutely clear and to rule out any heretical distortions, they added a special anathema of the Arian doctrines. "Those who say 'Once He was not,' and 'Before He was begotten, He was not,' and 'He came into existence out of what was not,' or those who profess that the Son of God is a different 'person' or of different 'substance,' or that 'He was made' or that He is 'subject to change'—all these are anathematized by the Holy, All-embracing (Catholic) Church."

They ended the Creed with a specific reference to the All-embracing

Church. "and I believe in one, Holy, Catholic [all-embracing] and Apostolic Church..."

The supporters of Arius, as well as the moderates such as Eusebius of Caesaria, found the special anathema too harsh and for a moment it appeared that the agreement might unravel. Eusebius asked to have one day to think about his position. But he had already struck a friendship with Constantine and he had no illusions about the emperor's wishes. He signed in the end but then he found it necessary to write a letter to his flock in Caesaria justifying his conduct and explaining why he considered the *omoousion* acceptable.

Eusebius of Nicomedia, Theognis of Nicaea, and Maris of Chalcedon, all old friends of Arius and his fellow students at the school of Lucian, made an effort to salvage whatever could be saved of the Arian doctrine. Apparently, Eusebius of Nicomedia talked to his friend, the Augusta Constantia, Constantine's stepsister, and tried to enlist her help in modifying the word *omoousios* to read *omoioousios* (of like substance) but Constantine adamantly rejected the suggestion. They, too, signed the statement.

Arius did not surrender. Constantine had to step in and openly threaten the rebels. Another historian, Philostorgus, has left this report. "When Arius' supporters refused to adhere to the faith of the synod, the emperor declared that those who refused to accept the general ruling of the bishops, whether they were priests or deacons, or other members of the clergy, would be exiled. Philomenos, the *magister officiorum*, the chief of the civil service, was assigned the implementation of this order. He presented the formal statement of faith to Arius and those with him and gave them the choice of signing or going to exile. They chose exile." Arius was sent to Illyricum, too far from Egypt to cause more trouble. But it will be a mistake to assume that this was the end. His ideas remained powerful for more than two hundred years after his sudden death in 336.

On the Celebration
of Easter

O nce the Creed was adopted, the synod turned to the other major feud that marred the unity of the Christians in Egypt: the Meletian dispute.

Very much like the feud of Donatus and Caecilianus, the dispute between Meletius and his opponents had strong personal overtones. And just as in the case of the Donatist schism, Constantine turned the matter to the assembled bishops asking them to settle the disagreement and restore the unity of the Church.

At the time of the Council of Nicaea, the initial protagonists had changed. Peter of Alexandria was no longer alive, beheaded in 311, but Meletius had survived the horrors of the salt mines and was still leading his "Church of the Martyrs," mostly in Upper Egypt, in direct opposition to the "legitimate Catholic Church" which at the time was led by Alexander, the bishop of Alexandria.

The bishops at the Council of Nicaea rejected most of the charges brought by Meletius against Alexander but at the same time refused to take a strong stand against Meletius. They ruled that he should stop ordaining new bishops in competition with Alexander's, but they proposed the integration of the "Church of the Martyrs" into the Catholic Church by giving the right of succession in Catholic sees to bishops already ordained by Meletius. A similar effort at Arles to bridge the gap between Caecilianus and the Donatists had failed. This conciliatory judgment was to be just as ineffective. The differences between the churches in Upper Egypt and the churches in Lower Egypt were too deep to be settled by a decision reached in far-off Nicaea. The feud lasted for almost two hundred years. But for the moment, Constantine was pleased with the Council's efforts to bring unity to the Church.

He must have been relieved when discussion turned away from the internal divisions of the Church to the question of the celebration of Easter. In many areas in the East, especially in the dioceses led by Antioch, the day of Easter was set by the day of the Jewish Passover. Quite often, then, Easter was celebrated on a weekday, not on Sunday. Alexandria, Rome and the West in general followed a different approach altogether. Easter was to be celebrated on the Sunday after the full moon, following the Spring Equinox. The synod at Arles had decreed that Easter should be celebrated on that Sunday throughout Christendom but the ruling had not been accepted by all. This issue may seem unimportant today but at that time it was a burning issue. Constantine asked the Council to establish a universal system so that all the Christians would celebrate Easter on the same day every year.

The eastern churches in Asia Minor, Syria, and Palestine were not willing at first to change their traditions and accept the system followed by the church of Alexandria. In a way, they saw the issue as a matter of prestige.

In the end, Constantine himself had to intervene. He had gone back to Nicomedia soon after the end of the discussions over the Arian dispute, so he sent to the Council a letter. It is revealing about his view of the Jews. The pagan Romans had never taken a hostile stand against the Jews because they considered their religion to be old and sanctioned by a long tradition. The Christians, however, considered the Jews to be the murderers of Christ. Constantine's letter to the council reflected this view.

"It seems inappropriate," he wrote to the Council, "to calculate the most holy feast in accordance with the customs of the Jews who, having stained their hands with the lawless crime, remain blind in their soul...What right opinions can they have, those who, after the murder of the Lord went out of their minds and now live not by reason but by uncontrolled hatred." (Later, however, he exempted by law Jewish rabbis from public service just like the Christian clergy.) For the assembled bishops, this was an argument of great force. The partisans of Antioch could not continue to claim that they were right to calculate the Easter by the calendar of those "who had murdered Christ." This was a turning point in the life of the Jews throughout the Roman Empire. The tolerant indifference of the pagan Romans turned slowly but steadily into hostility throughout the Christian world, east and west.

Unanimously the Council of Nicaea decided that Easter should be celebrated on the first Sunday after the full moon following the Spring Equinox.

After approving a number of "canons" designed to strengthen the discipline and regulate certain practices within the Church, the Council concluded its deliberations. Delighted with the results, Constantine invited the prelates to take part in the celebration of his Vicennalia, the twentieth anniversary of his investiture with the purple. It had been on the 25th of July in the year 305, immediately after the death of his father, that he had been acclaimed Augustus by the army in far-off Eboracum on the British Isles.

Eusebius describes the emotions of the bishops as they entered the Imperial Palace, on the way to the banquet, "passing without fear in their hearts the anterooms which were lined along the walls with guards their swords drawn," welcomed by the palace officials, and escorted with great honor to the inmost hall where the emperor was waiting for them. "It felt," Eusebius writes with flair, "as if we were seeing a picture of the kingdom of Christ, and that what was happening was no reality but a dream."

Constantine acting as the highest *episkopos*, the highest overseer of God's domain on earth, announced to all the dioceses in a circular letter the decision of the Council, adding to them in effect the stamp of his imperial authority. He concluded by declaring that "all the dissensions, schisms, disturbances and fatal poisons of discord have, by the Will of God, been overcome under the brilliant light of Truth." It would soon prove to be a rather optimistic assessment.

Chapter XIII

The Murders

A Specter of
Conspiracies

O nly three months had passed since the end of the Council of
Nicaea, when something changed in the man who had
thrown into the fire unread the scrolls with the charges and
counter-charges of quarreling bishops and who had spoken with such
reverence for God and with such force for unity in the Church. On
October 1, he issued an edict from Nicomedia asking all his subjects
to become informers and report to him any secret plot against him
that came to their knowledge, no matter how high the status of the
conspirator, even if the traitor was an intimate of the emperor himself.
Anyone discovering such a threat to the emperor should report what
he knew and the emperor would reward him generously. "Let him
come without fear and let him address himself to me. I will listen to
all. I will personally conduct the investigation and search for the
truth."

What had provoked this edict? We have no written record, but
such far-reaching edicts were not issued without reason. Constantine
had eliminated all his rivals. Licinius was under guard in
Thessaloniki, no longer a threat to Constantine. Yet in the fall,
Constantine ordered his execution, breaking his solemn promise to

his stepsister Constantia. Was Licinius executed because he was involved in a conspiracy against Constantine? He did have friends he might have asked for help to escape. But if he had become entangled in such a plot, he was writing his death warrant since all his moves were closely watched by his guards.

One can easily imagine Constantine's reaction if he was told that Licinius was plotting to escape and possibly resume the fight. With his open and forceful embrace of the Christian Church at the Council of Nicaea, Constantine had angered and frightened the pagans who still represented a majority in the population and even in the army. Licinius could become the champion of the ancient religion and try to turn the clock back.

If Licinius was indeed plotting for another round, then both his death and the edict begin to make sense. Moreover, Constantine's open invitation to informers may be the missing clue behind the murders of Crispus and Fausta a few months later.

THREE WOMEN

Constantine had celebrated his twentieth anniversary as emperor in Nicomedia, not in Rome. Rome was no longer the capital of the empire but it had never ceased to be its spiritual and symbolic heart. Even Diocletian had gone to Rome to celebrate his twentieth anniversary. It is true that he had left in disgust as soon as he could, but still he had paid homage to the eternal city.

Quite possibly, Constantine was advised that he should go to Rome to celebrate but also to reaffirm his control as the sole emperor. Since his twentieth anniversary had already passed, he decided to combine a second celebration with the festivities for the tenth anniversary of the elevation to the rank of Caesar of his sons Crispus and Constantine.

By this time, young Constantine was some fourteen years old, a mere boy, but Crispus was thirty-one, a man who had shown his mettle in Gaul against the Franks and in the Hellespont against the powerful triremes of Licinius. Eutropius, a pagan chronicler, tells us that Crispus was a man of the highest merit (*vir egregius*). We can find nowhere in the ancient sources, both Christian and pagan, a single word of criticism or condemnation of Crispus. In fact, many saw him as a worthy successor to his father. But such acclaim had its downside because it was bound to rouse the enmity of Fausta who saw Crispus as a threat to her own sons.

The imperial train left Nicomedia in February of 326 as soon as the weather had improved enough for the imperial ladies to travel in comfort. They first stopped at Serdica, a palace Constantine liked, and then by March they reached Sirmium, another of his familiar places. One month later they came to Aquileia, to the old palace Maximian had used and where reportedly a mosaic of the Herculian family hung, including Fausta as a child handing a helmet to Constantine as a young boy.

The imperial family traveling with Constantine included Fausta, Constantine's mother Helena, his stepsister Constantia, and of course Crispus and young Constantine. The three women in the imperial household must have made for a rather tense company.

Two years earlier, Constantine had given his mother the title of Augusta, a gesture that must have angered Fausta who considered herself the only Augusta. Religion may have also been another source of mutual dislike. Helena, now seventy, had accepted the Christian faith but there is no record anywhere that Fausta had abandoned the ancient gods.

Fausta was only thirty-six years old, eighteen years younger than Constantine, the daughter of an emperor, an attractive, proud, strong-willed woman, anxious to secure her own future after Constantine was gone by having her sons succeed him. She probably looked down on Helena, to her always the innkeepers daughter. If she behaved decently at all toward the old lady, she did so only because of Constantine.

Crispus, too, was another cause of simmering friction between the two women. Helena had brought up the boy after his mother Minervina died, and her love for him knew no bounds. Like herself, Minervina was of humble origin and Crispus was like her son Constantine, the offspring of a *matrimonium concubinatum*. That Fausta considered Crispus a potential threat could not have escaped Helena's watchful eye.

Constantia, the third imperial lady, herself an Augusta as the wife of Licinius, could not have been very good company during the journey to Rome, considering that her stepbrother had ordered her husband's execution only a few months before, leaving her a widow at thirty-one. She may not have been in love with her husband, since their marriage was arranged by Constantine for reasons of state, but his killing must have cast a dark shadow.

Certainly the imperial family on its way to Rome to celebrate the great anniversaries could not have been in a very festive mood.

A WRONG START

The imperial family came to Rome in June. The celebrations were scheduled for the month of July. The first jarring note came on the day of the Procession of the Knights, an ancient ceremony celebrating a Roman victory with the aid of the twin gods, Castor and Pollux, the Dioscuri of ancient Greek mythology, who tradition held fought at the side of the Romans on that day and then brought the news of victory to the city. On the day of annual celebration, the men who belonged to the equestrian class paraded, riding their horses through the great avenues of Rome in one of those resplendent pageants the Romans knew how to stage so well. Traditionally, the emperor was expected to review the parade if he were in town. When Constantine stayed in the palace, pointedly ignoring the festivities which included a sacrifice to Jupiter Maximus on the Capitoline Hill, the people of Rome were angered. Rome continued to be a pagan city, emotionally attached to the ancient gods who were so closely connected with the city's past glories and with its festivals and celebrations. Riots broke out near the emperor's palace, and in fact one of Constantine's statues was pelted with stones, the face battered and disfigured. John Chrysostom left us the story that when Constantine was told of the incident, he stroked his face and said: "I am not able to see any wound inflicted on my face. Both the head and the face appear to be quite sound." Constantine did have a rye humor and he may have well said what Chrysostom reports. But his mild words were probably an effort to veil his real feelings, because he did not accept an insult easily. The anniversary celebrations had not started on a happy note.

This time, the ancient sources do not have any dazzling descriptions of triumphal celebrations. The traditional festivities called for sacrifices to the ancient gods and Constantine did not want to participate, although he let the pagans go freely through their rituals. Since the Christian Church had not developed as yet religious ceremonies for such events, he simply stayed away, closeted in the palace most of the time. But that was not the only reason for the dark mood that had settled over the Palatine.

Intrigue and Violence

Eusebius in his *Life of Constantine* casts total silence over the tragic events. Lactantius ended his *Death of the Persecutors* with the death of Maximin Daia so had nothing to say. Only those who wrote after the death of Constantine have allowed a fragmented and convoluted picture to emerge. Zosimus claims that Fausta was in love with Crispus and tried to seduce him. They were both in their thirties—he around thirty-one, she around thirty-six—and such an illicit affair was certainly possible. Crispus, we are told, rejected Fausta's enticements and the scorned woman turned on him with vengeance. Here is part of what Zosimus had to say. Being a pagan, he was not among Constantine's admirers. "Now that the whole Empire had fallen into his hands, he no longer concealed the evil dispositions and vicious inclinations...When he came to Rome he was filled with pride and arrogance. He decided to begin his impious acts at home, for he put to death his son Crispus, on suspicion of debauching his step-mother Fausta without any regard to the ties of nature. And when his own mother Helena expressed deep sorrow for this atrocity, lamenting with great bitterness the death of the young man, Constantine, pretending to comfort her, applied a remedy worse than the disease. He ordered a bath to be heated to an extremely high temperature, had Fausta thrown in it, and a short time later she was taken out dead."

Sextus Aurelius Victor in his book *De Caesaribus* admits that he does not know why Crispus was executed. In the *Epitome*, we read the rumor that "it was on the instigation of Fausta that Constantine ordered his son Crispus to be killed." He adds that "afterwards he had his wife Fausta herself killed in a boiling bath, when his mother Helena accused her for having done her grandson a grave injustice".

Eutropius, another pagan, writing in his dispassionate fashion, had this to say: "To tell the truth, being somewhat unaccustomed to his good fortune [Constantine] changed radically from his good nature which had made him popular. He persecuted first and killed his son Crispus, a man of high merit, a youth of agreeable nature; then, soon (*mox*) [he killed] his wife."

Two facts are beyond dispute. Constantine in late July ordered the arrest of Crispus who was executed. Then, within a short period of time, he ordered the killing of his wife Fausta in a scalding bathtub. What had led Constantine to commit those crimes? The victims were not strangers. They were persons he loved. The provocation must have been beyond endurance, otherwise we will have to accept that the killings were the deeds of a madman. Eutropius implies something of the sort. But practically everything else Constantine did during the same period and till the end of his life reveals no trace of mental imbalance. The opposite is true. The murders were the acts of a sane man who had to set aside personal feelings and send to their death the two people closest to his heart.

It will not be easy to uncover the tragic mystery, but we do know enough to piece together a pragmatic scenario.

Constantine had no intention of abdicating on his twentieth anniversary like Diocletian. He was only fifty-four years old, at the prime of his life. The master now of a great empire, he did need help. It would have been only natural to make Crispus his fellow Augustus, in charge of all the territories in the West, just as Diocletian had done with Maximian. The empire was certainly much too large to be governed from Nicomedia. Coins issued at that time bear the inscription "Augusti" in plural. Was this a hint that Constantine was thinking of elevating Crispus to the rank of Augustus?

We know that, on the 21st of July, Constantine gave a lavish banquet in the palace. Crispus was there. In fact, the poet Optatianus Porphyrius, a Christian, read a poem in which he spoke of Constantine's glorious victories but also of "the courage, the merits, the handsome youth of his older son, Crispus, who had the noble bearing and the majesty of his father." The poet had a favor to ask of the emperor, and a pleased emperor gladly granted it. Clearly, Crispus enjoyed his father's affection until that day. Did the praise given Crispus at the banquet add one more straw to Fausta's fear for the future of her sons?

Although Constantine was not an old man at the time of his Vicennalia, he would be well over sixty in less than ten years. If he died, Crispus would be in a strong position to become his successor. Although we know very little about Crispus' personal relations with his stepbrothers, a long tradition backed Fausta's fear that her children might be in mortal danger as potential rivals. Worse, as the new master, Crispus might send Fausta to her death or at the very least to exile—possibly with the blessings of his grandmother Helena. Very likely the moment appeared critical in Fausta's eyes, critical enough for her to make a desperate move to eliminate Crispus before it was too late.

It was no secret that Constantine was very proud of Crispus. Still, he had shown no less love and affection for his sons with Fausta. At the beginning of the tragic year 326, he had ordered the casting of medals showing together the Caesars Crispus, Constantine II, and Constans II, then a boy of five or six. Clearly, he loved all his children. The only difference was that Crispus was already old enough to be of real help to him.

Sozomenus, a Christian writer, asserts that Crispus was "the hope of the Catholics, the only one, with his father, being their favorite." If that is true, then Constantine had one more reason to love Crispus. Yet, we know that within days after the banquet, he ordered his arrest. For Constantine to do so, the charges must have been horrid and the proof unassailable. If Fausta was the one who brought the charges, then Constantine had a most highly placed informer complying with the dictates of his edict of the previous October. Still, the fact that the informer was the empress herself would not have been enough. Constantine would have demanded proof. What proof did she offer? Did she tell Constantine that Crispus had indeed tried to seduce her? A few days after the arrest of Crispus, unknown persons hung on the gates of the Palatine palace a plank with the words *"Saturni aurea secula quis requiret? Sunt heac gemmea, sed Neroniana"* (Who will search now for the golden centuries of Saturn? They are back again gem-studded, but reminiscent of Nero). The reference to Saturn, who according to the ancient myth had devoured his own children, was also a transparent allusion to Constantine's killing of Crispus. Even more tantalizing was the reference to Nero. There was an old rumor that he had an incestuous relation with his mother. Did this couplet refer to a similar liaison between Fausta and Crispus? What was happening inside the imperial family could not have remained completely in the dark. Servants do have ears and they do talk. It may be then that the story about Fausta's charges has some basis in truth. It would not have been an effective argument on her part to accuse Crispus of conspiring to take the crown from his father. Constantine knew better. But the charge of seduction was more plausible in the eyes of a man with a much younger wife.

Certainly such a charge would have enraged Constantine. The chroniclers of the time tell us that shortly afterwards he had several other persons executed. Were those persons the witnesses Fausta had brought to Constantine to support with their testimony her accusations? Constantine would have demanded proof, and persons claiming to have been eyewitnesses could have provided the proof Constantine needed. Crispus was arrested and taken to Pola (near today's Trieste) where he was put in prison.

The cruelty of Fausta's death clearly shows that Constantine was seething with anger when he ordered the manner of her execution. The ancient writers imply that she was punished because she had unjustly accused Crispus. But was she guilty of something more than false accusation? Constantine did not restore Crispus' memory after his death which means that he did not think he was innocent. What then was Fausta's terrible crime? With Helena there, Constantine would not have moved so hastily to issue the order to kill her beloved grandson. Yet Crispus was executed only a few days after his arrest.

We are told by Aurelius Victor that Helena "upbraided Constantine" when she heard of Crispus' death. We can understand her "unbearable grief for the killing of the young man" (ασχετως την αναιρεσιν του νεου φερουσης). But this cannot explain Fausta's gruesome death. Helena could not have easily disproved Fausta's allegations of seduction, especially in the face of witnesses. She could have only sown enough doubt into her son's mind to stay his hand from signing Crispus' death warrant. If the evidence was later found to be false, Constantine could have closed the matter by giving Fausta a severe tongue-lashing for her false accusations and her excessive hatred of Crispus. Then Crispus would have been set free and the entire sordid episode would have ended. It did not happen that way.

Constantine's insane rage when he ordered Fausta's savage execution shows that something much more terrible than false accusations had provoked his ire. What if Crispus had been executed so soon after his arrest—without his orders? Crispus' jailers would have never acted on their own, without a death warrant bearing the Emperor's signature and seal. If he did not sign it, then who did? Who could have used the imperial seal other than Fausta or someone following her orders? If this is what actually happened then everything else falls into place. Her savage punishment is easier to understand if she was indeed responsible for Crispus' death. The other persons who, we are told, were executed shortly afterwards, could have been Fausta's witnesses and those who had misused the emperor's signature and imperial seal. There is not ancient testimony to support this scenario. But it fits the scattered allusions and fragmentary reports, and parts away somewhat the cobwebs that have kept the mystery covered for so many centuries.

But still one question remains. Was there any truth to Fausta's story about a seduction? Very likely yes. The ancient sources tell us that shortly after the tragic events the names and the images of Fausta and Crispus were removed from every place of honor and never reappeared on coins or medallions. (A later chronicler, Codinos, wrote that Constantine erected a golden statue of Crispus but this may be only a legend.) Clearly Constantine did not consider Crispus to be entirely innocent. Otherwise, he would have kept his name in the places of honor. It is quite possible that Fausta had initiated the affair in a scheme to implicate Crispus and then accuse him of trying to seduce her. Very likely Crispus imprudently fell for it and let himself be left open to the charges of seduction. If that is what happened then we can understand why Constantine erased not only Fausta's but also his sons' name and image. All this is speculation, of course, but speculation which seems to reflect the known facts.

The killing of Licinianus is another mystery. The boy Licinius had with Constantia was only twelve years old at the time and could not have been involved in any palace intrigue. Besides, it would have been too much, even for Constantine, to kill his sister's son after he had killed her husband.

What did actually happen? It appears that Licinius, long before he married Constantia, had with a concubine a son also named Licinianus. He would have been in his early twenties at the time of Crispus' death, old enough to have been involved in a conspiracy. The pagans were searching for a new leader to fight off the "atheist" Constantine and his "Catholic Church." It would be totally unrealistic to expect the pagan priesthood and the millions of those who worshipped the traditional gods to remain indifferent while their world was dissolving before their very eyes, its age-old edifice crumbling under the blows struck by Constantine and his Christians.

Licinius was now dead but his son, even the son of a concubine, could serve as a rallying point. Such a son, if he did indeed exist as some ancient sources imply, was potentially a dangerous rival. If informers came to Constantine with some evidence that the man was entangled in a conspiracy, his execution in the fall of 326 would make sense.

Constantine left Rome depressed and angry, hating the city as much as its pagan citizens hated him. He would take revenge by building a new Rome on the banks of the Bosporus. He had already started some construction in the town of Byzantium which he valued because of its strategic location. Now he would go back and turn the humble town into a magnificent capital that would bear his name.

CHAPTER XIV

BACK TO
THE EAST

The "New Rome"

Constantine, Helena and Constantia were the only adults now traveling back from Rome to Nicomedia. The celebration of the imperial anniversaries had been covered with blood. Young Constantine, who was traveling with them, must have been in an emotional turmoil after his mother's horrid death by orders of his father. Helena, too, must have had a broken heart, mourning with bitter tears the young man she had raised from the time he was an infant. These people may have claimed imperial rank but they did not cease to be human beings with emotions and feelings.

It seems that during the long journey Constantine reached a momentous decision. He was going to build a "new Rome." Soon after his victory over Licinius he had started some construction work in the small but strategic town of Byzantium. He knew the area well, since for more than ten years he had lived there in the service of Diocletian and then, briefly, of Galerius. The town's unique strategic value could not have escaped a keen mind like that of Constantine. The two continents of Europe and Asia are separated at that point by less than two miles, at some points by less than one. The inlet known as the Golden Horn is a natural harbor. The small peninsula from the Golden Horn to the Propontis is surrounded by water on three sides, leaving only one side to be buttressed with strong walls.

The original town of Byzantium was founded in the seventh

century before Christ by Byzas, the legendary king of Megara, a city just a few miles to the west of Athens. Already some other settlers from Megara had set up a colony on the Asiatic side, which became the town of Chalcydon. When Byzas asked the Oracle of Delphi for advice, the priestess Pythia replied that they should build their new settlement "opposite the land of the blind." Byzas interpreted the oracle to mean that the blind men were his compatriots who had settled in Chalcydon. They must have been blind not to see the unsurpassed advantages of the small peninsula with its precious inlet. He named the small settlement Byzantium after himself.

We are told that Constantine laid the first stone for his "new Rome" on the 4th day of November of 326. Considering that he must have come to Nicomedia from Rome in October, he clearly had made up his mind and was anxious to get the work started.

Several charming legends were crafted by later chroniclers, evidence of the fascination the city of Constantine inspired in East and West for centuries. They are legends without foundation in truth, but they tell us what people thought at the time.

Sozomenus in his *Ecclesiastic History* claims that Constantine first thought of building his new Rome at the plain below Troy, since the ancient Romans claimed that Troyans who escaped the sacking and burning of Troy by the Greeks had come to Italy to found Rome. There is no evidence that Constantine even thought of Troy but the fable was attractive in itself. Sozomenus goes on to explain why Constantine abandoned the site and went to Byzantium.

> "...God appeared to him by night and commanded him to seek another site. So led by God's hand he came to Byzantium in Thrace, and was ordered to build his city there, making it worthy of the name of Constantine."

Of course, Sozomenus can be excused for seeing divine guidance because another legend claimed that as Constantine was walking, tracing with his spear the boundaries of his new city, he replied when one of his companions asked how much further he intended to go since he had already covered a large area: "I shall continue until the one who is walking ahead of me stops." The "one" of course was no other than God himself.

Sozomenus' tale was later embellished by another more colorful story. When Constantine stopped uncertainly at Chalcydom, the eagles from the mountains, no doubt by divine inspiration, flew down and picked up with their beaks the builders' tools and carried them to the acropolis of Byzantium.

Legends also sprang up in the West. One of them, embellished over time, claimed that "as Constantine was sleeping he saw an old woman standing before him, her forehead furrowed with age. But then, suddenly she turned into a beautiful maiden, so charming that Constantine could not refrain from kissing her. His mother Helena who was also present in the dream told her son: 'she shall be yours forever, and shall not die till the end of time.' When he awoke, the emperor implored heaven by fasting and praying for an explanation of the dream."

Then the Western influence is showing. Constantine had another dream, a week later. He saw Sylvester, the bishop of Rome who had died some time earlier. The bishop told him the meaning of his dream. "The old woman is this city [meaning Byzantium], worn down by age, her walls eaten by time, threatened by approaching ruin, waiting for a restorer. You, having renewed its walls and its prosperity, shall make it famous with your own name, and the descendants of emperors shall reign there forever." The final prophesy was not to be fulfilled, but at the time of the dream, the fall of the city to the Turks was still over a thousand years away.

In another, more prudish version of the same tale, the kissing of the maiden by Constantine is modestly omitted.

Constantine, certainly a very superstitious man, may have been strengthened in his resolve by the old oracle given to Byzas from Delphi. The oracle seemed to imply that the city would be built twice, the second time by a fish, a rather mysterious prediction. The Christians, however, could find a clear meaning. A mystical sign of Christ was in the form of fish. For the initiated the sign implied the letters of the word fish in Greek. These letters formed the initials of the words (in Greek) Jesus Christ, the Son of God, Savior (I. Ch. Th. Y.S.). Here was an ancient prophesy that could not be ignored, even though it was the saying of a pagan priestess in Delphi. The new Rome was to be a Christian city built with the blessings of the Christian God.

THE CITY OF CONSTANTINE

A fter four years of work, the city was officially opened in May 330. It would remain the "Queen of Cities" (*Vassilis ton Poleon*) until it was conquered by the Turks in May 1453, one thousand, one hundred and twenty-three years later.

The celebrations for the inauguration lasted forty days. During one of the festival days a statue was brought to the Hippodrome. It was a colossal statue of Apollo removed from Athens where it was believed to have been sculptured by Pheidias himself. The head of the statue had been removed and replaced by that of Constantine. After the parade, the statue was placed on a tall column made of red marble (porphyry), in Constantine's Forum. The column was made up of eight marble drums brought from Rome, each about ten feet in height, connected with wide bands of bronze wrought into the shape of laurel leaves. The eighty feet tall column rested on a pedestal of white marble, some nineteen feet high, which in turn stood on a base composed of four wide steps. (The column still stands today though badly damaged by fire. The statue is long gone. It came crushing down to earth in 1105, killing a number of persons in its fall.) At the foot of the column, we are told, there was this inscription: "Oh Christ, Ruler and Master of the world, to Thee I have dedicated this obedient city. Guard and deliver it from every harm." For many centuries, the statue was held in superstitious reverence, with horsemen dismounting as they passed by. Every year on the first day of September, Constantine's successors, with the Patriarch of Constantinople at their side and with priests chanting hymns, assembled in front of the column to pay homage to the founder of the city.

On the last day of the inaugural festivities, columns of soldiers in dress uniform, carrying white candles, escorted a statue of the goddess Fortuna now under its Greek name "Tikhy", symbolizing the good fortune of the new city. Large crowds of spectators along the avenue of the Hippodrome acclaimed the procession. It circled the Hippodrome and stopped before the imperial box, the *kathisma*. Constantine rose from his seat, hailed the statue and commanded it to be placed in the new chapel he had built for the purpose. Then he proclaimed that this parade was to be held every year on the city's inauguration anniversary. The festivities ended with the traditional chariot races in the magnificent circus, to be known by its Greek name Hippodrome (Hippodromos, the Horse Track). At the same time coins were minted showing Constantinople with a ship as the Queen of the seas.

Writers critical of Constantine complained that the construction of the city was done too hastily, that the work was so shoddy that buildings crumbled with the mildest earthquake and they had to be torn down and replaced. We may assume that there was some truth to those statements. An entire new city could not have been built in just four years without cutting corners.

Still, the new city was a magnificent sight. Constantine had removed statues and works of art from Greece and other parts of the empire to embellish his city. Many were statues of ancient gods but Constantine apparently saw in them only the beauty.

In the center of the city he constructed a vast plaza, the Augusteum, paved in marble, adorned with classical statuary, surrounded by imposing buildings. To the north was the church of Saint Sophia (Holy Wisdom) still under construction at the time of the inauguration, and to the east was the building of the Senate. To the south, overlooking the Propontis, was the imperial palace (the palace was located where the Blue Mosque is today.) next to the Hippodrome. To enter the palace one had to pass through an enormous bronze gate known as *khalki* (of bronze). Right next to the palace were the so-called baths of Zeuxippus.

In the Augusteum, Constantine had installed a marble column known as the Million, to measure the distances of all parts of the empire from Constantine's city. A wide avenue, the *mesi*, the middle street, connected the Augusteum with the Forum of Constantine, an elliptical plaza surrounded by colonnades. They ended at either end in two spacious porticos in the shape of a triumphal arch. In the middle, which tradition held was the exact spot where Constantine had pitched his tent when he was besieging Licinius inside Byzantium, Constantine had installed the column of red marble we mentioned earlier.

The imperial palace, known as the Great Palace (*Mega Palation*), was really a cluster of buildings spread over a large area, a city in itself, strongly protected with walls and towers. One of the buildings, covered in red (porphyry) marble brought from Rome, was reserved for pregnant ladies of the imperial household, to provide for them serenity and comfort, away from the cares of everyday life. Sons of emperors born within this porphyry palace were distinguished by the title "*Porphyrogenitos*," a title often encountered in Byzantine history.

Below the city, Constantine built underground cisterns to provide water for the inhabitants. The water was brought in over a long aqueduct but it was also collected from rainfall because Constantinople had few natural springs. The colonnaded cisterns, many of them enormous in size, must have cost a fortune to build. Two of the largest are still in good condition, even after so many centuries. One, the so-called Cistern of Philoxenos, had eighteen feet tall columns in sixteen rows of fourteen columns each. The cistern was named after Philoxenos, a wealthy Greek who paid for its construction. Constantine had many wealthy Romans and Greeks contribute large sums for the construction of the cisterns in exchange for having their names chiseled on stone. Practically all the names are Greek, an interesting piece of evidence that the new Rome was rapidly becoming a Greek city. The second cistern, known as the Underground Palace, is three hundred and ninety feet long and a hundred and seventy-four feet wide and still supplies water as clear as when it was first opened. Both cisterns can be visited today by tourists.

From the famous Hippodrome, renowned around the world, little remains today—an Egyptian obelisk, a marble column in the shape of a twisted serpent (brought in from Delphi where it was erected centuries ago to commemorate the victory of the Greeks over the Persians at Plataea in 479 B.C.) and a crumbling stone pillar. These three stone monuments that have survived define the outline of the *spina*, around which the charioteers raced their chariots. The obelisk stood in the exact center of the racing track which followed the traditional lines of an elongated ellipse. Tiers of marble seats were on both sides of the racetrack, adorned with statues, and works of art. At the northern end of the *spina* was a large building housing the stables and the storehouses where the supplies and the chariots were stored.

At the middle point of the long side of the arena adjacent to the Great Palace was the imperial box, with the *kathisma* (Greek for seat), the emperor's throne, with a pillared platform right in front of the throne, for the emperor's standard-bearers. Right behind the imperial box was the Church of St. Stephen as part of the Great Palace. To reach the imperial box the emperor went through the church down a spiral staircase. It was designed for an impressive entry of the emperor. Around the *kathisma* were seats for high ranking dignitaries.

The first tier of seats, reserved for the more distinguished spectators, was some thirteen feet above the arena, with several more tiers rising behind. Right above and behind the seats at the top was a wide promenade which ran all around the arena, a spacious avenue of some two thousand, seven hundred feet long, forty feet above ground, with a magnificent view of the Bosporus. People walking on it were protected from falling off by a solid marble railing reaching almost to a man's breast.

The Hippodrome was to become a focal point in the life of the city. Eighty thousand people could easily find a place in it, and in the excitement of the race all distinctions of rank and wealth were forgotten, as all those thousands of people, fused into a common passion, shouted for their favorite team to win. At times, the Hippodrome was also to become the arena where political passions erupted and history was written.

Constantine spent large sums for the construction of churches. One of them, Saint Sophia (Holy Wisdom)—half-finished at the time of the inaugural celebration—was burned to the ground during the Nika rebellion in the reign of Justinian, who replaced it with the present magnificent edifice which became the most renowned church in the East. Saint Sophia has not been used as a church since the fall of Constantinople to the Turks, and today it is sort of a museum.

Another important church was dedicated to the Holy Peace (*Aghia Eirini*), the Peace of God. It, too, was half finished at the time of the city's inauguration. One church that was finished was that of the Holy Apostles, initially dedicated to the Holy Trinity. Buried under the great High Altar were the remains of Timothy, Andrew, Luke, Mathias, James the brother of Jesus and the head of St. Euphemia. One may question the authenticity of the relics but Constantine and his fellow Christians believed them to be genuine. Around a rotunda inside the church stood the memorials of the Twelve Apostles, and in their midst Constantine had placed the sarcophagus where his body was to be placed after his death. In later years, the Church would accord him the title *Isapostolos* (equal to the Apostles). The placement of the sarcophagus implied that he already considered himself to be one. In a way he deserved the title more than any other man on earth. With his actions he had lifted the Christian faith from obscurity and persecution and made it the dominant religion in the Roman Empire and eventually one of the principal religions in the world.

To bring people to his city, Constantine used every practical inducement. To the poor, he promised handouts of food and clothing; to the rich, tax relief. He required all the officials in the imperial administration to reside within the walls of the city. He invited old patrician families from Rome to move to his new city and receive large tracts of land in Asia Minor, but not many responded. He created a new aristocracy, the class of *clari*, and elevated new senators for his Senate. Within a short time, many Christians, especially from Asia Minor and the Balkans, moved to the city on their own to live in a place where the emperor and the majority of the residents shared their religious beliefs.

Using the Greek language, Constantine named the city after himself, CONSTANTINOUPOLIS, the City of Constantine, eventually to be called simply "the Polis," the City. Even when the Turks changed the name to Istanbul, they still used, somewhat distorted, the Greek words *is tin poli*, meaning "to the City."

HELENA GOES
TO THE HOLY LAND

Helena was approaching seventy-one when she came back to Nicomedia after the horrible events in Rome. She had known moments of happiness but also much sorrow in her long life. It had been so very long since the time when as a humble girl of sixteen she was seduced by the dashing tribune and fell forever in love with him. She had known the wrenching distress of a divorce neither of them wanted, but which affairs of state dictated, and which she had seen as a mother's sacrifice for the future of her beloved son. She had spent many years of loneliness at Drepanon, the village near Nicomedia, which her son, the emperor, had since renamed to Helenopolis in her honor. In those years at Drepanon, the joy of her life was her grandson Crispus, the boy with the curly hair. She had lived long enough to see her son Constantine win one battle after another, becoming the sole emperor of the Roman Empire, and her grandson Crispus raised to the rank of Caesar. She should have now looked forward to the last years of her long life ending in peace. But the execution of her beloved Crispus shattered all hope. It is not surprising that she sought solace in the Christian Church and that she decided to visit the Holy Land, ignoring her old age and the rigors of such a journey.

399

Eusebius, in his *Life of Constantine*, has covered in great detail Helena's pilgrimage. She stopped in many cities on the way to Jerusalem, distributing charity to the poor, visiting the local churches for prayer, meeting with the clergy. When she came to Jerusalem, she visited the places where according to the Gospels Christ had walked, and she arranged the construction of a church in Bethlehem, next to the cave where she was told Christ was born. "On the Mount of Olives, in memory of the event, she constructed at the very top a sacred house of worship with a temple." Eusebius goes on to describe in two long passages the ornaments of the two churches, which he found quite impressive.

Helena apparently voiced her desire to find the cave where Christ had been interred after the crucifixion. The search was not easy because no one remembered exactly where it was. According to one story, which may or may not be accurate, it was a Jewish inhabitant of Jerusalem who came to tell her that from his ancestors he knew where the tomb was. The location had long been buried under new construction "done by atheists and impious men and was no longer visible" (Αθεοι τινες και δυσεβεις, αφανες το σωτηριον αντρον εποιησαντο). In fact, right above the cave a temple dedicated to Aphrodite had stood for a long time.

Helena had enough clout to get the temple torn down. Then, the area was cleared until she found the cave. Evidently, she immediately wrote to Constantine, because Eusebius has this to say: "In a letter to Makarios, the bishop of Jerusalem, Constantine gave instructions for the construction of a church over the sepulchre. He added that he had already given orders to Drakilius, the provincial governor, to provide technicians and workers and all the necessary materials [Makarios] might need. He matched his words with deeds and the work moved forward."

In the next passage, Eusebius tells us of Helena's death. "Since she had spent the length of her life, she was called to the better end (κρει τονα ληξιν), being almost eighty years old...and so she arranged her last will, distributing her own possessions to each of her descendants. When all was done, she left this world as her son was by her side holding her hand." She evidently died in 333 when she was seventy-seven to seventy-eight years old, close to eighty as Eusebius tells us.

Some eighteen years after Helena's death a strange story surfaced, a story the Church has fully embraced since. It is the story of the discovery of the cross on which Christ died.

A first hint appears in a letter sent by Kyrillos, the bishop of Jerusalem, to Constantius, one of Constantine's sons.

This is what the bishop wrote:

> "In the days of the God-loving and of blessed memory Constantine, your father, the saving wood of the cross was found in Jerusalem (Επι μεν γαρ του Θεοφιλεστατου και του μακαριας μνημης Κωνσταντινου, του σου πατρος, το σωτηριον ξυλον του σταυρου εν Ιεροσολυμοις ηυρηται.)

The bishop of Jerusalem goes on to say that Constantius, "the most reverend king," not on the earth but "on the sky saw the miraculous sights." It appears that during a visit to Jerusalem, Constantius had witnessed a brilliant sight in the sky, resembling a cross extending from the hill of Golgotha to the Mount of Olives. The significance of the passage lies on Kyrillos' clear statement that the cross had been discovered during Constantine's reign.

Socrates, a Christian and a native of Constantinople, born around 380, wrote a history of the Church (in Greek) some seventy years after the death of Helena. In it we find this passage: "Helena, the emperor's mother, being divinely directed by dreams, went to Jerusalem...There she searched for the tomb of Christ and after much difficulty, with God's help, she discovered it. What the difficulty was I will explain in a few words. Those who embraced the Christian faith

401

greatly venerated the tomb, but those who hated Christianity, having covered the spot with a mound of earth, erected on it a temple of Aphrodite, and set up her image (*xoanon*), endeavoring to abolish the memory of the place. This they succeeded doing over a long period of time, but at last the location became known to the emperor's mother who, having caused the statue [of Aphrodite] to be thrown down and the earth removed, and the ground completely cleared, found three crosses inside the tome; one of the three was the blessed cross on which Christ had hung...A dying woman was brought in by Makarios, bishop of Jerusalem, and when she was touched by the true cross she was immediately healed, and recovered her former strength."

Hermias Sozomenus, in his history of the Church, covering the period between 324 to 440, gives practically the same story as that of Socrates. Sozomenus, a Christian, was born in Palestine and was educated at Gaza and Berytus (Beyrut). In the early part of the fifth century, he was practicing law in Constantinople. Socrates writes that he received his information from "an old man." Sozomenus also states that "we have related the above incidents precisely as they were delivered to us by men of great accuracy, who had received the information as it passed from father to son."

Since both Socrates and Sozomenus wrote many decades after the events they describe, it is only natural that they received their information from other people who had heard the stories from their parents or grandparents. This in itself would not be a good reason for questioning the accuracy of their stories. The problem is really caused by Eusebius. Neither in his *Life of Constantine* nor in his *Ecclesiastical History* does he say one word about a discovery of such tremendous significance for the Christian world. Why does he ignore such a momentous event like the discovery of the cross, which presumably occurred during his lifetime? He writes in such detail about Helena's visit to the Holy Land, about the removal of the temple of Aphrodite and the discovery of the cave and the construction of the church right above the tomb, yet he has nothing to say about the discovery of the cross. Nor do we find one letter from Constantine—and he was a prolific letter-writer as we know—mentioning the discovery, let alone the miraculous recovery of the half-dead woman. Evidently he said nothing about the discovery of the cross to Eusebius during the long interviews that helped Eusebius write his life.

Eusebius has described Helena's death when "she was almost eighty," which means that he was following very closely the life of the imperial family. After all, since the Council of Nicaea he had become an intimate and trusted friend of the emperor. Is it possible that he knew nothing of such a tremendous event when he had been for a long time bishop of Caesaria in Palestine? Why then this strange silence?

The story given by Socrates and Sozomenus seems to have some other weak points. Why should the crosses of the two thieves be kept inside the tomb, together with that of Christ? Even the reference to the image of the cross is suspect. People were not crucified on a cross as we visualize it today. The vertical pole was kept more or less permanently at the execution site, securely embedded in the ground. The condemned man walked to the place of the crucifixion carrying on his shoulders a long, heavy plank which was then attached to the vertical pole forming a cross. It was removed after the death of the person to be used again. The Church had adopted the image of a cross because of its obvious emotional and symbolic value. But if custom was followed in the case of Christ, the plank would have been taken back to the barracks to be used again until eventually it was cut to pieces to be used for firewood.

The facts seem to indicate that the story about the discovery of the cross by Helena may be one of the many legends that sprang up through the centuries around Constantine and his life.

CHAPTER XV

CONSOLIDATION

AN ELABORATE PYRAMID

In the remaining eleven years of his life after the Vicennalia in Rome, Constantine worked hard to build an elaborate pyramid of administrative control over his far-flung empire. The years he had spent near Diocletian had not been wasted. He had learned that the power of the emperor rested on a complex network of officials who owed their position, well-being, and future advancement to him. Disloyalty carried a heavy price.

In many ways, Constantine built and expanded on the basic structures introduced by Diocletian, but change breeds change and what emerged in the end was the edifice of an absolute monarchy the ancient Roman emperors would not have recognized.

At the apex of the administrative pyramid was, as in the days of Diocletian, the Praetorian Prefect, the emperor's prime minister. He oversaw the four "prefectures," in which Constantine grouped Diocletian's twelve dioceses, each under its own "Praetorian Prefect." The title was ancient but the functions of these high officials were quite different from those of the Praetorian Prefect in Rome (the commander of the Praetorian Guards). Directly under the emperor and his Praetorian Prefect, these four prefects were the supreme administrators of their large areas. And they were large indeed. One covered Gaul, Spain and the British Isles; a second, Italy and North Africa with the exception of Egypt; a third, Illyricum, Pannonia, Dacia,

Moesia, Macedonia and the Greek peninsula (today's Balkans); and a fourth, the Orient (Asia Minor, Syria, Palestine, Mesopotamia). Egypt was kept separate, governed by a proconsul because it was a major source of grain for the capital.

The four prefects had no military authority. Prudently, Constantine kept the command of the military forces in separate hands. But their civil functions were quite extensive, highlighted by their symbolic insignia which were a large silver inkstand and a golden pencase, a hundred pound in weight. They had their own finance ministers to supervise the collection of taxes and to transfer the money to the imperial treasury, and they were the final court of appeal in both civil and criminal cases. To avoid the nuisance of appeals to the emperor, Constantine had issued an edict making the decisions of the Praetorian Prefects final. They even had the authority to issue decisions with the force of an edict in dealing with major problems in their own areas.

They were certainly powerful within their prefectures, but they served at the pleasure of the emperor and could be replaced without even an explanation; some actually found out that they had been replaced when their successor arrived and showed them the imperial documents for their dismissal. During the last years of his reign, Constantine raised his sons and nephews to the rank of Caesar and sent them to the major prefectures in the empire. We have to understand, however, that they were not to impose their authority on the Praetorian Prefects or the senior military commanders. At the time, his sons were much too young and inexperienced to actually govern or command troops—with the exception of Crispus who actually served as an active Caesar for a few years before his execution.

Below the four prefects came the vicars of the twelve dioceses: Orient, Pontica, Asiana, Thracia, Moesia, Pannonia, Italia, Gallia, Viennensis, Brittania, Hispania, and Africa. Each diocese was divided into provinces under a provincial governor. When Constantine came to the purple, there were one hundred and ten provinces, but as the years went by, the number of provinces increased not because new territories were added into the empire but because some provinces appeared much too large to Constantine or because he wanted to reward a particular favorite. To quote Eusebius, "the king invented various positions in order to honor more people (εις γαρ το πλειονας τιμαν διαφορους επενοει βασιλευς αξιας)

Apparently not all provincial posts carried the same rank, or at least the same symbolic status. Some of the governors had the title of *rector* or *corrector*, others were called *praesides*, and those governing the most important provinces had the title *consulares*. Each governor had his own administrative staff, with officials in charge of the major departments, all based on a rigidly observed hierarchical principle. The system of having the lower officials subordinate to their superiors was not new; it was only made more strict and much more elaborate under Constantine. In this pyramid, with its multitude of coveted positions, ambitious men could make a career for themselves and find loyalty to the emperor not merely an obligation but the best way to serve their own interest.

Constantine had understood that this officialdom was the most reliable foundation for his rule. But he also realized that men can abuse their authority and oppress the weak and ordinary people in their charge. In the edict which he had issued in October 325, inviting informers to report any conspiracies, he had also invited every citizen with sufficient evidence of abuse or corruption to report an official's misdeeds to Constantine himself.

This administrative structure was only one of the major pillars of the edifice. For centuries the legions had overthrown emperors and had acted as king-makers. To curb this dangerous habit, Diocletian had separated in his days the civilian governors from the command of military units. Constantine went even further. He formalized even more this separation of military and civilian functions throughout the bureaucratic structure, from the Praetorian Prefects to the vicars to the provincial governors, but he did not stop there. He restructured the army.

He created two high level positions, that of the Master of Infantry (*Magister Peditum Praesentalis*) and that of the Master of Cavalry (*Magister Equitum Praesentalis*). The Master of Infantry was regarded as the more senior although both were ex officio members of the Emperor's Council, the *Consistorium*. This division between the foot soldiers and the cavalry was carried all the way down to the provincial level. It made for a more efficient military organization but most important it worked against a treasonous rebellion since, especially at the highest levels, both masters would have to agree and cooperate in committing treason.

Constantine introduced many other structural changes. He cut down the size of the legions from their traditional strength of approximately 5,500 men to 1,000. Then, he divided the army into three categories: the units which were to guard the frontiers (*limitanei* or *riparienses*, the second referring to those units which were stationed along the Rhine and the Danube); those which were to serve as a "rapid deployment force", highly mobile infantry and cavalry units (*comitatenses*) ready to move and attack an invading force, if the frontier troops had been forced to fold back; the third branch, which was made up of small garrison units stationed in almost every city and major town in the empire, acting as a local police force ready to assist the local magistrates in the collection of taxes, in apprehending criminals, and in putting down any riots or disturbances.

When the old ponderous legions were replaced by the smaller units, Constantine had to establish many new ranks in the chain of command, giving many more capable men the opportunity to move up in the ranks. There were now many more *duces* (*dux*, leader) and *comes* (from the word *comites*, companions of the emperor). In later centuries, the titles of Duke and Count would become familiar in the kingdoms that emerged after the Dark Ages in Europe. The masters of the Infantry and of the Cavalry at the highest level were usually officers who had served as *comes* with distinction and had performed services Constantine regarded as of great value to him. Many of those who were promoted to dukes or counts had served in the elite Imperial Guard, the *Palatini*, crack troops serving primarily as protectors of the emperor.

It was an expensive army and a heavy burden on the taxpayers who had to support it. But the existence of this army had brought years of peace and security which, for the people who had suffered for so long, were benefits they valued. They grumbled and tried to evade the payment of taxes, and many authors critical of Constantine claim that the burden was intolerable, but this should not surprise us. Seldom does one find taxpayers who gladly transfer their money to the public treasury. On the whole, the general population accepted Constantine's rule without strong or vocal opposition. We have no record of public unrest, not even in the writings of his critical chroniclers.

An impressive building for the Senate was one of the first that were completed in Constantinople. It was more a symbolic imitation of the Senate in Rome than an institution of debate and legislation. Like the Senate in Rome in those days, it had hardly any political power. It merely gave a symbolic sanction to the imperial decrees and it provided ceremonial dignity to state functions. But it would be a mistake to think that it was a useless ornament.

Because membership in the Senatorial Order was a distinction that might be accorded to a man who lived far away from Constantinople, a new aristocracy of state officials, former officials, distinguished citizens, imperial favorites, wealthy men, and men of letters was formed. Not all of them came to Constantinople to participate in the work of the Senate, in the same way that today's titled Britons do not often take part in the deliberations of the House of Lords. Membership in the Senatorial Order often involved additional burdens of taxation or contributions to the emperor's private purse, but the emotional satisfaction (and possibly the material advantages) of belonging to a distinguished group was sufficient compensation.

Faithful to his penchant for titles and honorific distinctions, Constantine had devised a whole new list, and not only for the members of the Senatorial Order. The title Most Noble (*Nobilissimus*) was reserved for the members of the imperial family. But he had enough other titles to meet the need for distinction. The members of the Senate, individuals elected as consuls, high administrators such as Praetorian Prefects or proconsuls, and the highest palace officials were addressed as Most Distinguished (*Clarissimi*). Officials of lower levels such as vicars or members of the Senatorial Order who were not actual members of the Senate were known as Most Perfect (*Perfectissimi*). Later Constantine created two higher orders, the *Illustres* and the *Spectabiles*, for individuals who had been Most Distinguished or Most Perfect and who, because of special achievement or merit in the eyes of the emperor, were elevated to the two, even higher ranks.

Titles of high ranking palace officials were given to distinguished citizens as an honor with no requirement that they were to perform the duties associated with the position. Those were honorary *archons*, a Greek word found in ancient Greek literature attached to officials of the Athenian city-state. All these "titled" men, prominent in their cities and towns, became members of an elite group that felt attached to the emperor and his political system. In addition to the administrative apparatus and the army, this new aristocracy became a third pillar in Constantine's political edifice.

There was a fourth pillar, the Christians who had a strong reason to favor Constantine. In fact, the Christians, in the eyes of Constantine, were to serve as a unifying force holding together the sprawling empire. This explains why he was so intent on preserving the unity of the Church.

THE COURT

R ight above the four Praetorian Prefects and the Masters of the Infantry and the Cavalry and the members of the Senate was the Emperor, assisted by his Praetorian Prefect and the other palace officials. In the last few years of Constantine's life, the court acquired a mystique all its own, and became a world in itself, a legacy Constantine left to his successors and to the European courts of the following centuries.

In the conduct of state affairs, Constantine was assisted by an imperial council, the *consistorium principis*. It included ex-officio his Praetorian Prefect, the four Praetorian Prefects and the Masters of Infantry and Cavalry; the *Quaestor* who acted as a general secretary; the *Magister Officiorum*, the Master of Offices, who was not only the general overseer of the palace administration but also the minister of police for the imperial capital; the Presiding Official of the Sacred Chamber (*Praepositus Sacri Cubiculi*), the Grand Chamberlain of European courts in later centuries.

Included in the Consistorium were also the two ministers of finance. One had the title *comes sacrarum largitionum*, the count of the sacred treasuries, in charge of public finances. The other was the count of private properties (*comes rerum privatarum*), in charge of the emperor's personal finances. Several other officials were in charge of subordinate departments, all of them with impressive titles.

413

Many of the officials in the palace were eunuchs because they were considered to be, as a rule, efficient and capable civil servants. Constantine did not introduce the practice; it had a long tradition going back to the days of Diocletian and before. He only expanded the numbers, possibly because so many more good civil servants were needed in the palace bureaucracy.

When the imperial court moved to Constantinople in 330 the changes which were already underway began to take a more pronounced shape. Constantine was no longer the soldier-emperor he was during the first twenty years of his rule. For more than three centuries the Roman emperors had been, in their majority, soldiers vested with the imperial purple and the illusion of divinity. Diocletian had moved away from this mold by introducing an almost oriental mystique to the imperial office, wearing elaborate, impressive robes, and surrounding the palace in Nicomedia with an atmosphere of mystery and awe.

Constantine apparently saw merit in Diocletian's innovations, and when he became the sole emperor, he decided to carry them even further. The protocol, the official language of the court, the use of flowery and extravagant salutations, the almost religious reverence accorded to the emperor far exceeded anything Diocletian had used in his time. The emperor himself became a remote, aloof presence, seen by the public only on special occasions and then in robes encrusted with precious stones, surrounded by officials in impressive attire denoting their status, Christian bishops in religious vestments, and military escorts in multicolored tunics and shining helmets and shields. The simplicity of the Roman times was subtly being replaced by the trappings of oriental despotism. A new world was coming into existence.

THE ECONOMY

To provide for a large army of more than 300,000 men and for a vast bureaucracy, not to mention the special expenditures of a generous emperor—including the building of new churches and assisting the Christian clergy—the public and the emperor's private treasury had to be filled with monies collected through taxation or special contributions. The primary source of revenue was, as it had been for centuries, the tax on the production of the land. The old *tributum soli* had been replaced by the *capitatio terrena* but there was little difference between the two. Diocletian had introduced a more equitable evaluation of landholdings and households, using the *jugum* as a basic unit and assessing more such units to a piece of land equal in size but much more productive or valuable than another—a vineyard as compared to an equal acreage of poor quality arable land. Constantine kept this method of assessment and, with many more bureaucrats to work for him, he was able to collect the taxes more efficiently.

The emperor's finance ministers calculated each year the amount of revenue needed to cover the expenditures of the empire. The overall sum (the imperial budget) was then subdivided into four parts, one for each of the four prefectures. The Praetorian Prefects had now their marching orders. It was their responsibility to bring the money in.

Their finance ministers calculated how much each of the dioceses in their area should collect and they communicated the news to the vicars who calculated in their turn the levy for each of their provinces. At that level, the governors assigned the task of actually collecting the taxes to the *decurions* of the cities and towns and to the landowners, both big and small. Very often, the actual collection was taken over by private individuals who agreed to pay the state a certain amount in exchange for being allowed—with the assistance of the state authorities—to collect as much as they could.

When the harvest was good, the tax burden was bearable, but in bad years many small farmers could go under and join the landless peasants who had to work as share croppers (*coloni*). Slowly a form of serfdom was emerging as many a *colonus* became an *ascripticius*, a share cropper "assigned to the land." If there was any bright side to losing the land, it was that the share cropper had no longer the obligation to pay the land tax. It was paid by the landowner.

The land tax was not, of course, the only tax supporting the empire although it was the principal source of revenue. Constantine did not spare his new aristocracy. Every member of the Senatorial Order had to pay every year a special tax known as *follis senatoria* as well as "voluntary" gifts in gold. The wealthy and prominent citizens in every town and province were also expected to contribute "voluntarily" between one thousand and two thousand gold *solidi*, the so-called *aurum coronarium* on festival occasions such as the celebration of the emperor's or a Caesar's five or ten years of rule. Some chroniclers claim that Constantine invented a special tax known by its Greek name *chrysargyron* (gold-silver) paid every five years by all shopkeepers and money-lenders according to their means in addition to the annual tax paid by the head of every household. People were certainly taxed heavily. Zosimus in a bitter attack on Constantine's fiscal policies wrote that even prostitutes and beggars had to pay. Maybe Zosimus exaggerates but there is no doubt that Constantine deliberately tried to finance state expenditures with tax revenue, not with the debasement of the currency.

Constantine had not forgotten the failure of Diocletian's attempt to fight inflation with a rigid control of prices for every commodity and every service. He had understood that a stable economy requires a stable currency, money people can accept for their goods or their services confident that others, too, will accept it for their goods and services. Already in 309, he had minted in Treves a gold coin he named *solidus* with the inscription "victories everywhere." But the solidus did not become the basic imperial currency until later in Constantine's reign. By then he had more gold—some of it stripped from the pagan temples—and he established the solidus at seventy-two coins to a pound of gold. The solidus was given a fixed value to the silver *milliarences*, twenty-four milliarences to one solidus. The copper coins, the *denarii*, were a problem but most important transactions were paid in gold or silver coins so that for all practical purposes Constantine had now a stable currency. The *solidus* remained a coin with a stable value for several centuries, a remarkable feat in itself.

THE ROLE OF THE CHURCH

B y the time Constantine moved his capital to Constantinople, the Christian Church had become a major force in the empire. Other mystery cults such as that of Mithras were losing their faithful to Christianity because Christ's message was not much different and, besides, it had the support of the emperor himself. Although Constantine continued to employ pagans in high places—and two prominent pagans, the augur Sopater and the High Priest Praetextus participated in Constantinople's dedication ceremonies—many pagans were embracing the Christian religion because they could see that the emperor favored the Christians and that it was prudent on their part to join the Church. In fact, Eusebius expressed regret for the large numbers because he saw the action of those new members of the Church as hypocritical and self-serving. But many joined because they were attracted by the message. True, to many pagans the moral strictures of the Christian Church were a far cry from the mild demands of the pagan gods, but, on the other side of the coin, the promise of eternal life was a prospect few were prepared to ignore in that superstitious age.

Whatever their motives, they were joining by the thousands, strengthening the public image of the Christian Church as the "wave of the future." In less than a generation, the obscure, persecuted Christian cult had emerged, with Constantine's help, as the new religion of the Roman Empire.

Christ's message "to love each other" could not turn Constantine into a saint because the demands of governing could not fit to the prescriptions of the Christian code. But Constantine could not remain totally untouched. Whenever he could, he issued decrees which provided for the more humane treatment of prisoners, he abolished crucifixion as a method of execution, he banned the separation of slave families by selling family members to different owners, he banned the killing of slaves by their owners, and he ended the fights and the killings of gladiators at the amphitheater. He himself gave generously to the needy from the private treasury, to the point that many, knowing that the money came from their taxes, condemned the emperor's acts of charity (his *filanthropia*) as too excessive. We find in Constantinople old-age homes (*geirokomia*), orphanages (*orphanotropheia*), hospitals and other institutions, in addition to the regular handouts of food to the poor of the city. It was to be expected that his example would be imitated by the local magistrates and the wealthy Christians in many cities and towns.

Among the edicts that were inspired by the Christian religion is the one commanding that the Lord's Day (Κυριακή) should be observed and honored by all as the day of rest. The soldiers, too, whether pagan or Christian, were entitled to that day of rest and worship. He even prepared a prayer to the "Supreme God" that all soldiers should use in offering thanks to the "Giver of Victory, their Protector, Guardian, and Helper." Prudently, it was a prayer all could use.

> "Thee alone we know to be God; Thee alone we recognize as the Celestial King' from Thee we have gained our victories; through Thee we are superior to our enemies. To Thee we give thanks for the benefits we now enjoy; from Thee we look for benefits to come. All of us pray that Thou wilt guard our king Constantine and

his pious sons long, long to reign over us in safety and victory."

The style is unmistakably Constantine's. The prayer is also cleverly worded. No pagan soldier could find anything wrong with a prayer addressed to the Supreme God. If he were a true believer he could hope that his prayer would reach Jupiter. If he was a Christian he could certainly hope his prayer would reach the Christian God, since often in the church hymns, the term "Celestial King" (επουραν-ιος βασιλευς) was frequently used.

In spite of his strong attachment to the Christian religion, Constantine did not forcibly eradicate the old gods. Although Eusebius in his *Life of Constantine* writes that "he alone brought down every multi-god error" (μονου τε πασαν πολυθεον πλανην καθελοντος), he dutifully quotes in full the text of an edict addressed to the governors of the East in which Constantine clearly reaffirms the principle of religious freedom he had first set at Milan. "Let no one interfere with another; each should do what his soul wishes" (μηδεις τον ετερον παρενωχλειτω; εκαστος οπερ η ψυχη βουλεται τουτο και πραττετω). Still, responding to the teachings of the Church against sexual laxity, he closed some temples of Aphrodite or Venus because of reports that acts of sexual depravity were committed behind their walls.

Nevertheless, throughout his reign, Constantine never forgot that the majority of his subjects were still pagan, and was careful not to press them too hard and push the more fanatical among them to acts of despair. He knew well that with the imperial favor withdrawn from the old religion, the vine would sooner or later wither.

CHAPTER XVI

THE LAST SEVEN YEARS

Trouble Along the Danube

While Constantine was busy with the construction of his city, the frontiers in Gaul, along the Danube, in the Orient and in Africa were quiet for a change. An incursion of the Franks into Gaul in 324 had been beaten back by Crispus and the legions, and the Franks had decided to remain in peace and rebuild their forces.

Along the Danube, after the defeat of the Sarmatians and the death of their king Rausimond in 322, the frontier had been peaceful. Even the borders with the Persian empire had been calm for over three decades, since the time Galerius had broken the back of the Persian army. Egypt had been safe ever since Diocletian destroyed the black raiders, when Constantine was in his twenties. Constantine could reasonably hope that the last years of his life would be free of serious upheavals. By 332 he had reached the age of sixty and the many years of toil and hardship on the battlefield had taken their toll.

New signs of trouble along the Danube had appeared in the summer of 331. New Slavic hordes from the flatlands (today's Ukraine) were pressing from the north on the Goths who lived in what is today south Poland, Moldavia, and north Rumania. In their turn, the Goths threatened to push southward the Sarmatians and the Vandals. It was just the opening scene of the great migrations of the people from the steppes who would in the next century move on to the West and together with Germanic tribes destroy the western half of the Roman Empire.

The Sarmatians and the Vandals had never been friends but in the face of the threat from the north they joined forces and asked Constantine for help. He received their envoys in the Great Palace which dazzled them with its magnificence, and promised to send his son Caesar Constantine II with an army to protect them. Before the legions had time to reach the Danube, Araric, the king of the Goths, broke through the area of the Sarmatians, crossed the river, and galloped with his men into Moesia (today's northern Bulgaria) spreading death and destruction. Their joy ride did not last long. When they saw the legions, they turned around and tried to find safety beyond the Danube but the legions followed in hot pursuit until they caught up with the tribesmen and forced them to battle. On April 20, 332, the forces of Constantine II cut the Goths to pieces. One chronicler of the period claimed that in addition to those killed in battle, around hundred thousand more died of hunger. The figure may be too high, but there is no doubt that the Goths suffered a devastating defeat. A proud Constantine bestowed on his son the title "Gothicus." The young Caesar agreed to stop the fighting in exchange for the surrender of hostages including king Araric's son. Constantine had a good reason to be pleased.

We may assume that the Sarmatians gave a sigh of relief but their troubles were not over. Two years later they faced new threats, first from the Limigantes, a subordinate tribe, and then again from the Goths. This time many Sarmatians were taken deep into the territory of the Goths where they were gradually absorbed. Others trekked toward the Germanic lands in today's Austria. The majority, however, asked Constantine to allow them to settle peacefully south of the Danube. He agreed. Then, under a new treaty, he allowed Goths to join the imperial army and serve as frontier guards along the Danube. The great river was peaceful again and would remain so for quite some time. But then, less than two hundred years later, strong Slavic tribes would come from the north and eventually settle permanently throughout the Balkans.

Constantine's critics accused him of turning the empire over to the barbarians but at the time his was a practical policy. The year before, a bad harvest had caused near-famine in many areas, including the very city of Constantinople. Constantine needed more farmers to grow food on lands that had been neglected for very long. By accepting the Sarmatians he had brought in new farming hands. By the following year, farms in Illyricum and Moesia which had been vacant for years produced the first harvest. Constantine had also added robust soldiers to his army and had pacified the frontiers on both sides of the Danube. The bridge over the river was again open to traffic. Constantine had a good reason to feel satisfied.

THIRTY YEARS
AT THE HELM

The general public must have been fairly pleased with Constantine's rule because only one significant revolt broke out during the last seven years of his life. It happened on the island of Cyprus in 335. A man by the name of Kalokeros, the master of a herd of camels, if we are to believe Aurelius Victor, "insanely dreamed of becoming a king" and proclaimed himself Augustus. It must not have been such an idiotic affair, however, because Constantine had to send an expeditionary force under his nephew Dalmatius, the son of his stepbrother Dalmatius the Censor. Evidently Kalokeros had an armed force strong enough to challenge the local garrison. Dalmatius landed in Cyprus and in a short time broke up Kalokeros' force. Kalokeros was captured in midsummer and taken in chains from Cyprus to Tarsus of Cilicia where he was executed. "While he was tortured to death, as the law prescribes for slaves or bandits, the whole world agreed that the man must have been insane."

The Kalokeros rebellion must have been a cause of especially violent anger for Constantine because it happened at the very time he was preparing to celebrate his thirty years as the emperor. The great anniversary fell on the 25th of July of the year 335, and was celebrated with magnificent festivities in Constantinople, in Rome and in other major cities of the empire. Certainly each Praetorian Prefect, every vicar, and every provincial governor made sure that the day was properly celebrated by their citizens. In Constantinople, the clergy with the patriarch at the front participated with hymns and prayers for the emperor's long life and happiness. Delegations from Armenia, Persia, even Ethiopia and India came bringing exotic presents. Constantine, a generous man, reciprocated with lavish presents of his own. It was a happy time.

Before the Persian delegation left for home, Constantine sent a personal letter to the Persian king. It was a strange letter addressed from one sovereign to another. If the letter as reported by Eusebius is genuine, then Constantine spoke more as a Christian bishop than as an emperor. In the letter, Constantine told the Persian king that the Supreme God had punished severely those who denied Him and rewarded abundantly those who worshipped Him. In forceful language, he declared his personal horror at the sight and smell of blood in pagan sacrifices. "The God I serve," said Constantine, "asks nothing from His worshippers but a pure mind and an undefiled spirit." The letter was long and tedious and we may assume that the Persian king was puzzled when it was read to him in translation. He could have ignored it, except for one paragraph in which Constantine told Sapor that "he confidently committed the Christians who honor with their presence some of the fairest regions of Persia to the generosity and protection of their sovereign." They were Christians in Persia, to be sure, and on the whole they were not repressed, but Sapor certainly did not think that they honored his country with their presence. But was Constantine trying to tell him that he held him responsible for their safety and well-being? Was there a veiled threat in this religious sermon? Sapor did not react right away.

On the 25th of September, Constantine elevated Dalmatius to the rank of Caesar. Dalmatius and his brother Hannibalianus had remained out of the spotlight until now. Constantine was on good terms with his stepbrothers and their families, but his mother Helena resented the sons of her former husband, Constantius. The situation changed when Helena died in 333 at the age of seventy-seven. A year later Constantine called his two nephews to his side.

At the same time Dalmatius became Caesar, his brother Hannibalianus married Constantine's daughter Constantina and was appointed to the region of Pontus—today's northern Turkey along the Black Sea—as king. In fact, Constantine gave him the title "king of kings"—a title traditionally claimed by the Persian monarchs. Apparently, Constantine chose this title because the area had been governed by kings in the past and the inhabitants were accustomed to it. Sapor must have seen it as an insult.

Constantine was already thinking of his succession but apparently he did not consider any of his sons or nephews capable of filling his shoes alone. Treating the empire "as if he were giving the paternal property as inheritance to his beloved persons," (οια τινα πατρωαν ουσιαν τοις αυτου κληροδοτων φιλτατοις), to quote Eusebius, he assigned his elder son Constantine as the ruler of the West, including the British Isles, Gaul, and Spain. To his second son, Constantius, he gave the rich provinces of the Orient, including the part of Asia Minor bordering on the Aegean, Syria, Mesopotamia and Egypt. The youngest, Constans, a teenager now, received Italy, Illyricum and North Africa west of Egypt. The sensitive area which included Constantinople, that is, Moesia, Thrace, Macedonia, and the Greek peninsula, Constantine gave to his nephew, Dalmatius. The northern section of Asia Minor which was known as Pontica and which included Cappadocia, he gave to his nephew—and now son-in-law—Hannibalianus. For a man of his experience in the exercise of power and statecraft, Constantine had planted with this distribution, however well-meaning, the seeds of violent conflict. Zosimus, writing a few decades after Constantine's death, when he had already seen the bloody fighting among the heirs, accurately blames Constantine for the massacre. But this was in the future. In

September 335 the festivities for the wedding of Hannibalianus and Constantina, and the elevation of the two new Caesars were happy and joyous events as recorded in the Paschal Chronicle. We have no record that at the time Constantine's three sons expressed any resentment for the elevation of their two cousins to royal rank. No doubt Constantine's sons would have never dared to criticize openly or voice disagreement with any of their father's decisions—at least for as long as he was alive.

In 336 another happy event was lavishly celebrated in Constantinople; the wedding of Constantine's second son, Constantius, to the daughter of his stepbrother Julius Constantius. Already Constantine was setting a custom which was to be followed by the royal families in Europe for centuries: Young men of royal blood should marry to other persons of royal status. In Constantine's case, there were no royal families in other kingdoms suitable for a matrimonial union. So, he had to find for his daughters husbands from inside the family.

TROUBLE WITH THE PERSIANS, AGAIN

The first heavy clouds in the East appeared in the spring of 336. A delegation of Armenian nobles came to Constantinople to tell Constantine that a Persian satrap by the name of Waras had seized by treachery the Armenian king, Tiran, and had taken him to Persia where both of his eyes were put out. The Armenian kingdom had been largely Christian since 309, when king Tiridates had embraced the Christian faith. Armenia had been an independent kingdom for centuries and a close friend of the Romans. The Armenian ambassadors asked for Constantine's help.

While the delegation was still in Constantinople, the Persian army invaded Armenia and seized the country. The treaty Diocletian had signed with the Persians after their defeat by Galerius was violated after almost forty years.

The Persian king, Sapor, had come to the throne at the death of his father, when he was still in his mother's womb. During his childhood and adolescence, the Persian kingdom had remained quiet. Now Sapor had grown up and appeared determined to recover the territories Narses had lost almost forty years ago. The invasion of Armenia was the first step.

It is difficult to tell how much Sapor was influenced by

Constantine's veiled support for the Christians in Persia, judging by the rambling letter his envoys brought to him upon their return from Constantinople. Maybe it was not what Constantine said about the Christians but the total tenor of the letter which for a non-Christian sounded almost silly. It is quite possible that he interpreted the content of the letter as a veiled threat.

Whatever the answer to this question, Sapor, with the invasion of Armenia and the fomenting of unrest in Mesopotamia, seemed to strengthen the arguments of those who wanted a pre-emptive war against the Persians. Constantine decided to lead the military expedition himself.

BANNING THE HERETICS

I n the midst of all his other preoccupations—the construction of his "new Rome," the resettling of barbarians on imperial lands, weddings of family members, the loss of the mother he loved so deeply, the celebration of great anniversaries, and renewed problems with the Persian empire—Constantine had to spend much time trying again to reconcile divisions within the Church. To him the Christian religion could be the new, unifying force that could keep the sprawling empire together, and he considered the unity of the Church a key element in his imperial policy. This explains his involvement and his actions during the last twenty-three years of his life.

He had hoped that after the Council in Nicaea and the exile of Arius, the "all-embracing" Church would be truly united around the Statement of Faith the Council had adopted with such solemnity. A little over a year later, in September 326, he had decreed that Novatians, Valentinians, Marcionites, Paulinians and Cataphrygians were not allowed to congregate in their churches because they were "heretics." He wrote:

> "Let no one of you dare, from this time forward, meet
> in congregations. To prevent this, we command that
> you will be deprived of all the houses in which you
> have been accustomed to meet, and those places

should be handed over immediately to the all-embracing Church."

He further ordered the burning of all heretical writings. The heretics Constantine banned were relatively small groups of Christians, either following a charismatic leader or born out of some local experience. They were not a real threat to the Christian religion but to Constantine they were a blemish to his vision of a united Church. A few weeks later he issued another order exempting the Novatians from the ban because someone convinced him that they were not really heretics but extremely puritanical and ascetic believers.

Eusebius, ignoring the tragic killings of Crispus and Fausta which had taken place only weeks earlier, wrote a very flattering and rather overly optimistic passage in his *Life of Constantine*, hailing the unity Constantine's actions had brought to the "all-embracing" Church.

> "The members of the whole Church were united and made to one harmonious whole at unity with itself, shining with an unblemished radiance, while no heretical or schismatic group remained anywhere...the credit for this mighty achievement going solely to our God-protected king."

True, for the first three years after the council of Nicaea the situation appeared calm. Those who were unwilling to accept the Nicaea Creed kept their views to themselves. But it was a deceptive unity.

ATHANASIUS IS
ELECTED BISHOP

The first signs of trouble appeared shortly after the death of Alexander, the bishop of Alexandria, in 329. He had been the man who had started the initial feud with Arius. His death might have signaled an end of the dispute, now that Arius was also out of the way, an exile in far-off Treves in Gaul. But a potent supply of oil was thrown into the simmering fire with the election of Athanasius as the new bishop of Alexandria.

Athanasius was the most fanatical enemy of Arius and an uncompromising opponent to his theological views. His election to the throne was not accomplished without much wrangling, but in the end public acclaim for the man who had shone with his eloquence at the Council of Nicaea swept away all opposition and Athanasius became the new patriarch of Alexandria.

Within months, the dispute flared up again. Certain bishops and priests in Egypt and Libya refused to obey instructions from Athanasius (they claimed that he had been elected by only two bishops hiding in a dark corner of the church) accusing him of arrogant and dogmatic behavior.

The reports reached Constantine while he was happily overseeing the last stages in the construction of his new city on the Bosporus.

Osius was no longer at his side to guide him with his well-informed and moderate advice. Apparently, he had left Constantine's court after the violent deaths of Crispus and Fausta, unable to forgive Constantine for what he had done. It is a pity that he did not write a chronicle of his years with Constantine or if he did that no copy has been found. He had a great deal to say because he had been there, next to Constantine, for the sixteen crucial years between 310 and 326.

Without the wise counsel of the experienced and moderate cleric from Spain, Constantine had to rely on his own judgment. When he received the reports of renewed disagreements in Egypt and Libya, he ordered the few bishops and priests who opposed Athanasius to come to Nicomedia—Constantinople had not been inaugurated yet at the time—and explain their actions. Maybe Constantine hoped that in Nicomedia they would see the light and abandon their "error" (πλάνην). Instead they found influential friends. Strange as it may seem, Helena, the emperor's mother, had become very devoted to Lucian the Martyr and had a church built to his memory. Lucian was one of the victims of Diocletian's persecution, but he was also the teacher of Arius and of Eusebius, the bishop of Nicomedia. Long after his death on the block, Lucian's influence remained strong among the pro-Arius Christians.

Was Helena an Arian Christian? Her devotion to Lucian may give that impression, but one cannot say so with certainty because most of her other actions appear to have been in line with the teachings of the "all-embracing" Church. Helena was not the only person in the imperial family that may have looked at the opponents of Athanasius with a friendly eye. Constantia, the emperor's stepsister, was also friendly to the Arians. She was extremely fond of Eusebius, the bishop of Nicomedia, ever since the days when her husband Licinius had been the ruler of the eastern part of the empire. Eusebius had survived the elimination of Licinius only because Constantia had spoken strongly in his favor to Constantine. Eusebius favored Arius and at the Council of Nicaea had tried to shift the current in the direction of his idol.

Even this did not affect his standing within the imperial court.

The record is not entirely clear but it appears that the anti-Athanasius clerics from Egypt and Libya formed close ties with Eusebius of Nicomedia and Theognis of Nicaea, and with their help passed on to Constantine proof that it was Athanasius who should be blamed for the disunity and unrest in the churches of Egypt and Libya. Knowing that they could find friendly support within the imperial family, Eusebius and Theognis wrote to Athanasius asking him to restore Arius to communion. Athanasius flatly refused. Arius, he said, had started a deadly heresy and he had been anathematized by an ecumenical synod in Nicaea. How, then, could he be restored to communion?

Probably on the advice of Eusebius and Constantia, Constantine himself wrote also to Athanasius virtually ordering him to accept Arius to communion. "Now that you have been informed of my will, see that all who wish to enter the church are provided unhindered entry. If I hear that you have prevented any one from joining the services, I will immediately send someone to remove you from Alexandria." Athanasius was not scared by the imperial command and bravely replied that there could not be fellowship between heretics and true believers. Although no imperial emissary was sent at this time to deport Athanasius, the Arian party seemed to be dominant within the imperial court less than four years after Nicaea.

Then, for reasons not entirely clear, Constantine changed course again. It appears from what followed that the proof he had been given to put the blame on Athanasius proved false, and Constantine did not like to be deceived. Was Eusebius guilty of lying to the emperor? Very likely. Whatever the reasons, Constantine, ignoring this time his sister's pleas, issued an order deposing both Eusebius and Theognis and calling for a synod of bishops to fill the vacant sees. The area bishops held back, arguing that under the canons of the Church, the emperor did not have the right to remove a Christian bishop. Angered, Constantine wrote a letter to the people of Nicomedia accusing

Eusebius of being "a traitor to the all-embracing Church". He added for good measure the charge that as bishop of Nicomedia, Eusebius had cooperated with Licinius in organizing his oppressive persecution. He went on to say that Eusebius and Theognis had been plotting with the Egyptian and Libyan dissidents to undermine the Creed of Nicaea and to sow discord in the churches of Alexandria. In the end, enough bishops bowed to the emperor's orders and elected Amphion as bishop of Nicomedia, and Chrestus, bishop of Nicaea. Eusebius and Theognis went into exile. The pendulum had now swung against the friends of Arius.

CONSTANTINE
PARDONS ARIUS

The ancient sources show clearly that Constantine was not entirely certain about the course he was following. He wanted to preserve unity within the Church because he firmly believed that God would be displeased with him if he failed to act against those who undermined unity. But his strong actions had not been serving the "celestial quest" for unity. Only if all Christians—including above all the followers of Arius—accepted the Creed of Nicaea would unity be real.

Quite possibly his mother and his stepsister, who could talk to Constantine freely almost daily, tried to persuade him that Arius was not such a dangerous heretic after all, and that he should make an effort to see if a common ground could be reached. No doubt Constantia wanted also to see her favorite bishop, Eusebius, return from exile. Sozomenus, in his *Ecclesiastical History*, claims that Constantia was told "in a vision from God" that the exiled bishops held the true doctrine and that they had been unjustly banished.

Even before the death of Alexander and the election of Athanasius, Constantine had written letters to both Arius and Alexander urging them to come to terms and restore unity among the Christians. They both had refused using the best diplomatic language they could so that they would not offend the emperor. Then, after Alexander died, Constantine had written to Athanasius hoping that reconciliation could be possible. Athanasius proved more adamant than even Alexander.

In 330, as the festivities for the dedication of Constantinople were approaching, Constantine, evidently in a happy mood, wrote again to Arius. Socrates Scholasticus quotes the letter in his *Ecclesiastical History*.

> "Constantine, Victor, Augustus Maximus, to Arius. Long time ago, your Reverence received an invitation to come to me so that you might enjoy my presence. I have been surprised that you did not come forthwith. Take now a public carriage and hurry to my court so that having enjoyed my benevolence and solitude, you may return to your native city. May God keep you, most dear friend (φιλτατε).

This was a clear message that Constantine had decided to end Arius' exile. Arius could hardly ignore the invitation. But being always the stubborn theologian, he wrote back a carefully worded letter explaining his beliefs. He gingerly avoided the word *omoousion*, but still managed to give the impression that he was accepting the Creed of Nicaea. "Because our faith and our thoughts," he wrote, "are those of the Church and of the holy Scriptures, we pray that by exerting your peace-loving and Godly piety you will unite us to our mother Church...so that we may all pray as one for the peace of your kingdom and for that of your family." A few weeks later, Arius, riding a state supplied carriage, left Treves, a free man.

With Arius pardoned, Eusebius and Theognis could not remain in exile. Probably they returned to their sees even before Arius arrived.

THE ARIANS GAIN
MORE GROUND

Once again Constantine was moving away from the spirit of Nicaea. The next sign, after the release of Arius and the return of Eusebius and Theognis to their sees, came when Eustathius, the patriarch of Antioch, a staunch anti-Arian, was removed from his throne by his fellow bishops, accused of a scandalous life.

The move against Eustathius started in 330 while Constantine was busy inaugurating his new city. Certain pro-Arian bishops in Syria accused Eustathius of insulting Constantine's mother Helena, and of fathering an illegitimate son.

He vehemently denied the charges but to no avail. It is quite doubtful that, even if he believed that the emperor's mother favored the Arians, he would have spoken against Helena in front of witnesses. But false witnesses were never hard to find. It appears that no actual proof was presented to the synod of bishops which assembled in Antioch to try the case; nevertheless, a majority of bishops accepted the charge. They also accepted the charge that he had an illegitimate child. Although the mother later admitted that the father of the baby was another Eustathius, working as a coppersmith in Antioch, at the council of bishops she insisted that bishop Eustathius was the father of her son.

While the work of the synodical tribunal was in progress, riots roared through the streets of the city and fights broke out between supporters and opponents of Eustathius. "The argument would have been settled with swords if the watchful eye of Divine Providence," wrote Eusebius, "as well as the fear of the emperor's anger, had not quelled the fury of the mob." In the end, Eustathius was deposed.

When Constantine received word that some of the bishops had proposed his friend Eusebius of Caesaria as a candidate, he sent a letter advising his friend to decline because, as he wrote, both synods at Arles and at Nicaea had clearly stated that bishops should not be transferred from one see to another. Before the emperor's letter arrived, the synod elected Eusebius, but he prudently and properly declined. It was at that point that Constantine suggested as candidates the presbyters Euphronius and Georgius. Euphronius was a fanatical supporter of Arius, while Georgius had no strong views either way.

Constantine's letter to the bishops deserves special note because, in it, the emperor set a precedent for imperial interference in Episcopal elections.

> "...Having informed myself of the circumstances in this case...and having probed the matter deeply, I have written to the people of Antioch suggesting a course of action which will be pleasing to God and to the benefit of the Church...My information is that Euphronius, presbyter from Caesaria in Cappadocia, and Georgius a presbyter of Arethusa, appointed to that position by Alexander of Alexandria are both men of true faith..."

In his reference to Alexander of Alexandria, Constantine was subtly establishing his impartiality by offering as one of the two candidates a man appointed by the opponent of Arius. In reality, Geogius was not a strong opponent of Arius. In any event, half of the assembled bishops voted for Euphronius while the other half complained of imperial interference and refused to recognize the election as valid. Constantine sent to them strongly worded letters but he failed to change anyone's mind. With Athanasius' encouragement, the anti-Arians elected their own bishop and for the next eighty years Antioch had two camps, each electing a new bishop whenever its own died. Instead of unity, Constantine's intervention had resulted in further disunity.

ATTACKS ON ATHANASIUS

Constantine did not blame himself for what had happened in Antioch. He blamed Athanasius. To the emperor the litmus test was unity. Anyone who appeared at the moment to undermine the unity of the Church would feel Constantine's anger, regardless of his religious beliefs. This time it was Athanasius' turn again. The pro-Arian forces, seeing that they had gained Constantine's support or at least his benevolent neutrality, launched a relentless campaign to unseat the fiery patriarch of Alexandria.

Later Athanasius accused Eusebius of Caesaria of being behind the conspiracy. It will be difficult to argue that the charge was without foundation. In spite of the decisions in Nicaea, the Church, especially in the East, continued to be divided into two camps—in reality two political parties—vying for supremacy. Constantine was the man each camp wanted to win to its side and during the years after Nicaea, he was leaning to one or the other, reacting to what he was told, by whom, and under what circumstances.

In 331, the Arian partisans had decidedly the upper hand and their target was the elimination of Athanasius. This time, they joined forces with the supporters of Meletius who had established, as we know, a separate congregation in Upper Egypt, the "Church of the Martyrs." Meletius had died by this time, but another man by the name of John Arkaph had been elected in his place. Arkaph hated

Athanasius as much as the Arians did, so he had no problem in join-ing forces with them.

Arkaph and his friends first accused Athanasius of illegally imposing a tax so he could buy striped linen for use in the churches. The charge was rather ridiculous so they soon added two more charges, one of bribery, the other of sacrilege. They said that Athanasius had paid a large sum of money to one named Philomenos to intrigue against the emperor who, they argued, in the eyes of Athanasius had fallen under the spell of the Arians. They were appar-ently hoping that Athanasius would be brought before an imperial magistrate to answer the charge. Even if he were acquitted for lack of evidence, they were ready to bring up the second charge of sacrilege and force a synodical tribunal to examine the charges. Charges of vio-lating the ethical laws of the Church had worked well in the case of Eustathius in Antioch. The stratagem could succeed against Athanasius as well.

This charge of sacrilege would haunt Athanasius and the Church for years. The story comes, piece by piece, from both pro-Arian sources and from Athanasius himself, and we can reconstruct its essentials with some accuracy.

It appears that while Athanasius was visiting the Mareotis dis-trict, in Egypt, he sent a priest named Macarius to bring for question-ing a certain Ichyras who continued to officiate as a priest although even Meletius had asked him to stop doing so because he had not been ordained. Macarius went during mass to the house Ichyras used as his church and asked the man to come to see the patriarch. Ichyras refused, and in the scuffle that followed, Macarius overturned and smashed the wine cup Ichyras used as a chalice during the service. The Meletians, ignoring that Ichyras was not an ordained priest and that the wine cup could not have been considered a chalice, accused Athanasius of sacrilege since under the law he was responsible for the action of his agent.

Apparently the pro-Arian forces thought that this was a good time to bring Athanasius down. It was the spring of 332, when Constantine was busy with the invasion of the Goths under Araric. Athanasius would have no chance to appeal to the emperor for justice because the emperor would have no time to listen to him. But Athanasius was not an easy target. Without delay he left for Constantinople ready to answer the charges. When he was received by the emperor, he produced a document signed by Ichyras himself stating that he had been pressured to make the initial accusations and that nothing had really happened in his house of worship. Later he was to claim that he had signed the document under pressure from Athanasius, but at the time Constantine was convinced by the document and with the advice of his Praetorian Prefect, Ablavius, an admirer of Athanasius, dismissed the charges and sent Athanasius back to Alexandria in time to celebrate Easter.

Athanasius in his Κατα Αριανων Απολογια (Treatise Against the Arians) claims that Constantine in a sharp reversal of policy gave him a letter warning the people in the city of Alexandria "to avoid any disturbances" and telling them that "I have received your Bishop Athanasius with a large measure of benevolence and have treated him as a man of God." The events that followed show that the Arians had suffered a temporary setback. Apparently Athanasius, with his magnetic personality and mesmerizing eloquence, had not only persuaded the emperor of his innocence but had raised doubts in his mind about the honesty of the Arians.

Athanasius' return to Alexandria sparked some riots in spite of Constantine's warning, but it also prompted Arius to pass to the attack personally. After his release from exile, Arius had returned to Alexandria, and he had tried to resume his work. Athanasius had refused to let him go back to his parish in Baucalis. To counter the effect of Athanasius meeting with the emperor, Arius sent a letter to Constantine, claiming that all the Christians in Libya and most of those in Egypt were behind him, and that Constantine should force Athanasius to let him go back to his parish. Arius, convinced that he had friends in high places, wrote with a certain tone of arrogance which must have irritated Constantine. But it had been his position that for the sake of unity Arius should be allowed to return to his parish, so he decided this time, instead of clerics, to send two officials from the department of the Master of Offices with letters addressed to both Athanasius and Arius asking them to end their quarrel.

It appears that Constantine was still under the influence of Athanasius, because in his letter to the patriarch of Alexandria, he spoke harshly of the Arians, identifying them with the followers of Porphyrius, one of the most virulently anti-Christian pagans. Whatever his intention, Constantine with his words appeared to encourage Athanasius to take a harsh line against the Arians. Not surprisingly, Athanasius went as far as having their writings burned as blasphemous and heretical.

Even under the best of circumstances, Constantine's letters and their delivery by government officials could not have helped the cause of unity. The emperor was losing his touch, vacillating from one side to the other and back. Age and success had changed him. He had become more arrogant, but also more susceptible to people who had his ear at the moment, or who flattered more effectively his vanity and encouraged his almost fanatical belief that he was God's appointed vicar on earth "to protect the true religion and assure unity in the holy all-embracing Church."

For at least another twenty months, Athanasius remained in the emperor's favor. But his good fortune could not last. His enemies were only waiting for the next opening.

ATHANASIUS ACCUSED
OF MURDER

In 334, John Arkaph, the Meletian bishop, accused Athanasius of complicity in the murder of Meletian bishop Arsenius of Hypsela. He even offered as evidence a blackened human hand which, he claimed, was what was left of Arsenius. Athanasius protested that the entire story was a lie but Arkaph came up with specific details saying that bishop Plusianus, on orders from Athanasius, had captured bishop Arsenius and had tied him to a pillar in his own house. After Plusianus and his thugs had beaten Arsenius to death, they chopped up the body, set the house on fire and left. The blackened hand was the proof.

By the time these charges reached Constantine, more than a year had passed since his meeting with Athanasius, and apparently the effect of the bishop's eloquence was fading. Maybe Constantine's mother, during her final days, had asked him to be more protective of those who followed the teachings of her favorite saint, Lucian the Martyr. They were called Col-Lucians but in effect they were supporters of Arianism. Maybe Constantine was convinced by Arius' friends in the imperial court that where there was smoke there was fire and that maybe Athanasius was not an innocent man.

Constantine was thinking of the celebration that was coming in a few months, in the summer of 335—his thirtieth year as emperor. He wanted it to be the most magnificent Christian festival, to be crowned with the dedication of the Church of the Holy Sepulchre in Jerusalem, the church his mother had started but had not lived to see completed. He did not want the festivities to be marred by nasty quarrels within the Church. The enemies of Athanasius within the imperial court had a good argument. Whatever the truth, the case against the patriarch of Alexandria should be closed one way or another. They advised the emperor to summon Athanasius and thrash out all the accusations. Constantine finally agreed to investigate the case of the murdered bishop but he refused to reopen the question of the broken chalice. The murder of the Meletian bishop, if proven, was not only an issue for the Church but also a crime punishable under the laws of the empire.

Constantine asked his half-brother Dalmatius, who was the Praetorian Prefect for the Orient, to investigate the case. Clearly Constantine regarded Athanasius' status as being high enough to have the case investigated by the highest official in the Orient, right below the nominal authority of his young son Caesar Constantius. At the same time he wrote letters to the area bishops asking them to assemble in Caesaria for a synod to take up the charges against Athanasius. The synod did not take place until the following year, 335, and it met not in Caesaria but in the town of Tyre.

Athanasius appeared before the synod accompanied by some fifty clerics, prepared to defend himself. He found that the synod was packed with his enemies, but he had a surprise in store for them. When Arkaph produced with great drama the blackened hand, accusing Athanasius of murdering Arsenius, the accused punctured the charges in a most spectacular way. Here is the story as given by Theodoretus in his *Ecclesiastical History* and by Athanasius in his *Treatise Against the Arians*.

After the accusers had enjoyed a moment of triumph as they passed the blackened hand around, Athanasius asked in a quiet voice if any of those present knew Arsenius personally. A number of bishops claimed to have known the murdered bishop well. Would they recognize him if they saw him, Athanasius asked. Certainly they replied "if he were alive." At that point Athanasius signaled to a man who was standing near the doorway, his face covered with his cloak. The man, his face still covered, moved to the front. "Lift your cloak," Athanasius said. The man removed the cloak and "lo and behold it was Arsenius himself". Athanasius moved closer and drew first one and then the other sleeve. Arsenius had both his hands. "Has God given any man more than two hands?" Athanasius asked with a sarcastic smile.

What had happened? Theodoretus explains. "Arsenius had been persuaded by his friends to go into hiding" and stay out of sight until Athanasius was sent to the block for murder. "Then they cut off the right hand of a corpse, embalmed it, put it in a box, and carried it around saying that it was the hand of Arsenius." Athanasius, however, had discovered the place where Arsenius was hiding and had forced him to come to Tyre to tell the truth.

For a moment there was stunned silence. Then one of the accusers declared loudly that all this was sorcery and devil's work. The man was not Arsenius although he had his face, he was not even human but an illusion produced by Athanasius with his knowledge of black magic. Athanasius asked the bishops to come and touch the man he was accused of having murdered. The meeting turned into a brawl and Dionysius, the imperial officer attending the meeting on orders form Constantine, had to hurry Athanasius out to save his life.

In the face of the reappearance of Arsenius, the bishops could not condemn Athanasius. Still, his enemies were not prepared to give up their campaign to unseat him. Claiming that matters were still obscure and unresolved, they asked the synod to appoint a special commission to go to Egypt and investigate matters on the spot. In a secret meeting, the bishops selected a six member commission. Athanasius protested in vain that all six members were his avowed enemies.

Athanasius had no other recourse but to go to Constantinople to see the emperor and clear matters in a face to face meeting. In a letter Constantine sent to the bishop of Tyre after the synod, he described in colorful detail his meeting with Athanasius. Here is the story in the emperor's own words:

> "As I was returning on horseback to the city which bears my name, Athanasius, the bishop, presented himself in the middle of the road, accompanied by certain individuals, so unexpectedly that I felt very surprised by the sight. The all-seeing God is my witness that at first I did not know who he was, but some of my attendants gave me the information after having ascertained who he was and the reason for coming to me. I did not grant him an audience but he persisted and although I had refused him and I was about to have him removed from my presence, he told me with greater boldness than he had ever before shown, that all he wanted was to have you come over here so that he might in your presence complain of the injustice done to him."

Constantine, impressed by Athanasius' willingness to defend his innocence in a face to face confrontation with his accusers, asked Dionysius to submit a report on what had happened at Tyre. Told that the synod there had been a travesty, Constantine dispatched letters to the bishops asking them to come to Constantinople. Before his instructions could reach them, they received the report of the commission which had gone to Egypt to investigate the charges. The report was critical of Athanasius. On the strength of that report, the bishops condemned Athanasius by a majority of votes, declared the Meletians to be true believers in the "all-embracing Church," and then moved on to Jerusalem to dedicate the church of the Holy

Sepulchre. At the synod they held in Jerusalem, they pronounced Arius to be in full communion with the "all-embracing" Church. The Arian party appeared to be triumphant. They evidently thought that they had the emperor on their side.

They were wrong. Constantine hoped to have the celebration of his thirtieth anniversary as emperor free of Church quarrels. Instead the chasm was deepening. Thoroughly disgusted he wrote angrily to the bishops that he was disturbed by the "tumult and disorder" which had marred their councils. He had sent those letters soon after their synod at Tyre, but the letters summoning them to Constantinople reached them when they were already in Jerusalem. It was clear to them that Constantine was in a vile mood. Prudently, they decided not to go to Constantinople. Instead, a small delegation including Eusebius of Nicomedia and Eusebius of Caesaria traveled to the new capital. Both of them knew Constantine well. They realized that he had been leaning on their side only because he had thought that this would help the unity of the Church. They had gone too far, and now the emperor was mad at them. Wisely they did not try to bring up the old discredited charges against Athanasius. Instead, speaking not as enemies of Athanasius but as devoted friends of the emperor, they told Constantine that they had been informed that, if Athanasius did not get his way, he was planning to call on his followers and have them prevent the shipment of grain from Alexandria to Constantinople. Athanasius protested vehemently that he had no such designs. He was just a bishop, he said, with no political ambitions or taste for intrigue. Did his enemies offer proof, corroborated by imperial officials in Alexandria? The sources do not say. But we know that in the spring of 336, Constantine exiled Athanasius to the court of his son Constantine II. The Caesar of the West received the bishop of Alexandria as an honored guest. Most likely, Constantine had not sent Athanasius away because he had given much weight to the accusation regarding the grain shipments, but because he wanted to get Athanasius away from Alexandria and end the turmoil. This exile turned out to be a blessing for Athanasius. With his personality and forceful defense of the doctrines enshrined in the Creed of Nicaea, he won over young Constantine who after the death of his father became the strongest supporter and protector of the patriarch of Alexandria and of his anti-Arian convictions.

THE DEATH OF ARIUS

With Athanasius out of the way, the Arian party could look forward to the quiet consolidation of its influence in the Eastern Church. Of course, they were not going to challenge the Creed of Nicaea, which Constantine held as the focal point of Church unity. But by now the dispute had become as much a matter of personalities and competing factions with vested interests as of questions of doctrine.

The removal of Athanasius did not end the strife. His many followers in Alexandria remained as faithful as ever and clashes between the two camps erupted time and again. Antonius the hermit—later St. Antony—wrote repeatedly to Constantine praying for the return of Athanasius to his see. The emperor refused to reconsider Athanasius' exile but he banished John Arkaph from Alexandria to even the score.

But the success of the Arian party remained incomplete as long as Arius continued to be excommunicated. A majority of the bishops assembled in Jerusalem to dedicate the church of the Holy Sepulchre had declared Arius to be in good standing but many more churchmen throughout the Orient considered him to be a heretic. His friends at the imperial court, with the bishop of Nicomedia taking the lead, persuaded Constantine to summon Arius to Constantinople and there, in the emperor's presence, to clear his name of the dark stain of the heretic.

Constantine, now an old and troubled man, finally agreed. In the fall of 336, Arius came to Constantinople. The encounter, as reported, shows that Constantine, in spite of his vacillation between Athanasius and Arius, remained at heart the champion of the "holy all-embracing (Catholic) Church" and of the Nicaean Creed.

In a face to face confrontation, Constantine asked Arius point blank if he accepted the faith of the all-embracing Church. Arius nodded in the affirmative.

"Can I trust you?" Constantine persisted. "Are you really of the true Faith?"

Arius solemnly affirmed that he was indeed of the true Faith.

Constantine was not convinced. "Have you renounced the errors (*planin*) which you held in Alexandria in the past?"

Arius again declared that he had accepted the true Faith.

"Will you swear it before God?" Constantine asked.

Arius took the required oath, and Constantine, satisfied but clearly still uncertain, said, "Go, and if you are not true to the Faith, may God judge you from Heaven."

This strange scene is described by Socrates in his *Ecclesiastical History* , by Sozomenus, and by Athanasius himself in a letter to Bishop Serapion of Thmuis. Athanasius told his friend that he had been given the details by a priest who was present at the interview.

Before he left the palace, Arius begged the emperor to ask the patriarch of Constantinople to admit him to communion as a solemn testimony that he was now fully accepted into the Church. Alexander, the bishop of Constantinople, was very old and feeble but he did not lack courage. He told the emperor that he could not in good conscience offer the sacraments to one who, in his eyes, was a heretic. To quote Socrates, Alexander "was not concerned with his own fate being so advanced in years." His main concern was the protection of the principles of Faith of which he regarded himself to be the appointed guardian.

For days Bishop Alexander went through an agonizing ordeal of conscience locked in the church of Aghia Eirini (Holy Peace) which was the official church of the patriarch. Prostrate before the altar he prayed that he might not live to see the heretic enter the church, and that if he himself held the true Faith, Arius the impious be punished for his impiety (ασεβειαν).

Constantine brushed aside the patriarch's objections and set the day, a Sunday, for the public offering of the sacraments to Arius. On Saturday, the day before the appointed Sunday for Arius' appearance to the church of Aghia Eirini, the controversial cleric went to the palace for last minute instructions from the court officials. Socrates describes in considerable and colorful detail what happened.

Arius left the palace accompanied by several friends and was passing through the center of the city, very conspicuous (περιοπτος) to bystanders, evidently happy and proud that the hour of his triumph was approaching. As the group came to the Forum of Constantine and was passing by the Porphyry Column with Constantine's statue at the top, Arius felt a stabbing pain in his abdomen. He walked a few more steps, but then he asked to be taken to a nearby public latrine (αφοδευτηριον), his face pale and his body doubling in pain. He went inside the latrine while his friends stayed outside waiting. When much time passed and Arius did not come out, alarmed, they opened the door. They found Arius sprawled on the ground in a pool of blood, dead of a violent hemorrhage.

One can imagine the sensation the news must have caused as it traveled through the city. Not only patriarch Alexander but all the faithful attributed the death of Arius to divine retribution in answer to their prayers. Within minutes excited worshippers filled the churches which were ablaze with lighted candles as if they were celebrating a great holiday.

The sudden death of Arius made also a strong impression on Constantine's superstitious mind. Arius had been punished by God because he had taken a false oath. Now Constantine was fully convinced that what the Council of Nicaea had decided was what the Supreme God really wanted. Arius was indeed a heretic.

The partisans of Arius naturally hinted that he had been poisoned, and in whispers they blamed his death on his enemies in the palace. Is it not true that he had just left the palace, they asked. Others spoke of some magic (βασκανια) performed by Athanasius. Certainly there is no evidence whatever that either Constantine or Athanasius—who was hundreds of miles away—had any part in Arius' death. If he was indeed poisoned, some anti-Arian officials in the palace must have acted without the emperor's knowledge. Constantine would not have ordered the poisoning of Arius because he could never be sure whether Arius was "a man of God." In his superstitious mind he would have never dared risk displeasing the Supreme God with such a deed. In any event, the accepted view at the time and for many years to come—especially among the faithful of the all-embracing Church—was that Arius had died struck by God for his impiety and perjury.

The death of the gifted heretic did not signal the end of his influence or the continuing feud of the two religious parties. In less than seven months, Constantine too would be dead, and the strife would continue under his successors for another hundred years of more.

Preparing for War
with Persia

W hile Constantine was struggling with the disunity inside the Church, other crucial problems called for his attention. Sapor, the Persian king, was definitely on the move. The seizure of Armenia was a first step. Rebellious uprisings in Mesopotamia was a second. Constantine could not let the Persian get his way. Throughout the year 336, he sent orders to his sons and their Praetorian Prefects to step up the recruitment of soldiers under the direction of the high military officers in their regions. For the aging Constantine, the preparations for a campaign against the Persians brought back memories of his years of military glory. After more than ten years of dealing with the administration of the empire, its economy, the building of his new city, and the thorny religious quarrels, Constantine was again in his element. By all accounts, he welcomed but did not provoke the Persian challenge.

Although he spoke so many times of peace, Constantine always found war exhilarating. His personal life since the ill-fated Vicennalia in Rome had not been very happy. There is no evidence anywhere that another woman entered his life. As a man, of course, he used *palakides* (odalisks) for his pleasure, but those were purely physical encounters with no meaning. The only two women who were close to him in the last ten years of his life were his mother Helena and his stepsister Constantia. His entire life was devoted to the governing of the empire. A war with Persia would make him feel young again. Ignoring his old age—he was now sixty-five years old—he decided to lead the campaign himself.

In late February 337 he invited to the palace the area bishops and spoke to them of the forthcoming campaign. Sapor was a nonbeliever, and an enemy of the Christians within his realm. The war Constantine planned would deserve the blessing of the Almighty God (την του παντοδυναμου Θεου ευλογιαν). The bishops expressed their support and offered to accompany the emperor to the battlefield to assist him with their prayers.

In the rapidly changing empire, especially in the East, with Christianity gaining converts by the thousands, a war crowned with a religious halo had a much better chance to receive popular acclaim and infuse the troops with religious fervor. As a symbolic sign, Constantine ordered a large tent to be made in the shape of a church so that he could pray in it during the campaign.

Eusebius reports that Sapor, alarmed by Constantine's preparations for war, sent a delegation to Constantinople with assurances of peaceful intentions. Maybe he was still unprepared for a head-on clash with the mighty legions. Although Eusebius claims that "the most peace-minded king" (ειρηνικωτατος βασιλευς) accepted Sapor's assurances at the moment, we cannot be sure that Constantine had given up his campaign plans. We will never know because a few weeks later he was dead.

CONSTANTINE FALLS
SUDDENLY ILL

The first reported sign that the emperor was not well came on April 1st, Easter Sunday of 337. Easter, coming after forty days of fasting, was a day of joyous celebration, a feast with a great deal of food and wine. From the description of Constantine's final weeks, we can rule out cancer, a stroke, or any infectious disease. He most likely suffered a mild heart attack after heavy eating and drinking on Easter day, "splendidly enjoying the holiday" (λαμπραν την εορτην καταφαιδρυνας). The attack was mild enough for him to think that he might be able to travel all the way to the Jordan river to be baptized, a move he himself said he had contemplated for a long time.

During the first week after the heart attack, he was advised by his physicians to take hot baths to find relief. He did, but if anything he felt weaker. Then he decided to go south. Did he expect to go as far as the Jordan river? In any event, accompanied by many palace officials, clerics, and servants, Constantine crossed the Bosporus and traveled on a litter going south. He only managed to reach Drepanon, the little town where his mother had spent so many years after her divorce from Constantius. Constantine had renamed the town to Helenopolis, the town of Helena, in honor of his mother.

Apparently he suffered there another heart attack because prayers for his recovery were offered at the church of Lucian the Martyr his mother had build in honor of her favorite saint. His condition showed no improvement. While he was still inside the church, he felt that the time was near. He fell on his knees and asked the clergy to accept him as a member of the Church, and to baptize him so that he could receive absolution for the sins he had committed in his life.

He confessed as it was required, and with the laying on of hands he was accepted as a catechumen. All these years he had not even become a catechumen—a prospective member of the Church. Now there was not much time left for procrastination. Since Drepanon did not have proper accommodations for the comfort of the dying emperor, and since Nicomedia was only a stone's throw away, they moved him to an imperial palace in the outskirts of the old imperial capital.

Laying in bed, he called to his side Eusebius of Nicomedia and other bishops, and in a halting voice told them that the moment he had "thirsted and prayed for" had come at last and he was begging them to give him "the seal which confers immortality" (της αθανατοποιητου σφραγιδος). To explain why he had not asked to be baptized earlier, he told them that he had hoped to be baptized in the river Jordan but "God has willed otherwise and I bow to His will." The Church had been very critical of people who were asking to be baptized while they were on their deathbed. Many believed that with the baptism all their sins were washed away, so they waited until the last moment when they were fairly sure that they were not going to sin any more. Maybe Constantine had delayed his baptism with something of the sort of mind, because to reassure the bishops he told them that if he were to recover and live longer he would set for himself "rules of life that will be proper for God" (θεσμους βιου Θεω εποντας εμαυτω διατεταξομαι).

Constantine was then baptized by Eusebius, the pro-Arian bishop of Nicomedia. After the ceremony he was dressed in shining and royal garments and lay down on a bed covered with sparkling white linen sheets. He said that if he recovered he would never again wear the imperial purple but instead would always wear the simple garments of a repentant man. As was the custom, officers of his army passed by his bed to see him for the last time. Many were weeping.

More than forty days had passed since his first heart attack and Constantine was growing weaker by the day. It was now clear that he was dying. At last, word was sent to his son Constantius in Antioch that his father was gravely ill. Constantius left Antioch immediately, but before he could reach Nicomedia, Constantine, possibly after suffering a third massive attack, died "around noon" (αμφι μεσημβρινας ηλιου ωρας προς τον αυτου Θεον ανελαμβανετο) on the 22nd day of May, which that year happened to be the holiday of the Pentecost. He had survived the first heart attack by only seven weeks.

THE FUNERAL

As soon as Constantius reached Nicomedia, he took over the arrangements for his father's funeral. After the embalming, the attendants "placed the body in a golden catafalque" (χρυση κατετιθεντο λαρνακι) which they covered with a deep red imperial cape. They placed the catafalque on a carriage and, with columns of soldiers with shining spears leading the procession, the funeral train started for Constantinople.

Thousands of grieving people from the nearby towns and villages lined the way. The procession crossed the Bosporus on barges and then walked up to the imperial palace. It seemed that every person living in Constantinople had come out to pay their respects to the dead emperor. Constantine, before he died, had given instructions to the palace officials to distribute food and other goods to the people from his private purse. He was generous to the very end. But the handouts were not the only reason for the popular reverence. Although Constantine's popularity had lost much of its luster in the last years of his life—many in the marketplace called him *trakhalos*, referring with a sneer to his thick neck—to millions in the empire he was an almost mythical person. To the Christians, of course, he was the man who had ended their persecution and had embraced the Church with his imperial authority. And, if we are to believe Eusebius, even the people in Rome, many of them pagans, as soon as

462

they learned of the emperor's death, by decision "of the Senate and the People of Rome (SPQR) they ordered the closing of the public baths and of the marketplaces and everything that they used to make life pleasant. And with long faces the erstwhile joyful, honored the departed with offerings..." Eusebius further claims that the citizens of Rome asked "with loud voices to have the body taken to Rome to be interred in the imperial city (βασιλίδι πόλει)."

The request of the Romans was not fulfilled. Constantine had long ago made clear where he wanted to be buried. The sarcophagus was waiting for him in the church of the Holy Apostles.

When the procession reached the palace, the armed units paused and the golden catafalque was taken through the "Khalki" Gate into the imperial palace, placed on a high pedestal in the great hall. The body was adorned with the royal insignia, the diadem and the deep red imperial cloak. Hundreds of candles were lit and were kept burning day and night, while a large number of officials stood around as an honor guard. We may let Eusebius describe the viewing of the body. "The leaders of the army, the counts, and all from the order of the *archons*, who in the past under the law were required to bow before the king came and, did not change their customary ways, but kissed the hem of the purple with bent knees bowing to the king on the catafalque, acting after death as they did when he was alive. After the officials of the highest rank, the members of the Senate and all those who had official positions passed in front of the bier, and after them the people from all the municipalities with their wives and children passed by to view the body. It took so long for all of them to pass by that the military discussed whether they should preserve and guard the body until the king's sons arrived to honor their father by escorting him to his burial." The funeral had been delayed for several weeks in the hope that his other two sons would come. They did not.

In the end, the funeral could not be postponed for much longer. The summer heat was not helping matters. The Christian Church did not allow the type of embalming that could prevent the decomposition of the body. The religious saying was that "man is of the earth and to the earth he must return" (χους ει και εις χουν απελευσει). After so many days the body must have begun to show signs of progressing decomposition. Finally Constantius decided not to wait for his brothers any longer.

With Constantius leading the funeral procession, the cortege left the palace for the church of the Holy Apostles. It was a military, not a religious funeral. "A long line of thick columns of military battalions was leading the way, followed by lines of guardsmen with glittering spears, flanking on both sides the body of the king." Many palace officials in their splendid robes and impressive insignia followed, while thousands of people stood reverently on both sides of the street, the Christians among them making the sign of the cross as the catafalque passed by.

When the cortege reached the church of the Holy Apostles, the pallbearers took the catafalque inside the church where the patriarch, flanked by many bishops and presbyters in their religious vestments, waited to perform the last rites for the first Christian emperor. Constantius did not go into the church because he had not been baptized yet. According to Sulpicius Severus "Constantius was still a catechumen" (*Constantius erat tamen catechumenus*).

After the funeral service, the body was placed into the impressive sarcophagus Constantine had prepared for himself.

THE AFTERMATH

In the 9th day of September 337, the three sons of Constantine, Constantine II (Flavius Claudius Constantinus), Constantius II (Flavius Julius Constantius), and Constans (Flavius Julius Constans), moved to the rank of Augustus in military ceremonies, acclaimed by the troops in keeping with the earlier tradition. This must have been arranged in secret correspondence among the three brothers.

They had a problem. Constantine had raised to the rank of Caesar his nephew Dalmatius and had given him control over the Balkans including the area of Constantinople. He had also installed as king of Cappadocia his son-in-law and nephew Hannibalianus. The three brothers were in agreement that the empire belonged to them. The fate of Dalmatius and Hannibalianus was sealed.

Strangely the slaughter started with Constantine's step-brothers, Julius Constantius, known as the Patrician because of his slender and aristocratic bearing, and Dalmatius, known as the Censor, an honorary title with a high tradition in ancient Rome. Caesar Dalmatius and King Hannibalianus were his sons.

The first signs of trouble appeared a few weeks after Constantine's funeral. Eusebius, the bishop of Nicomedia, we are told by Philostorgus, went to Constantius and told him a chilling secret. His father had not died of natural causes. He had been poisoned by his two stepbrothers, Constantius the Patrician and Dalmatius the Censor.

Philostorgus goes on with a rather tall story. He writes that Constantine, "upon learning of the plot, wrote his Will, demanding that vengeance be launched, commanding his sons to see this was done lest evil men should do the same to them. He then gave his Will to Eusebius, the bishop of Nicomedia. To prevent the emperor's brothers from finding the Will, if they suspected anything, he folded the scroll and put it in the dead emperor's hand and covered it with the clothes. And when the brothers commanded him to reveal the Will to them, he handed them a scroll similar to the one the emperor held. Afterwards, Eusebius gave Constantius the Will the emperor had written."

How much truth is in this fascinating story? Eusebius of Nicomedia two years later became patriarch of Constantinople, the highest honor a Christian bishop could hope to receive. Was this a reward for some extraordinary service? Eusebius was indeed a survivor and an astute politician. He had started as a bishop of Berytus (Beyrut) and then, back in the days of Licinius, he contrived to be elected bishop of Nicomedia, the imperial capital of the East where he became a close friend of Licinius and his wife Constantia, Constantine's stepsister. He survived the fall of Licinius and continued as bishop of Nicomedia even when Constantine was there as the sole emperor. At the Council of Nicaea he sided with Arius and refused to sing the *anathema*, excommunicating Arius for his heretical views. Yet, he remained bishop of Nicomedia. His close friendship with Constantia, a pro-Arian herself, was certainly an asset. He had a falling off with Constantine and was briefly expelled and exiled but he soon returned back and became an even more influential adviser of Constantine who was at times leaning toward the Arian party himself. Then, irony of ironies, it was he, an Arian bishop, who baptized the dying Constantine, the champion of the Nicaean Creed. Did Eusebius forge a Will of the dead emperor knowing that Constantius would welcome the information? Was that the extraordinary service which justified his transfer to the see of Constantinople—a transfer which was not in keeping with the Nicaean and Arletian canons of the Church? Those canons did not permit the transfer of bishops from one see to another to avert rivalry and intrigue among bishops to move to more attractive sees. Zonaras, writing later, claims that Constantius accused his uncles of poisoning his father, but Zosimus does not give a reason for the killings. He simply speaks of the killings with undisguised distaste.

It is very unlikely that Constantine's stepbrothers would have plotted to poison him. Julius Constantius, the Patrician, was a refined man, enjoying a life of comfort as a member of the imperial family. Married in his younger days to Galla, the sister of Senator Rufinus, a most prominent member of the imperial Court, he had one son with her, Gallus, and a daughter, Eusebia. When Galla died, he married for the second time to Basilina, the daughter of Praetorian Prefect Julius Julianus. She died soon after giving birth to a boy named Julian, the future emperor that came down in history as Julian the Apostate. Constantine had also arranged the marriage of his son Constantius to the daughter of Julius Constantius, Eusebia. No, the Patrician had nothing to gain and much to lose if Constantine died, because the emperor's sons were selfish and arrogant and apparently had no genuine affection for their uncles.

Dalmatius the Censor, too, had no reason to harbor ill will toward Constantine. Constantine had raised one of his sons, Dalmatius, to the rank of Caesar, and his other son Hannibalianus to king of Cappadocia while giving him as his wife his daughter Constantina. He had nothing to gain by poisoning Constantine.

Still, Constantius may have welcomed the false evidence that his father had died of poisoning. He wanted to eliminate his cousins and with them their fathers and several other high officials who had been close to his father. The rumor about the plot to poison Constantine was a useful excuse.

In the early part of September, a military detachment, on direct orders from Constantius, arrested Julius Constantius and a few days later executed him by beheading in one of the wine cellars of the palace, without trial or even an interrogation. He was Constantius' father-in-law. How did his wife Eusebia react to her father's execution on orders from her husband? The chroniclers do not say, but it was not the first time that such cruel killings had happened in the family and probably after much weeping life returned to normal.

Anastasia, Constantine's stepsister, who had been married back in 312, to Bassianus only to become a widow a few months later when her husband was killed by Constantine for treason, was now married to Flavius Optatus, a tutor in his early days to Licinius' son Licinianus, who by gaining Constantine's favor he had risen in the Court, had married Anastasia, and had even received the honor of being elected consul in 334. We have no word of what his crime was, but he, too died on the block, leaving poor Anastasia a widow for the second time, this time by a decision of her nephew.

Within days, Constantius ordered the arrest of Ablavius who was Constantine's last Praetorian Prefect. Ablavius came from a poor family and had started his career as a scribe in the office of the governor of Crete at the beginning of the century. He rose through the ranks, especially after 326 when, by then a high official, he was with Constantine in Rome. Rumors have it that he was the one who told Constantine about Fausta's tryst with his son Crispus. There is no written proof of this, but Ablavius' meteoric rise in the following eleven years may give credence to the rumor. Shortly before Constantine's death, Ablavius' daughter Olympias was betrothed to Constantine's third son, Constans, the Caesar of Italy and Africa. Did Constantius punish him for his actions in Rome, which, as the rumor had it, had provoked the gruesome death of Constantius' mother Fausta? Every scrap of evidence we have shows that Fausta was very close to her children. Was the punishment of Ablavius an act of revenge? Evidently Constantius was not stopped by the thought that Ablavius was his younger brother's prospective father-in-law. Did

Constans also know why Ablavius was being punished? Be that as it may, Ablavius was exiled to Bithynia and his property confiscated. Then, a few months later he was executed without any formal charges brought against him.

But the main targets were the two cousins, Caesar Dalmatius, and Hannibalianus the king of Cappadocia. With them, Constantius faced a problem. They commanded their own legions. For a man of twenty, Constantius proved that he was quite mature, both in cruelly eliminating his relatives, and also in planning his moves with a great deal of cunning when direct force was not the best solution.

He apparently found willing officers in the armies of his cousins to help him eliminate them. Both of them had been in command for a rather short time, with no opportunity to build the type of loyalty that is the foundation of imperial rule over the soldiers. Constantius' agents could point out that the great Constantine had three sons and only they were entitled to inherit his imperium. Dalmatius and Hannibalianus should be decent enough to step down on their own. It was an argument that made sense to the men in the legions. When Dalmatius and Hannibalianus showed no intention of stepping down, Constantius' agents cleverly inflamed the soldiers' feelings against them. In brief rebellions, in Thrace and Cappadocia, the angered troops seized and killed them, only days apart from each other, in the spring of 338, less that ten months from the death of Constantine.

Now, in addition to Constantine's three sons, only two young boys remained alive from all the male descendants of Constantius Chlorus, the father of the great Constantine. The two boys were Gallus and Julian, the son's of Julius Constantius, the Patrician. Gallus was sixteen, Julian only six.

The three brothers came together for a conference in Pannonia, a location convenient to Constantius coming from Constantinople, Constans coming from Mediolanum, and Constantine II coming from Treves. They were much too young all three of them to rule the mighty empire. Constantine II was a little over twenty-two, Constantius just over twenty, and Constans eighteen. Still, they acted sensibly and divided the empire without violent disagreements.

Constantine II kept the lands he already had under his control, the British Isles, Gaul, Spain. Constantius for some reason did not take the lands which his father had given to Caesar Dalmatius, now dead. These lands included Constantinople. Instead, he asked for all the Orient including Egypt and Mesopotamia, and the kingdom of Cappadocia which brought the entire Asia Minor under his control. Constans, the youngest, was treated very well by his older brothers. They gave him, in addition to the lands he already had—Italy and Africa from Libya to Mauretania (today's Morocco)—the entire Balkan peninsula, including the city of Constantinople. For some reason, Constans did not move his court to that city but instead stayed on in Mediolanum.

The three brothers did not let their religious differences interfere with their amicable distribution of the empire. Constantius, already under the influence of Eusebius of Nicomedia, was leaning toward the Arians. Constantine II had been with the exiled Athanasius for the past two years and had been impressed by the man's personality and theological views. He ended Athanasius' exile and the prominent prelate returned to Alexandria without delay. Since Egypt was part of Constantius' domain, he must have raised no objection to the return of the patriarch of Alexandria to his see. Constans also favored Athanasius, and disliked Arius. In this, he was in agreement with his subjects because the Arians had found little support among the Christians in Italy.

Athanasius now became the major figure in the campaign to restore the supremacy of the Nicaean Creed. His efforts did not succeed until some years after his death in 373. In the thirty-five years after his return from exile, Athanasius was forced three more times to abandon his see, twice finding refuge in the desert. During the reign of Constantius, Arianism had the support of the emperor and it was mainly because of the uncompromising efforts of Athanasius that the Nicaean Creed survived and, after the death of Emperor Valens in 378, gained ground throughout the empire.

The three brothers remained on good terms with each other for no more than three years. In 339 Constans offered the Balkan peninsula including the city of Constantinople to his brother Constantius. The youngest son had a reason for his generous gesture. He needed his brother's help because their older brother Constantine II was showing dangerous signs of greed and arrogance. Constantine II regarded himself as being the senior Augustus, entitled to interfere freely with the affairs of his brothers. Constantius in the Orient was rather far way, but young Constans was much too close and he was the one who felt most directly his big brother's meddling.

The simmering conflict exploded in 340. Young Constans was engaged in a fight with unruly tribes along the Danube and had marched with his legions to restore order. While he was preoccupied there, his brother Constantine II marched into Italy bent on conquest. Constans swiftly returned from the Danube, determined to fight for his lands. Apparently he had good scouts, because they located the whereabouts of Constantine II. Constans ordered his men to set up an ambush. As the Augustus of Gaul galloped through the woods near the town of Aquileia, he was suddenly attacked by archers hiding behind the trees and was killed.

With this, Constans inherited the domains of his older brother. The empire was now divided between Constantius and Constans almost along the same lines Diocletian had initially divided the empire between himself and Maximian.

For the next ten years, the two brothers ruled the empire. Constantius, an imperious presence in spite of his short legs, proved a good administrator and a fairly good soldier with several victories against the Persians. He loved ceremony and protocol even more than his father. During his reign, the Master of the Sacred Chamber, a eunuch called Eusebius, became so powerful that a chronicler,

Ammianus, caustically remarked that if anyone wanted a favor "he would have to speak to the emperor because the emperor had considerable influence with [the eunuch]." Constans was physically an attractive young man, muscular with broad shoulders, and in spite of his young age a fairly capable administrator. But he loved the pleasures of life too much, and according to Aurelius Victor he knew no bounds "in avarice and contempt for the soldiers." Evidently the chronicler was not exaggerating. In 350, when Constans was twenty-seven years old, several of his legions rebelled and raised to Augustus one of the senior officers named Magnentius. He received such strong support from the legions that Constans lost his nerve, left Mediolanum and tried to reach Spain where he expected to find loyal troops. As he was trying to cross the Pyrenees, he was intercepted by rebels who captured and killed him. Only Constantius remained now. But before he could become truly the sole emperor, he had to put down the rebel Magnentius. And this he set out to do without delay.

In March 351, Constantius was at Mediolanum, preparing to launch the campaign against Magnentius, when he summoned his cousin Gallus, the son of Julius Constantius, the Patrician. Now that he faced a serious challenge in the western part of the empire he needed someone he could trust to oversee the affairs in the East. By now Gallus was thirty years old, living in obscurity at the family estate in Bithynia. A summons from the cousin who had sent his father to the block without a trial must have been a frightening experience. It could mean death. But it could also mean an end to all those years of isolation and fear. Whatever the reason for the call, Gallus had to obey.

When he came to Mediolanum, he was greeted cordially by the courtiers, and especially the powerful eunuch Eusebius—a good omen. In the next few days, he was received by his imperial cousin and his wife Eusebia (who was Gallus' sister). His life was about to take a spectacular turn. In a ceremony appropriate for the occasion, Constantius raised Gallus to the rank of Caesar. There was also a wedding. Gallus was married to the emperor's sister, Constantia, who had been a widow since 338 when the rebellious troops had killed her husband, Hannibalianus. A few days after the happy festivities, the new Caesar left with his bride for Antioch to govern the Orient for his cousin.

Fortune had smiled on Gallus but he did not prove worthy of the favor. Within three and a half years, he managed to alienate almost everyone with the exception of some troops that admired him for his handsome face and athletic physique, and for his way of giving the impression that he was a soldier's soldier. He would have probably proclaimed himself Augustus of the East but he did not have the military forces to face his imperial cousin.

Constantius, who had by then put down the rebellion of Magnentius, turned his attention to his cousin. The reports from the Orient were disturbing and he decided to have a face to face meeting to clear the air. Gallus, fearful of his cousin's wrath, asked his wife Constantia to go to Mediolanum and try to calm her brother. She left Antioch in September, but somewhere in Bithynia she fell ill. After several days suffering with high fever, she died. Gallus had lost the one person that could have saved him.

In a letter amiable in tone, with expressions of sorrow for the loss of their beloved Constantia, Constantius reminded Gallus that under Diocletian a Caesar always obeyed the Augustus and that he expected him to come so that they could discuss the affairs of the empire. He sent the letter with one of his eunuchs, a high official and a born diplomat. The envoy assured Gallus that the emperor wished him no harm.

To everyone's surprise, Gallus agreed to go to Mediolanum. On the way from Antioch, he stopped for a few days at Constantinople and watched the races in the Hippodrome from the imperial box, as the Caesar of the East, acknowledging the customary cheers of the jubilant multitude. It was the last glorious day he was to know. When he came to Mediolanum he was placed under arrest and a few weeks later, at the beginning of December, he was beheaded. Now only two men were left alive from the line of Constantius Chlorus, Constantius and Julian who was twenty-four years old, spending most of his time in studying philosophy and living the life of a young scholar.

Julian—Flavius Claudius Julianus being his formal name—was enchanted with the Hellenic culture, and although he had received instruction by none other than Eusebius of Nicomedia, he retained a healthy skepticism about the Christian faith. In 355 Julian was initiated into the mysteries of Mithras and to the Eleusinian mysteries. It was also the year that Constantius called him to Mediolanum. Julian had a good friend in his stepsister Eusebia, the emperor's wife.

In a military ceremony held outside of Mediolanum, Constantius raised Julian to the rank of Caesar. Again there was a wedding. Julian was married to Helena, the emperor's younger sister. She was Constantine's second daughter and, it is said, she looked too much like her illustrious father to be called an attractive woman. The demands of the imperial mantle are often too heavy. Julian lived up to his duties and Helena became pregnant only to die at childbirth.

Because Eusebia was tired of the cold weather in Europe and wanted to return to the more agreeable climate in Constantinople and Antioch, Constantius sent Julian to Gaul so he could return to the East. In the next five years, the young scholar proved a very capable and courageous soldier in fighting the German tribes along the Rhine. The effect of Greek philosophy and culture became evident in his policies. He rebuilt the towns which had been laid waste, restructured the administration on a just and efficient footing, and streamlined as much as possible the collection of taxes making the burden somewhat less onerous. For the most part he stayed in Lutetia which because of his presence began to grow and to rise in importance.

Inevitably Julian had his enemies at Constantius' court, who made every effort to poison the emperor's mind against his cousin. At first they failed, but in 360 the first serious clouds appeared on the horizon. Constantius was facing a stubborn enemy in Persia. He needed more legions to protect the grain fields of Mesopotamia, and wrote to his cousin Julian asking for several legions to move to the East. At first Julian objected, arguing that the situation along the Rhine required their presence in Gaul. Later he agreed but the soldiers refused to leave. The legions came to Paris, and there they proclaimed Julian Augustus. The wild cheers "Hail Flavius Claudius Julianus, Augustus" had a familiar ring. Julian accepted his elevation to Augustus and the die was cast.

The messages he sent to Constantius, explaining what had happened and offering to resolve the issue in negotiations, were ignored. Constantius was furious. To him the events in Paris were nothing but treason. A clash was now inevitable. In a rapid march, through the Black Forest and down the Danube, Julian and his legions reached Sirmium. Constantius, too, set out from the Orient to meet his cousin on the field of battle. He was angry but he was also full of optimism. His wife Eusebia, after so many years, was pregnant and Constantius hoped for a son. But by the time Eusebia gave birth to a girl she named Constantia Posthuma, Constantius was already dead. He died of illness on the march through Asia Minor as Julian was preparing to march on to Constantinople. He was only forty-four years old. The date was November 3, 361. Julian was now the legitimate sole emperor.

During his brief reign, Julian tried to revitalize the ancient pagan religion which in his mind was entwined with the glamour of ancient Greek philosophy, culture and art. He did not last long enough to have a serious impact. The tidal wave the great Constantine had set in motion could not be reversed.

After a year in Constantinople, he moved to Antioch and then, disgusted with the city and the continuing feuds among its Christians, he went to the city of Tarsus in Cilicia to prepare for a war against Persia. In the spring of 363 he set off for Mesopotamia at the head of a strong and well-organized army. His force was accompanied by a fleet down the Euphrates. His legions advanced through Mesopotamia as far as Ctesiphon, crossed the Tigris and engaged a strong Persian force in a great battle. It was a bloody encounter with heavy casualties on both sides but at the end of the day the legions had won. The Persian king ordered his generals to retreat into Persian territory.

In years past, after such a victory, the next step was a call to peace. This time Julian did not follow tradition. It is said that he accepted the advice of a captured Persian nobleman who told him that the Persian king and his forces were demoralized and could be destroyed easily if forced to do battle one more time. Hoping for a decisive victory, such as that of Galerius, he ordered his troops to pursue the enemy deep into the Persian lands.

After many days of marching through a desolate country of sand and stone in the summer heat, searching in vain for the enemy, Julian ordered his troops to start back for Mesopotamia. It was too late. The Persian army, familiar with the terrain, had managed to envelope the legions. Julian's army fought with the tenacity of a cornered wild beast but to no avail.

In one of the skirmishes, Julian, who was as ever fighting at the front, was mortally wounded. A spear had pierced his side. It is said that he had been fighting without the protection of armor because the straps of his cuirass had broken the day before and he had given it to his servant for repair. A rumor was heard later that the spear that wounded him was a Roman spear and that it was thrust by a Christian soldier. We will never know. The legend that he said just before he died *Nenikikas me Galilee* (You beat me, Galilean), a reference to Christ, is most likely just a legend. He struggled with death for two days. But the internal bleeding could not be stopped and shortly after midnight, in the early hours of June 26, 363, he died. The male line of Constantius Chlorus had come to an end.

A legion commander named Jovian was proclaimed Augustus by the army, and the Roman Empire, now a Christian empire, continued in the eastern half its march through history for another one thousand years.

THE ADMINISTRATIVE SUBDIVISION
OF THE ROMAN EMPIRE

(At the time of Diocletian and Constantine, based on the Verona List)

DIOCESE OF ORIENT

Libya Superior
Libya Inferior
Thebais
Aegyptus Jovia (created 314-315)
Aegyptus Herculia
   (created 314-315)
Arabia Nova
Arabia
Augusta Libanensis
Palaestina
Phoenice
Syria Coele
Augusta Euphratensis
Cilicia
Isauria
Cyprus
Mesopotamia
Osrhoene

DIOCESE OF PONTICA

Bithynia
Cappadocia
Galatia
Paphlagonia
Diospontus
Pontus Polemonianus
Armenia

DIOCESE OF ASIANA

Lycia and Pamphylia
Phrygia Prima
Phrygia Secunda
Asia
Lydia
Caria
Pisidia
Hellespontus

DIOCESE OF THRACIA

Europa
Rhodope
Thracia
Haemimontus
Scythia
Moesia Inferior

DIOCESE OF MOESIA

Dacia
Dacia Ripensis
Moesia Superior
Dardania
Macedonia
Thessalia
Achaea
Praevalitana
Epirus Nova
Epirus Vetus
Creta

DIOCESE OF PANNONIA

Pannonia Inferior
Savensis
Dalmatia
Valeria
Pannonia Superior
Noricum Ripense
Noricum Mediterraneum

DIOCESE OF ITALIA

Venetia and Istria
Aemilia and Liguria
Flaminia and Picenum
Tuscia and Umbria
Campania
Apulia and Calabria
Lucania and Bruttii
Sicilia
Sardinia
Corsica
Alpes Cottiae
Raetia

DIOCESE OF GALLIA

Belgica Prima
Belgica Secunda
Germania Prima
Germania Secunda
Sequania
Lugdunensis Prima
Lugdunensis Secunda
Alpes Graiae and Poeninae

DIOCESE OF VIENNENSIS

Viennensis
Narbonensis Prima
Narbonensis Secunda
Novem Populi

Aquitania Prima

Aquitania Secunda

Alpes Maritimae

DIOCESE OF BRITANNIA

Britannia Prima

Britannia Secunda

Maxima Caesariensis

Flavia Caesariensis

DIOCESE OF HISPANIA

Baetica

Lusitania

Carthaginiensis

Gallaecia

Tarraconensis

Mauretania Tingitana

DIOCESE OF AFRICA

Africa Proconsularis

Byzacena

Tripolitana

Numidia Cirtensis and Militania

Mauretania Caesariensis

Mauretania Sitifensis

(From Stephen Williams *Diocletian and the Roman Discovery,*
op. cit. pp. 221-223)

COINS FROM THE
CONSTANTINE PERIOD

Courtesy of Dumbarton Oaks Collection

CONSTANTINE THE GREAT
Gold coin Reverse shows the standard figure of Jove (Jupiter) the Preserver.

Courtesy of Dumbarton Oaks Collection

DIOCLETIAN
Gold coin Reverse the standard figure of Jove.

Courtesy of Dumbarton Oaks Collection

FLAVIUS CONSTANTIUS, CHLORUS AS CAESAR
Gold coin Reverse shows Hercules, a reference to Maximianus Herculius who at the time was the Augustus in the West.

483

Courtesy of Dumbarton Oaks Collection

MAXIMIANUS HERCULIUS
Gold coin struck c.291 soon after Maximian was proclaimed "son of Hercules" (see p. 32), the legendary Greek hero who killed the many-headed Hydra; reverse shows Hercules killing Hydra.

Courtesy of Dumbarton Oaks Collection

GALERIUS MAXIMIANUS
Gold coin. On the reverse the figure of Jove the Preserver.

Courtesy of the British
Museum Collection

CARAUSIUS
The usurper who established the *Imperium Bretanniarum* over Britain and northern Gaul, which ended with the invasion of Britain by Constantine's father, Flavius Constantius Chlorus in 296 A.D.

Arras Medallion, Museum of London
Collection

FLAVIUS CONSTANTIUS LIBERATING LONDON

Obverse side, Constantius, head and upper chest, in military uniform and the golden diadem of Caesar; reverse, Constantius on horseback receiving thanks from a man kneeling, the walls of London in the background and the words *Redditor Lucis Aeternae*; (Restorer of Eternal Life).

Courtesy of Dumbarton Oaks Collection

LICINIUS

Gold coin. Reverse, the familiar figure of Jove.

Courtesy of Dumbarton Oaks Collection

MAXIMIN DAIA

Gold coin. Reverse, the figure of Jove.

485

Courtesy of Dumbarton Oaks Collection

MAXENTIUS
Silver coin

Courtesy of Dumbarton Oaks Collection

CRISPUS AS CAESAR
Gold coin Possibly struck after the naval victory in Helespont against the fleet of Licinius in 323 A.D.

CRISPUS AND CONSTANTINE II
Circular pendant with a double *solidus* of Constantine the Great wearing a radiating crown. On reverse side the busts of Constantine's two sons, Crispus and Constantine II as Caesars. The coin was struck at Sirmium, possibly around 324-325, shortly before the tragic events in the summer of 326 in Rome.

NOTES

Page	Quote	Source
23	"he was gruff"	Victor, *Epitome*, 40, 10-11; also Victor, *De Caesaribus*, 39; *Pan. Lat.*, 10(2)
24	"Carausius rebellion"	Victor, *De Caesaribus*, 39; *Pan. Lat.* 10(3)
26	"when did the Rhine"	*Pan. Lat.* 11(7)
26	"naval failure"	*Pan. Lat.* 11(3)
30	"the closer you came"	*Pan. Lat.* 11(3) 10
30	"she sent the"	*Pan. Lat.* 11(3) 11-12
42	"four seasons"	*Pan. Lat.*, 8(4) 4
43	"Galerius was a tall"	Malalas, *Chronogr.* XII, 414
45	"new, imposing"	Lact. *De Mort. Pers.* VII
46	"*duces* and *judices*	*Pan. Lat.*, 10(2)
51	"these bandits"	*Oxyrhychus Papyrus*, 2, 142
52	"Manicheans"	P. Brown, JRS (1969)
57	"a heavy fog"	*Pan. Lat.*, 8(5) 15
58	"he failed to"	*Pan. Lat.*, 8(5) 16
64	"we saw him"	Eusebius. *Vita Constantini*, I, 19
68	"Manicheans founder"	FJRA II, 544
71	"*De Pretiis*"	JRS (1970), (1971), (1973)
89	"has been better expressed"	Celsus, *The True Doctrine* 8.68 from Origen's *Contra Celsum* trans. Chadwick
95	"a superstitious woman"	Lact. *De Mort. Pers.* X
95	"as was his custom"	*ibid.*, XI
96	"extirpate the"	*ibid.*, XI
97	"Apollo spoke"	Eusebius, *Vit. Const.*, I, 50
98	Porphyrius' letter	Wilken, p. 134
98	"remained firm"	Lact. *De Mort. Pers.* XI

Page	Quote	Source
99	*"ille dies"*	*ibid.*, XI; Eusebius *Historia Ecclesiastiki*, VIII, 2.4 Constantine's *Oratio ad Sanctorum*, 25
102	"is this all true?"	*The Passions of the Saints*, in Firth, p. 35
105	"the palace on fire"	Lact. *De Mort. Pers.* XIV; Eusebius. *Hist. Eccl.* VIII, 6.6
107	"to roast him alive"	Lact. *Divines Institutiones*, VII; Euseb. *Hist. Eccl.* VIII
112	"filthy dungeons"	Euseb. *Hist. Eccl.* VIII
114	"some had their hands"	*ibid.*,
124	"on the triumph"	Lact. *De Mort. Pers*, XVII Eutropius, IX; *Pan. Lat.* 6(7) 10
125	"oath before Jupiter"	Lact. *De Mort. Pers.* XVII, Eutropius, IX
131	"young man"	Zosimus, *Hist. Nov.* II, 7
132	"Galerius who forced"	Lact. *De Mort. Pers.* XXIV
147	"fearful that he"	Zosimus, *Hist. Nov.* II, 8; Eusebius *Vit. Const.* I, 21
154	"Jupiter himself"	*Pan. Lat.* 7(7)
154	"legitimate children"	Zosimus *Hist. Nov.* II, 7
154	"the soldiers in"	*ibid.*
155	"spurs to his horse"	*Pan. Lat.* 7(7)
156	"bust to Galerius"	Lact. *De Mort. Pers.* XXV
158	"his soul was"	*Pan. Lat.* 10(8)
164	"the Senate has"	Vopiscus Florianus quoted in Firth, p. 4
165	"the census was"	Lact. *De Mort. Pers.* XXIII

Page	Quote	Source
166	"the conspirators were now"	*ibid.* XXVI
170	"troops of Mauretania"	Zosimus, II.9; *Lact. De Mort. Pers.* XXVI
170	"Well fortified"	Zosimus, II. 10
172	"wedding Fausta"	Lact. *De Mort. Pers.* XXVII
174	"no one could have"	*ibid.* XXVI
174	"giving back the purple"	*ibid.*; Zosimus, II. 10
176	"taking the flocks"	Lact. *De Mort, Pers.* XXVII
177	"childishly jealous"	*ibid.,* XXVIII
183	"Domitius Alexander"	Victor, *De Caesaribus* 39, 8
186	"that divine statesman"	*Pan. Latin.* 7(15)
188	*"fillii Augusti"*	Lact. *De Mort. Pers.* XXXII
192	"they did not want"	*Pan. Lat.* 7(20)
198	"you saw Apollo"	McMullen, p. 65
211	"malignant ulcer in"	Euseb. *Hist. Eccl.* VIII, 16
211	"Galerius was in"	Lact. *De Mort. Pers.* XXXIII
213	"among the measures"	Euseb. *Hist. Eccl.* VIII, 17; Seston, p. 210
222	"Const. took pity"	Euseb. *Hist. Eccl.* IX, 9
225	"170,000 foot soldiers"	Zosimus, II. 15
225	*"non solem tacite"*	*Pan. Lat.* 9(2)
232	"like an angry torrent"	*Pan. Lat.* 9(9)
239	"realizing that he needed"	Euseb. *Vit. Const.* I, 27
240	"Const. was directed"	Lact. *De Mort. Pers.* XLIV

Page	Quote	Source
240	"while he was"	Euseb. *Vit. Const.*I, 28 and 29
242	"Const. feeling sorry"	Euseb. *Hist. Eccl.* IX, 9
242	"all Gaul was talking"	*Pan. Lat.* 10(14)
242	"we see Constantine"	*ibid.*
243	"not exclusively"	*The Catholic Encyclopedia* Vol. IV, p. 518; Holsapple, p. 164
249	"with captive chiefs"	*Pan. Lat.* 10(31)
249	"entry into Rome"	Zosimus, II. 29; Euseb. *Vit. Const.* I, 39; *Pan. Lat.* 12(9)
253	"was reconstituted"	Zosimus, II. 27; *Pan. Lat.* 10(2)
254	"Lateran palace"	The Lateran Palace remained the official residence of the Pope for a thousand years. According to *Liber Pontificalis* Pope Miltiades held a Synod *"in domum Fausta in Laterano"* in A.D. 313
256	"if there have been"	Euseb. *Hist. Eccl.* IX, 7
258	"with his spirit"	Lact. *De Mort. Pers.* XLII
260	"already long ago"	Euseb. *Hist. Eccl.* X, 5; Lact. *De Mort. Pers.* XLVIII
267	"heavy snowfall"	Lact. *De Mort. Pers.* XLV
270	"Supreme God"	*ibid.*, XLVI
271	"must have had angelic"	Holland Smith, p. 127
272	"threw his imperial"	Lact. *De Mort. Pers.* XLIX
273	"having covered"	*ibid.*, L
274	"unable to find relief"	*ibid.*, LI
282	"Licinius not responsible	Zosimus. II, 18
283	"Const. a mighty man"	Eutropius, X, 5

Page	Quote	Source
284	"as their enmity became"	Zosimus, II, 18-20; Eutropius, X, 5; Anonymus Valessianus, V, 14-15
284	"Licinius assembled his"	Zosimus, II, 19
304	"since I know"	*Constantinus Augustus Episkopis Excerpta*, p. 789
307	"with the favor"	*ibid.*, p. 790
320	"ordered general"	Euseb. *Hist. Eccl.* I, 48
320	"Vetius Rufinus"	Paully-Wissowa, IA, col 1186
322	"which is formed in"	*Codex Theodosianus*, IX, xl, 2
329	"filling his young"	Pan. Lat. 10(17)
329	"Crispus Caesar"	Zosimus, II, 20; Euseb. *Vit. Const. IV, 40*; Idatius, *Chronicon*, I, 8
334	"Const. realizing"	Zosimus, II, 22
335	"the next day"	*ibid.*,
335	"chose only eighty"	*ibid.*, II, 23
339	"he pitched his tent"	Euseb. *Vit. Const.* II, 12
340	"breaking his oath"	Zosimus, II, 28
343	"Constantine, Victor"	Euseb. *Vit. Const.* II, 42
350	"even in the pagan"	*ibid.*, II, 61
353	"the ally of my endeavors"	*ibid.*
354	"therefore let each"	*ibid.*, II, 71-73
358	"Christ and the"	Socrates Scolasticus, *Hist. Eccl.* I, 8
359	"in proper decorum"	Euseb. *Vit. Const.* III, 10-11
369	"it seems inappropriate"	Theodoretus, *Hist. Eccl.* I, 9; Galasius, *Hist. Eccl.* II, 37; Euseb. *Vit. Const.* III, 17

Page	Quote	Source
380	"Crispus rejected the"	Zosimus, II, 29
381	"it was on the instigation"	Victor, *Epitome* 41, 2
381	"to tell the truth"	Eutropius, X, 4
382	"the courage, the"	P. Optatiani, IV, 1
383	"Saturni aurea"	Apolinaris Sidonius, *Epistolae* V, 8
384	"upbraided Constantine"	Victor, *Epitome* 41, 2
385	"Crispus golden statue"	Firth, p. 248
390	"God appeared"	Sozomenus, *Hist. Eccl.* II, 31
391	"as Const. was sleeping"	Malmesbury, *Chronicle*, p.373
400	"on the Mount of Olives"	Euseb. *Vit. Const.* III, 43
400	"done by atheists"	*ibid.*, III, 48
401	"in a letter to"	*ibid.*, III, 46
401	"in the days of"	*Kyrillou Apanta* in J.P. Migne *Patrologiae Graecae* Vol. 63, Column 1165
401	"Helena, the"	Socrates, *Hist. Eccle.*, 14
419	"thee alone we"	Euseb. *Vit. Const.* IV, 36
420	"he alone thought"	*ibid.*, IV, 23
420	"let no one interfere"	*ibid.*, IV, 56
426	"while he was tortured"	Victor, *De Caesaribus* 41, 11
428	"as if he were giving"	Euseb. *Vit. Const.* IV, 54
432	"let no one dare"	"Epistole to Heretics" in Euseb. *Vit. Const.* III, 64-65
433	"the members of the"	*ibid.*, III, 66

Page	Quote	Source
437	"a traitor to the"	Theodoretus, *Hist. Eccl.* I, 25
439	"because our faith"	Sozomenus, *Hist. Eccl.* II, 27
441	"the argument would"	Euseb. *Vit. Const.* III, 60
441	"having informed"	*ibid*, III, 61
447	"he even offered"	Theodoretus, *Hist. Eccl.* I, 28 Athanasius, *Treatise Against Arians*, 64-68
450	"as I was returning"	Sozomenus, *Hist. Eccl.* II, 28
454	"can I trust you"	Socrates, *Hist. Eccl.* I, 37; Athanasius, *Epistola ad Episkopos*; Sulpicius Severus, *Historiae* II, 71
458	"the most peace-minded"	Euseb. *Vit. Const.* IV, 56
459	"splendidly enjoying"	*ibid.*, IV, 60
460	"the seal which confers"	*ibid.*, IV, 61
460	"rules of life"	*ibid.*, IV, 62
463	"of the Senate and the"	*ibid.*, IV, 69
466	"upon learning of"	Philostorgus, *Hist. Eccl.* II, 16
472	"he would have to speak"	Ammianus, 18, 4.3
570	"avarice and contempt"	Victor, *De Caesaribus* 41.23

BIBLIOGRAPHY

ORIGINAL SOURCES

(Note to the reader: Those who wrote about Constantine during his lifetime and in the early decades after his death fall into two main groups: those who loved him for embracing the Christian Church and those who hated him for the same reason. In using those sources one has to tread carefully, reading between the lines, comparing their stories, acting almost like a modern day investigative reporter. Still, no matter how biased, unclear on their prose, prone to exaggeration, or unreliable about dates they may be, those writers cited below are primary sources of information and if used carefully they can be invaluable in our effort to reconstruct and bring to life the story of Constantine.)

Eusebius Pamphilus. He came from Syria Palaestina (today's Israel) and wrote in Greek. For his support of Constantine, he was elevated to bishop of Caesaria after the Christian Church was accepted as a legitimate religion in A.D. 312. His *Ecclesiastiki Istoria* (Ecclesiastical History) is divided into ten books and covers the history of the Church from its beginnings to the early fourth century. It can be found today in *Patrologiae Graecae* ed. by J. P. Migne, Paris 1857-1866; also in *Berlin Corpus* vol 8, a French translation in *Sources Chretiennes,*

Paris Editions du Cerf 1958; and an English trans. by Lawlor *Eusebius; Ecclesiastical History*, Loeb Classical Library 1932. His other major work is the *Bios Constanttinou* (The Life of Constantine, Vita Constandini) written also in Greek, contained in *Patrologiae Graecae* ed. by J. P. Migne; English trans. in *Library of the Nicene Fathers*, Vol. I. (all volumes available at the Dumbarton Oaks Library in Washington D.C.)

Lactantius (Lucius Caelius Firmianus). He was born in Africa but he taught rhetoric in Nicomedia during Diocletian's reign. It is possible that during that time he met Constantine because later he moved to the West and served as the tutor of Constantine's son Crispus. Lactantius wrote in Latin and in spite of his violent hatred of the pagan emperors, his works are informative. Very likely he was converted to Christianity by his teacher Arnobius. He was with Constantine during the A.D. 312 invasion of Italy. His work *De Mortibus Persecutorum* (On the Death of the Persecutors), a book designed to prove the dismal end of the emperors who persecuted the Christians during his lifetime, is edited by Samuel Brant, Leipzig, 1897; we have a French trans. in *Sources Chretiennes*, Paris 1954; and an English trans. in the *Library of the Ante-Nicene Fathers*, Vol 73. His other work *Divinae Institutiones* (Divine Institutions) is full of praise for Constantine. An English translation can be found in the *Library of the Ante-Nicene Fathers*, Vol 7; also in sister Francis McDonald, Catholic University Press, 1964 and in Rene Pichon, *Lactance* Paris, Librairie Hachette, 1901.

Socrates Scholasticus. A lawyer in Constantinople (born c. 380), he wrote in Greek his *Ecclesiastiki Istoria* (Ecclesiastical History) in which he carries on Eusebius' work to A.D. 439. He lived a generation after the death of Constantine and his work is primarily useful because of his verbatim quotations of original texts. An English translation can be found in the *Library of the Nicene Fathers*, Series II, Vol. 2.

Sozomenus. Also a lawyer in Constantinople born in today's Gaza, (died c. A.D. 450) he wrote his *Ecclesiastiki Istoria* in Greek covering the period A.D. 324 to 439. In his work he relies heavily on the work of Socrates Scholasticus but his work is useful because it offers some additional information. The original in Greek can be found in *Patrologiae Greacae*, Vol. 67; an English trans. in the *Library of the Nicene Fathers*, Series II, Vol. 2.

Theodoretus. His *Ecclesiastiki Istoria* in Greek offers some valuable information about Constanine. The Greek original can be found in *Berlin Corpus*, Vol. 19, 1911. Also in *Excerpta Valesiana*, edited by H. Valesius in 1636.

Theophanes. His *Ecclesiastiki Istoria* in Greek is found in *Patrologiae Graecae* ed. J. P. Migne, Vol. 108.

Theophilos Ioannou. *Mnimeia Aghiographica* Venezia 1884, the source for Michelangelo Guidi ed. *Un Bios Constantino*, Academia dei Lincei, 1908, in Greek.

Optatus. Bishop of Mileve. His *De Schismate Donatistorum* in Latin is a major source on the Donatist Schism; in *Patrologiae Latinae*, Vol. 43; also S. Optati Milevitani, Libri VII, ed by Carolus Ziwse, Prague, 1893.

Other authors worth mentioning include Philostorgus with fragments of his Ecclesiastic History found in *Berlin Corpus*, Vol 21; Sextus Aurelius Victor who served under Julian the Apostate, with his *De Caesaribus* covering the period from Augustus to Constantius II, ed. by Pichlmayr and Gruendal, Leipzig, 1961; and *Epitome* ed. by Pichlmayr and Gruendal, Leipzig, 1961; and Ammianus Marcellinus, a good historian whose work, *Istoria*, did not survive in full. Also Ioannis Malalas, *Chronographia*, in *Patrologiae Graecae*, Liber XIII; and Stephanus Byzantinus, *Annotationes* ed. by L. Holsten et als. Leipzig, 1825. Also,

Zonaras, *Epitome* ed. by Lindorf, Leipzig, 1875. Another source is the *Liber Pontificalis; De Gestis Romanorum Pontificum*, especially the early sections, edited by L. Duchesne, 2 Vols. Paris, 1886-1892.

Eunapius. A pagan critic of Constantine, he wrote in Greek a *Istoria* (History) in fourteen books covering the period from A.D. 270 to 404, of which only fragments survive.

Eutropius. This author who served under Julian the Apostate and under his Christian successor Valens takes a more impartial view of Constantine and thanks to his position as *Magister Memoriae*, a high ranking keeper of records, he probably had access to official documents. His *Breviarium ab Urbe Condita*, a review of Roman history since the founding of Rome, is found in *Compendio di Storia Romana*, ed. by P. Parducci, Cita di Castello, 1913; a French translation is in *Eutrope, Abrege de l'Histoire Romain* by Maurice Rat, Paris, Garnier, 1934; and an English translation in *Breviarium ab Urbe Condita*, by S. Hallidie, London, Welch and Duffield, 1892.

Zosimus. He wrote in the sixth century and like Eutropius held senior official posts although he was a pagan. His *Historia Nova* (New History) covers the period from Augustus to A.D. 410. It was edited by Ludovicus Mendelssohn, Leipzig, 1887. He is not a friend of Constantine but he writes with a certain degree of impartiality. His work is very useful in evaluating historical events reported by other pro-Constantine authors.

We should also draw attention to the panegyrics, orations offered on important occasions by contemporary orators. In spite of the flowery language and the inevitable flattery, they are very useful for the information they contain both in relation to specific events and to social and other conditions at the time. *Panegyrici Latini* ed. R.A.B. Mynors. Oxford, 1964.

The study of Constantine's life and times is assisted by the coins issued during that period. Coins reflected prevailing policies, major events, and the ascendancy or fall of major personalities.

MODERN SOURCES

For readers who wish to learn more about Constantine and his times the following modern sources and texts will certainly be useful. In addition to the books listed below, significant articles appear in the *Journal of Roman Studies* and in *Revue des Etudes Byzantines*.

Alfordi, A. *The Conversion of Constantine and Pagan Rome*, 1969.

Anastos, N. "The Edict of Milan", article in *Revue des Etudes Byzantines*, 1968.

Anderson, J.G.C. "The Genesis of Diocletian's Provincial Reorganization", art. in JRS 1932.

Arnold, W.T. *The Roman System of Provincial Administration*, 1906.

Attridge, H.W. and G. Hata (eds). *Eusebius, Christianity and Judaism*, 1992.

Baker, C.P. *Constantine the Great and the Christian Revolution*, 1931.

Barnes, T.D. "Lactantius and Constantine", art. in JRS, 1973.

Barnes, T.D. *Constantine and Eusebius*, 1981.

Barnes, T.D. *The New Empire of Diocletian and Constantine*, 1982.

Baynes, N.H. "Three Notes on the Reforms of Diocletian and Constantine", JRS, 1925.

Baynes, N.H. *Constantine the Great and the Christian Church*, 1972.

Bowder, D. *The Age of Constantine and Julian*, 1978.

Brogan, O. *Roman Gaul*, 1953.

Broglie, Albert de. *L'Eglise et l'Empire Romain au IV Siecle*, 1877.

Brown, P. "The Diffusion of Manicheanism in the Late Roman Empire", JSR, 1969.

Brown, P. *The Making of Late Antiquity*, 1978.

Brown, P. *Power and Persuasion in Late Antiquity*, 1992.

Bruun, P.M. *Studies in Constantine Chronology*, 1961.

Bruun, P.M. *Studies in Constantine Numismatics*, 1991.

Burch, Vacher. *Myth and Constantine the Great*, 1927.

Burckhardt, J. *The Age of Constantine the Great*, 1927.

Bury, J.B. *History of the Later Roman Empire*, Vol. I, 1923.

Bury, J.B. *The Invasion of Europe by the Barbarians*, 1928.

Chadwick, H. *The Early Church*, 1967.

Chadwick, H. *Heresy and Orthodoxy in the Early Church*, 1991.

Cons, Henri. *Dalmatia*, 1882.

Crook, J. *Concilium Principis*, 1955.

Cumont, Franz. *The Mysteries of Mithras*, trans. 1903.

Cumont, F. *The Oriental Religions and Roman Paganism*, 1911.

Cunliffe, B. *Greeks, Romans and Barbarians*, 1988.

Dagron, G. *Naissance d'une capitale: Constantinople et ses institutions de 330 a 451*, 1974.

Davies, J.D. *The Early Christian Church*, 1963.

Desroches, J. *Le Labarum*, 1894.

Dorries, H. *Constantine and Religious Liberty*, 1960.

Downey, G. *The Late Roman Empire*, 1969.

Drijvers, J.N. *Helena Augusta*, 1991.

Duncan, J.R. *Pay and Numbers in Diocletian's Army*, 1978.

Eadie, J.W. *The Conversion of Constantine*, 1977.

Eichholz, D. "Constantius Chlorus' invasion of Britain", JRS, 1953.

Ferguson, J. *The Religion of the Roman Empire*, 1970.

Ferrill, A. *The Fall of the Roman Empire; The Military Explanation*, 1988.

Firth John, B. *Constantine the Great*, 1905.

Fox Lane, R. *Pagans and Christians*, 1986.

Frank, T. *Economic Survey of Ancient Rome*, 1940.

Frend, W.C. *Martyrdoms and Persecutions in the Early Church*. 1965.

Frend, W.C. *The Donatist Church*, 1985.

Frye, R. *The Heritage of Persia*, 1962.

Gibbon, E. *The Decline and Fall of the Roman Empire*, 1776-1788; 1836; abridged version, 1960.

BIBLIOGRAPHY

Gibbon, E. *History of Christianity*, Harper edition, 1836.

Gill, C. and T.P. Wiseman, *Lies and Fiction in the Ancient World*, 1993.

Grant, Michael. *The Climax of Rome*, 1974.

Grant, M. *The Fall of the Roman Empire*, 1990.

Grant, M. *Augustus to Constantine*, 1990.

Grant, M. *Readings in the Classical Historians*, 1992.

Grant, M. *Constantine the Great*, 1994.

Grant, R.M. *Eusebius as Church Historian*, 1980.

Greenslade, S.L. *Schism in the Early Church*, 1953.

Gregg, R.C. and D. Groh. *Early Arianism*, 1981.

Harries, M. *Religious Conflict in Fourth Century Rome*, 1982.

Harries, M. *Towards a New Constantine?*, 1985.

Heinichen, F.A. ed., *Constantini: Ad Sanctorum Coetus Oratio*, 1830.

Hendy, M. "Mint and Fiscal Administration under Diocletian", JRS, 1972.

Holsapple, Lloyd. *Constantine the Great*, 1942.

Holland, Smith J. *Constantine the Great*, 1971.

Houlden, L. (ed.) *Judaism and Christianity*, 1991.

Howe, L. *The Praetorian Prefect from Commodus to Diocletian*, 1941.

Hunt, E.P. *Holy Land Pilgrimage in the Later Roman Empire*, 1982.

Johnson, P. *A History of Christianity*, 1978.

Jones, A.H.M. *Constantine and the Conversion of Europe*, 1948.

Jones, A.H.M. *The Decline of the Ancient World*, 1975.

Jones, A.H.M. *The Later Roman Empire*, 2 vols., 1964, 1986.

Jones, A.H.M. *The Roman Economy*, 1974.

Kee, H.C. *Constantine versus Christ: The Triumph of Ideology*, 1982.

Krautheimer, R. *Early Christian and Byzantine Architecture*, 1965.

Lees-Milne, J. *L'Eglise et l'Empire au IVe Siecle*, 1989.

Lieu, S.N. and M. Dodgson *The Roman Eastern Frontier and the Persian Wars AD 226-363*, 1991.

Luttwak, E. *The Grand Strategy of the Roman Empire*, 1976.

MacMullen, R. *Soldier and Civilian in the Late Roman Empire*, 1963.

MacMullen, R. *Constantine*, 1969.

MacMullen, R. *Christianity and the Roman World*, 1974.

MacMullen, R. *Paganism in the Roman Empire*, 1981.

MacMullen, R. *Corruption and the Decline of Rome*, 1988.

Mann, A.J. *The Persecution of Diocletian*, 1876.

Marasovic, T. *Diocletian's Palace*, 1968.

Markus, R.A. *The End of Ancient Christianity*, 1991.

Mazzarino, S. *The End of the Ancient World*, 1966.

Millar, F. *The Roman Empire and its Neighbours*, 1967.

Millar, F. *The Emperor in the Roman World*, 1977.

Mommsen, Theodore. *The Provinces of the Roman Empire*, 1886.

Neusner, J. *Judaism and Christianity in the Age of Constantine*, 1987.

Nischer, E. "The Army Reforms of Diocletian and Constantine and their modifications up to the time of the Noticia Dignitarum", JRS, 1923.

Oliva, P. *Pannonia and the onset of the Crisis of the Roman Empire*, 1962.

Owen, F. *The Germanic People*, 1990.

Parker, H.M.D. "The Legions of Diocletian and Constantine", JRS, 1933.

Paschoud, F. *Cinq Etudes sur Zosime*, 1975.

Perowne, S. *The End of the Roman World*, 1966.

Pieterse, J.N. (ed), *Christianity and Hegemony: Religion and Politics as the Frontiers of Social Change*, 1992.

Piganiol, A. *L'Empire Chretien*, 1972.

Puech, H.C. *Le Manicheism, son Fondateur, sa Doctrine*, 1949.

Rostovsteff, M. *Social and Economic History of the Roman Empire*, 1957.

Salway, P. *Roman Britain*, 1981.

Schutz, H. *The Romans in Central Europe*, 1985.

Shiel, J. *Greek Thought and the Rise of Christianity*, 1968.

Sperber, D. "Denarii and Aurei in the time of Diocletian", JRS, 1964.

Sordi, M. *The Christians and the Roman Empire*, 1986.

Stevenson, J. *A New Eusebius*, 1987.

Sutherland, C.H.V. "Diocletian's Reform of the Coinage", JRS, 1955.

Thiede, C.P. *The Heritage of the First Christians*, 1992.

Thompson, E.A. *Romans and Barbarians: The Decline of the Western Empire*, 1982.

Todd, M. *The Everyday Life of the Barbarians*, 1972.

Vogt, J. *The Decline of Rome*, 1964.

Vryonis, S. *Byzantium and Europe*, 1967.

Wade, W.V. "Carausius, Restorer of Britain" art. in *Numismatic Chronicle* 12, 1953.

Wallace-Hadrill, D.S. *Eusebius of Caesaria*, 1960.

Williams, R. *Arius: Heresy and Tradition*, 1987.

INDEX